WITHDRAWN

# PIETIST AND WESLEYAN STUDIES
Editors: David Bundy and J. Steven O'Malley

This monograph series will publish volumes in two areas of scholarly research: Pietism and Methodism (broadly understood). The focus will be Pietism, its history and development, and the influence of this socio-religious tradition in modern culture, especially within the Wesleyan religious traditions.

Consideration will be given to scholarly works on classical and neo-Pietism, on English and American Methodism, as well as on the social and ecclesiastical institutions shaped by Pietism (e.g., Evangelicals, United Brethren, and the Pietist traditions among the Lutherans, Reformed, and Anabaptists). Works focusing on leaders within the Pietist and Wesleyan traditions will also be included in the series, as well as occasional translations and/or editions of Pietist texts. It is anticipated that the monographs will emphasize theological developments, but with close attention to the interaction of Pietism with other cultural forces and to the sociocultural identity of the Pietist and Wesleyan movements.

1. Gregory S. Clapper, *John Wesley on Religious Affections*. 1989.
2. Peter Erb, *Gottfried Arnold*. 1989.
3. Henry H. Knight III, *The Presence of God in the Christian Life: John Wesley and the Means of Grace*. 1992.
4. Frank D. Macchia, *Spirituality and Social Liberation: The Message of the Blumhardts in the Light of Wuerttemberg Pietism*. 1993.
5. Richard B. Steele, *"Gracious Affection" and "True Virtue" according to Jonathan Edwards and John Wesley*. 1994.
6. Stephen L. Longenecker, *Piety and Tolerance: Pennsylvania German Religion, 1700–1850*. 1994.
7. J. Steven O'Malley, *Early German-American Evangelicalism: Pietist Sources on Discipleship and Sanctification*. 1995.
8. R. David Rightmire, *Salvationist Samurai: Gunpei Yamamuro and the Rise of the Salvation Army in Japan*. 1997.
9. Simon Ross Valentine, *John Bennet and the Origins of Methodism and the Evangelical Revival in England*. 1997.

10. Tore Meistad, *Martin Luther and John Wesley on the Sermon on the Mount.* 1999.
11. Robert C. Monk, *John Wesley: His Puritan Heritage.* 1999.
12. Richard B. Steele, *"Heart Religion" in the Methodist Tradition and Related Movements.* 2001.
13. Diane Leclerc, *Singleness of Heart.* 2001.
14. Charles Yrigoyen Jr., *The Global Impact of the Wesleyan Traditions and Their Related Movements.* 2002.
15. Laurence W. Wood, *The Meaning of Pentecost in Early Methodism: Rediscovering John Fletcher as John Wesley's Vindicator and Designated Successor.* 2002.
16. Floyd T. Cunningham, *Holiness Abroad: Nazarene Missions in Asia.* 2003.

# Holiness Abroad

## Nazarene Missions in Asia

Floyd T. Cunningham

*Pietist and Wesleyan Studies, No. 16*

The Scarecrow Press, Inc.
Lanham, Maryland, and Oxford
2003

# SCARECROW PRESS, INC.

Published in the United States of America
by Scarecrow Press, Inc.
A Member of the Rowman & Littlefield Publishing Group
4720 Boston Way, Lanham, Maryland 20706
www.scarecrowpress.com

PO Box 317
Oxford
OX2 9RU, UK

Copyright © 2003 by Floyd T. Cunningham

*All rights reserved.* No part of this publication may be reproduced, stored in a retrieval system, or transmitted in any form or by any means, electronic, mechanical, photocopying, recording, or otherwise, without the prior permission of the publisher.

British Library Cataloguing in Publication Information Available

**Library of Congress Cataloging-in-Publication Data**

Cunningham, Floyd Timothy.
   Holiness abroad : Nazarene missions in Asia / Floyd T. Cunningham.
      p. cm. — (Pietist and Wesleyan studies ; no. 16)
   Includes bibliographical references and index.
   ISBN 0-8108-4564-4 (alk. paper) — ISBN 0-8108-4565-2 (pbk. : alk. paper)
   1. Church of the Nazarene—Missions—Asia. 2. Asia—Church history.
I. Title. II. Series.
BV3151.3 .C86 2003
266'.799'095—dc21                                            2002030246

∞™ The paper used in this publication meets the minimum requirements of American National Standard for Information Sciences—Permanence of Paper for Printed Library Materials, ANSI/NISO Z39.48-1992.
Manufactured in the United States of America.

# Contents

| | | |
|---|---|---|
| | Foreword  *J. Steven O'Malley* | vii |
| | Preface | ix |
| | Acronyms and Abbreviations | xiii |
| 1 | Policies and Philosophies | 1 |
| 2 | India | 49 |
| 3 | Japan | 95 |
| 4 | China | 143 |
| 5 | Korea | 205 |
| 6 | The Philippines | 237 |
| | Conclusion | 269 |
| | Bibliography | 281 |
| | Index | 307 |
| | About the Author | 319 |

# Editor's Foreword

With the publication of Floyd T. Cunningham's study of Nazarene missions in Asia, the Pietist and Wesleyan Studies Series directs its focus upon the international and intercultural dissemination of the Wesleyan tradition, with reference to a major holiness denomination, the Church of the Nazarene. This work departs from the standard model of an institutional history of a denominational mission program. It is an empathetic and intensive analysis and interpretation of the distinctive Nazarene goal of building a single, international holiness body.

Cunningham's examination of the strategies designed to achieve that goal includes an in-depth look at the cultural identity and self-understanding of the home church in North America and the influence of those factors upon its Asian missions, as well as the impact of those missions upon the home church. He brings to the discussion the perspective of one who has given service in this denomination, as both missionary and educator. The interaction between its explicit theology of missions and its mission practice amid the social and political conditions of its Asian fields provides a leitmotif for the study.

Our expectation is that this work will prove useful for readers beyond the denomination under consideration. It should contribute to a greater understanding of the interaction of theological and cultural themes that accompanied the development of the Christian world movement in the twentieth century.

> J. Steven O'Malley
> Co-editor
> The Pietist and Wesleyan Studies Series

# Preface

This book began with questions I had when I started teaching the course in the history of Nazarene missions at Asia Pacific Nazarene Theological Seminary some years ago. The sources I used initially were the same as the students'. They included R. V. DeLong and Mendell Taylor, *Fifty Years of Nazarene Missions* (1955), and J. Fred Parker, *Mission to the World* (1988), neither of which was annotated. These works depended upon several generations of missionary books that had been written from the 1930s onward, and, especially for the early years, upon Roy Swim's *A History of Missions of the Church of the Nazarene* (1936). These texts, like the missionary books upon which they were based, were written with a specific and legitimate purpose: to generate interest in and support for Nazarene missions among Nazarene laypersons. The authors centered upon what missionaries had done and how fields had progressed. They did not explore relationships among missionaries or emphasize national leadership development, and they left unexplained many things about which I was curious.

The answers to my questions were beyond the books at hand and led me to the Nazarene Archives in Kansas City. The Archives contain many of the reports and other papers of missionaries, particularly letters to and from general church leaders. In addition to finding material in the Nazarene Archives, I was given access for a short period of time to microfiche kept separately in the World Mission Division offices. This was extremely helpful as I researched Taiwan and Korea.

I found data not explored by DeLong and Taylor or Parker, especially concerning personality conflicts on mission fields. Authors writing official histories for laypersons in order to boost and promote missions could not very well be expected to tell the whole story. The more I thought about it, and the more I lived it as a missionary myself, the more I became convinced that the church was not well served by having only one official, and for the most part triumphal, side of the story. The not-always-so-glorious internal story created a more realistic picture for my students of the kinds of issues and struggles missionaries underwent in order to establish the Church of the Nazarene in the area of the world from which they came.

My students, some of whom intended to become missionaries themselves, were not well served by having only laudatory accounts of missions and missionaries. My task as a teacher and missionary was to produce self-confident as well as academically prepared local leaders. They needed to see that missionaries were not super human, that they quarreled among themselves over petty as well as grand issues, and that their accomplishments often came in spite of their many personal foibles.

Along the same lines, I wanted to lift into greater prominence the roles that indigenous leaders played in building the Church of the Nazarene in various countries. I found that information on local leaders was much more difficult to acquire than that on missionaries, but I seized on what I could find. Admittedly, what I grasped came mostly (though not altogether) from the missionaries' perspectives. I weighed their perceptions and assessments. In some cases Asian leaders did write to the Church of the Nazarene's headquarters and leaders in Kansas City, and their reflections on the church and its missionaries were illuminating. Local leaders felt themselves capable of fulfilling the tasks of the Church of the Nazarene in their countries and furthering its mission, and sometimes believed that missionaries were inhibiting their development.

This history that I tell is still missionary-centered. Even at the present time Asian historians are writing histories of the Church of the Nazarene in their own countries in their own languages. Their perspectives will give a more completely orbed picture than mine. However, much I might try to be objective as a historian and sympathetic as a human being to indigenous perspectives, I remain not only a Westerner but a missionary myself.

I realize that the history that is told here will be re-written not only because of its orientation but also because it covers only through the early 1970s. There needs to be about a generation for perspective and, since many of the topics deal with interpersonal issues, it is good that missionaries about whom this is written are no longer active (and are in most cases dead). I did not attempt to examine correspondence and papers of missionaries presently serving.

The chief questions are the development and implementation of the church's philosophies and policies of mission; the rise of local leadership; and conflicts and tensions on mission fields. This "inner" history of the Church of the Nazarene in Asia is important not only for what it says about human nature, but for what it says about how American-based denominations construct missions and overseas churches. I have not focused so much on institutional development, partly because this is less interesting than the human drama and partly because this is told well enough by the official histories.

Other questions deal with broader issues. How conscious were missionaries and missions leaders of other churches' policies, and of the strategies being developed by various theorists? More particularly, how did the Church of the Nazarene balance its attempts to evangelize the world as effectively and quickly as possible with its holiness message? Did Wesleyan theological presuppositions and holiness practices inform and shape the church's mission in the world? How did the Church of the Nazarene develop its distinctive policy of "internationalization"? Were Nazarene missionaries conscious of their Western worldview? Were they agents in some witting or unwitting way of American interests abroad? Were they empathetic with those of other cultures?

John Wesley, whom Nazarenes consider their theological mentor, wrote that his purpose was "not to form any sect; but to reform the nation, particularly the Church; and to spread scriptural holiness over the land" (*The Works of John Wesley*, third ed. [reprint, Kansas City, Mo.: Beacon Hill, 1979], 8: 299). Nazarenes believed that they were taking up Wesley's mantle, at least in the sense of extending the message of entire sanctification around the world.

This book is written as a case study of an American denominational mission's work in Asia. I am writing with historians and missiologists in mind, yet also for those laypersons who might wish to be more acquainted with the inner history of twentieth-century missions, and Nazarene missions in particular. This book, however, is written for, and dedicated to, my students.

I wish to express my indebtedness to others who have either shaped this project particularly, or my historical skills more generally. The late Timothy L. Smith was my mentor at Johns Hopkins University, the model of an honest and thorough historian of American religion and a committed churchman. I profited by my year as missionary-scholar-in-residence at Nazarene Theological Seminary and from conversations with Professor Paul Bassett and the Nazarene Archivist, Dr. Stan Ingersoll. I have shared several of these chapters with my colleagues at Asia Pacific Nazarene Theological Seminary. Dr. Donald Owens read and commented on the Korea chapter; Dr. John Holstead, who served at APNTS as visiting professor of missions, was helpful on the Taiwan section. Both Rev. Shigeru Higuchi and Dr. Hitoshi Fukue read and offered helpful comments on the chapter on Japan. Wes Tracy, Beverly Gruver, and Paul Leclerc provided helpful comments on the manuscript. A long series of student assistants and others who typed and processed these pages, and helped in other ways, are deserving of mention: Linda Perez, Angeline Lacamen, Lillian and Emmanuel Jatayna, John Gois, Garry Bernabe and Peter Paul Domen.

I must not forget to mention the support and encouragement of my mother, Eleanor Cunningham, and sisters, Mrs. Janice Leaman and Dr. Diane Leclerc.

Taytay, Rizal, Philippines

# Acronyms and Abbreviations

| | |
|---|---|
| APCA | Association of Pentecostal Churches of America |
| APNTS | Asia Pacific Nazarene Theological Seminary |
| CEHA | Central Evangelical Holiness Association |
| CMA | Christian and Missionary Alliance |
| ENC | Eastern Nazarene College |
| HCC | Holiness Church of Christ |
| NHA | National Holiness Association |
| NNC | Northwest Nazarene College |
| NTC | Nazarene Theological Seminary |
| OMS | Oriental Missionary Society |
| PCI | Pentecostal Collegiate Institute |
| SDA | Seventh-day Adventists |
| SVM | Student Volunteer Movement |
| YMCA | Young Men's Christian Association |

# Chapter 1

# Policies and Philosophies

The Church of the Nazarene was one of scores of American denominations that exported its own distinct theology and practices to various countries throughout the twentieth century. The denomination spread its organization along with the gospel and its distinct message of holiness around the world. Unlike most other denominations, the goal of the Church of the Nazarene was not to establish or enable autonomous national churches. Rather, the church's goal was to build one international holiness body. To do that, Nazarene missionaries bound converts to the church itself as well as to its message. More than they realized, Nazarenes' understanding of how they were to demonstrate holiness and to proclaim it abroad depended on the times in which they lived.

Nazarenes never felt completely at home in their own cultures. In America, the first Nazarenes had left Methodism and other denominations around the turn of century over the theological issue and experience of entire sanctification; but, more than that, they had rebelled against the *embourgeoisement* of the older denominations, their appeasement with culture. The new holiness groups readily assumed denominational form. They sponsored colleges as well as urban and foreign missions. The associations that formed the Church of the Nazarene already had sent missionaries to various countries. They did not ask what John Wesley and his theology had to do with Asia or Africa. They took it for granted that his, and their, interpretations of Christian faith and life were biblically and universally true. To them "second blessing" holiness was for all. The first goal was to "get people saved," and their second to lead converts into entire sanctification.

As former members of larger denominations, early leaders felt themselves to be guardians of an older personal and social morality. They took this sense of moral custodianship with them to various places around the world. Members understood themselves to be part of a grand if small enclave within Christendom. They saw American culture and American Christianity as in need of great moral transformation. Like others influenced by Wesleyan Arminian theology, Nazarenes understood that the evangelization of the world depended upon human cooperation with God's initiatives. However, the denomination had little influence beyond its own boundaries. Interests in society declined after the First World War, while the church's list of prohibited behavior lengthened.

Both the church's home constituency and the missionaries it sent out after the war tended to be from humble, though not necessarily impoverished, positions in society. Some were poor, others prosperous. They were average citizens, for the most part not economically marginalized or "disinherited." Their "outsiderness" came not primarily because of their social and economic position in society, but because of their belief in holiness and their practice of strict moral codes.[1]

Nazarenes felt themselves to be "called out" ones, and gloried in their separateness. In the first five decades of the twentieth century, they and holiness people in general attempted to maintain nineteenth-century moral traditions. Especially in the 1920s and 1930s, Nazarenes were sub-cultural and self-contained. They had risen to protest "worldliness." Thus, when entering mission fields, Nazarenes set up "called out" spiritual communities that had as little as possible to do with the cultures of the world. Since their purpose was to build an international church rather than national ones, they took little heed of cultures.[2]

Missionaries presented the Church of the Nazarene as one worldwide family. Leaders idealistically supposed that Nazarenes would have more in common with each other than with their own local societies. One church leader boasted that "if you enter a thatched roof in the jungles of Africa, or an open tent in the steaming forest of Central America, or an ice-domed igloo in Alaska, or a store-front church in one part of America, wherever you see the sign 'Church of the Nazarene' you will hear the same message of full salvation."[3]

Certain philosophies and policies undergirded this culture-transcending sense of oneness among Nazarenes. By the 1960s church leaders were articulating a process of worldwide church organization they called "internationalization." This idea rationalized the type of church government that mission work had formed, and, at the same time, assured control by headquarters in Kansas City over emerging local churches. Self-governing national churches were not the goal. Rather, the goal was to have local churches and districts bound to each other by holy fellowship and governed by one general assembly, a church *Manual*, and general superintendents, who remained the only ones allowed to ordain ministers.

The church's view toward the world was both missionary-oriented and American-centered. As such, the Church of the Nazarene emphasized that though missions were integral to its nature, persons volunteered for missions based on an individual call, and the church supported the missionaries through its Missionary Society, which was a voluntary association. Like other American missions, the Church of the Nazarene raised (for its size) a considerable amount for missions. Like other American missions, the Nazarene church was intensely pragmatic when it came to creating methods that served the ultimate aim: to gain converts. Likewise, because of the church's belief in the separation of church and state its missionaries remained aloof from political and social issues.[4]

Though diverse cultural conditions on mission fields influenced the practice of missions, they had only an indirect impact on the church's early philosophies of missions. Leaders assumed that Christian values should be equated with holiness movement mores. The centralized nature of Nazarene church government made denominational and theological loyalty a higher value than cultural relevance. The very reason-to-be of the denomination was theological and moral. Fidelity to holiness doctrine and holiness ethics, as defined by the church, remained the standard for all converts to follow. The missionaries' task was not just to make converts and leave them to their own devices. It was to make knowledgeable and loyal Nazarenes of converts. The processes of becoming Nazarene took believers beyond conversion to discipleship.[5]

The church's leaders were not thinking of overall aims when they set out at the turn of the century to do their part to convert the world, and, moreover, to contribute their distinct emphasis upon the sanctification of believers to the global endeavor of evangelical Christians. Policies followed the desire to evangelize. Hiram F. Reynolds, the chief administrator responsible for mission work throughout the early decades of the church, was eager to get at the task of world evangelization in his generation. He was a pragmatist more than a theorist. When problems arose he addressed them. Policies developed on the basis of his responses. It was not until the 1960s that leaders analyzed the implications for the entire church of these processes.[6]

The development of Nazarene missions was influenced by what was happening within the American Nazarene church. There the denomination underwent marked transitions of leadership at intervals of about thirty years. It also experienced marked demographic changes. The church's beginnings were in the associations of urban churches centered in Brooklyn, New York; Boston, Massachusetts; Los Angeles, California; and Nashville, Tennessee. However, by the 1920s the denomination had become predominantly rural. By then the church was led by those who had matured in holiness groups rather than larger denominations. They had been educated in small holiness colleges. Thirty years later, by the 1950s, the church was increasingly suburban. It also had become bureaucratic. The church moved from exhibiting mostly churchly characteristics in its early period to more sectarian ones by the 1920s, and toward more churchly ones, again, by the 1950s. These transitions followed the deaths or retirements of significant leaders in 1915-1918, to mark the end of one era; 1946-1947, another; and the mid-1970s the third.[7]

## Mission Policies to the First World War

The pioneer leaders of the denomination were consolidators. They had been put out of or had voluntarily left established denominations—mostly the Methodist churches—and had organized the Association of Pentecostal Churches of America in the Northeast, the Church of the Nazarene in California, the Holiness Church of Christ in Texas, Tennessee and Arkansas, and the Pentecostal Mission in Nashville. Their visions remained broad and socially engaged. They sought the reformation of the American church. Like other holiness people in the late nineteenth century, they maintained numerous gospel missions and other agencies such as homes for unwed mothers and orphanages that kept them involved in American social issues. Revivalism and social reform remained tied in both their minds and actions.

A. M. Hills, the most influential theologian of this first period of Nazarene history, was a former Congregationalist who had studied under both Charles G. Finney at Oberlin and New School theologians at Yale. Like other founders, Hills viewed the "journey back to Pentecost" as a means of social as well as personal renewal. He saw temperance as a moral reform movement. To the embarrassment of post-World War I Nazarenes, Hills defended infant baptism and remained ardently post-millennial. Hills criticized the low spiritual state of the American churches. Many preachers won few converts. They themselves had not been baptized with the Holy Spirit. Though Hills rarely wrote about missions directly, the implication of his theology was that Spirit-baptism impelled the church forward into evangelism with a boldness it otherwise lacked.[8]

## The Association of Pentecostal Churches of America

The language and image of the baptism with the Holy Spirit, and its implications for world missions, greatly influenced the Association of

Pentecostal Churches of America. While still a group of urban missions centered in Brooklyn, leaders expressed their global concerns in an early (1895) mission statement: "We will cheerfully contribute of our earthly means as God has prospered us, for the support of a faithful ministry among us, for the relief of the poor, and for the spread of the Gospel over the earth."[9] The Association formed a missionary committee and, almost immediately, in December 1895, also a women's auxiliary.

The Association united in 1896 with the Central Evangelical Holiness Association (CEHA) of New England "for the purpose of increased efficiency in the advancement of the Redeemer's kingdom, by the spread of scriptural holiness in home and foreign fields."[10] Like other organizations of the era, the CEHA and other holiness bodies were seeking greater "organization, efficiency and power."[11] In the case of CEHA, this meant increased possibilities to evangelize the world. Sometime before the merger, the CEHA congregation in Malden, Massachusetts, had sent D. J. McDonald as a missionary to India. Unfortunately he died soon after arriving in India (about 1895).[12]

The constitution of the united body stated that the Association's duty was "to suggest to the churches such measures as may be judged wise and proper to promote the interests of the Messiah's kingdom and the spread of scriptural holiness throughout the world."[13] Local manuals, which varied from congregation to congregation, were explicit in understanding the church's global mission. Whether related to foreign or home missions, members of the Association aimed at people and places seemingly neglected by others. At the same time, leaders knew that it was necessary for the advancement in other places for there to be solid home congregations.[14]

In April 1897 the Association elected Hiram F. Reynolds home and foreign missionary secretary. Born near Chicago, Reynolds was raised on farms in Illinois by strict and at times abusive foster parents after his father's death when he was six. As a young man Reynolds lived the kind of immoral life (enjoying the "roaring night life," and other "popular sins" of the times, as he described it to J. B. Chapman) that he later admonished others to avoid. In December 1874 he moved to Vermont, where his now remarried mother was living. He was converted soon after, married, and felt called to ministry. Reynolds attended local theological schools and joined the Methodist Conference. He pastored a series of rural churches, and was ordained in 1886. Soon he became an active part of the holiness movement in the state. In 1892 he helped to organize the Vermont Holiness Association, affiliated with the National Holiness Association. In 1895 Reynolds decided to leave the Methodist Church. He moved to Brooklyn and joined the Utica Avenue congregation of the Association of Pentecostal Churches of America. He was the first ordained minister to join the Association and quickly became a leader. After being elected home and foreign missionary secretary, he held rallies and campaigns in Association churches to raise money to send missionaries abroad.[15]

The Association was not very strong when it sent out its first missionaries in December 1897. They arrived in Bombay in January 1898. Just before the missionaries left, the Foreign Missions Committee hastily compiled a mission policy. It formed the basis for all future policies in the Church of the Nazarene. The essence of the mission, the policy stated, was "to use every endeavor to bring lost souls to Christ, and to labor to bring every believer into the experience of entire sanctification." As long as the focus remained salvation, "every endeavor" included social as well as directly evangelistic ministries. It was equally evident that imparting the distinctive message of entire sanctification depended upon there first being converts to lead into the experience. The policy put control of the mission under the Missionary Committee at home. It restricted actions of missionaries on the field. Funds for the mission were not to be sent directly to missionaries, but, rather, channeled through the Association's treasurer.[16]

In 1899 the Woman's Foreign Missionary Society of the Pentecostal Churches of America was formed. Unlike the separate organization of women in the Methodist Church and other denominations, women in the Association chose not to establish their own missionary-sending agency. Led by Susan N. Fitkin, a former Quaker, the women decided, instead, to cooperate with the Association as a whole. Some of the leaders of the Women's Missionary Society were ordained ministers themselves. There were only twenty churches in the Association. The women sensed less distance between themselves and denominational programs than their counterparts in the Methodist Church.[17]

Though small, the APCA manifested concerns for society as a whole. In 1901 the Association's Annual Meeting sent a letter to President William McKinley protesting prostitution being licensed by American forces occupying the Philippines.[18] Association and, later, Nazarene, missionaries undertook educational, medical and other compassionate work. Because the New England setting out of which they came, and because it was common among holiness people in the nineteenth century to establish both schools and rescue missions, it seemed a natural part of the Association's responsibility abroad.[19]

In 1901, a congregation in the Association, the "People's Evangelical Church" in South Providence, Rhode Island, sent John J. Diaz—

one of its members and a native of the Cape Verde Islands—back to minister to his own people.[20]

Even though the local congregation guaranteed the support of Diaz, the "faith missions" idea never stood a chance under Reynolds's leadership. The pull was in the opposite direction, away from unbridled independency and congregationalism and toward superintendency. Reynolds suspected claims to the leadership or guidance of the Holy Spirit on some project unless they were backed up with the planning and finances necessary to get the job done. To him, the Spirit worked through structure.[21]

Reynolds inspired people with his seemingly boundless energy and enthusiasm for world evangelism and his organizational acumen. The policies developed under him did not come, at least explicitly, from contemporary theories of mission; but Reynolds clearly imbibed the missions spirit of his age. Like missions executives of larger agencies, Reynolds was held in high esteem among the churches, and like other leaders, Reynolds had to manage not only missionaries on the field, but public relations at home. Yet he was more known for his organizational efficiency than for his preaching. At least two movements clearly influenced him: the Student Volunteer Movement and the independent work of Methodist Bishop William Taylor.[22]

Reynolds possessed the kind of optimism characterized by the Student Volunteer Movement—that with sufficient planning and hard work Christians could evangelize the world within a generation. The SVM had begun in 1888 and was at its height around the turn of the century. The SVM was "higher life" or Keswickian in theology during these years. The "consecration" it called young Christians to make regarding their vocation came after their conversion and was not unlike the call holiness people made for entire sanctification. The SVM also talked about the power for witnessing that came through the Holy Spirit.[23]

Although Reynolds owned (and presumably read) books by Taylor, a strong advocate of holiness, he did not impose Taylor's policies and practices on the church's missionaries. Both Taylor and Reynolds were pragmatists. But Reynolds was more cautious than Taylor. Paradoxically, for one who rejected the church in which Taylor remained, Reynolds was more attached than Taylor to home-based financial stability, organizational system and hierarchical methods of control over both missionaries and mission fields.[24]

While Reynolds instructed missionaries to lead converts on to entire sanctification, he believed that they should abide by comity arrangements (by which denominations remain within mutually agreed-upon geographic boundaries). When Reynolds became aware that comity arrangements existed in India, for instance, he directed that missionaries work harmoniously with churches already in the area. The same respect for comity held true in China and other countries.[25]

The presupposition behind Reynolds's agreeing to abide by comity was that the "second blessing," the denomination's distinctive doctrine, was *not* essential for salvation. If leaders had believed that entire sanctification was necessary for salvation, they would have advocated evangelizing Episcopalians, Presbyterians, Methodists or Baptists who did not claim the experience. The Seventh-day Adventists, for instance, aggressively proselytized other Protestants out of the belief that otherwise these individuals would be eternally lost. Some in the holiness movement, indeed, held to an aberration of Wesley's doctrine of holiness, and suggested that the Bible verse "without holiness no one shall see the Lord" restricted salvation to those who had experienced entire sanctification in this life. However, this was not the position of Wesley or the model the Church of the Nazarene followed. Reynolds's willingness to cooperate reflected a more churchly than sectarian tendency.[26]

The Association also demonstrated its "churchliness" by engaging in compassionate ministries. In this period of high colonialism, social ministries were an inevitable component of mission work. Education and forms of social work were legitimate, "civilizing" components of the church's task in the world, according to contemporary missions theorists such as James Dennis. Among critics, the uplift of others reflected ideas of the superiority of Western civilization and the white race. Missions theorists Henry Venn and Rufus Anderson in the mid-nineteenth century, and Roland Allen later in the century, rejected institutional work and stressed that the church's attention must not drift away from preaching, evangelism and church planting.[27]

Holiness people never decided fully whether educational, medical and other such enterprises were ends in themselves, as expressions of hearts made perfect in love, or means toward evangelism. Reynolds seemed not to mull over the issue. "Duty" more than "love" motivated social activities in Reynolds's mind. Yet it was not "duty" springing out of a sense of noblesse oblige that motivated Nazarenes, many of whom were on common ground with those they sought to help.[28]

Reynolds sanctioned literacy training, elementary schools, clinics, flood relief projects and other such enterprises in countries such as India and China, where he considered these to be needed. Simply, these were the church's "duty" under God as part of a nation destined, so he thought, to redeem the world.[29]

Reynolds sensed a responsibility to maintain church order. Often he faced problems created by leaders desirous to go their own ways apart from the wisdom and counsel of the church. Problems of this sort emerged at Pentecostal Collegiate Institute in Saratoga Springs, New York, under Principal Lyman Pettit and in India under M. D. Wood. These situations convinced not only Reynolds but others in the Association of the necessity of greater superintendency, and were strong factors pulling the Association in the direction of denominationalism, Methodist polity, and union with the Church of the Nazarene in 1907. American social trends moved in the same direction, from independency to order.[30]

The paradigm Reynolds molded for the church emphasized world evangelism, Christian responsibility and organization. He appreciated the need for efficiency, procedures and frugality. One of the chief characteristics of a holiness church to him was one endeavoring by the power of the Spirit to do its part for the evangelization of the world. In doing so, Reynolds in effect emphasized the "cardinal" doctrine of the church, justification by faith, rather than its "distinguishing" doctrine of entire sanctification.

## The Holiness Church of Christ

The inadequacy of "faith" alone to finance foreign missionaries in the Holiness Church of Christ (HCC) was a factor that led this group toward union with the Church of the Nazarene in 1908. Many holiness people in the South remained within their churches, mostly Methodist, and some, such as Henry C. Morrison, established nondenominational mission agencies that promoted holiness. Those who either came out of or were put out of older denominations for propagating holiness feared ecclesiastical hierarchy on one hand and spiritual disorder on the other. However, as the groups grew, the fear of disorder outweighed fear of hierarchy. At the same time, leaders did *not* view the centuries following the apostolic era as ones of declension and apostasy and sought, in their own years of organization, to avoid the evils of "sectarianism." On the fringes, but perilously close to Southern holiness camp meetings and churches, was fire-baptized "fanaticism," which began giving way in some places to tongues-speaking Pentecostalism.[31]

The Holiness Church of Christ, and its forerunners, energetically sent out missionaries—primarily to Mexico, Central America and the Caribbean. Two representing the HCC worked in Japan. Unlike either the Association of Pentecostal Churches or the Church of the Nazarene in California, the HCC subscribed to the "faith mission" principles circulating among evangelical groups enamored over the success of J. Hudson Taylor's China Inland Mission. The right of any congregation to send out missionaries was stated explicitly in HCC council proceedings and governing documents. Members guarded and cherished this privilege. It was part of the congregationalist principles held dear in these years of exodus from denominations. There was something exciting to local laypeople in rural Southern towns linking their faith directly to missionaries around the globe. Young people from their churches who expressed a missionary call sailed abroad with prayers and promises of support from their congregations. But the small bands sending them out were themselves struggling financially. They not only supported numerous pastors and evangelists, but a Bible school, a rescue mission for unwed mothers and an orphanage.[32]

Until 1905 there were no means of systematically promoting, financing or supervising missionary work in the HCC. Then, realizing the disservice this did to the missionaries themselves as well as to local churches, leaders set up provisions for the licensing and commissioning of missionaries and centralized missions giving. But they also reaffirmed their commitment to the right of local congregations to send money for missions directly to the field, and not necessarily through the organization's general treasurer. Leaders sensed, by 1906, the need for a missions secretary. After sending observers to the union of the Association of Pentecostal Churches of America with the Church of the Nazarene in 1907, Holiness Church of Christ leaders strengthened the role of the committee on missions to select, send and support missionaries. S. M. Stafford, superintendent of the work in Mexico, recommended to the Eastern Council: that all money for missions pass through the church's committee on missions; that all persons claiming a call to the mission field be carefully examined by the same committee; and that, if accepted, missionary candidates be both appointed and ordained by the committee. Though the HCC did not act upon these before its merger with the Pentecostal Church of the Nazarene at Pilot Point, Texas, in October 1908, the recommendations demonstrated the changed sentiment of the church toward the organization and leadership of its missions program.[33]

Just before the merger, certain HCC leaders and missionaries boosted an encomienda-like enterprise in Chiapas, southern Mexico. They believed this "self-supporting" mission would require fewer foreign dollars by supplying its own needs. In addition, HCC leaders hoped to set up a printing press and publish a missions magazine in Chiapas, where labor and other expenses were cheap. After the union at

Pilot Point, Reynolds became involved. He strongly opposed the idea, primarily because there was no way to adequately supervise it. Nevertheless, Reynolds agreed to allow the Southern churches to support it for a year. Soon political crises in Mexico made the issue moot. All missionaries were forced out of Mexico in 1910.[34]

Members of the Holiness Association of Texas preferred to send out missionaries through existing holiness missions agencies rather than to establish their own. They supported missionaries sent out by Henry C. Morrison's Holiness Union, and J. O. McClurkan's Pentecostal Mission as well as the Holiness Church of Christ. More than any of these other Southern groups, the Holiness Association of Texas attended to domestic social issues. In 1907 members issued a sharply worded denunciation of race relations in the South and condemned lynching in particular. Many Association members became Nazarene—some through the Holiness Church of Christ, and others through membership in the college church at Texas Holiness University in Peniel, which united with the Church of the Nazarene in April 1908.[35]

## The Church of the Nazarene

While holiness people were forming the Association of Pentecostal Churches in the East and the Holiness Church of Christ in the South, Phineas Bresee began the Church of the Nazarene in Los Angeles. Like the Texas Holiness Association, Bresee focused on American society's needs for moral reform rather than on foreign missions. Soon after the beginning of the Church of the Nazarene in October 1895, members drew up Articles of Faith that included a statement of purpose: "The field of labor to which we feel especially called is in the neglected quarters of the cities and wherever else may be found waste places and souls seeking pardon and cleansing from sin. This work we aim to do through the agency of city missions, evangelistic services, house to house visitation, caring for the poor, comforting the dying."[36] The people felt that other denominations were abandoning urban centers, and believed God leading them, as they said, to a "mission in the midst of the other churches: to preach and bear its testimony to the cleansing blood of Jesus as a second distinct experience of grace," and "to take up mission work in the heart of the cities."[37]

Like Reynolds, Bresee was a former Methodist minister. Reynolds was set to evangelize the world, Bresee to reform the nation, beginning with its churches. He possessed strong memories of the successful cause that eradicated slavery, and maintained Methodism's grand confidence that other evils also could be defeated. In the 1890s Bresee was active in California's Prohibition Party. He admitted to the social, even class, origins of evils such as alcoholism and poverty. Like those of his era who became Progressives, Bresee was optimistic that good would triumph and that middle-class people possessing purity and moral virtue would lead the way to social reform.[38]

The Church of the Nazarene would attempt to "christianize Christianity." Different metaphors described this mission. Nazarenes would be as leaven or as salt in the church as well as in the world. Bresee thought of the Church of the Nazarene as a divine "knighthood." It was a kind of religious order within Protestantism. In fact Bresee compared Nazarenes to the Franciscans, bearing the message of divine love to all.[39] He considered the church born "with broad, generous, brotherly impulses . . . at once free from narrow sectarianism and from fanaticism; liberal as to non-essentials, tenacious for all that is absolutely necessary for holiness."[40]

Nazarenes would transform Christianity through their witness. Perfect love, the heart of holiness, was to flow particularly in compassion to the poor, toward "the outcast, the lowly, the downtrodden; to those in greatest need, and those in deepest sorrow."[41] There was a preferential bias in Bresee toward the poor. "We have no war on people because of wealth but I would rather have the thousands of the poor coming around the cross," he said, "than to have all the gold of the rich."[42]

Bresee believed that establishing a strong, holiness denomination, centered in America's cities, was the immediate and primary task. Nazarenes, Bresee believed, should "tarry" (as Jesus had told the disciples to tarry in Jerusalem before taking the gospel to other parts of the world).[43] He stressed that revival in American churches and society should precede emphasis upon world evangelism. If American churches and members became Spirit-filled, world revival would follow. "Our great life work lies close to us," he said, "to preach to the heathen of our own city, those who speak our own language, the real American heathen who come nearest to us."[44] Bresee further stated, "Perhaps no missionary work needs more to be done than the planting of centers of fire in this country to preach and lead people into holiness, and help christianize Christianity, and save America from going utterly into worldliness and paganism."[45]

Bresee's church set up procedures by which its General Board appointed both home and foreign missionaries after first examining candidates' doctrine, call, gifts, preparation, and personal experience of salvation. The home church itself needed to prepare and plan for missions. The faith missions idea had no more of a chance under Bresee than it did under Reynolds.[46]

Bresee's church stated its mission in language similar to the Association of Pentecostal Churches: "We seek holy Christian fellowship, the conversion of sinners, the entire sanctification of believers and their upbuilding in holiness, together with the preaching of the Gospel to every creature." Their sense of having a distinct mission to the American church was so extreme that the Missions Committee itself reported to the 1904 Annual Assembly: "As strange as it may seem, God is more anxious for a holy church than he is for the conversion of the heathen."[47]

The same year, 1904, the church began a mission in Los Angeles led by Mae McReynolds among Mexicans, and another led by Ko Chow among Chinese.[48]

By 1905, nonetheless, many of Bresee's people longed for their own missions abroad. The Missions Committee now asked how long they should wait to go outside America. Individual members already were giving liberally to other missions and independent "faith" missionaries. Giving for home mission boards would not decline, the committee believed, if work started overseas.[49]

Two members of Bresee's own congregation already were missionaries. One, Jacob Kohl, had gone to China in 1903 with Horace Houlding, the founder of the South Chili Gospel Mission. Another, Mary Hill, a former missionary to China, played a role in the beginning of the church's college and then returned to China in 1904. She also worked under the South Chili Mission. The church supported neither of these directly or officially.[50]

The Church of the Nazarene finally entered foreign missions work after being presented in 1906 with the needs and preexisting ministries of an Indian, Sukhoda Banarjee. She had established in Calcutta the kind of work that was dear to Bresee. It was urban and focused on social needs neglected by others, in this case the plight of child widows and orphans. The ministry of Banarjee appealed to Bresee's reformist as well as evangelistic impulses. Furthermore, Bresee had learned from his mentor in the Methodist church, Bishop Matthew Simpson, the importance of local leaders. Bresee commissioned both Banarjee and P. B. Biswas—her son-in-law, who was traveling with her—as missionaries. Later, operating under the same philosophy, Bresee appointed Pasadena College–trained Japanese workers as missionaries to their own country.[51]

Bresee's understanding of the Church of the Nazarene was both sectarian and churchly. Its beliefs, he said, were "the common orthodox doctrines of the church" on the trinity, sin, the atonement, justification and sanctification. The Church of the Nazarene championed nothing new. Like National Holiness Association leaders, Bresee admonished holiness people not to concentrate upon or to divide over "nonessentials" such as divine healing and millennial doctrines.[52]

Like John Wesley, whose idea was for the Methodist societies to be a leavening influence within the Church of England and within British society as a whole, Bresee hoped that the Church of the Nazarene would reform American Christianity. In a sense, in emphasizing the "distinguishing" contribution of the church's mission in the world rather than its common mission with other denominations, Bresee was more sectarian than Reynolds. Bresee's intent was not that the Church of the Nazarene simply join with others for world evangelization. Although evangelism concerned him greatly, the Church of the Nazarene carried a unique message. His primary aim was to renew American Protestantism, both by preaching holiness and by manifesting it through concern for the neglected urban masses.[53]

A holiness church signaled to Bresee one freed from the worldliness and worldly values that mired other denominations. Both evangelism and social concern, for Bresee, were manifestations of perfect love. Those who professed holiness needed to demonstrate it through deeds. These deeds flowed not so much out of duty as out of love made perfect. Holiness was more than doctrine and more than spiritual experience. "We are to give," Bresee said, "not because it is charity, but because it is right, and the working out of our righteousness."[54]

## Missions Policies of the United Denomination

The 1907 and 1908 mergers of these three groups to form the Pentecostal Church of the Nazarene continued the movement each had undergone from "boundlessness" to "consolidation."

Like the earlier groups, the united Church of the Nazarene remained interested in social issues beyond its boundaries. Under the editorship of B. F. Haynes, a former Southern Methodist, the church's official paper, the *Herald of Holiness*, manifested support for women's suffrage, anti-lynching laws and military disarmament. It addressed issues of labor rights and urban crime. Pre-war Nazarenes, like nineteenth-century evangelicals, tended to be moral reformers rather than reactionaries, still more optimistic than pessimistic about the future. Missionaries who went out during or who were shaped by this era, carried with them concerns about the social conditions of the people among whom they ministered. Unlike some other missions, the Church of the Nazarene appointed women as full, not "associate" missionaries.[55]

The 1908 Assembly gave one year after the union for missionaries sent out by the three uniting bodies to continue to be supported by their original constituencies. This gave Reynolds time to bring the Southern "faith" missionaries under a more controlled system of appointment and guidance as well as financial support. In the meantime, as both general superintendent and foreign missions secretary, H. F. Reynolds set up channels of support among the districts for missions and screened missionary applicants.[56]

Reynolds's vision was expansive. At the same time, he was pragmatic. He affirmed that God had providentially called the church into existence in order to spread scriptural holiness throughout the world. In order to do so most effectively, Nazarenes, he believed, should avoid supporting independent missions and missionaries, give only to commissioned Nazarene missionaries, and send their money for missions through the church's central office (then located in Chicago). In turn, Nazarene missionaries were not to solicit funds directly from churches without authorization from headquarters. This ensured proper accountability, something dear to Reynolds.

The General Missionary Board (which at that time was the only general board of the church) was elected by the General Assembly. From 1907 to 1911, it was made up of two representatives from each district. After 1911, the North American church was divided into six zones. Each zone elected members of the Missionary Board. Additional general boards were created.[57]

The Missionary Board set a missions budget, with certain amounts apportioned to each of the districts. The board reported to the church how much was distributed to each mission field from the budget. This had been Reynolds's method with the Association and its constituents, to be as open and forthright as possible regarding finances, as well as firm regarding missions policy.

Reynolds called Nazarenes to "the speedy evangelization of the whole world with the full gospel." Yet it was not Reynolds's aim for the church to immediately enter new fields. This would wait until there were greater means. The church must "conserve" its resources. Very importantly in line with both financial frugality and missions policy, the church—in Reynolds's mind—had no intention of retaining missionaries on mission fields once they had established self-functioning national churches. Eventually, Reynolds envisioned, each mission field would be able to function without missionaries and financial support from headquarters.[58]

The January 17, 1914, policy for Japan, built upon the one that Reynolds had helped to write for India many years earlier, stated that missionaries were "on the field to get souls saved and sanctified, and trained for the kingdom of God on earth," and must focus on preaching "full salvation." The latter was a coded phrase among holiness people for entire sanctification. The means of spreading the message were those being used in the American church: visiting house-to-house, organizing Bible classes, establishing Sunday Schools, opening preaching stations and missions, and distributing literature. When either missionaries or national leaders established a local congregation, they were to encourage it to be self-supporting and self-governing, the policy stated. When a local congregation raised enough for half of its own support, including its pastor's salary, it had the privilege of electing a church board. When several local churches collectively achieved self-support, "missionary control shall be relinquished except such superintendency as is provided for in the *Manual*."[59]

The policy reflected Reynolds's idea of the dispensability of the "mission" and missionaries. Even this early, he considered the mission a preliminary stage toward the development of indigenous districts. However, this did *not* mean autonomous national churches with their own manuals and general assemblies. The church's government was to remain centralized.

Reynolds raised interest and support throughout the denomination for missions. His world vision and optimism challenged the young church. With the right organization, Reynolds believed, God would use wonderfully Nazarene efforts to win the world. The industrial, agricultural and engineering advances that awed Reynolds and others in his generation contributed to this faith in progress, consolidation and organization. Through the Church of the Nazarene people with little voice in the world could transcend their day-to-day lives and become part of what Reynolds told them was the greatest enterprise on earth, the expansion of God's kingdom.[60]

Though Reynolds emphasized evangelism, he understood that the church would minister in material ways to destitute and neglected people. In India it took the form of famine relief, an orphanage, primary schools and a farm. In Japan, it included urban slum and leprosy work. In China, it meant building roads, dams, schools and a hospital, and teaching old women how to read. To first-generation Nazarenes these were both the imperatives of Christian duty, and evidences of holiness.[61]

Reynolds began making personal visitations to mission fields in 1909 when he visited Mexico City. In December 1913 he began a round-the-world tour that took almost a year to complete. He stopped in Japan, China (where he spent a month) and India (four months) before making his way to Nazarene missions in Swaziland and the Cape Verde Islands. For his time, Reynolds's experiences in these countries made him an "expert" on Asian affairs.[62] Similar trips abroad followed during his general superintendency. He visited Japan and China again in 1919 and 1922.[63]

## The Pentecostal Mission

After previous futile attempts at union, the Pentecostal Mission, headquartered in Nashville, joined the Church of the Nazarene in 1915. This was shortly after the death of it founder, J. O. McClurkan, a former Cumberland Presbyterian active in the Southern holiness movement since the 1890s. The stated purpose of the Pentecostal Mission was "to seek the salvation of the lost; the sanctification of believers; the deepening of the spiritual life; the dissemination of scriptural knowledge of the Lord."[64]

Like Bresee, McClurkan saw the necessity of establishing strong holiness congregations at home in order to push the work of "the Full Gospel to the uttermost parts of the earth."[65] Like the Association of Pentecostal Churches in New England and Bresee's work in California, the Pentecostal Mission was urban in orientation. However, McClurkan was not as hesitant as Bresee to send out missionaries. Like the Holiness Church of Christ, the Pentecostal Mission sent out missionaries on faith. In fact one of the chief reasons for the Pentecostal Mission's merger with the Church of the Nazarene was that its missions program had been overextended and needed a firmer financial base.[66]

Its first missionary, W. A. Farmer, went to China in 1900 co-sponsored by the Pentecostal Mission and the Christian and Missionary Alliance. Others followed. When the Pentecostal Mission did not join the CMA, some of its missionaries, already scattered around the world, continued under the CMA board. Like the CMA, and more so than the other holiness groups that eventually formed the Church of the Nazarene, the Pentecostal Mission was intensely pre-millennial.

The Executive Committee of the Pentecostal Mission spent many long hours over problems with missionaries. It forged policies as time went on and problems arose—much as the Association of Pentecostal Churches had done. Sometimes several local churches pledged support for a certain missionary. Each missionary before going out confessed "a personal trust in God for financial support."[67]

Like other holiness groups and various other sectors of society in the same period, the Pentecostal Mission moved toward "consolidation."

Leaders attempted to gain more centralized control over both home and foreign missions projects. Taking organizational steps like the other groups that became part of the Church of the Nazarene, the Pentecostal Mission eventually guaranteed its missionaries a monthly income ($25), which it solicited through the *Living Water*. This paper circulated far. Persons of various denominations supported Pentecostal Mission missionaries. In time, the Missions Committee thought it wise to interview and commission prospective missionaries rather than to leave this to local churches. The 1906 Pentecostal Mission Convention established policies and guidelines that stated, first, that, regardless of the missionary's source of income, each was responsible in conduct, doctrine and work to the Mission's Executive Committee. Policy directed missionaries to plant churches along "New Testament" lines. It gave the ordained missionaries the right collectively to ordain local workers. Pentecostal Mission missionaries served in Japan, China, India, Persia, the Sudan, Cuba and Guatemala.

In 1908 the Pentecostal Mission was far ahead of the already united Church of the Nazarene in both the size of its missions budget and the number of missionaries it was supporting. By 1911, however, when the Nazarenes held their General Assembly in Nashville, the new denomination had already doubled what the Pentecostal Mission was doing in both regards. Merger talks, however, stalled. The Pentecostal Mission wanted the Church of the Nazarene to take a strictly pre-millennial stand on Christ's Second Coming, and it wanted to prohibit women from being ordained. McClurkan also felt that union would not offer anything to the Mission's foreign work. In fact, according to one observer, "it was the frightening picture of failing in their avowed responsibilities to their missionaries" that kept them at that time away from union, since they feared the Nazarenes would not support them all.[68]

However the next four years were ones of financial crisis in the Mission. The Mission barely maintained its commitments to its missionaries. When McClurkan died, the remaining leaders, led by John T. Benson, decided it was time again to approach the Nazarenes. Leaders won assurances from the Nazarenes that Pentecostal Mission missionaries would remain in India, Cuba and Guatemala. They decided to support union—although each local mission decided whether or not to join the Church of the Nazarene.[69]

The addition of these missionaries added strength to Nazarene missions. It also reinforced Reynolds's efforts to establish control and clear policies along with a sufficient financial base for Nazarene missions.

## Philosophies and Policies 1915 to 1945

The Pentecostal Church of Scotland, which was organized in 1909, also united with the Church of the Nazarene in 1915. This signified that the Church of the Nazarene was a merger of international and not just American holiness bodies. The Pentecostal Church of Scotland had been using the Nazarene *Manual* and supporting Nazarene missions even before the union. By 1924, missionaries from Scotland were appointed by the general church.[70]

Union, church growth and economic prosperity led the Nazarenes to dramatic increases in giving to missions in the years immediately after the First World War. Giving through the general headquarters in 1908 totaled only $12,000, and reached over $22,000 in 1911, and more than doubled this in 1916. By 1919 the total for missions was over $122,500. Giving peaked in 1921, when about 45,000 Nazarene members contributed a total of $203,000 to world misisons. This postwar peak in giving reflected a trend in American missions giving as a whole. Nearly all mission societies peaked during these same years, and then declined in revenues.[71] The Church of the Nazarene sent out missionaries based on anticipations of continued increases, which could not be sustained. The economic hardships of the Midwest during the 1920s and, later, the Depression, led to reverses. Giving to both foreign missions and home missions projects declined. At the same time, the church developed other priorities. Districts planted dozens of new churches in the 1920s and 1930s, mostly in rural areas. Members sacrificed to maintain the church's liberal arts colleges, which, they believed, protected their children from the world and kept them in the faith. They concentrated on nurturing a holy environment and a holy faith for their children. It was a priority like those of many second-generation religious movements.[72]

Some who defended the necessity of missions did so in terms rich with meaning in both American social reform and Wesleyan theology. Near the close of the First World War, C. J. Kinne raised support in the church for a hospital in China based on Bresee's sense of the mission of the Church of the Nazarene. Kinne was a prominent California layperson and publisher who eventually went to China himself to help build the hospital. "To love my neighbor is the test of whether or not I love God," Kinne wrote.[73] Christians should seek to rectify social conditions not merely out of a sense of duty, Kinne believed, but out of love. "The church greatly needs this form of service in order to develop and increase the gift and graces which will make her Christlike. If we are to be like our Lord, then we shall have to possess and exercise the same compassion and love which he had for all who were in distress."[74] Kinne emphasized that charitable work must be undertaken with disinterested benevolence. A religion, he said, "which does not flow out of the heart and life in streams of blessing unto needy souls is a poor thing in which to invest either time or money." Though Kinne mentioned the evangelistic impact of such service, this was not, for him, the primary motivation for such ministries.[75]

The leaders of the church in the years between the world wars were not, for the most part, ones who possessed Bresee's and Kinne's wedding of social compassion and urban evangelism with the mission of the Church of the Nazarene in the world. Leaders such as Roy T. Williams and James B. Chapman possessed less interest in and optimism toward reform either in society or in the church at large. They were determined before all things to evangelize. The Secretary of Home Missions, N. B. Herrell, stated it well in 1923: "Our vision, passion and heart cry should be 'Give us souls! Give us souls!' For this purpose we exist, and when we fail in this we have no right to continue as a church."[76] These leaders heightened sectarianism while strengthening denominational loyalties. Persuasive and trusted administrators in Kansas City gave weight to the episcopal side of the church's government. At the same time the church rapidly became rural in orientation. This was a result not only of aggressive church planting by zealous district superintendents, but also a result of an influx of Midwestern Methodists concerned as much about Modernism and "Social Gospel" trends in their former church as holiness. Nazarene leaders focused on evangelism and conformity to holiness mores.[77]

Sectarianism was evident in a number of ways. Breaking with Methodist tradition, increasingly, baptism was only for adult believers, and was only by immersion. Numerous popularly written books evidenced fundamentalist views toward biblical inspiration and the second coming of Christ. Nazarene placed little emphasis on the sacraments or the need for spiritual growth and maturity following entire sanctification. Theologians emphasized the second crisis of entire sanctification to the neglect of living out the experience in perfect love. Nazarenes in the 1920s and 1930s were more legalistic than many who had earlier joined the church. They added to the number of rules in the *Manual*. Even more taboos prohibited women from "bobbing" their hair or wearing jewelry, including wedding rings. Nazarenes looked, talked and behaved differently from the world. It was not just looking plain for the sake of looking plain, however, that was important. The evangelists who preached against jewelry sent rings, necklaces and bracelets to Kansas City so that the church could sell the jewelry and use the proceeds to keep missionaries on the field. These were means through which Nazarenes linked themselves to a common cause and forged a communal identity.[78]

In the years following the First World War, increased pessimism about social morality and the rise of pre-millennialism accompanied the church's sense of urgency to evangelize the world. In part because of fundamentalist "leavening," pre-millennialism eclipsed post-millennialism during these years. This intensified the sense of necessity to evangelize the world quickly. Even Reynolds, whose nineteenth-century Methodist roots disposed him toward post-millennialism, used the rhetoric of pre-millennialism to prod church members to work as energetically as they could and to give as much as they could for the redemption of the world. "What if there is a gracious and world-wide revival within the next few years, and then the rapture? Don't we want the biggest possible part in the first that we may be found in the second? With all these solemn responsibilities upon us, and the Lord's coming imminent, how can we hoard up money?" Duty demanded the pursuit of lost souls who would perish forever unless the gospel reached them in time.[79]

The Church of the Nazarene never sharpened its Article of Faith on the Second Coming to exclude post-millennial or a-millennial interpretations, though delegates hotly debated this at the 1928 General Assembly. However, General Superintendents Williams and Chapman and other former leaders in the Holiness Church of Christ who moved into influential positions were strongly pre-millennial, as was J. G. Morrison, who brought the mostly Methodist Laymen's Holiness Association, centered in the Dakotas, into the denomination in 1921. Morrison rose to become secretary of foreign missions in 1928, and general superintendent in 1936.[80]

The missions policy statements of the 1920s, still either written or guided by Reynolds, affirmed that: "The primary object of our work is spiritual, namely, the salvation of sinners, the sanctification of believers and building them up in the holy faith." At this level the church seemed to follow the anti-institutional perspectives of Henry Venn and Rufus Anderson. Yet the Nazarene policy went on to affirm what these two nineteenth-century strategists had warned against. Orphanages, schools, industrial and medical work, translation and publication all were legitimate insofar as they served the primary, evangelistic objective. As well as this cardinal mission, the church's policy also voiced its distinguishing mission to keep the doctrine and experience of entire sanctification "to the front."[81]

The policies also maintained that the "work and manifestations of the Holy Spirit are practically the same in all countries." Reynolds's ministry in various countries seemed to confirm this. He never mentioned adapting or contextualizing the message for his audiences. Yet, under his preaching, people around the world testified to a "second blessing" and left their vices. That was sufficient enough evidence for him for the universality of his revival methods as well as the holiness message.[82]

Mission policies continued to affirm the goal of establishing local churches with their own leaders: "We must guard against the danger of keeping the native congregation in baby clothes too long. This will hinder the Holy Spirit in His freedom of operation among the people." Yet the 1923 policy also stated that it would be an error to release "our parental control over them before they are able to stand alone." Church leaders worried over "doctrinal confusion, and a low standard of experience" in the mission churches. These shortcomings would lead the church to be ashamed to call its progeny "Nazarene." Until churches paid their pastors and shouldered other responsibilities befitting organized congregations, mission councils functioned as district assemblies.[83]

In order for the districts in mission fields to reach maturity, the policy charged missionaries with the task of raising up converts who would be not only saved and sanctified, but also trained for leadership. This required Bible schools, and missionaries established these in nearly every country the Church of the Nazarene entered. Nevertheless, leaders felt that if the Church of the Nazarene were to err it would be better for it to err in keeping missionaries in control too long rather than in releasing them too quickly, before local leaders were adequately prepared. Of course, Nazarenes were hardly alone in this practice in the annals of missions history.[84]

By the late 1920s, a more detailed policy (still developed under Reynolds's guidance) clarified the relationship between the mission council and the District Assembly. However, the goals of the church remained unchanged: "to secure the conversion to Jesus Christ our Lord of the people of foreign lands, lead them into heart holiness as a definite work of grace, and establish them in local church membership, on each foreign mission field." The mission council was to station both foreign and national workers, supervise, employ and dismiss national workers, develop a clergy-training program, and transact business. It was, in short, "to supervise all of the work of the church on the mission field"—until the local churches were able to establish a "missionary district." The latter could be organized upon the recommendation of the council and upon the approval of both the department of foreign missions and the general superintendents.[85]

According to the same policy, the mission council's powers and prerogatives would, one day, be superseded by the organization of a District Assembly. The missionaries would organize a council separate from the district when a local minister was appointed as district superintendent. When this occurred the local leadership and the missionaries endeavored to "work in close fellowship and harmony with the other, and render respect to each other's wishes and feelings." In both cases, whether under missionaries or local leaders, with the approval of the general superintendents the district could elect delegates to represent it at the church's quadrennial General Assembly.

The policy set no criteria as to when a work might reach "missionary district" status. Missionaries proved slow in recommending their organization. General church leaders such as Chapman, after he became general superintendent in 1928, often had to prod them in this direction.

Beyond this "missionary district" status, the policy also stated, was a full or "regular" level of district organization. A district could achieve this when it became fully self-supporting, although the General Assembly would still need to approve it. A "regular" district was entitled to proportional representation at the General Assembly, based on membership, according to *Manual* guidelines.

Thus the policies of the late 1920s described three stages for districts: a mission council-controlled district; a "missionary" district under national leadership; and a regular district. Policies linked measures of self-government to self-support and maintained the vision of an international church.[86]

Though Nazarene leaders could not foresee all of the implications of this, by the 1930s policy-makers such as Reynolds were envisioning a church made up of self-supporting districts located around the world that one day would need no missionary supervision, and that would have equal rights, privileges and responsibilities with any American district. Leaders did not aim toward the development of autonomous national churches. At the same time, they did not plan for indefinite missionary control, Without a great deal of thought about where this would lead, without consciously copying any other denomination's model of church government, and without much theological reflection, the Church of the Nazarene headed toward being an international body.[87]

As fields developed in the 1930s and the world situation darkened, leaders gave increased attention to the evangelistic purpose of the Church of the Nazarene in the world. Many Nazarene writers of the era echoed A. M. Hills in seeing Pentecost as the link between the distinguishing doctrine of entire sanctification and the cardinal mandate of evangelism. Pentecost, Nazarenes understood, gave the early church in the first century and gave the present church now its power to witness, and impelled it to go into all the world with the gospel.

J. Glenn Gould, a pastor and theologian associated with the Eastern wing of the church, wrote that the Holy Spirit gave power both to cast out demons and to translate the gospel into many languages (the then-current Nazarene version of the Pentecostal gift of tongues). The central connection, to Gould, between the mission of the church in the world and its distinctive doctrine lay in the power that entire sanctification bestowed on believers to witness boldly to the unconverted. He advised the church to concentrate on evangelism. "The Nazarene work is an evangelistic movement," he wrote, "our genius lies along this line. To this end were we called forth." Nazarenes, he warned, must avoid allowing church buildings, schools, colleges, hospitals or orphanages, at home or abroad, to become ends in themselves. "Evangelism," Gould said, "has been the church's central objective. God grant it may never change."[88]

Gould's comments were in part a reaction to the interdenominational Laymen's Report, *Re-Thinking Missions*, published in 1932. Gould devised his thoughts within a religious climate uneasy with anything that seemed like a "social" gospel. He wanted Nazarene missionaries to be convinced of the complete lostness of people apart from faith in Christ. Gould and others pushed into the background anything distinctive about the Nazarenes' mission in the world. Gould's position fell within the Reynolds paradigm that emphasized evangelism.[89]

Other Nazarenes emphasized the distinguishing or "special calling" of the Church of the Nazarene. Roy Swim, for example, in his *History of Nazarene Missions*, linked sanctification directly to compassionate deeds. For Swim the educational, medical and other activities of Nazarene missions flowed out of hearts made perfect in love and needed no justification as means toward evangelistic ends. They were ends in themselves. Pentecost, to Swim, was less of an empowering and more of a purifying event in connection with missions, allowing the disciples to be loosed of prejudices, antagonisms and selfishness. Swim, a former student of H. Orton Wiley at Northwest Nazarene College, served the church as a pastor, college teacher and, later, assistant in the Church Schools Department at headquarters. In Swim's understanding, God had entrusted the Church of the Nazarene with a singular and distinct "message to tell to the nations," which was that human beings "may by the grace of God and the baptism with the Holy Ghost be made holy in this life." Swim believed that the world sorely needed this unique message, which was not being emphasized by other denominations. "We dare not detain it. We must not limit it by territorial bounds." Swim lauded efforts such as those of Congregationalist missionary Frank Laubach and included literacy programs like the one Laubach began in the Philippines as legitimate manifestations of the gospel.[90]

Basil Miller was another writer who refused to repudiate the reformist impulses of Wesleyanism in the 1930s. Miller, an enigmatic figure, as well as the most prolific Nazarene writer of the times, railed against modernism and biblical criticism and strongly preached a premillennial interpretation of the Second Coming. Yet he linked social betterment and technological improvements to the transforming power of the gospel. As it was with James Dennis, to Miller it was good that missionaries introduce "civilizing" measures. Through missionaries, "shocking inhumanities" such as infanticide, footbinding, prostitution, and the oppression of women were being replaced by "the more gentle spirit of Christianity."[91] He lauded Roger Winans, Nazarene missionary to Peru, for introducing mills and machinery to the remote Aguaruna tribes among whom he worked. Such missionaries, Miller said, were on the forefront of bringing a new social order into the world. Miller compared their efforts to the antislavery movement. At the same time, like most American Christians, he exalted General and Madame Chiang Kai-shek as "Christian liberators of China."[92]

The roots of Miller's ideas were in the nineteenth-century evangelical synthesis of social and personal transformation. Despite his many diatribes against modernists, Miller stood closer than perhaps he realized to their position on missions. Like modernists, Miller believed that social betterment was a legitimate part of the Christian endeavor.[93]

J. B. Chapman succeeded Reynolds as the general superintendent most involved in establishing missions policies. Chapman was a native of Illinois who migrated in boyhood to Oklahoma and then to Texas. He quickly affiliated with small independent holiness churches, and by the time he had reached twenty he was married, an ordained minister, and secretary of the Pilot Point, Texas–based Independent Holiness Church. Chapman rose in positions of leadership after the merger with the Church of the Nazarene in 1908. A popular camp meeting preacher, folk theologian and homespun philosopher, he was editor of the *Herald of Holiness* when elected general superintendent in 1928. As general superintendent, Chapman's concerns were to boost the denomination's work among African Americans, and to establish a graduate level theological seminary.

Like Reynolds, though Chapman was not against medical and educational enterprises, the development of strong local churches and leaders was his primary concern in missions. Chapman was in tune with the "Wilsonian" goals of "self-determination."[94]

Chapman sensed that the "pioneer" stage of Nazarene missions had already passed. As he traveled around the world he was impressed, as Reynolds had been earlier, with local preachers' abilities. "All we want to do," he wrote, "is to start the work and stand by it until the people get their feet down, then we want them to develop a self-supporting and self-directing church." Dependency was not healthy. Missionaries, Chapman believed, needed to develop and use local workers, and to push them forward as district leaders. As did Basil Miller, Chapman believed that missions lifted people out of "the dungeon of economic and intellectual poverty."[95]

Though he was nearer Reynolds and Gould than Kinne and Swim in stressing that the church's goals must remain evangelistic, to the point of obscuring the message with sectarian language, Chapman stressed the distinguishing doctrine of the Church of the Nazarene. He understood the church's task as being twofold: both to "Christianize Christianity" (as Bresee had said), and to preach Christ to those who had not yet found him (as Reynolds emphasized). In 1946, shortly before his death, Chapman encouraged a denomination-wide "Crusade for Souls."[96]

During the 1920s and 1930s the general superintendents were like Bresee in preferring home missions projects to foreign missions. Especially during the Depression, they realized the financial limitations of the church. It did not need to enter new territory. There were ten million people in areas where the Church of the Nazarene already worked by comity and other arrangements who still had not accepted the gospel. C. Warren Jones, who served as both foreign and home missions secretary for eight years after 1936, tried to balance these two areas of outreach. The church, Jones said, had to fulfill both its general calling as an "evangelizing agency," and its particular mission "to preach holiness."[97]

## Policies in the Post-War Era

The leaders who took over important roles in the post-war years were conservative and stable, made up of corporate or "organization-type" men (and few women), who stood together on issues. The denomination became increasingly bureaucratic. As the first generation had been predominantly urban in outlook, and their successors rural in temperament, the church quickly accommodated to suburbia. Even in Kansas City, Nazarenes fled with other whites to the suburbs when African Americans began to buy homes near them in the mid-1950s. At the same time, radically legalistic leaders began to leave the church to form their own denominations, which had the effect of moving the majority of the Nazarenes closer to the social and religious mainstream. Nazarenes became more aware of and more influenced by the opinions of others outside of themselves. Nazarenes expanded their missions dramatically in the post-war years and at the same time initiated ethnic ministries at home—ironically, to the African Americans from whom they fled. American values placed emphasis upon economic laissez-faire and personal self-reliance, and these continued to abet mission policies aiming toward self-sustaining churches and fields.[98]

There was both a spirit of community among Nazarenes, and a greater feeling of belongingness to both society and the broader church. Through theologian H. Orton Wiley, who published a three-volume systematic theology near the beginning of this period, the denomination affirmed that its roots were deeply set in the Christian tradition. Wiley subtly yet firmly repudiated both sectarianism and fundamentalism. But he was unwilling to see the theological boundaries of the church pushed too far in the direction of neo-orthodoxy. Wiley wrote of social ethics as "duties we owe to others," motivated out of love. The Christian church functioned best as a "missionary institute," or "institute of evangelism."[99]

Jones had been standing poised and waiting for peace before sending out a backlog of waiting, eager and green missionary recruits at the end of World War II. During the global conflict, the church had amassed financial resources for expansion. Giving to the foreign missions program of the church more than doubled during the war, reaching well over a half-million dollars by 1943–1944. The opportunities to enter new countries excited church leaders and laypeople. The number of missionaries stood at 78 in 1944, but surpassed 200 by 1948, 300 by the close of the next quadrennium in 1952, and over 400 by 1960. In 1976 there were 549 Nazarene missionaries.[100]

Just as it was the theme of other evangelicals, the Church of the Nazarene took Matthew 28:23–28 as its "Great Commission." As others, Nazarenes interpreted the verses to emphasize the making of converts. "God has called the Church of the Nazarene to this one task, we have nothing else to do," said C. Warren Jones.[101] Schools and other auxiliaries must fit into these goals, since the "primary objective" was spiritual.[102]

Although the post-war impetus of Nazarene missions was strongly evangelistic, Nazarene leaders were conscious of the political impact of missions. The Truman Doctrine and the Marshall Plan stabilized Europe militarily and economically. Americans believed that their cultural values were superior to others, while at the same time paranoid, to use Richard Hofstadter's analysis, over the threat of "godless" communism in the world. When China fell to communism in 1949 and soon closed its doors to missionaries, religious aims and American foreign policy both seemed defeated.[103]

Though missionary policies continued to forbid missionaries' involvement in any political activity in the countries that they served, fear of communism lent impetus to the rapid deployment of missionaries, and in some places to an emphasis upon the indigenization of the work. The Philippines, where the church sent some former China missionaries, and where there was a strong Communist insurgency, was one such case. The missionaries sensed that they must educate Filipinos as quickly as possible and make sure that they were able to lead if political expediencies forced missionaries to withdraw. "Great areas of the world," said General Superintendent Hugh C. Benner, "are now open to the gospel, but any or all of these may be closed at an early date."[104] Missions leaders used this fear and anti-Communist rhetoric to win greater support for Nazarene missions.[105]

In Asia, the Nazarenes' pre-war work included only India, China and Japan (and from Japan, work in Korea). Like other American agencies, Nazarenes heavily invested in these countries. The situation changed after the close of China. Nazarenes continued to minister in India, resumed work in Japan and Korea, and expanded to the Philippines, Australia, New Zealand, Papua New Guinea, Taiwan and, in 1960, Samoa. At the same time, like other American mission agencies, the church sent more missionaries to Africa and Latin America after World War II than it had before. After 1960 the Nazarene church did not open work in another Asian country until it entered Indonesia in 1973.[106]

By the time C. Warren Jones retired in 1948, he had become more cautious and wary about the church's rapid deployment of missionaries and the entry of the church into new fields. Church leaders replaced him with Remiss Rehfeldt, the young and energetic Iowa district superintendent. Rehfeldt became the chief booster for the rapid expansion of the church. Though he was ardently anti-Communist, for Rehfeldt evangelism was the overriding aim of the church. Rehfeldt closely regulated the type of missionaries who went out under the church. Women were supposed to abide by the strictest standards of dress, could not wear jewelry, including wedding rings, and could not cut their hair. Eventually, as the Church of the Nazarene moved closer to main currents of American life in the 1950s, Rehfeldt's legalism on these points and others led him into conflict with the general superintendents, who were relieved when he left the missions office in 1960.[107]

Another prominent booster of Nazarene missions and evangelism in the 1950s was Russell V. DeLong, a writer, evangelist, and professor at Nazarene Theological Seminary. DeLong's *We Can If We Will*, a "required" denomination-wide study book in 1947, extolled the church's rapidly expanding missionary force. His position was that the Church of the Nazarene should do its part in cooperation with other evangelical denominations to evangelize the world. DeLong was as optimistic as Reynolds had been. What world evangelism required was the power of the Holy Spirit and efficient organization. DeLong, from the East like both Reynolds and Gould, had an expansive world vision. He believed that with only a fraction of the resources that the Allies had used to defeat evil during the Second World War, within a generation everyone around the world could have the gospel preached to them. DeLong argued that though there might be "secondary" motives for missionary efforts, such as concern for the social and physical welfare of individuals, the primary motive must always be evangelism. A firm belief in the eternal lostness of people apart from faith in Christ compelled the church to send missionaries.

DeLong mentioned little about entire sanctification or a distinctive message or mission that the Church of the Nazarene might have in the world. But his optimism about world evangelism stemmed from his confidence that a genuine baptism with the Holy Spirit would lead men and women toward deeper commitment to the missions effort. He believed that the Holy Spirit would give the dynamics to achieve the goal. Yet, overall, it seemed that DeLong (who had earned a Ph.D. in philosophy from Boston University) placed a great deal of emphasis upon human will and effort, and upon the fortuitousness of the times that allowed for world outreach.[108]

The church maintained the hospitals it had begun in India and Swaziland, undertook responsibility for an additional one in South Africa, and began a new hospital in Papua New Guinea. Yet Nazarenes in the 1950s did not often link educational or medical work to holiness. The reasons given for these efforts related to evangelism, not holiness.

Others attributed more importance than DeLong to medicine and education. William Esselstyn, a long-term missionary to Africa, emphasized that in the African context medicine was necessary to defeat belief in witchcraft. He linked medical work to evangelism. However, Esselstyn said, if the church diverted all the money and effort of the mission to evangelism, there would be an influx of new converts for a time, but they would be shallow in faith and commitment. Education produced more lasting results.[109]

Similarly, General Superintendent G. B. Williamson argued for the necessity of strong educational programs around the world. He also reminded the church that holiness consisted not only in avoiding the evil, but also in doing the good. In carrying out the Great Commission, Williamson said, the church must give a place not only to the preaching of the gospel but to "ministries of mercy," including healing the sick.[110]

David Hynd, long-time Scot missionary and medical doctor serving the church in Swaziland, believed that mission hospitals by their very work testified to the "regenerating power of the gospel with its spirit of divine compassion." He argued that medical work was nothing less than the Spirit of Christ at work in the church. Christians must not consider medical work only as a proselytizing tool. It was to Hynd, as it had been to Kinne, the "most effective interpretation of the Christlike Spirit."[111]

Meanwhile, some emphasized ministries to neglected sectors of American society. S. T. Ludwig, the church's general secretary, cited Bresee's commitment to American cities and the church's desire to be broad rather than narrow, partisan or sectarian. The mission of the church, Ludwig wrote, quoting Bresee, was to establish "a thousand centers of holy flame in this country," with the belief that "from them the streams will flow to the world."[112] Similarly, Roy Smee, home missions secretary from 1948 to 1964, and before that a successful district superintendent in Northern California, dusted off Bresee's statements about the church ministering first to the great cities of America.[113] Alpin Bowes, Smee's assistant, argued that the church must minister to transient agricultural workers as well as to areas of cities wracked by racial conflict. Echoing Bresee, Bowes wrote that "perhaps the Church of the Nazarene, in the white-hot intensity of holiness evangelism, has the responsibility, not only to the lost, but to act as leaven among the denominations, proclaiming God's call to his people to be holy and zealous of good works."[114]

As always, policy statements entreated missionaries to lead converts on into the experience of holiness. However, both the presentation of the gospel and its basic core were little different for Nazarenes than for other evangelicals. Except for Hynd and a few who thought like him, if there was any distinctiveness in the message of holiness it was related to the power to witness and to the trenchant moral legalism that leaders even less extreme than Rehfeldt thought integral to it—not to merciful deeds.[115]

The views of Nazarenes and their missionaries about the world were similar to those prevailing in American culture, although on the mission fields women retained more freedom to minister than in the

United States. In the 1950s American women went back into the kitchens, so to speak, away from the public roles they had assumed in earlier decades and during the war. In the Church of the Nazarene the percentage of women preachers and evangelists decreased. Women who in previous decades might have become pastors or evangelists in the church at home now felt called to foreign missions. In spite of Rehfeldt's strict views toward women's dress and in spite of trends in the American church, women on mission fields remained pastors, evangelists, church planters, field superintendents, and college administrators as well as teachers, doctors, nurses and accountants.[116]

In 1958, as the church faced the fiftieth anniversary of its union, there was concern among leaders about whether it had maintained its reason-to-be. General Superintendent Hugh C. Benner, for instance, stated that God had given the church a "particular" mission to spread the message of holiness, "as a second definite work of divine grace, over all the earth." The Church of the Nazarene was not to be like other Protestant denominations, suffering spiritual decline in the second or third generations. How the church was to give this message to the world was perhaps to Benner and his listeners self-evident. It was by preaching and evangelizing—by "telling" the gospel well.[117]

During the 1960s, the church continued to hear voices of dissent to the idea that the church's holiness mission could be divorced from a social witness. Carl Bangs (a former student of Wiley, with a Ph.D. from the University of Chicago, and then teaching at Olivet Nazarene College) questioned the church's identification with the "present order" and accused it of lacking concern toward the suffering of others. The call to sanctification, he stressed, surely repudiated class interest along with self-interest. "Perfect love," Bangs said, demanded a concern for the "whole" person: social, economic and intellectual as well as spiritual. Love was not "timid" in the face of injustice, but rather witnessed to the mercy of God. The good news was told by "loving word and deed, relating this gospel to the real needs of real people."[118] Though Bangs left the Church of the Nazarene to become a Methodist, these sentiments continued to beat among some Nazarenes.[119]

Under World Mission Directors George Coulter, E. S. Phillips and Jerald Johnson, who served from 1960 to 1980, Nazarenes articulated more consciously a philosophy of internationalization. By this time the church had effectively proved its point that those outside of North America could equally receive the message of holiness, articulate it appropriately, and live it according to the church's expectations. Churches on mission fields were meeting all the requirements the church had placed upon them to become partners on an equal footing with those who were sending missionaries to them. They were becoming self-supporting and self-propagating, and had reached the levels of self-government the church required. Coulter, who had emigrated from Northern Ireland to Canada, instructed missionaries to make the development of self-supporting churches the priority.[120]

Phillips, who led the Missions Department from 1964 until his death in 1973, encouraged local leadership and solicited advice from those outside North America. That the age of colonialism was over changed the face of missions, Phillips realized. The role of the missionaries must change from church planters and evangelists to advisers.[121]

Even before Phillips, H. T. Reza had become an influential spokesperson for the international church. In 1946 Reza became director of the Spanish Department in the Department of Foreign Missions and moved to Kansas City. Over the years his ministry involved a number of duties and titles, and was broader than any of them signified. Reza served as an adviser to general superintendents on issues related to Latin America, explained policy to local leaders, and influenced mission theory. He increased the church's sensitivity to its non-North American members and promoted the use of local workers rather than missionaries. Local leaders could live more cheaply and could adjust more easily, knew the language, and could communicate the gospel to their people in ways missionaries never could. They did not bring customs and aspects of culture that might be confused with the gospel.[122]

At the Central American Pastors' Conference in 1969, Federico Guillermo, district superintendent in Guatemala, stated that although the missionaries had been amiable, altruistic, generous and long-suffering, they were still outsiders. Nationalism and "Latino pride," he said, longed for Central American leadership, and for those reasons as well as economic and political ones, missionaries needed to transfer leadership to Central Americans.[123]

These sentiments came at a time of heightened racial conflict and soul-searching in the United States. A Missionary Study Commission in 1972 recognized "the clamor of men of every race and culture and of differing systems of government and of different stages of development to be heard and to have a voice in the determination of their own destiny." The commission recognized "that the gospel has too often been thought of as a white man's religion," and urged that more non-North Americans be appointed to missionary service and that districts be granted increased autonomy.[124]

Before the 1972 General Assembly Phillips met with leaders from churches outside of North America in order to listen to their perspectives, facilitate better relationships between them and missionaries, and take steps that might enable the church to become truly international. Phillips believed that the church was at a turning point. It would have to decide whether to allow its mission fields to become autonomous national churches, or to create a federation of national churches, or to continue being an international church with an administrative and theological connection maintained through its *Manual*, General Assembly, General Board, and General Superintendents—a structure in which each regular district had equal rights, privileges and responsibilities.[125]

The 1972 General Assembly established four levels of districts based on financial self-sufficiency, local leadership, and growth. A Pioneer District was organized when the church was just entering a new area. A district reached National-Mission level when there were measures of growth and self-support, and a local district superintendent. The intent here was for missionaries to step aside from leadership early in a district's development. At the next, Mission District, level there was to be 50 percent self-support and an elected national district superintendent. At the second and third stages the duties of the mission council were separated from those of the local superintendent. However, the mission council president served on the District Advisory Board and the district superintendent presented budget needs to the mission council. The District Advisory Board and the Executive Committee of the mission council jointly approved how money from Kansas City was apportioned. General Board funds used for building projects and institutions remained under the mission council. Both the district superintendent and the mission council president submitted regular reports to the Department of World Missions.[126] At the fourth level, a district achieved Regular status when it became fully self-supporting and there were at least 1,000 members. The number of delegates to the General Assembly depended on the level and membership.

When, after the 1972 General Assembly, districts were evaluated by these criteria, the World Mission Division identified 32 Pioneer districts, 29 National-Mission districts, 5 Mission districts, and only 1 district, the Northeast Guatemala District, at Regular district level. Missionaries in Guatemala had intentionally prepared the church for self-support. A careful policy that led to self-reliance had been prepared in the 1930s. But not until 1963, in part due to "internal strife" among missionaries, was a Guatamalan, Federico Guillermo, appointed district superintendent.[127]

Though the church was a long way from promoting non North Americans to positions of leadership in the church, local leaders like Guillermo appeared around the world with increasing regularity. There were only fifteen national district superintendents in 1970, but the number had risen to seventy-five by 1980.[128]

## Conclusion

The church's leaders presumed that the holiness message was democratizing. In theory, there were no spiritual hierarchies based on history, culture, language or ethnicity. Holiness was for all. Just as Phineas Bresee had opened the doors of his church to the poor, and had given them privileged seats, all were equally entitled to participation in the life of the Church of the Nazarene. Yet, in spite of these ideas, the church was slow to transfer responsibility and trust to local leaders. Inevitably, at different times, the church had to recognize the "clamor" of those from "every race and culture and of differing systems of government and of different stages of development to be heard and to have a voice in the determination of their own destiny." A 1972 report went on to affirm that the gospel must not be thought of as a "white man's religion."[129]

Reynolds himself and his successor saw that men and women of various countries around the world could respond to the message of holiness and manifest the presence of the Holy Spirit. It was a matter—a large matter—of when and how to bring those who were spiritual equals (if not betters) into positions of influence and leadership in the denomination as a whole. That later leaders could pose the question of equality even if it remained unanswered, was evidence of decades of work of missionaries and their co-laborers.

On the side of local Nazarenes, questions remained as to whether denominational loyalty could really become more important than nationalism. Could there be (or should there be) both contextualization of the gospel and fidelity to second blessing holiness? Could missionaries develop strong, self-reliant local leaders while encouraging them to remain indebted to Nazarene principles of church government and theology? The policies and philosophies that had characterized Nazarene missions from the beginning as well as the doctrine of perfect love made the issue of equality integral to the very soul of the church.

## Notes

1. Compare Amy Hinshaw, *Messengers of the Cross in China* (Kansas City, Mo.: Nazarene Publishing House, n.d.), *Messengers of the Cross in Latin*

*America* (Kansas City, Mo.: Woman's Foreign Missionary Society, 1927), *Messengers of the Cross in Africa* (Kansas City, Mo.: Woman's Foreign Missionary Society, [1928]), and *Messengers of the Cross in India* (Kansas City, Mo.: Nazarene Publishing House, n.d.), to the similar profile of missionaries to China in Valentin H. Rabe, *The Home Base of American China Missions, 1880–1920* (Cambridge, Mass.: Harvard University Press, 1978), 93–107.

2. See Carl Bangs, *Phineas F. Bresee: His Life in Methodism, the Holiness Movement, and the Church of the Nazarene* (Kansas City, Mo.: Beacon Hill, 1995); Paul Bassett, "Culture and Concupiscence: The Changing Definition of Sanctity in the Wesleyan/Holiness Movement, 1867–1920," *Wesleyan Theological Journal* 28 (Spring/Fall 1993), 59–127.

3. Kimber Moulton, quoted in Donald S. Metz, *Some Crucial Issues in the Church of the Nazarene* (Olathe, Kans.: Wesleyan Heritage, 1994), 138.

4. Andrew Walls, *The Missionary Movement in Christian History: Studies in the Transmission of Faith* (Maryknoll, N.Y.: Orbis, 1996), 221–240.

5. R. Franklin Cook, *The International Dimension: Six Expressions of the Great Commission* (Kansas City, Mo.: Nazarene Publishing House, 1984), 30–35, 51–59. See also J. Fred Parker, *Mission to the World: A History of Missions in the Church of the Nazarene through 1985* (Kansas City, Mo.: Nazarene Publishing House, 1988), 36–47.

6. See *Ministering to the Millions*, comp. Department of World Missions (Kansas City, Mo.: Nazarene Publishing House, 1971).

7. Timothy L. Smith, *Called Unto Holiness; The Story of the Nazarenes: The Formative Years* (Kansas City, Mo.: Nazarene Publishing House, 1962), 266–271, 289–297, 315–321; W. T. Purkiser, *Called Unto Holiness*, vol. 2: *The Second Twenty-Five Years, 1933–1958* (Kansas City, Mo.: Nazarene Publishing House, 1983), 150–155, 161–173.

8. A. M. Hills, *Fundamental Christian Theology: A Systematic Theology*, 2 vols. (Reprint, Salem, Ohio: Schmul, 1980), 1: 117–135, 148, 370–375; 2: 261–265, 351–360; Hills, *The Secret of Spiritual Power* (Nashville, Tenn.: Pentecostal Mission Publishing, n.d.), 82, and throughout; Hills, *Pentecostal Light* (Reprint, Salem, Ohio: Schmul Publishers, n.d.), 24–26, and throughout. For analysis see Paul Bassett, "The Fundamentalist Leavening of the Holiness Movement, 1914–1940," *Wesleyan Theological Journal* 13 (Spring 1978), 80–81; George M. Marsden, *Fundamentalism and American Culture: The Shaping of Twentieth-Century Evangelicalism, 1870–1925* (New York: Oxford University Press, 1980), 55–62; L. Paul Gresham, *Waves Against Gibraltar: A Memoir of Dr. A. M. Hills, 1848–1935* (Bethany, Okla.: Southern Nazarene University Press, 1992), 124, 162–163, 194–195, 209.

9. Mendell Taylor, *Fifty Years of Nazarene Missions*, vol. 1: *Administration and Promotion* (Kansas City, Mo.: Beacon Hill, 1952), 11.

10. *History of the Foreign Missionary Work of the Church of the Nazarene* (Kansas City, Mo.: General Board of Foreign Missions, Church of the Nazarene, 1921), 7–8. See also Hiram Reynolds, "The Missionary Work," May 23, 1907, Nazarene Archives.

11. Samuel Capen, President of the American Board of Commissioners for Foreign Missions, quoted in Rabe, *The Home Base*, 154.

12. *Records of the Annual Meetings of the Central Evangelical Holiness Association* (Providence, R.I.: Press of George A. Wilson, 1896), 8, 21. On the increased organization of American society in the 1890s and 1900s see Robert Wiebe, *The Search for Order, 1877–1920* (New York: Hill and Wang, 1967).

13. Association of Pentecostal Churches of America, *Minutes of the Fourth Annual Meeting* (Providence, R.I.: Pentecostal Printing, 1899), 35.

14. *Manual of the First Pentecostal Church of Lynn, Mass.* (Providence, R.I.: Pentecostal Printing, 1898), 7–8; "Minutes of the Missionary Committee of the Association of Pentecostal Churches of America," December 15, 1899; Association of Pentecostal Churches of America, *Minutes of the Tenth Annual Meeting* (Providence, R.I.: Pentecostal Printing, 1905), 49.

15. For Reynolds see Amy N. Hinshaw, *In Labors Abundant: A Biography of H. F. Reynolds* (Kansas City, Mo.: Nazarene Publishing House, n.d.), and the "Autobiographical Memoirs" on which her book is based; J. Timothy White, "Hiram F. Reynolds: Prime Mover of the Nazarene Mission Education System," Ph.D. dissertation, University of Kansas, 1996, 38–88, especially pp. 53–56. See also Smith, *Called*, 60–61.

16. "Missions Committee of the Association of Pentecostal Churches of America," December 11, 1897, amended July 20, 1904, 3 pp.

17. Susan N. Fitkin, *Grace More Abounding: A Story of the Triumphs of Redeeming Grace Through Two Score Years in the Master's Service* (Kansas City, Mo.: Nazarene Publishing House, n.d.); Basil Miller, *Susan N. Fitkin: For God and Missions* (Kansas City, Mo.: Nazarene Publishing House, n.d.), 57–67, 70. Compare Patricia R. Hill, *The World Their Household: The American Woman's Foreign Mission Movement and Cultural Transformation, 1870–1920* (Ann Arbor: University of Michigan Press, 1985), 8, and throughout; Dana L. Robert, "Holiness and the Missionary Vision of the Woman's Foreign Missionary Society of the Methodist Episcopal Church, 1869–1894," *Methodist History* 39 (October 2000), 15–27.

18. *Association of Pentecostal Churches of America Minutes of the Sixth Annual Meeting* (Providence, R.I.: Pentecostal Printing, 1901), 45–46.

19. For the New England context see Clifton J. Philips, *Protestant America and the Pagan World: The First Half-Century of the American Board of Commissioners for Foreign Missions, 1810–1860* (Cambridge, Mass.: Harvard University Press, 1969), 22–23. See also Seth Cook Rees, *The Holy War* (Cincinnati: God's Bible School and Revivalist, 1904), 28–44; Paul S. Rees, *Seth Cook Rees: The Warrior Saint* (Indianapolis: Pilgrim Book Room, 1934), 64–77; Norris Magnuson, *Salvation in the Slums: Evangelical Social Work, 1865–1920* (Metuchen, N.J.: Scarecrow, 1977), 30–44.

20. *Records of the Annual Meetings of the Central Evangelical Holiness Association* (Providence, R.I.: Press of George A. Wilson, 1896), 8, 21. See Jose Delgado, "The Providence Connection: To Cape Verde and Back," *Holiness Today* (March 2001), 8–11.

21. L. S. Tracy to Reynolds, November 9, 1905; Smith, *Called*, 82–87; Russell V. DeLong and Mendell Taylor, *Fifty Years of Nazarene Missions*, vol. 2: *History of the Fields* (Kansas City, Mo.: Beacon Hill, 1955), 284–285.

22. Rabe, *The Home Base*, 72–75. See James McGraw, "The Preaching of Hiram F. Reynolds," *The Preacher's Magazine* 29 (April 1954), 3–5.

23. C. Howard Hopkins, *John R. Mott, 1865–1955: A Biography* (Grand Rapids, Mich.: Eerdmans, 1979), 22–23, 225–233; Michael Parker, *The Kingdom of Character: The Student Volunteer Movement for Foreign Missions (1886–1926)* (Lanham, Md.: University Press of America, 1998), 36–41.

24. Among the books by William Taylor that Reynolds owned, one was *Ten Years of Self-Supporting Missions in India*. Reynolds later drew together a missions library at Nazarene headquarters, to which he contributed his personal copies. See the accession sheets in the Nazarene Archives. But there are no certain indications of what he read, and there are no clues from Hinshaw, *In Labors Abundant*, from Reynolds's "Autobiographical Memoirs," or from other of his letters and papers. For Taylor see David Bundy, "Bishop William Taylor and Methodist Mission: A Study in Nineteenth Century Social History, Part I: From Campmeeting Convert to International Evangelist," *Methodist History* 27 (July 1989), 198–212, and "Bishop William Taylor and Methodist Mission: A Study in Nineteenth Century Social History, Part II: Social Structures in Collision," *Methodist History* 28 (October 1989), 3–21.

25. "Minutes of the First Meeting of the New Elected Missionary Committee of the Association of Pentecostal Churches of America," April 15, 1897; "Minutes of the Missionary Committee of the Association of Pentecostal Churches of America," January 18, 1905; L. A. Campbell, Secretary, "Recommendations of the [India] Missionary Meeting to the General Missionary Board, 1909"; L. S. Tracy to E. G. Anderson, December 27, 1911; Tracy to General Foreign Missionary Board of the Pentecostal Church of the Nazarene [1914]; and "China," n.d. (file 453-3); Hinshaw, *In Labors Abundant*, 156–157. See R. Pierce Beaver, *Ecumenical Beginnings in Protestant World Mission: A History of Comity* (New York: Thomas Nelson, 1962), 81–101.

26. On "holiness or hell" see J. Kenneth Grider, *Entire Sanctification: The Distinctive Doctrine of Wesleyanism* (Kansas City, Mo.: Beacon Hill, 1980), 144–146. On the Seventh-day Adventists see M. D. Wood, *Fruit from the Jungle* (Mountain View, Calif.: Pacific Publishing, 1919), 10–19, written by a Nazarene missionary pioneer in India who became Seventh-day Adventist; and P. Gerard Damsteegt, *Foundations of the Seventh-day Adventist Message and Mission* (Grand Rapids, Mich.: Eerdmans, 1977), 187, 283, 292.

27. William Hutchison, *Errand to the World: American Protestant Thought and Foreign Missions* (Chicago: University of Chicago Press, 1987), 99–102, 107–111, 118–124. See R. Pierce Beaver, ed., *To Advance the Gospel: Selections from the Writings of Rufus Anderson* (Grand Rapids, Mich.: Eerdmans, 1967), 97–102; Max Warren, ed., *To Apply the Gospel: Selections from the Writings of Henry Venn* (Grand Rapids, Mich.: Eerdmans, 1971), 74–78; Roland Allen, *Missionary Methods: St. Paul's or Ours?* (Reprint, Grand Rapids, Mich.:

Eerdmans, 1962), 151–163); Charles W. Forman, "A History of Foreign Mission Theory in America," in *American Missions in Bicentennial Perspective*, ed. R. Pierce Beaver (Pasadena, Calif.: William Carey, 1977), 80–95; and James Patterson, "The Kingdom and the Great Commission: Social Gospel Impulses and American Protestant Missionary Leaders, 1890–1920," *Fides et Historia* 25 (Winter/Spring 1993), 48–61.

28. Contrast Rabe, *The Home Base*, 63.

29. E. G. Anderson, *Annual Report and Survey of the Fields Occupied by Missionaries of the Pentecostal Church of the Nazarene, 1917–1918* (Kansas City, Mo.: General Foreign Missionary Board, [1918]), 7–8. Note also the Association's protest about "the horrible condition of affairs in the Philippines" under the Americans in *Minutes of the Sixth Annual Meeting* (Providence, R.I.: Pentecostal Printing, 1901), 45–46. On "duty" in Methodism see Olin A. Curtis, *The Christian Faith Personally Given in a System of Doctrine* (New York: Eaton and Mains, 1905), 63–67, 389f; and John H. Lavely, "Personalism's Debt to Kant," in *The Boston Personalist Tradition in Philosophy, Social Ethics, and Theology*, eds. Paul Deats and Carol Robb (Macon, Ga.: Mercer University Press, 1986), 23–38.

30. Compare Ben Primer, *Protestants and American Business Methods* (Ann Arbor: UMI Research Press, 1979), chs. 4–5.

31. *Holiness Association of Texas Yearbook 1904–05* (Greenville, Tex.: Texas Holiness Advocate Print, [1905]), 40–47; C. B. Jernigan, *Pioneer Days of the Holiness Movement in the Southwest* (Kansas City, Mo.: Nazarene Publishing House, 1919), 150–154; Joseph E. Campbell, *The Pentecostal Holiness Church, 1898–1948* (Franklin Springs, Ga.: Pentecostal Holiness Publishing House, 1951), 191–202, 211–212; Smith, *Called*, 174–176, 186–187, 198, 250–257; Vinson Synan, *The Holiness-Pentecostal Movement in the United States* (Grand Rapids, Mich.: Eerdmans, 1971), 125–139; Charles E. Jones, *Perfectionist Persuasion: The Holiness Movement and American Methodism, 1867–1936* (Metuchen, N.J.: Scarecrow, 1974), 93–95; John T. Benson, Jr., *A History 1898–1915 of the Pentecostal Mission, Inc. Nashville, Tennessee* (Nashville, Tenn.: Trevecca Press, 1977), 93–95; Stan Ingersoll, "Christian Baptism and the Early Nazarenes: The Sources That Shaped a Pluralistic Baptismal Tradition," *Wesleyan Theological Journal* 25 (Fall 1990), 25–28.

32. Smith, *Called*, 167–179; J. Fred Parker, "Those Early Nazarenes Cared: Compassionate Ministries of the Nazarenes," *The Preacher's Magazine* 59 (September/October/November 1983), 32P-32T, which mostly deals with the Southern groups; and Stan Ingersoll, ed., *Rescue the Perishing, Care for the Dying: Sources and Documents on Compassionate Ministry in the Nazarene Archives*, second ed. (Kansas City, Mo.: Nazarene Archives, n.d.). See Klaus Fiedler, *The Story of Faith Missions* (Oxford: Regnum, 1994).

33. *Government and Doctrines of New Testament Churches* (Milan, Tenn.: Exchange Office, 1903), 5. See also "Church Book of the New Testament Church of Christ, Milan, Tennessee, 1897–1905" [and later] regarding missionaries this congregation supported; "Minutes of the Seventh Annual Council of

the Holiness Church of Christ," Milan, Tennessee, November 16, 1905; *Manual of the Church of Christ* (Greenville, Tex.: Holiness Associates Publishing, 1905), 36f; "Minutes of the Eighth Annual Meeting of the Holiness Church of Christ," Jonesboro, Arkansas, November 14–16, 1906; *Minutes and Yearbook of the Eastern Council Holiness Church of Christ*, Little Rock, Arkansas, November 12–17, 1907 (Pilot Point, Tex.: Evangel Publishing, [1907]), 44–46.

34. DeLong and Taylor, *Fifty Years*, 2: 107–109; Smith, *Called*, 250–257. See also Deborah J. Baldwin, *Protestants and the Mexican Revolution: Missionaries, Ministries, and Social Change* (Urbana: University of Illinois Press, 1990).

35. *Holiness Association of Texas Yearbook 1906–1907* (N.p., n.d.), 67–69. The report on the "race problem" was signed by E. C. DeJernett, R. L. Averill and J. T. Upchurch. This evidence contrasts to Leonard Sweet, "A Nation Born Again: The Union Prayer Meeting Revival and Cultural Relativism," in *In the Great Tradition: Essays on Pluralism, Voluntarism and Revivalism*, eds. Joseph D. Bon and Paul R. Deckar (Valley Forge, Pa.: Judson, 1982), 207–208.

36. "Articles of Faith and General Rules of the Church of the Nazarene," November 26, [1895]; also in *The Manual of the Church of the Nazarene, Promulgated by the Assembly of 1898* (Reprint, 1995), 13.

37. "Church of the Nazarene" pamphlet published November 1895.

38. Reformist elements are evident in Bresee's *Sermons on Isaiah* (Kansas City, Mo.: Nazarene Publishing House, 1926), particularly the ones on "Righteousness in Politics," 61–69, and "Holiness and Civic Righteousness," 79–87. See also pp. 41, 56, 149, 167. See Bangs, *Phineas F. Bresee*, 90, 187–188, 200. Compare George E. Mowry, *The California Progressives* (Berkeley: University of California Press, 1951), 86–103; James H. Timberlake, *Prohibition in the Progressive Movement, 1900–1920* (Reprint, New York: Atheneum, 1970), 14–18, 29–30; Paul Boyer, *Urban Masses and Moral Order in America, 1820–1920* (Cambridge, Mass.: Harvard University Press, 1978), 195–204; Smith, *Called*, 199–204.

39. Ward B. Chandler, comp., *Sayings of Our Founder* (Houston: Chandler and Roach, 1948), 51.

40. Bresee, in *Nazarene Messenger* 11 (September 27, 1906), 6.

41. Bresee, *Soul Food for Today*, comp. C. J. Kinne (Kansas City, Mo.: Nazarene Publishing House, 1929), September 29 [no pagination]. See the 1898 *Manual*, 9–10, 23. Sandra Sizer Frankiel, *California's Spiritual Frontiers: Religious Alternatives in Anglo-Protestantism, 1850–1910* (Berkeley: University of California Press, 1988), 107–119, describes Bresee as a mystic.

42. Bresee, *Sermons from Matthew's Gospel*, 96.

43. Chandler, *Sayings*, 15.

44. Kinne, *Soul Food*, January 30.

45. Bresee, in *Nazarene Messenger* 11 (December 20, 1906), 7. Likewise, "Report of the General Superintendent," *Proceedings of the Tenth Annual Assembly of the Church of the Nazarene*, ed. Robert Pierce (Los Angeles: Nazarene Publishing House, 1905), 10; and *Proceedings of the First General*

*Assembly of the Pentecostal Church of the Nazarene* (Los Angeles: Nazarene Publishing House, 1907), 23–24, 47.

46. On Bresee's opposition to faith missions see *Nazarene Messenger* (December 8, 1904), 6.

47. *Manual of the Church of the Nazarene, 1903* (Los Angeles: Nazarene Publishing House), 7, 67–70; *Proceedings of the Ninth Annual Assembly of the Church of the Nazarene* (Los Angeles: Nazarene Publishing House, 1904), 37.

48. E. A. Girvin, *Phineas F. Bresee: A Prince in Israel; A Biography* (Kansas City, Mo.: Nazarene Publishing House, 1916), 236–237.

49. *Proceedings of the Tenth Annual Assembly*, 34–36. Among the signatories of the Missions Committee Report were stalwarts Leslie Gay, Mae McReynolds and E. A. Girvin. See *Nazarene Messenger* 11 (November 28, 1901), 6; and *Nazarene Messenger* 10 (October 19, 1905), 1; Girvin, *Bresee*, 340–341. See also Ronald Kirkemo, *For Zion's Sake: A History of Pasadena/Point Loma College* (San Diego, Calif.: Point Loma Press, 1992), 8, 23, 37.

50. L. C. Osborn, *Hitherto! 1914–1939: Silver Anniversary of the Church of the Nazarene in China* (Tianjin: Peiyang Press, [1939]), 1–3; W. W. Cary, *Story of the National Holiness Missionary Society* (Chicago: National Holiness Missionary Society, 1940), 7, 77–78; Kirkemo, *For Zion's Sake*, 8. See Bresee's remarks to the members of the Association of Pentecostal Churches of America in their *Minutes of the Tenth Annual Meeting* (Providence, R.I.: Pentecostal Printing, 1907), 17.

51. Hulda Grebe, "Minutes of the Assembly, October 3, 1906"; Girvin, *Bresee*, 182–186. See J. E. Kirby, "Matthew Simpson and the Mission of America," *Church History* 36 (1967), 305.

52. Bresee, "History of the Church of the Nazarene," *Nazarene Messenger* (July 4, 1907). Likewise see various articles defending "organized" holiness in the *Herald of Holiness*, April 17, 1912, and April 24, 1912, issues. See Girvin, *Bresee*, 238; Melvin E. Dieter, *The Holiness Revival of the Nineteenth Century*, second ed. (Lanham, Md.: Scarecrow, 1996), 251–255.

53. The distinction between "cardinal" and "distinguishing" characteristics was made by William Greathouse, "Nazarene Theology in Perspective" (Inaugural Address, Nazarene Theological Seminary, January 6, 1969), 15. Similarly, Geoffrey Wainwright, "Ecclesial Location and Ecumenical Vocation," in *The Future of Methodist Theological Traditions*, ed. M. Douglas Meeks (Nashville, Tenn.: Abingdon, 1985), 96–103.

54. Bresee, *Sermons from Matthew's Gospel* (Kansas City, Mo.: Nazarene Publishing House, n.d.), 128. See Smith, *Called*, 25–26; Magnuson, *Salvation in the Slums*, 34–39, 43–44; Diane Winston, *Red-Hot and Righteous: The Urban Religion of the Salvation Army* (Cambridge, Mass.: Harvard University Press, 1999), 18–23, 46, 114, 218–220.

55. *Proceedings of the Second General Assembly of the Pentecostal Church of the Nazarene* (Los Angeles: Nazarene Publishing House, 1908), 39, 43–47; "Rescue Mission" volume, *Herald of Holiness* (March 19, 1913); Haynes,

editorials in *Herald of Holiness*: March 19, 1913, 2; April 14, 1920, 3; May 12, 1920, 1; August 11, 1920, 2; September 22, 1920, 2; November 10, 1920, 1; April 6, 1921, 1; April 13, 1921, 2. See also Marsden, *Fundamentalism and American Culture*, 80–92.

56. Smith, *Called*, 250–257.

57. Taylor, *Fifty Years*, vol. 1: 15–20.

58. *Important Information Concerning Mission Work and Missionaries of the Pentecostal Church of the Nazarene, October 1, 1910 to September 30, 1911* (Chicago: General Missionary Board, [1911]), 22 pp.

59. "The Policy of the General Missionary Board of the Pentecostal Church of the Nazarene, to Govern the Work in Japan," January 17, 1914 (file 305-14).

60. Reynolds, "Missionary Sermon," June 10, 1917, Nampa, Idaho, transcription (file 183-9). See also sermons in file 183-6; and Reynolds, "With the General Secretary in Western India," *Other Sheep* (July 1914), 2–3.

61. See Magnuson, *Salvation in the Slums*, 30–44, 70–90; Jones, *Perfectionist Persuasion*, 71–77, 189–194.

62. James Reed, *The Missionary Mind and American East Asia Policy 1911–1915* (Cambridge, Mass.: Harvard University Press, 1983), 82–84.

63. See Reynolds's own account of his first world trip in *World-Wide Missions* (Kansas City, Mo.: Church of the Nazarene, 1915). See Reynolds's guidebook for his last trip to China, *Peking, North China, South Manchuria and Korea*, fourth ed. (N.p.: Thomas Cook and Son, 1920), in the library of Asia-Pacific Nazarene Theological Seminary. See also Hinshaw, *In Labor's Abundant*, 217–262.

64. *Zion's Outlook* (November 7, 1901), 10. See also "Minutes of [Executive Committee] Pentecostal Mission," November 6, 1902, for questions adopted for outgoing missionaries.

65. Benson, *Pentecostal Mission*, 118, 181–182, 192–193, 214.

66. *Zion's Outlook* (November 7, 1901), 9.

67. "State of Tennessee Charter of Incorporation," April 21, 1902. Compare Dana L. Robert, *American Women in Mission: A Social History of Their Thought and Practices* (Macon, Ga.: Mercer University Press, 1996), 204–205.

68. Benson, *Pentecostal Mission*, 113.

69. Benson, *Pentecostal Mission*, 30–31, 40, 45, 63–65, 81, 85, 101, 118, 120, 129, 151, 156, 161, 181, 192, 194.

70. Smith, *Called*, 238–242, 343; Jack Ford, *In the Steps of John Wesley: The Church of the Nazarene in Britain* (Kansas City, Mo.: Nazarene Publishing House, 1968), 58.

71. Rabe, *The Home Base*, 110–114, 169–171.

72. The statistics are from Chapman, *History*, 70. See Smith, *Called*, 86–90. Compare Edmund S. Morgan, *The Puritan Family: Religion and Domestic Relations in Seventeenth-Century New England*, rev. ed. (New York: Harper and Row, 1966), 173–186.

73. C. J. Kinne, *The Modern Samaritan: A Presentation of the Claims of Medical Missions* (Kansas City, Mo.: Nazarene Publishing House, n.d.), 10.

74. Kinne, *The Modern Samaritan*, 28

75. Kinne, *The Modern Samaritan*, 85. See Robert Jared, "The Formation of a Sunday School Philosophy for the Church of the Nazarene, 1907–1932," Ed.D. dissertation, Southern Baptist Theological Seminary, 1989, 125–144. On the connection between "disinterested benevolence" and social reform see Joseph A. Conforti, *Samuel Hopkins and the New Divinity Movement: Calvinism, the Congregational Ministry, and Reform in New England Between the Great Awakenings* (Grand Rapids, Mich.: Eerdmans, 1981), 121–124.

76. "What Is the Future of the Church of the Nazarene?" *Herald of Holiness* (September 12, 1923), 1.

77. Smith, *Called*, 305–321, 337–341; H. Ray Dunning, "Nazarene Ethics as Seen in a Theological and Sociological Context," Ph.D. dissertation, Vanderbilt University, 1969, 186–191; Purkiser, *Called*, 61–67, 70–78; Jones, *Perfectionist Persuasion*, 127–142. Also see Mildred Bangs Wynkoop, *The Trevecca Story: 75 Years of Christian Service* (Nashville, Tenn.: Trevecca, 1976), 144–145, which contrasts the "countrybred" C. E. Hardy (who served intermittently as president of Trevecca) to men of "city culture" such as H. H. Wise and John T. Benson. On the impact of World War I on Protestant thought see William R. Hutchison, *The Modernist Impulse in American Protestantism* (Oxford: Oxford University Press, 1976), ch. 7, and Timothy P. Weber, *Living in the Shadow of the Second Coming: American Premillennialism, 1875–1982*, revised ed. (Grand Rapids, Mich.: Zondervan, 1983), ch. 5.

78. A. J. Smith to J. G. Morrison, January 29, 1931, enclosing two rings to be sold. See Wallace Thornton, *Radical Righteousness: Personal Ethics and the Development of the Holiness Movement* (Salem, Ohio: Schmul, 1998), 223, and throughout.

79. Reynolds, "The Meaning of Present Conditions," n.d. (file 262-56). See likewise [Reynolds], *History of the Foreign Missionary Work* (Kansas City, Mo.: General Board of Foreign Missions, Church of the Nazarene, 1921), 58–59.

80. See B. W. Miller and G. F. Owen, *Behold He Cometh: Inspirational Messages on the Second Coming* (Kansas City, Mo.: Nazarene Publishing House, 1924), 38–39, 45–46, 57–58, 89; Basil Miller and U. E. Harding, *"Cunningly Devised Fables": Modernism Exposed and Refuted* (N.p., n.d.); and F. M. Messenger, *The Coming Superman* (Kansas City, Mo.: Nazarene Publishing House, 1928), for which William B. Riley wrote the introduction. See Smith, *Called*, 305–321; Kirkemo, *Zion's*, 87–94, 103–104, 139–140, 142–144, 150–153, 172–173; and Wynkoop, *Trevecca*, 118–119, on fundamentalism, and pp. 60 and 147 on pre-millennialism. See also James Moorhead, "The Erosion of Postmillennialism in American Religious Thought, 1865–1925," *Church History* 53 (March 1984), 61–77.

81. Undated policy, about 1921, very much like the previous policies issued for Japan and India in 1914, Reynolds papers (files 183-9 and 282-44).

82. For example, see Reynolds, "Around the World Trip," to the General Missionary Board of the Pentecostal Church of the Nazarene [1914]; Hinshaw, *In Labors Abundant*, 262.

83. "Policy of the General Board, 1923," December 8, 1923 (file 305-15).

84. "Policy of the General Board, 1923." After 40 years of work in India, in 1937 Nazarenes elected their first Indian district superintendent. The first Indian Anglican bishop, V. S. Azariah, was appointed in 1912 (and remained the only Indian Anglican bishop until his death in 1945), and the first Indian Methodist bishop in 1931, and both of these groups had been at work in India since 1813; 85 years longer than the Nazarenes. See Kenneth S. Latourette, *Christianity in a Revolutionary Age*, vol. 5: *The Twentieth Century Outside Europe* (New York: Harper and Row, 1962), 319–320; M. D. David, "American Missionaries in India: A Difference," *Indian Church History* 30 (December 1996), 117; Susan B. Harper, *In the Shadow of the Mahatma: Bishop V. S. Azariah and the Travails of Christianity in British India* (Grand Rapids, Mich.: Eerdmans, 2000), 97–100.

85. "Policy of the General Board of the Church of the Nazarene to Govern Its Work in Foreign Fields," undated (copy in file 305-15 was that of Reynolds), and the nearly identical "Policy" dated June 11, 1932 (file 764-27). Compare undated policy (in file 282-43), which was not adopted.

86. "Policy of the General Board" (file 305-15).

87. Chapman, *Thirty Thousand Miles of Missionary Travel* (Kansas City, Mo.: Nazarene Publishing House, [1931]), 62–67; [J. G. Morrison], "Minutes" of the Department of Foreign Missions, 1931 [file 451-35], 16; C. Warren Jones, "Quadrennial Report of the Department of Foreign Missions," *Journal of the Tenth General Assembly of the Church of the Nazarene*, eds. C. Warren Jones and Mendell Taylor (N.p., [1940]), 342–343.

88. J. Glenn Gould, *Missionary Pioneers and Our Debt to Them* (Kansas City, Mo.: Nazarene Publishing House, [1935]), 39. For the context see Joel Carpenter, ed., *Modernism and Foreign Missions: Two Fundamentalist Protests* (New York: Garland, 1988), including Carpenter's "Introduction."

89. Gould, *Missionary Pioneers*, 21, 35, 37–39, 180–189. See Gould, "The Holy Spirit and Missions," in Gould, Basil Miller and Amy Hinshaw, *The Dynamic of Missions* (Kansas City, Mo.: Nazarene Publishing House, [1932]), 20–21, 38, 41, 46–47, 54. See also L. A. Reed and H. A. Wiese, *The Challenge of China* (Kansas City, Mo.: Nazarene Publishing House, [1937]), 49–50, 71–72, 77–78, 100–101; Chapman, *History*, 64. See also General Superintendents' "Address," *Herald of Holiness* 12 (October 3, 1927).

90. Swim, *A History of Missions of the Church of the Nazarene* (Kansas City, Mo.: Nazarene Publishing House, 1936), 201, 204. See also pp. 3, 10.

91. Miller, "The Bible and Missions," in Gould, Miller and Hinshaw, *The Dynamic of Missions*, 98.

92. Miller, *Generalissimo and Madame Chiang Kai-Shek: Christian Liberators of China*, second ed. (Grand Rapids, Mich.: Zondervan, 1943), 7, 155–169; Miller, "The Bible and Missions," in Gould, Miller and Hinshaw, *The*

*Dynamic of Missions*, 94–100, 114. In the early 1950s Miller established his own mission agency, World-Wide Missions, which aimed to directly support national workers. See his four-part autobiography, especially *Those Were the Days: Remembering My Youth* (Pasadena, Calif.: World-Wide Missions, 1970), 116; and *Dreams Fulfilled: My Mission Career* (Pasadena, Calif.: World-Wide Missions, 1971), 47–48, 53, 67–73, 103–104.

93. Hutchison, *Errand to the World*, 138–145. But contrast Marsden, *Fundamentalism*, 80–93, 161–164, and Weber, *Living in the Shadow*, 96–104, for "moderate" pre-millennialists' continued moral reform concerns that parallel Miller's.

94. Compare Tony Smith, *America's Mission: The United States and the Worldwide Struggle for Democracy in the Twentieth Century* (Princeton, N.J.: Princeton University Press, 1994), 335.

95. Chapman, *Ask Doctor Chapman* (Kansas City, Mo.: Nazarene Publishing House, 1943), 191–192.

96. D. Shelby Corlett, *Spirit Filled: The Life of the Rev. James Blaine Chapman, D.D.* (Kansas City, Mo.: Beacon Hill, n.d.), 168–169. See also Jim Lehrer, *A Bus of My Own* (New York: G. P. Putnam's, 1992), 39–45, who describes his grandfather's books as "mostly religious gibberish" (p. 45).

97. General Superintendents' Quadrennial Address, 207, 214, 217, and Jones, "Quadrennial Report of the Department of Home Missions and Evangelism," 360–361, both in the *Journal of the Tenth General Assembly*.

98. The anxiety over leadership and generational transitions is seen in the General Superintendents' Quadrennial Address, *Journal of the Twelfth General Assembly of the Church of the Nazarene*, eds. S. T. Ludwig and Greta Hfamsher (N.p., [1948]), 154–156, 162, 164; and is described in Purkiser, *Called*, 161–168. On the bureaucratization of the church see Jerald Johnson, *Hardy C. Powers: Bridge Builder* (Kansas City, Mo.: Nazarene Publishing House, 1985), 51–58; Kirkemo, *Zion's*, ch. 10, "From Subculture to Mainstream," 180–201. On demographics see Armstrong, *Face to Face*, 7–17, and Robert L. Ingle, "The Changing Spatial Distribution of the Church of the Nazarene," M.S. thesis, Oklahoma State University, 1973. See also Purkiser, *Called*, 68–171, 204–211.

99. H. Orton Wiley, *Christian Theology*, vol. 3 (Kansas City, Mo.: Beacon Hill, 1943), 68–79, 126. See Ross Price, *H. Orton Wiley: Servant and Savant of the Sagebrush* (Kansas City, Mo.: Nazarene Publishing House, 1968), 42–43, 49–52; Bassett, "Fundamentalist Leavening," 65–67, 74, 79–80, 82–85; Carl Bangs, *Our Roots of Belief: A Biblical and Faithful Theology* (Kansas City, Mo.: Nazarene Publishing House, 1981), 70–79; Kirkemo, *Zion's*, 77–79, 87–94, 202–226. As to where the holiness movement stood on these issues see Bassett, "The Theological Identity of the North American Holiness Movement," in *The Variety of Evangelicalism*, eds. Donald Dayton and Robert K. Johnston (Knoxville: University of Tennessee Press, 1991), 72–108; and Susie C. Stanley, "Wesleyan/Holiness Churches: Innocent Bystanders in the Fundamentalist/ Modernist Controversy," in *Re-Forming the Center: American Prot-*

*estantism, 1900 to the Present*, ed. Douglas Jacobsen and William V. Trollinger, Jr. (Grand Rapids, Mich.: Eerdmans, 1998), 172–193.

100. Jones to H. V. Miller, May 28, 1943 (file 920-62); *Quadrennial Reports to the Eleventh General Assembly of the Church of the Nazarene* (N.p., [1944]), 75, 102; Jones, "A Plain Statement of Facts," *Other Sheep* (March 1947), 1. Purkiser, *Called*, 175–197, 245–255, 277–285, 291–293. See "The Woman's Foreign Missionary Society of the Church of the Nazarene," 12 [1948] (file 423-7); *Herald of Holiness* (February 11, 1959), 3–4; Parker, *Mission*, 635.

101. Jones, *Look on the Fields*, 91.

102. Department of Foreign Missions, General Board, Church of the Nazarene, *Missionary Policy* (Kansas City, Mo.: Nazarene Publishing House, 1951), 4–6, 46–48.

103. See the 1948 General Assembly resolution on communism, *Journal of the Twelfth General Assembly of the Church of the Nazarene* (N.p., [1948]), 59, which included a strong statement about a person's "right for justice without regard for race or creed." For the post-war context of evangelical missions see William R. Hutchison, "Americans in World Mission: Revision and Realignment," in *Altered Landscapes: Christianity in America, 1935–1985*, ed. David W. Lotz (Grand Rapids, Mich.: Eerdmans, 1989), 155–170; and Richard V. Pierard, "Pax Americana and the Evangelical Missionary Advance," in *Earthen Vessels: American Evangelicals and Foreign Missions, 1880–1980*, eds. Joel A. Carpenter and Wilbert R. Shenk (Grand Rapids, Mich.: Eerdmans, 1990), 155–179.

104. Benner, "The 'Go' in the Gospel," in *For the Healing of the Nations*, ed. Jones, 50.

105. Rehfeldt, "The Singing of the Waters," in *For the Healing of the Nations*, 58; *So Shall We Reap* (Kansas City, Mo.: Nazarene Publishing House, 1958), 29–30; "The Verdict Is Yours," tract [1958] (file 1382-9). Along with other evangelical missions agencies in the 1950s, Rehfeldt even was prepared for Nazarene missionaries to supply information to the United States government, although there is no indication that they did. Clyde Taylor to Rehfeldt, August 29, 1955, in Samuel Young Papers; and James Murch, *Cooperation Without Compromise: A History of the National Association of Evangelicals* (Grand Rapids, Mich.: Eerdmans 1956), 105–108.

106. Ruth M. Park, comp., *The Church Abroad: A Quadrennial Review of Missions, 1948–1952* (Kansas City, Mo.: Nazarene Publishing House, 1952), 40–41. Similarly, W. Richie Hogg, "The Role of American Protestantism in World Mission," in Beaver, ed., *American Missions*, 376–377.

107. On Jones's resignation see Vanderpool to Powers, Williamson, Young and Benner, April 31, 1959; Vanderpool to Benner, March 29, 1960; *Other Sheep* (August 1960), 4; Vanderpool to Young, September 27, 1960, Vanderpool to Young, August 9, 1961. See also *Herald of Holiness* (July 6, 1960), 14, and Taylor, *Fifty Years*, 1: 47–51; Parker, *Mission*, 38–40; and Purkiser, *Called*, 224. On Rehfeldt's political stance see Clyde W. Taylor to Remiss

Rehfeldt, August 29, 1955, and [Rehfeldt], "The Verdict Is Yours," tract [1958]. (Compare Clyde W. Taylor, *A Glimpse of World Missions: An Evangelical View* [Chicago: Moody, 1960], 22, 118–119.) See also Thornton, *Radical Righteousness*, 138.

108. DeLong, *We Can If We Will: The Challenge of World Evangelism* (Kansas City, Mo.: Nazarene Publishing House, 1947), 9–12, 58–74, 151–152, 218–242, 261, 266.

109. In DeLong, *We Can If We Will*, 191, 197–198.

110. G. B. Williamson, "Christian Education in Foreign Fields," in C. Warren Jones, ed., *Missions for Millions* (Kansas City, Mo.: Nazarene Publishing House, 1948), 14–15. See also Williamson, "The Mission of the Church," *The Preacher's Magazine* 29 (January 1954), 7–8; and, with Audrey Williamson, *Yesu Masiki Jay: A First Hand Survey of Nazarene Missionary Progress in India* (Kansas City, Mo.: Beacon Hill, 1952), 65–75. See also J. B. Chapman, "Educational Standards," *Herald of Holiness* 27 (October 6, 1920), 5, which argues for high expectations and requirements. See also books by H.T. Reza, *Our Task for Today* (Kansas City, Mo.: Nazarene Publishing House, 1963), 44–54, 81–86; and *Prescription for Permanence: The Story of Our Schools for Training Ministers in Latin America* (Kansas City, Mo.: Nazarene Publishing House, 1968), 16, 64–71.

111. Hynd, "The Healing Urge of the Church," in *For the Healing of the Nations*, 72–73. See also Hynd, *Africa Emerging* (Kansas City, Mo.: Nazarene Publishing House, 1959), 66–70, 75, 118–123, and note his anti-apartheid statements on pp. 88–89, 110, 126. Compare the purely evangelistic reasons for medical missions in Evelyn M. Witthoff, *Oh Doctor! The Story of Nazarene Missions in India* (Kansas City, Mo.: Nazarene Publishing House, 1962), 43, 83–88. She echoes the sentiments of Harold Lindsell, *Missionary Principles and Practice* (Westwood, N.J.: Fleming H. Revell, 1955), 163–164, 205–276, who lists education, medicine and literature as "means" to evangelistic ends. Indian intellectuals criticized mission hospitals for their ulterior, proselytizing aim. See Koji Kawashima, *Missionaries and a Hindu State: Travancore 1858–1936* (Delhi: Oxford University Press, 1998), 138–141. See also Eugene P. Heideman, *From Mission to Church: The Reformed Church in America Mission to India* (Grand Rapids, Mich.: Eerdmans, 2001), 513–514.

112. Roy Smee, S. T. Ludwig and Alpin Bowes, *Enlarge Thy Borders: The Story of Home Missions in the Church of the Nazarene* (Kansas City, Mo.: Nazarene Publishing House, 1952), 26.

113. Smee, Ludwig and Bowes, *Enlarge Thy Borders*, 20.

114. Smee, Ludwig and Bowes, *Enlarge Thy Borders*, 66–67. See also Purkiser, *Called*, 197–200, 300.

115. Rehfeldt, "Survival at Stake," tract [n.d.] (file 645-26); Earl Hunter, "Robbed," mimeographed [n.d.] (file 1026-21); Joseph Pitts, *Voices From the Philippines* (N.p., n.d.). See also Purkiser, *Called*, 60–67, 266–274.

116. Compare Rebecca Laird, *Ordained Women in the Church of the Nazarene: The First Generation* (Kansas City, Mo.: Nazarene Publishing House, 1993), 143–147; Phyllis H. Perkins, *Women in Nazarene Missions: Embracing the Legacy* (Kansas City, Mo.: Nazarene Publishing House, 1994); Margaret L. Bendroth, *Fundamentalism and Gender: 1875 to the Present* (New Haven, Conn.: Yale University Press, 1993), 89–96, 98–100, 105–117; Kirkemo, *Zion's*, 103–104, 193–194, 348, 384–385; Richard Houseal, "Women Clergy in the Church of the Nazarene: An Analysis of Change from 1908 to 1995," M.A. thesis, University of Missouri–Kansas City, 1996, 22, 72.

117. Benner, *Rendezvous with Abundance* (Kansas City, Mo.: Beacon Hill, 1958), 116–117. See John T. Seamands, *Tell It Well: Communicating the Gospel Across Cultures* (Kansas City, Mo.: Beacon Hill, 1981).

118. Carl Bangs, *The Communist Encounter* (Kansas City, Mo.: Beacon Hill, 1963), 67, 75–79, 83, 91–93.

119. See, for example, Neil B. Weisman, ed., *To the City with Love: A Source Book of Nazarene Urban Ministries* (Kansas City, Mo.: Beacon Hill, 1976); Paul Moore and Joe Musser, *Shepherd of Times Square* (Nashville, Tenn.: Thomas Nelson, 1979); R. Franklin Cook and Steve Weber, *The Greening: The Story of Nazarene Compassionate Ministries* (Kansas City, Mo.: Nazarene Publishing House, 1986). See also F. O. Parr, *Perfect Love and Race Hatred* (N.p., [1964]).

120. Coulter file 1269-14.

121. See Phillips, *Man of Missions: Messages from the Pulpit of E. S. Phillips* (Kansas City, Mo.: Beacon Hill, 1974), 59.

122. *Herald of Holiness* (July 5, 1961); Jerald Johnson, foreword to Cook, *Reza*, 7–8; Ray Hendrix, "Will You Help Us Celebrate Our Golden Anniversary?" *Herald of Holiness* (September 1996), 42–43; Stan Ingersol, "H. T. Reza," 30–31. For Reza's influence see Reza to George Coulter, March 9, 1966, and Reza to E. S. Phillips, June 3, 1966 (both in file 777-14); Reza to Phillips, October 2, 1969 (file 567-8). See Reza, *Washed by the Blood: Stories of Native Workers Connected with the Church of the Nazarene in the Mexican Field* (Kansas City, Mo.: Beacon Hill, 1953); Reza, *Our Task for Today* (Kansas City, Mo.: Nazarene Publishing House, 1963), 83; Reza, *After the Storm, The Rainbow: The Church of the Nazarene in Cuba* (Kansas City, Mo.: Nazarene Publishing House, 1994), 63–65; R. Franklin Cook, *Reza: His Life and Times* (Kansas City, Mo.: Beacon Hill, 1988).

123. Federico Guillermo, "El Superintendente Nacional en el Desarrollo de la Iglesia del Nazareno en Centroamerica," Conferencia Centroamericana Pastores, December 1–5, 1969 (file 553-9).

124. *General Board Proceedings*, 1972, 187–189.

125. "Quadrennial Plan 1968–1972," in, e.g., file 1359-9; R. Franklin Cook, *The International Dimension: Six Expressions of the Great Commission* (Kansas City, Mo.: Nazarene Publishing House, 1984), 15–19, 37, 52–54.

126. Mission Council of the Guatemalan Mission District, n.d. (file 2131-44); "Progress of the Indigenous Church Plan in the Guatemala Field," [1942]

(file 1269-14); G. B. Williamson, *Sent Forth by the Holy Ghost: The Life of R. C. Ingram* (Kansas City, Mo.: Nazarene Publishing House, 1960), 69; Cook, *The International Dimension*, 33–34.

127. Transcription of conversation between Powers and Guillermo, October 27, 1963, George Coulter to H. C. Powers, n.d., and Powers to William Sedat, October 31, 1963, all in file 2131-44. See Parker, *Mission*, 45–46. Compare 1968, 1972 and 1976 editions, *Church of the Nazarene Manual*, paragraphs 301.1 and 301.4.

128. Parker, *Mission*, 45.

129. "Report of the Missionary Study Commission," General Board Proceedings, 1972, 187–189.

# Chapter 2

# India

India was the first field entered by any group that became a part of the Church of the Nazarene. It was a proving ground for philosophies and policies that became integral to Nazarene missions. Missionaries tried various ways of ministering. A sense of Christian duty motivated missionaries to take up humanitarian ministries that included feeding the hungry, taking in orphans, tending to medical needs, and educating the illiterate children and adults. Missionaries suggested that the only way to Christianize the Indian people was through education. "Christianization" meant more than conversion. It was a change in values and ways of life. The church emphasized educational and medical work even in stressful times after World War II when institutions sapped the energy of the mission and diverted it away from more direct means of evangelism. Administrators approved these measures and devised rationale for the church's heavy investment in schools and medical work. These undertakings, leaders affirmed, demonstrated Christian love and brought men and women to Christ.[1]

Most missionaries who went to India during the first two-thirds of the century did not stay long. Both the climate and conflicts with other missionaries conspired against longevity. Both in Central India and in East India, the two early centers of the work, pioneer workers left under duress within the first decade of the mission. But those who replaced them were forward-looking men and women who desired to build a strong national church. With the additional prodding of church administrators such as General Superintendent J. B. Chapman, Indian leaders were in nearly all of the key leadership assignments by the late 1930s, and remained so during the Second World War. After the war, however, the church sent dozens of new missionaries to India, most of them to maintain its schools and hospital. Missionary dominance returned—until the Indian government itself began to curtail the activities and number of American missionaries throughout the country. Meanwhile, many young Indians moved out of the rural Maharastra area where Nazarenes worked to cities. Church growth was virtually nil in the late 1950s and 1960s.

## Establishing Church Authority in Central India

The April 1897 Assembly of the Association of Pentecostal Churches of America voted to send a group of missionaries to India. M. D. Wood, who had already served one term in India, had joined the Association at what seemed to be a providential time, and the Missionary Committee desired to send Wood with a team of sanctified workers to India. The Assembly put H. F. Reynolds, as home and foreign missions secretary under the Missionary Committee, in charge of raising the necessary funds. Reynolds traveled from church to church holding conventions.[2]

Whereas Reynolds and the committee members were new at the missions task, Wood had not only experience in India with the Christian and Missionary Alliance, but missions training. Born in 1867, Wood wandered throughout his life from one religious home to another. His parents were "first-day" Christian Adventists, and Wood had been converted at one of D. L. Moody's schools for boys in North Attleboro, Massachusetts. Wood attended Methodist churches and camp meetings, and studied at the missionary training school of the Christian and Missionary Alliance in Nyack, New York. Wood went to India under the CMA, arriving in Bombay in 1892. He studied Marathi in Bombay for two years and married another missionary. The couple was stationed in Buldana, Berar—east of Bombay. About 60 other CMA missionaries were stationed in the Berar district of Maharastra. Wood's wife died, however, in October 1895, and was buried in Buldana. In 1896 Wood traveled across India with the Salvation Army.[3]

Wood returned to the United States later in 1896 and attended the holiness camp meeting in Douglas, Massachusetts. Here he met people affiliated with the recently organized Association of Pentecostal Churches of America. Wood became a member of W. H. Hoople's Utica Avenue Tabernacle in Brooklyn and married Anna Matlack, a nurse, and a member of a Pentecostal Association church in Pennsylvania.[4]

The missions philosophies that Wood brought with him into the Association were indebted to the CMA and to the faith missions concepts of J. Hudson Taylor—both of which emphasized the leadership of the Holy Spirit rather than human beings, and the importance of prayer and faith. Even though CMA leaders emphasized purely "evangelistic" work, missionaries sponsored industrial work, orphanages, and ministerial education. By 1900 the CMA missionaries in Berar were supporting about 1,200 orphans.[5]

In addition to Wood and his wife, the Association appointed Lillian Sprague, Carrie Taylor and Fred Wiley as missionaries. On December 11, 1897, the same day that the missionary party set sail for India, the APCA Missionary Committee issued a policy statement. It tied the missionaries closely to the sending body. "No step of any importance" was to be undertaken without the prior approval of the Missionary Committee. Missionaries were *not* to act unilaterally on major issues. All money would be channeled through the Association's treasurer and not be sent directly to the field. There was to be one station, the permanent headquarters of the mission, which must be approved by the Missionary Committee in America, and not moved without its consent. Property must be held in ways consistent with the laws of the host country, but any books, papers and other material articles belonged to the Association. The Mission would be known as the Pentecostal Mission of the Association of Pentecostal Churches of America. Missionary officers included the superintendent, assistant superintendent, secretary, treasurer, business manager and medical missionary. The duty of the medical missionary was "to use every practical means to care for the physical needs of those with whom she may be brought in contact." Missionaries were to master the language.[6]

On the way to India, the group stopped in England, where it visited the grave of John Wesley. The band arrived in Bombay in January 1898. The group settled in Igatpuri, Berar, 85 miles inland from Bombay, where both the CMA and the Methodists were already at work. The area had deep ties to the holiness movement. The renowned Methodist Bishop William Taylor had organized a Methodist society in Igatpuri in 1873. Soon, Carrie Taylor and Fred Wiley married. But they left the mission in 1899.[7]

Almost from the time of Wood's arrival, struggle ensued between Wood and Reynolds. As he had been accustomed, and as many Protestant groups were doing in these years of intense famine in India, Wood immediately began to take in orphans. The purpose was twofold: not only would they be saved from almost certain starvation, but they might be raised by missionaries as Christians. Wood informed the Missionary Committee of his action, but the committee feared the excessive financial burden the orphans might create for the struggling churches at home and chastised Wood sharply. Nevertheless, since Wood had already acted, the Missionary Committee agreed to sponsor the orphans. It solicited pledges for the orphans through its magazine, the *Beulah Christian*.[8]

Wood chafed under such constraints, which would have delayed any action for at least two months due to the length of time for mail to be sent and received, and he pleaded with the committee for more freedom and trust. Wood addressed Reynolds as "my very dear little brother" (actually Reynolds was older by 13 years) and reminded the Missionary Committee of its own inexperience.[9]

The missionaries did not inform the Missionary Committee before deciding upon the official name of the orphanage (the "Pentecostal Mission School"), the official colors of the uniform for female missionaries (red, white and blue), and even the mode of baptism. In the absence of an official position from the Association, Wood adopted the Methodist ritual of sprinkling. On the matter of ordination, however, Wood refrained from ordaining a worker, his converted Marathi teacher, upon receiving Reynolds's negative response—negative because the candidate for ordination was not yet entirely sanctified. (At home, the Association ordained workers by elders laying hands upon them.)[10]

In September 1899, without giving any warning to the Missionary Committee, Wood moved the mission, including the orphans, further inland, to Buldana. The climate there was better and the famine not so severe compared to Igatpuri and other parts of India. Within a short time Wood negotiated for a seven-and-three-quarter-acre farm. With money donated by Association members for famine relief, he hired workers and bought materials to construct a mission compound.[11]

Protestants already had been at work in Buldana for a number of decades. The Church of England's Church Missionary Society had established a mission there in 1862. The Christian and Missionary Alliance, Wood knew very well, also maintained a strong work in Buldana. His first wife was buried in Buldana. For the next several years, as the Association established itself and the CMA continued to work in Buldana, there were strained relationships between the two missions. Whether comity arrangements were formal or not in 1899, Wood was marching his band into an already evangelized area. (It was not until 1900 that Protestant missions in India formally divided the field, and boundaries were still being arbitrated more than a decade later.)[12]

Wood desired for the mission to be self-supporting. It was one way he saw for it to get out from under the control of the Association. To Wood self-support meant that the mission find indigenous ways of supporting itself. From the beginning Wood's work was "self-supporting" in ways similar to those of William Taylor, who had angered fellow Methodists by his independency in India. The reason for the farm in Buldana was not only so that the orphans might raise cows and grow crops for their own sake, but also so that the mission might sell the excess butter, milk and produce for its own support. The orphans, Wood argued, could be taken care of through the tithes of the missionaries (and through catching frogs to eat, Wood said, if the Association was unable or refused to support the enterprise). Once the church in India was established, Wood envisioned, it would support the orphans itself. A medical clinic begun by Anna Wood was self-supporting from its inception. Being made up of frugal New Englanders, the Missionary Committee encouraged Wood to find ways of being self-supporting even before there was one convert.[13]

Social ministries continued to develop. The hesitancy of Reynolds and the Committee to undertake orphanage work was financial, not philosophical, for the Association soon rallied behind support for the children. Inevitably, as the needs presented themselves, the missionaries took up primary school education and famine relief. There was no suggestion from Reynolds that the mission should desist from institutional concerns in order to devote himself exclusively to preaching and evangelism. Both Wood and Reynolds, despite their differences on who should administer the mission, took for granted that social concerns were their Christian duty. There were no lofty discussions of Christian civilization between them, but both the holiness movement and the Methodist Church out of which Reynolds came eagerly engaged in social ministries at the turn of the century. There was not, at least not yet, a breakdown in the holiness movement's consensus that both social concern and evangelistic preaching accompanied perfect love. Out of both love and duty the mission in India clothed the naked, fed the hungry, visited the sick and supported the weak.[14]

By 1903, when M. D. Wood, Anna Wood and Lillian Sprague furloughed to the United States, the character of the Association missions had been clearly established in the minds of the Missionary Committee. Missionaries should be governed on major decisions by the committee and its secretary. Financial self-support should be achieved as soon as possible, but money should not be donated directly to the missionaries on the field. Social ministries were an integral and authentic part of the church's mission.

Wood returned to India with a new group of missionaries in 1904. The group included Leighton Tracy, Ella Perry, her daughter Gertrude (who soon married Leighton Tracy), Nellie Barnes, Julia Gibson, Priscilla Hitchens, and three others who soon left the mission because of the tense situation. Wood still chafed under the committee's desire for strict accountability. Reynolds demanded that Wood submit weekly detailed reports to him. These reports contained conflicting accounts about the foul actions of the newer missionaries, on the one hand, and descriptions of a revival in their midst on the other. One missionary, according to Wood, was "full of the devil," another was "living in sin," and a third was "full of herself." But he was optimistic that the revival was straightening them out. In news regarding the revival Wood stated his conviction that Christians needed to be filled with the Holy Spirit *after* they were cleansed. Was Wood teaching a "third" work of grace? Pandita Ramabai's mission near Bombay, and the Christian and Missionary Alliance area in Gudjerat were among the places where a revival involving "baptism with fire" broke in 1905 and where, by December 1906, tongues were being spoken.[15]

If Wood was being influenced by this movement of the Spirit, he was expressing it in ways that conflicted with the accepted holiness movement teaching that linked the baptism of the Holy Spirit with cleansing from inbred sin. Perhaps Reynolds feared Pentecostalism on the mission field as well as well as insubordination. Pentecostalism was appearing on the fringes of the holiness movement in different places at this time and was one factor that hastened the denominational organization of holiness groups. At the same time, Reynolds, who was well acquainted with the new missionaries, and respected their maturity, suspected that Wood may not have been in a position to judge them. Reynolds asked Tracy, a 22-year-old Canadian who had been a student at the Association's Pentecostal Collegiate Institute, to send him additional reports about what was going on.[16]

The Missionary Committee soon decided to reorganize the missionaries in India—to force Wood to share leadership under a three-person executive committee made up of himself, Sprague and Tracy. Reynolds also forced Wood out of the management of the farm and orphanage. Finally, Reynolds designated himself superintendent of the field while, of course, remaining in America. These actions proved to be the breaking point for Wood.

In a letter to the Missionary Committee, Wood, Anna Wood, and Sprague, who remained loyal to Wood, voiced their frustrations and put forward several demands: (1) financial freedom, under which contributors would be able to send money directly to them without having to go through the Association's treasurer; (2) "freedom of the press," in order to appeal directly to the constituency; (3) freedom from "opposition" from the Missionary Committee for major undertakings; (4) freedom to expand the work as God would lead; (5) freedom from sectarianism; and, (6) church freedom, or autonomy. Actually, Wood had already circumvented the committee in financial appeals and received money from individuals outside the Association.[17]

When Wood had been sent out in 1897 the Association was only a loose band of independent holiness congregations. But much had changed in eight years. The denominational and hierarchical character of the Association had been strengthened. Its leaders, themselves strong-willed pastors of local congregations, had been forced to deal with Lyman Pettit, the independent and feisty first principal of the Pentecostal Collegiate Institute. He had run the school, then located in Saratoga Springs, New York, into debt, and had failed to heed the advice of the Association's Education Committee. Association leaders had seen both the necessity of Pettit's resignation in 1902 and the reorganization and relocation of the school to North Scituate, Rhode Island. Reynolds had been actively involved in making these decisions and could easily draw parallels to the situation in India. Because of these very crises, the Association headed toward a Presbyterian-like polity of representative government, and away from a Congregationalist or Baptist polity. Tracy, a student at PCI under Pettit, himself saw the similarities between what had happened at the school and what was happening in India.[18]

Like Pettit, Wood believed that the Holy Spirit should control the work, not a committee. After all, Wood said, missionaries were not the "servants of men," but servants of God and the "government shall be upon His shoulders." Wood reminded Reynolds, "God called us here and not you."[19] But Reynolds was resolute. He saw the need for both superintendency and accountability; and independency to this former Methodist was as dangerous as anarchy.[20]

When Wood, Anna Wood and Lillian Sprague pressed their demands upon the Association, the Committee accepted their resignations. They instructed Wood to turn over administration of the mission to Tracy. Rather than doing so, in February 1906 Wood and the two women, along with younger missionary Nellie Barnes, abruptly left the mission—in the middle of the night—along with the orphans (whom they left in the care of the Methodist station in Washim).[21]

At first Wood claimed that he and his wife had offers to work with the famous Pandita Ramabai and her mission outside of Bombay, but that never materialized. It is uncertain what he did until his return to America in 1909. He then pastored a Methodist church in Minnesota, and, later, another in North Dakota. There, Seventh-day Adventists converted him, and in 1912 he went back to India under the SDA. He was stationed at Kalyan and then at Igatpuri, where both the Church of the Nazarene and the Nashville-based Pentecostal Mission (which united with the Nazarenes in 1915) had work. Wood persuaded some of the Indians with whom he had had earlier contacts while a missionary under the Association to join the SDA. Sometime after 1919 Wood attended a holiness convention in Yeotmal (where the Free Methodists had a mission) and recovered, he reported, his experience of holiness. He even asked the forgiveness of the church. Wood continued working as an independent missionary and, in the eyes of the Nazarene missionaries, "died a victorious death in the Lord," in India in 1926.[22]

Meanwhile, in order to prevent misunderstanding within the Association about what was transpiring in India and Wood's departure, the committee published large parts of the correspondence between Wood and the committee in the *Beulah Christian*. The openness of the committee contributed to sentiments in the Association to support the Missionary Committee. More deeply, members of the Association saw that a well-superintended organization would best contribute to the spread of holiness around the world. Tracy stayed with the Association—gladly, as he said, putting himself under the authority of holy men and women.[23]

Though it was difficult for both the missionaries and the Indian townspeople to forget the Wood affair, through the leadership of Tracy and others the church eventually regained its reputation. Workers were few. Leighton and Gertrude Tracy remained in Buldana. Ella Perry, a practical nurse, carried on medical work until her own death by cholera on the field in 1919. Priscilla Hitchens worked in Igatpuri, which the Association had returned to in 1906, and Julia Gibson worked, for the most part alone, in Chikhli. Seeing the plight of women around her, Gibson found herself praying for India's "blighted childhood, enslaved wifehood, sorrowing widowhood and weakened manhood."[24]

Tracy based the purpose and direction of the mission on loyalty to the home church, which in 1907 united in Chicago with Phineas Bresee's California-based Church of the Nazarene. The next year saw the merger with the Holiness Church of Christ. In Buldana, the addition of a band of workers sent by the Holiness Church of Christ, which had arrived in Bombay in early 1908, greatly strengthened the work. Included among these were L. A. Campbell and A. D. Fritzlan, both of whom were to serve the church in India for many years. Collectively the missionaries expressed their commitment both to establish Indian churches and to replicate Nazarene church polity by forming a District Assembly and electing a superintendent as soon as possible. As the Church of the Nazarene was organized around districts, so the mission in India must become a "district."[25]

Both missionaries on the field and Reynolds decided that the church should abide by comity arrangements. Relationships between the Association and the CMA improved after Wood left, and the CMA voluntarily discontinued its work in the Buldana area in 1913.[26]

Though the missionaries envisioned district organization, there still were no permanent Indian workers. A few Indian preachers had come into (and in most cases had already gone out of) the mission, each of them transferring from and to other denominations. This situation created problems. Campbell noted this in 1911: "After we have secured a reasonably good worker, which is difficult to do, our task is to get them saved. For they invariably come to us unsaved. And it is not easy task either to convince a proud preacher he is not saved."[27] Often the Indian brethren "backslid" (though Tracy reminded Reynolds that altars in the churches at home also were filled with those who had "lost out" spiritually). However, stable Indian leaders began to emerge during the 1910s, among them Lucas Waghamari and Waman Kharat. As a result, by 1914, during Reynolds's visit, the missionaries were ready to recommend to the General Missionary Board a comprehensive new policy to govern the work in India.[28]

## Searching for a Place of Ministry in Eastern India

A decade after the Association's missionaries began establishing work in Maharastra, Bresee's congregation in Los Angeles the Church of the Nazarene agreed to sponsor a girls' school and orphanage in Calcutta. The work came to the attention of Bresee through Emma Eaton, wife of E. G. Eaton, an Oregon fruit farmer who was also a minister in the Evangelical Church. They were not members of Bresee's church, but had acquaintances in it. Since the 1890s Emma Eaton had been hearing of and praying for the work Sukhoda Banarjee. After trying other ministries, in 1905 Banarjee started a refuge for young widows in Calcutta. Eaton was already helping to finance the work, when, in 1906, Banarjee traveled in the United States in order to further raise funds. With her was a young Indian preacher, her son-in-law, Promotha B. Biswas. Through Eaton's friends at the Church of the Nazarene, Banarjee was invited to speak one Sunday evening. After an impassioned plea, a "hallelujah march" brought in a good offering and the church's Mission Board agreed to carry a large amount of the financial responsibility for the work, its first commitment to an overseas mission. In fact, Bresee officially appointed Banarjee, Biswas, Eaton, and her husband as missionaries, and they were soon on their way to Calcutta. Although Bresee and leaders of the California wing of the church had given as little thought to missionary philosophy and policy as their Eastern brothers and sisters, at this stage they considered nationals to be their best prospects for leadership positions. Banarjee seemed ideally suited to spearhead the church's work with the assistance of lay American missionaries. Along with them went V. J. Jacques, a wholesaler and Nazarene layperson who initially supported himself. The group arrived in Calcutta late in 1906. A. A. Avetoom, a European woman, had superintended the work while Banarjee was in America.[29]

Banarjee's work was renamed the "Hallelujah Village," and included a school and orphanage for girls, and other work. The mission took in girls whose husbands had either divorced them or had died. Many had been married when they were still children to much older men, and their fate in Indian society was dismal. They normally were relegated to begging or to serving their in-laws for the rest of their lives.

Such accounts stirred the compassion of Bresee and the Nazarenes, who had given women in their own midst the right to preach and to be ordained. Women in Bresee's congregation had spearheaded ministries to Spanish-speaking people in Los Angeles, and to Japanese immigrants. Laywomen had led in the founding of what became Pasadena College. The plight of women in India was well known to American Protestants. It was a frequent object of concern among missions in India. It was not unusual, then, that the church support an Indian woman's ministry, especially one that targeted women and girls, and appointed Emma Eaton to be her co-worker.[30]

Bresee and others in the Los Angeles congregation were not overly concerned with denominational labels at either the college or the mission in Calcutta. This did not bother Bresee. He was still trying to tie together the various strands of the holiness movement in the United States and was hoping that his school in Pasadena would remain interdenominational. None of the leaders who were sent to India, with the possible exception of Jacques, even had much familiarity with Bresee's church. It is unlikely that Banarjee understood the nuances of entire sanctification. That was not the priority. Rather, the church in Los Angeles delighted in ministry to the urban poor as a demonstration of perfect love. Its original mission had been "to preach holiness to the poor." Presented with such a case overseas, the Nazarenes could not turn down Banarjee's pleas for help.

Within a few years, however, grave difficulties among the workers had begun. In 1912 Avetoom left the mission with some of the girls and began spreading rumors about the work. Banarjee was not even the Indian leader's real name, Avetoom asserted. Rather, it was Hermanto Ghose; and she was not a widow. She kept much of what she raised abroad for herself and for her family relations, Avetoom said. Banarjee was skilled in weaving fact with fascinating, but fictitious, stories whenever she spoke to audiences. Avetoom also accused Banarjee and Jacques of "immoral conduct." Basically, Avetoom believed Banarjee to be a fraud.[31]

Banarjee toured Europe in 1912 and 1913, raising more money for the work, and sent it to Jacques, who was treasurer of the mission. By this time, of course, the work had become part of the broader Church of the Nazarene, but Reynolds had not been able to impose the accountability structure upon Banarjee and the Calcutta work.

In early 1914, during his world tour, Reynolds himself visited the Calcutta station. Reynolds found the mission at a dismal ebb. Jacques already had returned to California. Emma Eaton had had a recent operation for a cancerous growth and this had aggravated a condition of the heart and kidneys. Her husband had suffered a sunstroke and was a physical wreck, in Reynolds's estimation. But that was hardly the worst. Banarjee was making allegations that her relations with Jacques were romantic and that Jacques had promised to marry her. She publicly confessed her sins and demanded that Jacques return to India to marry her, as only this would restore her reputation. If Reynolds would not agree with this, she was ready to break her relations with the Church of the Nazarene. Reynolds decided that the church would remain and that Banarjee would go. The property was not that of Banarjee, and if she and her staff decided to leave, the mission would remain. Reynolds conducted a conference at Hallelujah Village, April 7–8. By this time Reynolds had prepared a document for Banarjee to sign, consisting of her resignation as a missionary, her severance of all relations with Hope School and Hallelujah Village and a pledge not to interfere with the mission. She received a small severance of 300 rupees as a "gift." Reynolds decided to remain in Calcutta as long as necessary and remained until May 11. Eaton resigned as superintendent and her husband as treasurer. By this time they were so demoralized and physically debilitated that Reynolds sent them packing and personally made sure of their departure on April 24. (They took with them two Indian girls.) Biswas also left over disagreements related to the dismissal of a relative. Hulda Grebe remained to work in the school and her sister, Leoda, to head the dispensary, but they were inexperienced and did not know the language. Tracy arrived to take over the Calcutta station on May 2. Banarjee persuaded several Bible women and children to leave with her, and Tracy feared that she would retain the sympathy of European and American friends who had been supporting her financially. Ten Indian workers and 120 boys and girls remained.[32]

The situation reinforced to Reynolds the necessity of strong administrative oversight and strict accountability of the mission. It also gave Reynolds the experience, even if only for six weeks, of missionary life on the field.

The Eatons returned to India in 1920, but not under the Church of the Nazarene. Reynolds refused to reappoint them because of their health. Emma Eaton proved to be an energetic and deft fund-raiser. She and her husband formed a prayer and support group called the Heart of India Mission Band, based in Pasadena, California. The Eatons returned to India as associate missionaries with the Christian and Missionary Alliance. Jacques remained in California as the secretary of the Heart of India Mission. Nonetheless, the mission became entangled in some legal redresses, and the Eatons left the Heart of India and formed the India Gospel League in 1931, centered in Bangalore and organized to distribute Christian literature throughout India by mail. The headquarters of the India Gospel League was moved from India to Pasadena in 1946. By this time former Nazarene missions secretary E. G. Anderson was the administrator of it. Across the years the Eatons' independent work received the financial support of Nazarenes, to the chagrin of mission leaders in Kansas City. In all, Emma Eaton served in India more than forty years, retiring when past eighty.[33]

Meanwhile, despite these grave setbacks, Tracy was able to officially organize a church in Calcutta in 1916. Tracy, Gertrude Tracy, and four single women missionaries (including the Grebe sisters), who had joined the staff shortly before the schism, also maintained a few Sunday School out-stations that served Hindu seekers as well as Christians. They also continued work among the Garos, a tribal people located far to the northeast of Calcutta, in what is now Bangladesh. This outreach had begun through the efforts of Emma Eaton, Jacques and Biswas in 1912. The missionaries also opened a school for boys along with the one they continued for girls. The number of students in the mission station at Calcutta in 1916 was seventy-three, nearly all sponsored by North American Nazarene individuals, churches or Sunday School classes.[34]

Tracy also found problems in relation to the very location of Hallelujah Village, the condition of the remaining missionaries, and the work among the Garos. The Village, where the schools as well as missionaries' residences were located, was in a low-lying area near stagnant ponds. This added to the already prevalent possibility of malaria. Inches of water covered the floors of the buildings during monsoon season and the general condition was unsanitary. Missionaries frequently became ill and out of necessity took respite in the mountains. The condition was especially unsettling to the four single women missionaries, none of whom had been in the country more than two years. They had not progressed very far in their study of the Bengali language, Tracy found, and he described one of the women as being in precarious mental and emotional health. He had little hope that she could recover in India.[35]

The Garo work also had its problems. It was among a relatively small, animistic group. The church had a station in the town of Dharkua. Since the nineteenth century, however, the Garos had been evangelized by Australian Baptists, who initially recommended that the Nazarenes find an area not so worked. An Indian pastor who had been dismissed from the Baptist mission was in charge of the work after Jacques's departure, and the missionaries visited him whenever they could. However, so far as Tracy was concerned, the work never had been truly "Nazarene," and he advised moving the center of the work to Kishorganj, a larger city (also in what is now Bangladesh), and farther away from the Baptists. Reynolds gave his permission for this, especially as it followed his policy of maintaining comity arrangements wherever possible. George Franklin, a young widower, arrived in 1915, quickly married Hulda Grebe, and took over for Tracy in Eastern India the next year. He implemented the transfer to Kishorganj, and returned the remaining work at Dharkua to the Baptists.[36]

The Kishorganj station, which opened in 1916, proved comparatively successful and the church shifted the Calcutta work there—the orphanage in 1918 and the boys' school in 1919. Franklin transplanted the entire Calcutta congregation—all seven members, presumably the Indian workers associated with the orphanage and school—to Kishorganj. "While we have left Calcutta," Franklin remarked in his 1919 report, "our interest and burden for it have not died."[37] Though the missionaries tried to maintain most of the same ministries at Kishorganj, they eventually had to close the boys' school for lack of teachers. Evangelistic itinerancy remained impossible because no missionary knew the language well enough to preach in it.[38]

The general church appointed several new missionaries to the Eastern field in the post-World War I years. The mission continued to rely mostly upon single women missionaries. The small church at Kishorganj remained, along with the orphanage, and a primary school, both of the latter for girls. Given the predominance of women among the missionaries, the ministry involved "zenana" visiting among Moslem women who were virtually forced into seclusion in their own homes. Other missions were actively doing the same.[39]

Becoming active in the 1920s as national leaders were Dwarka Babu and Samed Babu, formerly a Moslem, who served as a colporteur. Dwarka Babu worked in villages among the low caste. In 1930 the entire mission of the Church of the Nazarene in Eastern India included only the church in Kishorganj, with 55 full and probationary members;

six acres of property; a government-recognized Middle English Girls' school; and five village Sunday Schools. The number of missionaries had dwindled to three—George Franklin, Hulda Grebe Franklin and Maude Varnedoe.[40]

During a trip around the world in 1929 and 1930, General Superintendents John Goodwin and Roy T. Williams visited the field and decided that because of the work's slow progress, and the financial outlay it required in the midst of the Depression, the Church of the Nazarene should close its Eastern India field and transfer the remaining missionaries to the Maharastra area. Through Franklin's entreaties, they gave the field a one-year reprieve. If dramatic revivals took place the superintendents might reconsider their decision. But growth proved elusive. In 1931 the church officially closed the work and the remaining missionaries went on furlough. George and Hulda Franklin found places of ministry in America. The property, however, could not be sold immediately.[41]

Samed Babu and Samed Choudhury, one of Franklin's converts, maintained not only the property but the spiritual work for several years. On a visit to Eastern India in 1935 Prescott Beals, by then superintendent of the Central India work, found interested Moslem inquirers and classes that Babu had organized. Babu and Choudhury continued to pastor the congregation in Kishorganj and preached throughout the district. Nazarene supporters in the United States sent funds directly to Babu with the knowledge of both Beals and administrators in Kansas City, despite this being against long-standing policies. Several members of the community in Kishorganj asked for the return of the mission. Beals was drawn to the possibility, especially since the sale of the property was proceeding so slowly. But he also made contacts with the Australian Baptists regarding the possibility of their taking over ministry in Kishorganj. Finally, in 1937, the Nazarene church sold the property, one portion to the government and the rest to the Australian Baptist Mission. Beals had some consolation that a Christian witness would continue. The Church of the Nazarene returned to both Calcutta and Bangladesh in the 1990s.[42]

Implications for Nazarene policy stemming from the Eastern India work are several. Though the church employed Indians as key leaders in initiating the work, negative experiences with some of these workers forced the church to reconsider the wisdom of this. The almost nondenominational character of the early years in Calcutta could not stand for long once Reynolds brought the mission under his control and transferred Tracy there. Yet the early commitments to a social ministry remained all through the decades of Nazarene work. The church was vitally interested in promoting the cause of women not only by giving them leadership roles, but by helping to alleviate their plight in Indian culture. Compassion for the suffering of Indian wives and widows fulfilled the original aim of the Nazarene mission in Calcutta. Throughout its ministry in this area of India, through the orphanage and school and through visitation to Moslem women missionaries maintained this vision. They deeply empathized with their Indian sisters, but church leaders felt that the mission must become more than this.

The closing of the work in Calcutta, however, is difficult to assess in relation to policy. The concerns about the health of missionaries were genuine and these in connection with the other problems in Calcutta were sufficient to prompt the move from this intensely urban area (though the Village was not in a densely populated section) to a remote rural area. The thought was that the church would have more opportunity for growth and evangelism in the rural region, and the Nazarene constituency in the United States was itself fast becoming proportionately more rural. This assumption that rural evangelism would be more productive did not prove to be the case. On other points of policy, both Tracy and Franklin emphasized denominational lines while at the same time abiding by comity arrangements. This was the chief reason for relocating the work from Dhakua to Kishorganj. When, after several years in Kishorganj, it seemed that the church would never thrive there, leaders decided to transfer the work, if possible, to the Baptists. From the global standpoint, in the Depression years, it was a strategic retrenchment. Effort could be concentrated in Central India.

## Toward National Leadership in Central India

In 1914, on his trip through India, Reynolds prompted missionaries in Central India to form a policy for their field. He had just come from Japan, where missionaries together with him had worked out a governing policy. At this time Reynolds considered national policies better than formulating a general policy to govern all the fields; although, because of Reynolds's influence, various policies were quite similar. In fact they were based on the Association of Pentecostal Churches of America's earlier (1897) Articles. The process of formulating a policy for themselves enabled the India missionaries to both internalize and articulate their goals, as well as to develop strategies to reach Indians.

The Nazarene missionaries to India stated in their 1914 policy that they looked forward to the establishment of a truly Indian church. But the fact that much of the missionaries' time was spent developing policies that governed themselves showed that they believed that national development would be a long time in the future. They recommended that Indian workers *not* be considered as missionaries—a response to the problems that had risen with Banarjee. On other policy matters, they decided that all missionaries would receive the same salary (a reflection of the merger of Association with Holiness Church of Christ missionaries). Missionaries were prohibited from engaging in secular business for profit. Furloughs would be fixed—six years for the first term, seven for the next. All would have a six-week annual rest period. No missionary would be appointed for life. The first year of missionary service should be devoted fully to language study; and the inability either to use the language or to adjust to the culture would be grounds for a missionary's recall. Missionaries were to be engaged in touring villages, in visiting house-to-house, in preaching in fairs and bazaars, and in both establishing and maintaining mission stations. They were to care for the Christians, also, through Bible classes, Sunday Schools and general pastoral work. The missionaries recognized that: "The primary object of our work is spiritual, i.e., the salvation of sinners, the sanctification of believers and building them up in the holy faith. Such auxiliary works as orphanages, schools, industrial and medical works, translation, publication and other usual branches of missionary effort may be opened whenever they can serve our primary object." [43]

The policy, thus, did not relinquish the mission's social ministries, but put them in the context of more "spiritual" endeavors. Social ministries were not ends in themselves. The church's primary concern was with the salvation of individuals through more direct means of evangelism. Intentionally or not, the missionaries reflected the thought of Henry Venn and Rufus Anderson in emphasizing evangelism rather than institutional concerns and in focusing on the development of an indigenous church. But, like other missions of their day, they did not take the position to the extreme of altogether giving up institutional tasks, which they considered their Christian duty.

The missionaries did not adopt the suggestion of Anderson and Venn that local churches take an indigenous form of organization or government. Their goal was that the churches in India function like Nazarene churches and districts in America. According to the 1914 policy, there were three stages of district development. At the first stage, missionaries and any ordained Indian elders, along with delegates from self-supporting Indian churches, would compose the District Assembly. Though there were not yet any Indian elders or self-supporting Indian churches, the thought was one of cooperation between missionaries and Indians. When Indian members of the assembly outnumbered missionaries a second stage became possible. Missionaries then would form a mission council apart from the District Assembly. At that time the assembly would deal with questions directly related to the self-supporting Indian churches, and the missionaries in their council would control only money coming to the mission from abroad. The council would also be in charge of assigning missionaries to stations around the field. The third stage of development would be a self-supporting district. Crossing this threshold would need the approval of the missionaries. At that stage, the District Assembly would station missionaries as well as national workers; employ, supervise and dismiss Indian workers; examine both missionaries and Indian workers in the course of study for ministers; audit mission accounts; elect a District Executive Board; and nominate a district superintendent to the General Missionary Board.[44]

From the beginning, then, policy formulations promoted both self-support and measures toward self-government. Indeed self-support was the prerequisite, the sign and symbol, of readiness for regular district status. It is remarkable that the policy envisioned Indians having rights and privileges over missionaries on the field once they reached the last stage. Even so, the policy left the ratification of the election of the district superintendent to the Missions Board, even though this had no precedent among similarly organized districts in North America that were entitled to elect their own superintendents. The missionaries envisioned cooperation in government with ordained and delegated Indians until the district achieved full self-support. At that time the Indians would be in control of their own affairs and the missionaries would concentrate their ministries on undeveloped areas of the field. The form or likeness of the Indian church's government was the American church, and it would follow its *Manual*. The expected patterns of leadership among Indians would have to fit the structure. Yet such advance toward Indian leadership was years away in 1914, and in the meantime the policy allowed missionaries to control every detail of the work.

It may have been after the policy statement of 1914 that the mission became less preoccupied with educational and medical work, and more focused on the planting of and the creation of a district. The church saw little growth after 1914, nonetheless, though missionaries persistently attributed this to the lack of workers, both missionary and Indian.[45]

The year after missionaries drew up this policy statement, the Pentecostal Mission, headquartered in Nashville, Tennessee, united with the Church of the Nazarene and merged its work in India with the Nazarenes. This group had established itself in 1903 in the Thana district, near

Bombay, and even had missionaries stationed in Igatpuri, where the Nazarenes also maintained a mission from 1906 to 1912. Included among the "new" missionaries was veteran Roy G. Codding, who had served for eight years in Sudan with both the YMCA and the CMA before pioneering the Pentecostal Mission work in India. He soon became superintendent of the entire Western and Central work when Reynolds called upon Tracy to straighten out matters in Calcutta. The Pentecostal Mission had a boys school in Khardi. After Tracy's presence was no longer needed in the Eastern field, and as a way of integrating the two works, the General Board stationed him in Khardi. He was disappointed, however, when it decided to close the school in 1918. He and his family furloughed the following year.[46]

The issue over the Khardi school forced Tracy to think deeply about the role of schools and other institutions in mission policy as it related to India. In a long reflective letter to Reynolds, Tracy developed a philosophy justifying the need for social and especially educational institutions as long-term methods of evangelism. Medical, industrial, social and educational work, Tracy reasoned, provided the "medium" for the gospel. They were not ends in themselves, as some might claim, but were approaches to the Indians, who could not comprehend a "bare" gospel. The Old Testament's concern, Tracy said, for the material as well as the spiritual welfare of human beings was applicable in India: "The blessing of God must be manifested in temporal prosperity and advancement." He observed that when Indians became Christians they lost their families and jobs, and became socially ostracized. Until a Christian community was able to stand alone amid the Hindu culture, the mission must provide schools, industries and even loans. Tracy wrote: "We could get them saved, and some of them sanctified after a time, but that would be only the beginning of our responsibilities, because . . . his religion means to him every department of his life as well as relation with God and he has left the old resources of his old religion, he looks to the resources of his new religion to take their places, and to whom must he look but to the missionary and to whom must the missionary look but to his home denomination?" Tracy advocated an educational system whereby the church would establish village primary schools and a central boarding school. The latter, which would go to the seventh standard and would be registered with the government, would in turn lead some into a ministerial training school. The boarding school was particularly necessary in order to develop Christian character. Left in old, Hindu environments Christians succumbed to its "inborn customs and prejudices," whereas completely removed from it they would have the opportunity to adopt new thoughts. Through a system of Nazarene schools throughout the field national leaders (both laypersons and preachers) would emerge. The present way of securing workers by taking the "off-scourings" of other missions had failed completely.[47]

Tracy found what many other missions in India also had found, the necessity of establishing Christian communities that would provide economic and social as well as religious support for converts. Nazarene missionaries were more concerned with transforming Indian lives than in comprehending Hindu religion.[48]

The Church of the Nazarene also was like other missions in India under British rule in stressing education. Just as the British envisioned home rule to be based on the education of Indian leaders, the missionaries saw education as preparing for the self-government of churches. Though Tracy noted that such schools were evangelistic means, they were more than this. It was not sufficient to make converts. Education effected Christianization. Especially in the Indian context, a nurturing environment was necessary if converts were really to be Christianized. In essence, Tracy advocated a new start toward the creation of a church that would be at the same time truly Nazarene and truly Indian.[49]

While Tracy was articulating these thoughts during his furlough in America, other shifts in leadership occurred in India. The Coddings, after twelve continuous years in India, furloughed in 1917 and did not return until 1924; the Tracys remained in America for ten years before returning in 1929; and the Fritzlans, another long-serving couple, furloughed in 1920 and remained home until 1924.[50]

A contingent of missionaries arrived soon after the Armistice ended the First World War, but all were new to the field and it would take years before they learned Marathi and India's customs. The young missionary placed in charge, K. Hawley Jackson, who had had some experience in Guatemala before arriving in India in 1919, nonetheless possessed a vision for an Indian church that would be both spiritually and financially stable. Indian workers who were both sanctified and efficient were necessary, he said. The mission must seek the salvation and sanctification of Indians, but, more than that, it must provide a way for the Indian church to be less dependent on the mission for physical sustenance.[51]

Tracy had seen the social necessities for the denomination to care for physical as well as spiritual needs, and the new missionaries were as impressed as him with the necessity of village school work. Products of existing Nazarene schools were already often the only ones able to read and write in local villages, and so naturally they became community leaders. This facilitated good will between the people and the church, opened doors to preaching, and encouraged missionaries to look forward to the emergence of Indian leaders to take over a regular district organization.[52]

Meanwhile, in the United States during the early 1920s, Tracy was instrumental in formulating with Reynolds a policy that would govern all Nazarene mission work around the world. Thus far Reynolds had only a collection of various field policies, and he leaned on Tracy to codify a policy for all the fields. Indeed, Tracy himself had come to certain conclusions, and now supported the view that national and missionary leadership must be separated. If missionaries continued to mingle in the affairs of the national church, he felt, self-support and measures of self-governance would not be reached, and these, after all, were the goals of the mission. Tracy did not have to defend the "three-selfs" principles, as they were so readily believed by Protestant missionaries, but only to apply them to the Nazarene context. The heretofore so-called "District Assembly," which in most countries had been composed solely of missionaries, under a missionary as superintendent, should rather be styled a "mission council" with a president. The District Assembly should be composed of the national church, and it would elect its own district superintendent without the interference of the missionaries. The mission must consider itself only temporary, whereas the national church was permanent. The national District Assemblies and all other forms of government would be forever under the *Manual* of the general church—this was inescapable in Nazarene polity. The *Manual* was an international document. But national churches were *not* always to be under missionaries. Once they had achieved regular status, based primarily on self-support, the national districts would be as entitled as any district to proportionate representation in the General Assembly.[53]

These ideas had a deep impact upon Reynolds and the General Missionary Board that was responsible for ratifying policy statements. The Church of the Nazarene was moving toward a uniquely international polity regarding church government. The structure would be universal, the leaders national. The underlying assumption, of course, was that church structure was both necessary for organization and order, and usable by non-Western peoples. Nazarene leaders, unlike those of some other denominations, did not attempt to justify Nazarene church polity as the only possible model based on the Bible. Yet no one, it seemed, questioned that the form of government of the Church of the Nazarene was suitable for all men and women around the world.

Though Tracy himself was absent from India for ten years before returning in 1929, the development of national leadership in the Maharastra area continued, along with an educational program like the one he envisioned. Nazarenes erected primary schools in several of the villages over which they had comity arrangements, as Tracy had hoped. The first Church of the Nazarene organized in Central India was in Buldana, in 1919. By 1921 it had eighteen full and twenty probationary members—a meager start, after so many years, toward an indigenous church. The Mission Council separated itself from the District Assembly for the first time in 1924, in accordance with the general missions policy written in part by Tracy.[54]

Another sign of the developing national consciousness of the Indian church was evident in regards to a controversy that developed around missionary Fritzlan. The most senior of missionaries when they returned to the field from furlough in 1924, the Fritzlans had taken residence in and oversight of the Buldana mission station. There Fritzlan angered both missionary colleagues and Indian church leaders by dismissing several Indian workers, including B. D. Amolik, a teacher, for no apparent reason. Amolik did not take the dismissal lightly. He gathered support for himself among Indian Nazarenes. The Buldana local church board sent a letter to the General Board in Kansas City accusing Fritzlan of several matters related to his disposition toward the Indian nationals and asking for his removal. Eight workers, eight students and twenty laypersons signed the letter.[55]

George Sharpe, the founder of the Pentecostal Church of Scotland—which had become part of the Church of the Nazarene in 1915—and then serving as regional superintendent, himself believed that Fritzlan had behaved improperly, and was ready to reprimand him. But Reynolds defended Fritzlan, especially after receiving a commendatory letter regarding him from S. D. Ghordpade, an Indian worker involved in evangelism, and another from Samuel Bhujbal, one of the original signatories of the Buldana church petition who now regretted his action. The general church took no action against Fritzlan. Nor was Amolik reinstated. Some years later Amolik returned to the mission and was in the first group of Nazarenes to be ordained.[56]

The incident was of no permanent detriment to the Nazarene work, but illustrated the heightened boldness of the Christian workers in India. That they felt entitled to challenge a senior missionary leader on moral and spiritual grounds indicated that the age of excessive missionary veneration was nearing an end. They also felt entitled to a say in the church in their own country. Partnership and cooperation could then proceed.[57]

In the context of India during the 1920s the incident is even more understandable. India nationalists had ambiguous feelings toward missionaries. For the most part, nationalists in Maharastra appreciated missionaries' attempts to alleviate suffering, hunger and poverty, and to educate Indians. They recognized that without missionary influence, women and Indians from lower castes never would have had a chance for education. Yet nationalists also debated whether intervention in the lives of widows was helpful. They certainly disliked any disparagement of Hindu culture made by missionaries. The rising nationalism took an increasingly vocal and even violent stand against British colonialism. Indians desired home rule. Even though, as American rather than British missionaries, Nazarenes were more ambivalent toward the continuation of British rule in India, those sentiments could not help but be translated into the church. It mattered little that Fritzlan was American rather than British. His manner and attitudes as well as actions seemed colonial to at least some of the Indian Nazarenes.[58]

Amolik's work after rejoining the mission was to evangelize among the high caste in Buldana. Similarly, Samuel Bhujbal ministered for a year among the high caste in Murbad, in the Thana area. The church recognized the social reality that caste distinctions made a difference in means of evangelism, though in the church itself, like most Protestant missions, Nazarenes emphasized the casteless nature of Christianity.[59]

The Nazarene mission was tied to British colonialism in its educational system. The primary school work received financial support from the British colonial system. Nazarenes had few problems conforming to the Education Code of the government, which integrated various castes. In spite of this, a Nazarene girls' school begun in 1921 in Buldana had to be disbanded in 1924 due to missionary retrenchment. The church sent some of the orphans who had been studying there to a Free Methodist mission school. In contrast, in 1928 the boys school's importance grew when a Bible training department was added for those who had finished the seventh standard. This was, at last, an initiative toward ministerial training. Its program involved two key Indian leaders: S. Y. Salve as master in charge of the boarding school, and Samuel Bhujbal—a product of Nazarene schools in the western, Thana district, and a student at Bombay University—as headmaster. The missionaries considered these two faithful, efficient, truly consecrated, sanctified men. Salve also taught in the Bible Training School along with Fritzlan. It enrolled five students in 1930.[60]

Leighton and Gertrude Tracy returned to India in 1929. During their long furlough both of the Tracys had attended Northwest Nazarene College to finish their bachelor's degrees and both had earned

M.A. degrees from the Kennedy School of Missions of the Hartford Seminary Foundation, at the time the leading missionary training school in the United States. They returned to India eager to implement their theories—consistent with the thrust of the church toward nationalization.[61]

The 1932 mission council meeting, led by Tracy and Prescott Beals who had been serving in India since 1920, reaffirmed that the ultimate objective of the mission was to establish a fully functioning group of Nazarene churches in India. The council envisioned a self-supporting Nazarene church in each village of size in the district. The Indian church workers could never aspire to positions within the mission, council members well knew, but should set their sights upon being no less than "apostles" in the Indian church. The mission was expendable. The church would go on with or without it. The council suggested that though the period of transfer of control from the mission to the Indian church still might be years away, until then "brotherly cooperation" must characterize the relationship between missionaries and national leaders. Missionaries affirmed these sentiments in a "Church Development Committee Report" the following year: "It is the stated purpose of our church to develop the Church of the Nazarene in India and get it on a self-propagating, self-supporting, and self-governing basis as soon as possible." Then the Indian church would shoulder "full responsibility" for the district.[62]

Missionaries confidently reiterated this three-selfs formula while knowing full well that there was a serious crisis going on among Indian leaders. The general church itself had precipitated the crisis, in part, by closing the Western, Thana field in 1931. The Thana field had been the province of the Pentecostal Mission primarily, and its missionaries had moved into positions of leadership in the Nazarene mission after the 1915 merger. In 1928 missionaries suggested closing the Thana field and the decision became final during the visit of General Superintendents Williams and Goodwin in early 1930. Nazarenes hoped that the CMA would take over the work in Thana. As a result, several of the pastors and workers in Thana transferred to the Buldana area in 1930. Actually such transfers had been occurring for years, and it seemed to the workers in the central area that missionaries gave the Thana-area workers the choice preaching posts and positions in the Nazarene schools. The "insiders" and the "outsiders" had polarized into opposing factions. At a Preacher's Convention held by Tracy in Buldana in November 1932 the Indian workers fully aired their grievances. The outsiders' spokesman was John Magar and the insiders' was Runza Tode. S. Y. Salve took minutes on the ensuing debate. Tracy explained the reason the mission began using those from outside the Buldana area—that there had been a time when no workers could be found from within it. Samuel Bhujbal, apparently respected by all sides, preached at the Convention. After the Indians had bared their grievances, Tracy asked that the minutes Salve had taken, along with the notes of any other worker, be put into a wire basket. To these he lit a fire. All joined hands around the meeting place as they sang a hymn. Tracy later remarked that "the Holy Spirit applied this symbol with telling effect."[63] The event did seem to bind the Indian church together more closely, as did the first "jungle camp meeting" soon following.[64]

At the Annual Preacher's Convention the next year, 1933, missionaries drew plans for the first Annual District Meeting, to be composed of Indian preachers, lay representatives, and Tracy. In Tracy's mind this was one more step toward the formation of a "Missionary District Assembly."[65] That same year the mission council voted to make Samuel Bhujbal an associate member of its executive committee. The missionaries intended by this both to allow the Indian church to know reasons for the decisions it made, and to receive advice from the Indian standpoint. Though they did not give Bhujbal a vote, they brought him into the inner workings of the council. Tracy also urged the general church to allow the Indian pastors to perform marriage ceremonies, give the Lord's Supper and baptize—in short, to serve as licensed ministers under *Manual* provisions for such who were pastoring. The general superintendents approved the plan. These actions signified the missionaries' desire to place increasing responsibility on the Indian church.[66]

Tracy further asked that the general church *not* send new missionaries until the field was prepared to place them advantageously.[75] It was a big change from earlier years, when missionaries regularly implored Kansas City with pleas for more workers. Now neither Tracy nor national workers any longer considered missionaries to be the answer to all of the needs on the field. In spite of these steps, when Tracy retired due to ill health in 1934 it was with great remorse and a "broken spirit" over the lack of progress in the Nazarene church in India.[67]

The church now had a philosophy of concentrating in one central area. By 1931 it had given up work in both Thana and Kishorganj. In 1935 an opportunity arose to expand the area of Nazarene responsibility in Berar. An adjacent area to the east of the Nazarene field was Methodist by comity arrangement. The Methodists were interested in consolidating their own work in India and offered the Nazarenes the opportunity to purchase buildings and properties centered around the town of Washim.

Actually this area had been Methodist only since 1895 and had been pioneered by an independent holiness mission in the late 1870s. Lucy Drake (later the wife of William Osborn, a well-known holiness leader in the Methodist Church) had been commissioned and even ordained for missionary work by an interdenominational group of holiness leaders around Boston in 1875. The group was led by Charles Cullis, an Episcopal physician and lay evangelist. Cullis had been swept into the holiness movement during the 1857–1858 revival, and later emphasized divine healing. With the support of this group and Cullis in particular, Drake set sail for India. She decided upon Washim as the place for her ministry because, as she understood it, the place had not yet been touched by the gospel. After studying Marathi in Bombay, she reached Washim in 1877 and witnessed to various poor women. Amanda Smith, the African American holiness evangelist, visited Wasim in 1880. Though Drake stayed only one year, before she left she was joined by other missionaries sponsored by Cullis. These included Laura Wheeler, who remained in Washim for more than twenty years. In 1884 Wheeler married William Moore, another missionary sent out by Cullis. Laura Wheeler Moore was instrumental in beginning a boarding school and orphanage in Washim, and itinerated within a 40-mile radius of Washim. She and her husband remained with the mission after it was transferred to the Methodists.[68]

Other missionaries serving for a number of years in Washim under the Methodist board included V. G. and Celia Ferries McMurry, both of whom had transferred to the Methodist Church from the Free Methodists. Celia Ferries, in fact, had served in India since the late 1880s and had been one of the founders of the Free Methodist mission in India. Both wife and husband had served at different times as superintendents of the Free Methodist work. After a few years with the Methodist Board in Washim, where they were in charge of evangelistic, educational, orphanage and industrial work, the McMurrys returned to the Free Methodists.[69]

This is to say that the Washim area that became part of the Nazarene field possessed a long history in the holiness movement, even predating the founding of the groups that formed the Church of the Nazarene in America. The last report of the Basim [Washim] District of the Bombay Conference of the Methodist Episcopal Church showed 180 active and 15 inactive members, 35 schools with 871 enrolled, and an estimated property value of 80,000 rupees (about $30,000). The Methodist Board refused the initial Nazarene offer of $10,000, but under financial straits during the Depression it accepted a second offer of $15,000. Thus, after 40 years of building upon the foundations of the

Cullis mission, the Methodists transferred their work in Washim to the Church of the Nazarene in early 1935.[70]

The Methodists had "laid a good foundation," in the estimation of the Nazarenes, who may not have been aware of its background as a holiness mission.[71] In Washim there were buildings already in use as a church, schools and missionary homes, as well one suitable for a hospital. There was a congregation with over 120 members—larger than the membership of the Nazarene church in Buldana. There were two other organized churches in the Methodist area, in Pusad and Umerkhed. This brought to eight the number of organized Nazarene churches in all India. In terms of leaders, the Methodists had only one or two ordained, and four or five other supply preachers. Most, including those ordained, decided to remain with the Methodists and transferred elsewhere. Among the lay preachers who decided to join the Nazarenes was Luther Manmothe, who was to play a significant role in the future. Indeed many of the Nazarene leaders from the Buldana area had family members active in the work on the Methodist side, and some had been born in Christian homes because of the Methodist work. So it was not difficult for the Nazarenes to transfer their own pastors to the area. Salve became the pastor in Washim. The common laypersons, the Nazarene missionaries felt, sensed little difference upon being transferred to the Nazarene church. Beals felt that the accession of the Methodist work helped to fulfill the goal set by Tracy: to "Indianize and not Westernize our Indian church."[72]

The missionaries also transferred the Bible Training School in Buldana to Washim, and soon began construction of a hospital, for which money had been donated in honor of Hiram F. Reynolds. In 1936 Dr. Orpha Speicher arrived. She had received a medical doctorate at Loma Linda University, and, after brief study in Scotland, had passed Triple Licentiate Board exams entitling her to practice medicine within the British Empire. Almost single-handedly, she built the hospital in Washim. It remained a hospital for women until after the Second World War.[73]

## Indian Leadership, 1937–1945

While India underwent political turmoil and external threat in the late 1930s and the 1940s, the Church of the Nazarene in India grew stronger. The preparations of slow decades finally saw fruition in the first ordination of Indians in 1937 and in their leadership of nearly every facet of the mission during the war years.

General Superintendent J. B. Chapman personally and officially organized the church in India as a "Missionary District" under an Indian superintendent in November 1937, and ordained six. By this time, the *Manual* had been translated into Marathi and the Indian church had organized both young people's and missionary societies. Each local church regularly sent delegates to district meetings and various committees were carrying on the business of the Indian church. Chapman's view was that the only task left for missionaries was to educate preachers, teachers and other Christian workers while giving general direction to the evangelistic program. Hereafter, according to Chapman, missionaries were to have "no direct voice in the direction of the India church." Theirs was only an advisory relation. Their joy was in seeing the work develop "to the place where they themselves [were] eliminated. Missionaries are John the Baptists, whose glory is to decrease as the national leaders increase."[74]

Though, as in the case of Reynolds, it is difficult to assess the origin of Chapman's missiological theories, they were consistent with the three-selfs principles laid out by Venn and Anderson in the nineteenth century. Those whom Chapman ordained in 1937 formed the backbone of the church in the next decade: Samuel Bhujbal, S. Y. Salve, W. H. Kharat, David Bhujbal, G. S. Borde and B. D. Amolik.[75]

The Indian assembly delegates proceeded to elect Samuel Bhujbal as district superintendent on the day after he was ordained. Bhujbal was a third-generation Christian. His father and mother had transferred to the Nazarene mission in Vasim from another Protestant mission many years before. His father died of malaria when Bhujbal, the oldest son, was eleven. His mother served many years as a Bible woman in the Nazarene mission in Buldana. Raised, then, in Nazarene mission schools, Bhujbal easily won the trust of the missionaries. He testified to being converted in 1921 under Reynolds's preaching and sanctified in a revival in Buldana in 1926. He attended a university in Bombay. He subsequently ministered for a year in Murbad, before the missionaries transferred him to Buldana to teach in the boys' school. He became headmaster in 1928. He proceeded on the course of study for ministers and served as a preacher and evangelist around the field.[76]

Of the others ordained in 1937, Salve also was born to Christian parents, and had been educated in Christian schools. He joined the Nazarene church in Khardi, in the Thana district, and taught in the boys' school there. He served later in both the boys' school and the Bible Training School in Buldana. After the accession of the Methodist work, missionaries assigned him to pastor the church in Washim. Kharat had joined the mission in 1906, after being educated in Christian schools, and ministered in Buldana. David Bhujbal, Samuel Bhujbal's uncle, had been reared by missionaries in Thana and educated in Nazarene and other Christian schools. However, he had rebelled against the missionaries, studied medicine and became an ardent nationalist. His conversion came about 1923, when he was 23 years old. He ministered in Buldana. Borde had been educated in another denomination and had transferred to the Nazarene work. Nazarenes stationed him principally around Chickli. Amolik, born of Christian parents, affiliated with the Free Methodists before becoming Nazarene in 1921.[77]

In short, Tracy's realization of many years before was borne true, that leaders would have to come from Nazarene or other Christian environments. None of the six ordained had ever been Hindu.

Bhujbal as district superintendent proved to be a strong leader. He impressed the missionaries as a soul winner in the revivalist American style, and a preacher of holiness. While his main activities involved touring the district and preaching evangelistically, he also organized evangelistic teams, gave instructions to pastors on evangelism, and remained as headmaster of the boys' school. He published a district newsletter, the *Nazarene Evangel*, and translated holiness books. Other denominations called him to hold revivals. He got along well with missionaries. Beals, who was mission director during these years, remarked: "Never once was there anything but the finest of fellowship and cooperation and brotherly love between them." Under his leadership finances from Indian churches rose and churches collected "thanksgiving" offerings for the spread of Nazarene missions around the world.[78]

Bhujbal's leadership marked the fulfillment of what Beals called the "new school" of missions. The "old school" philosophy was that the missionary was the only one capable of carrying the work, said Beals. Missionaries did not encourage the Indians to take over responsibility. Indeed, in the early days of the mission, due to the lack of Indian leaders, this was inevitable. But it could not continue. Indians themselves were becoming nationalistic, Beals admitted, and possessed new aspirations. The "new school" missionaries placed leadership roles upon the Indian church as quickly as possible.[79]

Indian leadership developed in the late 1930s with the blessing of the missionaries. Indians reelected Bhujbal as district superintendent on repeated occasions. Another emerging leader was Luther Manmothe, originally from the formerly Methodist area and a graduate of the Nazarene Bible Training School, who became district secretary and district young peoples' society president while pastoring the church in Mehkar. He also helped to translate Sunday school lessons. Missionaries recognized that the Indian ministers rightly were taking such active roles. The slogan among the missionaries, wrote Bessie Beals in 1941, in words reminiscent of Chapman's, was, "Our Indian church must increase, and our mission decrease."[80]

They perceived the educational system as vital to this intention. At the boys' school Nazarenes maintained government standards in the grade school and also taught trades such as carpentry and weaving. In one year nine Hindu boys attending the school became Christians. In the minds of the Nazarene workers this fact justified the school as an "agency for evangelism."[81] Meanwhile, all recognized that the continued development of the church depended upon "qualified, indoctrinated, [and] spiritual Indian leaders," educated in the church's own Bible Training School.[82]

World conditions during the Second World War forced the reduction of the missionary staff. Various ones had gone on furlough just before the war. The remaining staff included only the Bealses, Agnes Gardner, a nurse, and Leslie and Ellen Fritzlan, who had arrived shortly before the outbreak of the war. Leslie Fritzlan, the son of A. D. and Daisy Fritzlan, had grown up in India and was acquainted from childhood with many of the Indian leaders. This added to the trust already established between them and the missionaries. Gardner died in India in 1942.[83]

The Japanese threatened to invade India from the East. Some feared Indian nationalists would take advantage of the situation and press their demands for independence from British colonial rule. Both Mohatma Gandhi and the All-India Conference of Indian Christians called upon the British to "quit India" once the war was over. This made it dangerous for foreigners who remained in the country and also provided good reason for the further indigenization of the work. In preparation for their possible evacuation, Nazarene missionaries registered the District Assembly with the government so that Indian church leaders would be able legally to buy and sell property, and they handed over supervision of the schools to Indians. The American consulate at one point advised the remaining missionaries to leave the field. Meanwhile, Indian tithing greatly increased (a 35 percent increase during the war years), an Indian doctor carried on the hospital, and the church grew more rapidly than ever before, with a 23 percent increase in membership. The Indian members, Beals reported, were "surpassing our expectations and were ready for whatever is thrust upon them."[84] It became evident to the Indians during this time, according to Beals, that: "this was their organization, and their church, and that their leaders and pastors were their own duly chosen ones. [This] caused them to realize that the church—not only its survival but its progress—was their very own responsibility. . . . They rallied far beyond our expectation and proved to us that the Indian church is a living faithful church."[85]

If the missionaries had to leave due to the impending civil war, the church work would not suffer. In 1944 Beals asked the general superintendents for permission, given the emergency, to ordain six. He thought at the time that it might still be years before a general superintendent would be able to come and he reminded them that the six previously ordained were all from one geographic area. However, the general superintendents did not give Beals permission for this.[86]

## The Post-War Period

Like other missions, the Church of the Nazarene had difficulty adjusting to the post-war situation in India. As India gained independence in 1947 it seemed to some that the missionary enterprise was a remnant of colonialism. During these nationalist times Indians associated with missions would need to prove to their fellow citizens their loyalty to the new state. The Church of South India, a union of several churches, was formed under Indian leadership in 1947. Meanwhile, the number of Nazarene missionaries grew from four in 1944 to twenty in 1946, and many more arrived in the years following. The new recruits were zealous, but inexperienced. Their role in the church in India was less defined than those of missionaries in previous generations. Almost all were assigned either to the hospital or to schools. In the same years hundreds migrated from Buldana and Washim, as well as other provincial towns, to Bombay and other large cities.[87]

These factors had a devastating impact upon the Indian Nazarene church. During the war the Indian leaders had grown accustomed to the responsibilities of controlling the institutions and programs of the church. They had proven themselves successful at the task and they reeled, especially in these anti-colonialist times, at relinquishing these roles to missionaries younger than themselves who did not understand the language or culture of the people. At the same time, Indians jockeyed among themselves for leadership positions. The new missionaries would have to catch again the vision of Tracy and Beals for a truly Indian church, and it was not easy for them to place the same faith in Indian leaders that older leaders had.[88]

Prescott Beals helped to organize the post-war influx of missionaries as best he could and remained in India until 1952, when his wife's health prevented them from continuing. Actually Beals requested more missionaries, and hoped that they would add to the growing church. His emphasis was upon evangelism. "The educational and medical have their very important place," he wrote, "but all are agreed that these are only means to an end, viz. the salvation of souls, the sanctification of believers, and the building up of the church in India."[89]

Beals also believed that the influx of new missionaries and money from Kansas City should not retard the growth of the Indian church toward self-support as long as headquarters did not require the Indians to finance all of the church's educational and medical work. If it did, the Indian district would not be able to reach it. Though the hospital generated income and charged patients, the amount it received from Kansas City far exceeded these receipts. The salaries of missionary nurses and doctors came from America. Beals doubted that the hospital could be fully supported by the church rather than the mission. The same was true of education. Beals believed that the district could support the village schools, especially considering that the government still subsidized teacher salaries, but not the higher schools in Washim. Having seen the progress of the church under Indians during the war, the tides of nationalism did not threaten Beals and he continued to wish that more authority could be granted to Indian workers.[90]

But the anomalies were clear enough. How could the Nazarenes both increase Indian participation in and responsibility for the church while at the same time sending platoons of new missionaries and tens of thousands of dollars for educational and medical work that the Indian church could not hope to match?

As early as 1947, the year India won independence from Great Britain, Borde, Bhujbal and other district Indian leaders expressed their concerns over these issues to General Superintendent H. V. Miller. They advocated instructing missionaries to put their membership on the Indian district where they served so that they would be amenable to the direction, supervision and guidance of Indian leaders. If this were not acceptable to the general church (as indeed it was not, as it ran counter to long-standing missions policy) the Indian leaders felt that the missionaries, being largely unacquainted with local conditions, would benefit by having more Indian representation on the mission's executive council. They also wanted the church to strengthen its ministerial education program, and for the church to send some Indians to college or seminary in America. The requests indicate that the Indian leaders were restless under missionary leadership in these days. They pressed for ways to minister together with missionaries more cooperatively than they felt the church's missions policy actually promoted. But missions policy could not be bent in the direction they advocated. The church was unwilling to change its policy of separating the mission council and the District Assembly, and it had no intentions or plans of financing the theological education of Indian students in America.[91]

At the same time, on its own terms, and with resources saved during the Second World War, the Church of the Nazarene put great emphasis upon India. There were short-term rewards for the efforts. Between 1944 and 1948 India received over $333,000 from the general church. Only the Africa field received more. However, two-thirds of the money from Kansas City went for missionary field expenses, and most of the rest went toward the educational and medical work. The Indian church, by comparison, raised just $25,000 during the same four years, about half of which came from the hospital. The membership of the India district rose significantly, from 1,394 full and probationary members in 1944 to 2,217 in 1948. Among districts outside the United States only Africa had more members. On a visit to India in 1947 (the first of a general superintendent since Chapman's visit ten years earlier) H. V. Miller ordained three. There were thirty-two organized churches in 1948.[92]

Sunday School attendance in India, however, showed no growth during these same years. This fact was perhaps a portent of decline. General Superintendent G. B. Williamson visited the District Assembly in 1951, but he ordained no one. As a consequence he advised the field to concentrate on ministerial education. A Marathi-language radio program began in 1952, but it had limited success. The district lost members during the late 1940s and 1950s due to migrations, yet the Nazarenes decided not to move immediately into the cities, despite pleas from leaders such as Bhujbal for them to do so, and remained exclusively in Maharastra until 1962. Then leaders allowed Luther Manmothe to open a work in Aurangabad.[93]

Independence from Great Britain in 1947 heightened the distance between the mission and the church. Mohatma Gandhi earlier had recommended that proselytizing from one religion to another would be prohibited when India became independent. Though this did not happen, it represented the resentments toward Christian missionaries that went together with colonialism in many Indian leaders' minds. When the United States offered military aid to Pakistan in the 1950s, life became even more difficult for the American missionaries. Mary Anderson put it this way: in 1952 the Indians were begging the missionaries never to leave; in 1953 they were saying "if you leave"; and in 1954, "when you go." By 1952 the Indian government itself began refusing missionary visas. The government also occasionally harassed missionaries by opening and censoring letters. Government officials were known to become surly if a missionary refused to baptize a relative. At the same time, some young people in the Nazarene area embraced communism. These as well as others cried, "Missionary go home." Anderson summed, "Our days are definitely numbered."[94]

Meanwhile, institutional ministries occupied missionaries' attention. Half of the missionaries were stationed at the Reynolds Memorial Hospital and almost as many were engaged in education. Village evangelism, or "touring," common in earlier years, was rare. Missionaries seemed remote from the Indian church. A spiritual revival did break out in 1954. It felt like the old days. The District Assembly that year placed full responsibility upon the churches for paying their workers. But the lasting results of these events were negligible. General Superintendent Hardy C. Powers ordained only one on his 1957 visit, bringing the total of ordained national workers to 13. There were 24 missionaries. No one was enrolled at the Bible Training School and membership continued to decline. The next year the district began selling property owned by the church in towns where no churches were operating, while the mission transferred the remaining deeds it held to the Indian Assembly. In 1960 there were 1,051 full and probationary members (about half the number in 1948), 26 organized churches and 27 missionaries. The Missionary Council chairperson expressed thoughts similar to those that Tracy had years earlier, but that seemed novel in 1960, that the Indians must learn to "do things for themselves," and that self-support was not only a practical but a moral need of the church.[95]

Bhujbal's leadership continued into the 1950s, but fellow Indians challenged him. He had always been the darling of the missionaries. This did him little good in an era of nationalism. G. S. Borde defeated him for the district superintendency in 1945, and remained in office until 1949, when Bhujbal was elected again and Borde became headmaster of the Bible Training School. During his period out of office Bhujbal spent nearly three years holding conventions and rallies among Nazarenes in North America, and one year in India as "District Evangelist." The 1948 Nazarene Woman's Foreign Missionary Society Convention in St. Louis featured him as a speaker. He was voted in again as district superintendent in 1949, but the vote for his reelection as district superintendent in 1955 brought division. Neither Luther Manmothe, who led in the balloting, nor Bhujbal was able to secure the necessary two-thirds vote for election until the seventh ballot, when Manmothe won. However, he resigned the next day, apparently at the urging of missionaries. The district superintendency reverted to the missionaries for the first time since 1937. Indians reelected Bhujbal in 1956 after 27 ballots. Manmothe was again the principal contender.

Once again in 1959 Bhujbal was unable to win reelection, and the missionaries appointed S. T. Gaikwad in his stead. Bhujbal retired, finally, at age 53, to Bombay, where the Church of the Nazarene had not yet opened work. Nazarenes and other groups continued to use him as a preacher and evangelist until his death in 1978. The leadership instability and missionary intervention was a sign of the church's internal problems.[96]

The hospital took on a greater role in the overall mission of the church in the post-war years. Speicher returned after having furloughed during the war. In 1952, with the arrival of Dr. Ira Cox, the hospital expanded to two wings, and initiated the medical treatment of men. A nurses' training program began. The hospital remained a highly visible form of the church's witness. It also proved a means of evangelism. Speicher repeatedly emphasized that the hospital provided an opportunity for witnessing to people who otherwise would not approach Christians. In the public defense of the work, missionaries emphasized to leaders and to the North American constituency its evangelistic role, rather than its fulfilling the holiness mandate of perfect love. Cash receipts from patients rose steadily and gradually Indian nurses and doctors replaced missionaries. But for more than two decades after the war it required a great deal of the mission's personnel and resources.[97]

The educational program also was a high priority and required a great deal of missionaries' time and effort. Missionaries administered and taught at the girls' and boys' primary boarding schools (which merged soon after the war to form the Nazarene Christian Coeducation School at Chikhli) and at the Bible Training School. It used the Marathi language. Some, but not all, of the few students enrolled in the Bible school were high school graduates; so it could not claim to be of college level. There was still a difficulty, after all the years of working in the Maharastra area, of not having enough holiness literature in Marathi.[98]

Leaders at headquarters and missionaries on the field both desired self-direction as well as self-support in India and set goals toward such. The mission and church established a 25-year plan toward self-support in 1954, for instance, and saw gradual movement away from mission support. However, George Coulter, who became executive secretary of missions in 1960, wanted to see the goals intensified and advocated a 10-year plan like the one being used in Korea. In May 1961 the mission began to give subsidies to churches rather than directly to pastors. But the pastors complained that they already were receiving less than in earlier years due to inflation. In 1962 only four congregations were self-supporting. The plan for self-support did not work. In 1973 still only four of the then 23 organized churches were self-supporting.[99]

The district continued to close churches. Strong nationalist feelings remained. Indians blamed leadership in general and missionaries in particular for causing problems. One group in Buldana in 1975 saw missionaries as "the great obstacle for the growth of the church," and urged them to go back to their own countries. At the same time Indians evidenced feuding among their own factions and jockeying for leadership positions.[100]

Indians gained administrative positions of leadership, though perhaps more slowly than in other missions.[101] In 1967 D. M. Kharat (from a family with long ancestry in the Church of the Nazarene in India) succeeded Hilda Cox as principal of the Bible Training School. In 1970 S. P. Dongerdive became director of the coeducational school. In 1976, the year before Speicher retired from India, Dr. Kamalakar Meshramkar became superintendent of the hospital. When Kharat became district superintendent of the Eastern Maharastra District in 1972, Padu Meshramkar, who had been educated at Nazarene Theological Seminary in Kansas City, became the Bible school director. Like earlier missionaries, these Indian leaders had learned to connect institutional work to evangelism.[102]

The leadership transition to these and other Indian leaders was prompted not only by their own readiness and missions policy but—perhaps even more so—by the Indian government, which pressured missions to indigenize, and did not allow new American missionary appointments.[103]

Missionary Bronnel Greer believed that the reason for tepidness in the post-war strength and growth of the church after all these years was that it had lost its evangelistic edge. Greer went to India in 1944 and served for forty-six years. For most of those years Bronnel and Paula Greer were the only missionaries assigned to full-time evangelism and church planting. As such Greer often was sharply critical of the mission. Real evangelism—with the world—was not taking place, he said. A balance among education, medical work and evangelism had been lost. "All divinely ordained work of the church has its importance. But not all God given vocations are equally important. Evangelism holds the highest priority."[104] But, he complained, it received less than two percent of the mission's budget. The Great Commission of the church was not to heal the sick or to reform society, Greer admonished, but to preach the gospel.[114]

Much like Rufus Anderson and Henry Venn a century earlier, Greer believed that institutions were strangling the true work of the mission. They were unsustainable by the Indian church and a stumbling block to indigenization. Insofar as the evangelistic work was concerned, Indians were as they should be on the forefront. The problem, he said, was that the mission council gave no direction or foresight and planning to evangelism and advancement. At the same time he sensed that the council maintained too much power over church decisions, and prevented Indians from devising their own strategies. The mission developed institutions across the years, but, he believed, it had yet to raise up a truly Indian church.[105]

It was quite an indictment. Greer specifically cited Roland Allen to support his views, which in many ways re-echoed those of Nazarenes such as J. Glenn Gould and R. V. DeLong. Greer articulated a paradigm like that of Reynolds, but without Reynolds's understanding of medical and educational work as a part of Christian duty. Greer's fear was that the church would lose its first love by concentrating on institutions, and his hope was that the primary mission of the church would remain evangelism. Eventually the Greers were stationed outside of the Maharastra area and off of the missionary council responsible for that area. They helped to open the work in Bombay where two congregations, including one under Bhujbal, affiliated with the Church of the Nazarene. For several years the Greers worked jointly with the Evangelical Fellowship of India.[106]

At the close of the Second World War the Church of the Nazarene was on the verge of completing its long-articulated goal and policy of establishing an indigenous church with strong and capable leaders. The leadership roles that Indian leaders had assumed during the war diminished in the post-war era and missionaries had to learn the lessons carefully and sometimes agonizingly worked out by Tracy, Beals and others many years before. The extension of self-governing policies by the pre-war missionaries had been the result of a slow and painstaking process that had built upon trusted personal relationships implemented at the urging of Chapman and others in the general church. Political urgency also hastened the process. It had taken time, patience, common experience and mutual trials to build reliance upon the Indian church. Rather than helping to maintain that reliance, the influx of missionaries at the close of the war and the emphasis upon educational and medical work inadvertently helped to defeat it, as did many other factors. It would take another generation, and further government pressures in the 1960s and 1970s, for Indians to again take significant leadership roles. In the meantime the spiritual fervor and excitement of the Indians to build their own church in their own way subsided, and Indian leadership itself became embroiled in contests for church positions. Political unrest and migrations from rural areas to the cities were other obstacles to the growth of the Nazarene church in central India. Until the church expanded beyond central Maharastra where these patterns had been built across the years, growth remained slow.[107]

## Notes

1. For the context of these issues see William R. Hutchison, *Errand to the World: American Protestant Thought and Foreign Missions* (Chicago: University of Chicago Press, 1987), ch. 4.

2. "Minutes of the Missionary Committee of the Association of Pentecostal Churches of America," July 6, 1897, September 10, 1897, and December 9, 1897, Nazarene Archives; Roy E. Swim, *A History of Nazarene Missions* (Kansas City, Mo.: Nazarene Publishing House, [1936]), 24; Mendell Taylor, *Fifty Years of Nazarene Missions*, vol. 1, *Administration and Promotion* (Kansas City, Mo.: Beacon Hill, 1952), 12, 30.

3. *Report of the Third Decennial Missionary Conference*, vol. 2 (Bombay: Education Society's Steam Press, 1893), 839; *Our Missionaries to India: The Christian Experiences of the Four Persons Recently Approved by the Association of Pentecostal Churches of America for Missionary Work in India* (Providence, R.I.: Beulah Christian Printing, 1897), 5–21; Wood to Reynolds, November 4, 1898; G. P. Pardington, *Twenty-Five Wonderful Years, 1889–1914: A Popular Sketch of the Christian and Missionary Alliance* (New York: Christian Alliance Publishing, 1914), 163; M. D. Wood, *Fruit from the Jungle* (Mountain View, Calif.: Pacific Publishing, 1919), 7.

4. Wood to Reynolds, March 3, 1899; *Pentecostal Mission and Missionaries* (Providence, R.I.: Pentecostal Printing, [1905]).

5. Wood to Reynolds, November 20, 1905; Pardington, *Twenty-Five Wonderful Years*, 103–106, 111–114; Robert B. Ekvall, et al., *After Fifty Years: A Record of God's Working Through the Christian and Missionary Alliance* (Harrisburg, Penn.: Christian Publications, 1939), 127–134. See also Klaus Fiedler, *The Story of Faith Missions* (Oxford: Regnum, 1994).

6. "Minutes of the Missionary Committee of the Association of Pentecostal Churches of America," December 11, 1897 (Article 12), and April 15, 1898.

7. *Beulah Christian* (January 1898), 5; Lillian Sprague, "Minutes," February 2, 1898; Ekvall, *After Fifty Years*, 130; Wade C. Barclay, *History of Methodist Missions*, part two, *The Methodist Episcopal Church, 1845–1939*, vol. 3, *Widening Horizons, 1845–1895* (New York: Board of Missions of the Methodist Church, 1957), 553, 595, 645–646, 650.

8. Missionary Committee to Wood, May 2, 1898; Reynolds to F[red] Hillery, September 12, [1898]; H. B. Hosley to Wood, December 22, 1898; Wood, *Fruit from the Jungle*, 276–286; Timothy L. Smith, *Called Unto Holiness: The Story of the Nazarenes: The Formative Years* (Kansas City, Mo.: Nazarene Publishing House, 1962), 84–85. See also M. D. David, "American Missionaries in India: A Difference," *Indian Church History Review* 30 (December 1996), 115–116.

9. Wood to Reynolds, March 24, 1898; Wood to Missionary Committee, March 3, 1899; Lillian Sprague, "Minutes," September 2, 1898, and October 13, 1898; Wood to Reynolds, January 16, 1899.

10. Reynolds to Wood, April 23, 1901. On ordination see *Constitution of the Association of Pentecostal Churches of America* (Providence, R.I.: Beulah Christian, 1897), 8–9.

11. Wood to Reynolds, January 30, 1900; Sprague to Reynolds, March 21, 1900.

12. Wood to M. B. Fuller, December 12, 1904; W. B. Godbey, *Around the World: Garden of Eden, Latter Day Prophecies and Missions* (Cincinnati: God's Revivalist Office, 1907), 472–473; L. S. Tracy to E. G. Anderson, December 27, 1911. On comity in India see M. A. Sherring, *The History of Missions in India: From Their Commencement in 1706 to 1881*, new ed., ed. Edward Storrow (London: Religious Tract Society, 1884), 216, 225; R. Pierce Beaver, *Ecumenical Beginnings in Protestant World Mission: A History of Comity* (New York: Thomas Nelson, 1962), 85–90; Eugene P. Heideman, *From Mission to Church: The Reformed Church in America Mission to India* (Grand Rapids, Mich.: Eerdmans, 2001), 322–336.

13. Wood to Reynolds, July 1, 1898; Wood to Missionary Committee, March 3, 1899; Reynolds to Wood, September 6, 1900.

14. Anna Wood, "Fourth Annual Report," January 1, 1902. For background on the social interests of evangelicals, especially as related to missions, see Hutchison, *Errand to the World*, 118–124.

15. Wood to Reynolds, September 18, 1905; Reynolds to the Pentecostal Mission, Buldana, September 25, 1905. See also Helen S. Dyer, *Pandita Ramabai: The Story of Her Life*, new ed. (London: Morgan and Scott, 1907), 49–51, 74–75, 101–105; James R. Cameron, *Eastern Nazarene College: The First Fifty Years, 1900–1950* (Kansas City, Mo.: Nazarene Publishing House, 1968), 45–46; J. Edwin Orr, *Evangelical Awakenings in Southern Asia* (Minneapolis: Bethany, 1975), 144–147, 158; Gary B. McGee, "'Latter Rain' Falling in the East: Early-Twentieth-Century Pentecostalism in India and the Debate over Speaking in Tongues," *Church History* 68 (September 1999), 652–656; Stanley Burgess, "Pentecostalism in India: An Overview," *Asian Journal of Pentecostal Studies* 4 (January 2001), 88–89. On the worldwide revival, see J. Edwin Orr, *The Flaming Tongue: Evangelical Awakenings, 1900–* (Chicago: Moody, 1975), 147–151, 191–200.

16. "Minutes of the Missionary Committee of the Association of Pentecostal Churches of America," June 2, 1905; Wood to Reynolds, October 19, 1905; Reynolds to Wood, October 30, 1905.

17. M. D. Wood, Anna Wood and Lillian Sprague to Reynolds, November 8, 1905; Wood, *A Life Saving Station* (Igatpuri, India: Watchman Press, n.d.), 6 pp. The tract requested that money be sent to the Buldana post office.

18. Tracy to Reynolds, November 9, 1905.

19. November 8, 1905, letter.

20. "Minutes of the Missionary Committee of the Association of Pentecostal Churches of America," September 14, 1905, and December 15, 1905; Reynolds to Pentecostal Mission, Buldana, September 25, 1905. See Smith, *Called*, 74–90, and Cameron, *Eastern*, 27–29, regarding Pettit.

21. C. Howard Davis to Wood, December 21, 1905.

22. Olive G. Tracy, *Tracy Sahib of India* (Kansas City, Mo.: Beacon Hill, 1954), 49. Swim, *History*, 48, mentions that Wood met Reynolds on the latter's 1914 trip to India, and that Wood reacquired the experience of entire sanctification and apologized for his earlier actions. The incident related by Swim would have more credence if it took place during Reynolds's 1921 trip. See also Tracy to Reynolds and the General Foreign Missions Board, February 25, 1913; and R. G. Codding to Tracy, December 3, 1926. For Wood's work with the SDA see A. G. Daniels, "The Bombay Mission," *Adventist Review and Sabbath Herald* (April 29, 1915), 11; Wood, "Two Testimonies," *ARSH* (August 12, 1915), 11; Wood, "India Famine Conditions: How Charlie Found the Third Angel's Message," *Adventist Review and Sabbath Herald* (May 10, 1917), 14–15; Wood, *Fruit from the Jungle*, 10–14; M. Ellsworth Olsen, *A History of the Origin and Progress of Seventh-day Adventists* (Washington, D.C.: Review and Herald, 1925), 529.

23. Tracy to Reynolds, November 9, 1905; *Association of Pentecostal Churches of America Minutes of the Eleventh Annual Meeting* (Providence, R.I.: Pentecostal Printing, 1906), 24–38; Olive Tracy, *Tracy Sahib*, 45–47; Smith, *Called*, 77–81, 89–90.

24. Julia Gibson, *A Cry from India's Night* (Kansas City, Mo.: Nazarene Publishing House, 1914), 8; see also pages 109–115 on child widows, and pages 155–165 on child wives.

25. Campbell, secretary, "Recommendations of the Missionary Meeting to the General Board," June 26–30, 1909. See DeLong and Taylor, *Fifty Years*, 2: 25.

26. Tracy to Reynolds, February 23, 1906; Reynolds to Missionary Committee, June 25, 1906. Tracy to Reynolds, April 18, 1913; and Tracy to General Foreign Missions Board, July 31, 1913.

27. Campbell, "Report from the Marathi District, 1910–11"; see likewise A. D. Fritzlan, "Annual Report, Buldana Station, 1915."

28. Tracy to Reynolds, September 30, 1912, Tracy correspondence; Julia Gibson, "Notes, Buldana District" [1910]. On Kharat and other Indian leaders see Amy Hinshaw, *Native Torch Bearers* (Kansas City, Mo.: Nazarene Publishing House, 1934), 78–105.

29. Emma Eaton, comp., *Our Work in India: Hallelujah Village, Hope School Calcutta* (Portland, Ore.: Boyer Printing, 1913), 19–21; E. A. Girvin, *Phineas Bresee: A Prince in Israel. A Biography* (Kansas City, Mo.: Pentecostal Nazarene Publishing House, 1916), 182–186; Basil Miller, *Mother Eaton of India* (Los Angeles: Bedrock, 1951), 22–27.

30. See Leslie A. Flemming, "New Models, New Roles: U.S. Presbyterian Women Missionaries and Social Change in North India, 1870–1910," in

*Women's Work for Women: Missionaries and Social Change in Asia*, ed. Leslie A. Flemming (Boulder, Colo.: Westview Press, 1989), 35–58, especially page 40; Dana L. Robert, *American Women in Mission: A Social History of Their Thought and Practice* (Macon, Ga.: Mercer University Press, 1996), 239–240.

31. A. A. Avetoom, Calcutta, to Herbert Anderson, September 8, 1915.

32. Jacques to General Missionary Board, October 31, 1912, and July 30, 1913; Banarjee to Reynolds, February 13, 1913; Tracy to General Missionary Board, April 14, 1914; Reynolds, "Report on Calcutta Work #1 to the General Missionary Board," April 17, 1914; Biswas to Reynolds, May 9, 1914, enclosing his commission, dated May 1, 1906, signed by Bresee (on Biswas see also *World Mission* [January 1986], 13); Reynolds to Biswas [1914]; Reynolds, "Report to the General Missionary Board," May 7, 1914; General Missionary Secretary's Report, June 19, 1914; L. S. Tracy, Gertrude Tracy, Leoda Grebe, Hulda Grebe, and Myrtle Mangum to General Missionary Board, September 10, 1914; Tracy, "Report, 1914: Eastern India"; Reynolds, *World-Wide Missions* (Kansas City, Mo.: Pentecostal Nazarene Publishing House, [1915]), 150, 155; "Financial Record of Hope School and Hallelujah Village, 1911–1917," (file 416-19). This incident is discussed by J. Timothy White, "Hiram F. Reynolds: Prime Mover of the Nazarene Mission Education System," Ph.D. dissertation, University of Kansas, 1996, 124–142.

33. See "Heart of India Mission Band" pamphlet [1920]; J. G. Morrison, "Supported by Nazarene Money," *Other Sheep* (May 1933), 4; Tracy to Morrison, June 5, 1933; and Miller, *Mother Eaton*, 32–34, 37, 41–42, 49–52, and passim.

34. Tracy, "Annual Report: Calcutta," 1916; "Minutes of the First Session of the East India District Assembly," August 1917.

35. Tracy to General Missionary Board, May 25, 1914; "Report, 1914: Eastern India." In regards to the condition in Calcutta, Reynolds noted the same in his "Report of the General Missionary Secretary to the General Missionary Board, 1914."

36. George Franklin, "Annual Report: Calcutta," 1916; "Minutes of the First Session of the East India District Assembly," August 1917. Compare Orr, *Evangelical Awakenings in Southern Asia*, 188. For background see Krickwin Marak, "Christianity Among the Garos: An Attempt to Re-read Peoples' Movement from a Missiological Perspective," in *Christianity in India: Search for Liberation and Identity*, ed. F. Hrangkhuma (Delhi: ISPCK, 1998), 163–168, 180–181.

37. Franklin, "Missionary District Superintendent's Report, 1919."

38. Franklin, "Missionary District Superintendent's Report, 1919"; "Annual Station Report: Calcutta, 1919"; "Annual Station Report: Kishorganj," n.d.

39. Lou Hatch to E. G. Anderson, May 17, 1922. Compare R. Pierce Beaver, *All Loves Excelling: American Protestant Women in World Mission* (Grand Rapids, Mich.: Eerdmans, 1968), 118, 134; Flemming, "New Models, New Roles," 46–48; Heideman, *From Mission to Church*, 182–187; Maina Chawla

Singh, *Gender, Religion, and "Heathen Lands": American Missionary Women in South Asia (1860s–1940s)* (New York: Garland, 2000), 203–244.

40. Franklin, "Missionary District Superintendent's Report, 1919"; "Annual Station Report: Calcutta, 1919"; "Annual Station Report: Kishorganj," n.d; "Minutes of the Seventh Annual Assembly of the Eastern India District, 1923."

41. Roy T. Williams, "Notes on the Missionary Trip Round the World" (file 544-1); Christine M. Williams, "Nazarene Missions in India," M.A. thesis, George Washington University, 1930, 28–31; George Franklin, "Bangladesh," [1970s].

42. Beals to J. G. Morrison, January 29, 1935; Beals to C. Warren Jones, October 5, 1937; Beals to "Friends," December 28, 1937. Swim, *History*, 64–65. The Baptists, however, did not take in Samed Babu. On Choudhury, see John Haines, "I Knew You'd Come," *World Mission* 19 (February 1993), 2–3.

43. "Combined Policy Suggested to the General Missionary Board to Govern the Work in India," received in Kansas City, Mo., October 6, 1914. Note the errors in the dating of this policy: Swim, *History*, 53; Olive G. Tracy, *Tracy Sahib*, 109; Smith, *Called*, 256–257; J. Fred Parker, *Mission to the World: A History of Missions in the Church of the Nazarene 1985* (Kansas City, Mo.: Nazarene Publishing House, 1988), 220. See Wilbert R. Shenk, *Henry Venn—Missionary Statesman* (Maryknoll, N.Y.: Orbis, 1983), chs. 3 and 4; Hutchison, *Errand to the World*, 95–102.

44. "Combined Policy," 1914.

45. Gertrude Tracy to General Missionary Board, July 18, 1918; A. D. Fritzlan to "Friend and Co-laborer," June 17, 1919.

46. Codding, "Annual Report: Mehkar, 1916"; Tracy to General Missionary Board, July 13, 1917; Tracy, "Annual Station Report: Khardi, Thana District," 1918; Tracy, "Annual Report of the Superintendent of the Marathi Missionary District," 1918; Amy H. Hinshaw, *Messengers of the Cross in India* (Kansas City, Mo.: Woman's Foreign Missionary Society, Church of the Nazarene, n.d.), 43–49; Olive Tracy, *Tracy Sahib*, 57, 104, 109. See Smith, *Called*, 180–199; Robert L. Niklaus, John S. Sawin and Samuel J. Stoesz, *All for Jesus: God at Work in the Christian and Missionary Alliance over One Hundred Years* (Camp Hill, Pa.: Christian Publications, 1986), 88.

47. Tracy to Reynolds, April 17, 1918, Tracy correspondence; Tracy, "Western India," in "Folios for the History of the Foreign Missionary Work of the Church of the Nazarene," n.d. (file 262-56).

48. Geoffrey Oddie, "Introduction," in Oddie, ed., *Religious Conversion Movements in South Asia: Continuities and Change, 1800–1900* (Richmond, Surrey, England: Curzon, 1997), 5–6. See also Antony Copley, *Religions in Conflict: Ideology, Cultural Contact and Conversion in Late-Colonial India* (New Delhi: Oxford University Press, 1997), 254–257.

49. Similarly, Sundararaj Manickam, *The Social Setting of Christian Conversion in South India: The Impact of the Wesleyan Methodist Missionaries on the Trichy–Tanjore Diocese with Special Reference to the Harijan Communi-*

*ties of the Mass Movement Area, 1820–1947* (Wiesbaden: Franz Steiner Verlag, 1977), especially pp. 256–260.

50. Hinshaw, *Messengers of the Cross in India*, 9–19, 64–65.

51. Jackson, in "Minutes of the Thirteenth Annual Western India Marathi District Assembly," November, 1922, 26–27.

52. Prescott Beals and Amber Tresham, Education Committee, "Minutes of the Fourteenth Annual Western India Marathi District Assembly," July 1923.

53. Bessie Seay and F. Arthur Anderson, Committee on the State of the Church, "Minutes of the Fourteenth . . . Assembly," 1923. Compare the similar sentiments in N. K. Mukerji, "The Education Program," in *The Missionary Policy in India of the Methodist Episcopal Church: Recommendations of the Asanol Conference* (N.p., [1927]), 50–62, affirming the importance of boarding schools in building character and shaping society.

54. "Annual Station Report: Buldana," 1921; Tracy, Burns, Oregon, to "Co-laborer," November 18, 1921. The proposed policy and Tracy's comments were circulated to missionaries in various countries; see "Policies Governing Foreign Work" (file 282-44). Tracy was ready to go back to India in 1926, but the finances of the church prevented this. See Emma Word to Tracy, March 10, 1926; Fritzlan to Susan N. Fitkin, June 24, 1927; Leighton and Gertrude Tracy to Department of Foreign Missions, December 3, 1928.

55. "Minutes of the First Annual Council" (1924), and "Minutes of the Second Annual Council" (1925). On the Fritzlans see also J. B. Chapman to the General Superintendents, December 1, 1937 (file 472-22).

56. "Your Humble Servants in Christ" to Secretary, General Board, February 18, 1927, Fritzlan correspondence.

57. Reynolds to Fritzlan, September 24, 1927; Samuel Bhujbal to Superintendent of Foreign Mission, March 10, 1927.

58. Hinshaw, *Native Torch Bearers*, 103. For the context see M. D. David, "Indian Attitude Towards Missionaries and Their Work with Special Reference to Maharashtra," *Indian Church History Review* 29 (December 1995), 93–105, and David, "American Missionaries in India," *Indian Church History Review*, 117–119; Paul Martin, *The Missionary of the Indian Road: A Theology of Stanley Jones* (Bangalore: Theological Book Trust, 1996), 7–11.

59. Compare Henriette Bugge, *Mission and Tamil Society: Social and Religious Change in South India (1840–1900)* (Richmond, Surrey, England: Curzon, 1994), which at various places discusses the issue of caste; and D. Dennis Hudson, *Protestant Origins in India: Tamil Evangelical Christians, 1706–1835* (Grand Rapids, Mich.: Eerdmans, 2000), 130–131, 140–142, 153–172, which discusses how Tamil Indians in this early period defended the caste system against Western egalitarianism.

60. Hinshaw, *Native Torch Bearers*, 79–82, 87–89; "Minutes of the Fifth Annual Council" (1928), 17. See Bhujbal to Superintendent of Foreign Mission, March 10, 1927. Compare the discussion of James Davadasan, "Present Day India as It Affects Christian Missions," in *The Missionary Policy in India of the Methodist Episcopal Church*, 19–27, which suggested that the church

should be favorable toward nationalism and that missionaries should more completely identify with the people. See also Brian Holmes, "British Imperial Policy and the Mission Schools," in *Educational Policy and the Mission Schools: Case Studies from the British Empire*, ed. Holmes (London: Routledge and Kegan Paul, 1967), 7–8, 25, 30–34, 39; and Steve Bishop, "Protestant Missionary Education in British India," *Evangelical Quarterly* 69 (July 1997), 245–266; Koji Kawashima, *Missionaries and a Hindu State: Travancore 1858–1936* (Delhi: Oxford University Press, 1998), 110–112.

61. See Olive Tracy, *Tracy Sahib*, 129–130, 135, and clipping from the *Hartford Daily Times* in Tracy papers. Reynolds encouraged Tracy to pursue his academics in anticipation of his being the key missions professor in a training school either at Pasadena College or in Kansas City, where Reynolds believed as early as 1926 that a theological school would be located. See Tracy to Reynolds, December 14, 1926; Reynolds to Tracy, November 8, 1926.

62. "Minutes of India Mission Council, 1932," Field Policy Committee Report; "Indian Church Development Committee Report," September 9, 1933, signed by Tracy and Beals.

63. Tracy to Fritzlan, June 6, 1935. The incident is also related in Beals, *India's Open Door* (Kansas City, Mo.: Nazarene Publishing House, 1940), 146–148; and Olive Tracy, *Tracy Sahib*, 156–159.

64. Fritzlan to Department of Foreign Missions, January 20, 1928; and see the telegram rescinding this suggestion, February 4, 1928. See Beals to Department of Foreign Missions, November 23, 1934. See also Swim *History*, 57; Taylor, *Fifty*, 2: 31–33; Olive Tracy, *Tracy Sahib*, 170–177; Beals, *India's*, 148–149.

65. Tracy to Chapman, December 14, 1933.

66. Tracy to Chapman, February 10, 1934; Beals to Chapman, August 31, 1934; Beals to Department of Foreign Missions, November 23, 1934; Beals, "Squibs," *Other Sheep* 25 (June 1937), 21.

67. Tracy to Department of Foreign Missions, February 21, 1934, and May 23, 1934.

68. W. H. Daniels, ed., *Dr. Cullis and His Work: Twenty Years of Blessing in Answer to Prayer* (Boston: Willard Tract Repository, 1885; reprint, New York: Garland, 1985), 300–318; and on Cullis in the context of the holiness movement see Norris Magnuson, *Salvation in the Slums: Evangelical Social Work, 1865–1920* (Metuchen, N.J.: Scarecrow, 1977), 68–69, and Melvin E. Dieter, *The Holiness Revival of the Nineteenth Century*, second ed. (Lanham, Md: Scarecrow, 1996), 252. See Lucy Drake Osborn, *Heavenly Pearls Set in a Life: A Record of Experiences and Labors in America, India, and Australia* (New York: Fleming H. Revell, 1893), 211–247; Amanda Smith, *An Autobiography: The Story of the Lord's Dealings with Mrs. Amanda Smith, the Colored Evangelist* (Chicago: Meyer and Brother, 1893), 307–308. Several other holiness movement leaders visited Bombay and other places in India in 1880–1881. See William McDonald and John E. Searles, *The Life of John S. Inskip* (Reprint, New York: Garland, 1985), 326–343. On Laura Wheeler Moore see

Laura W. Moore to [Thomas S.] Johnson, June 22, 1901, and T. S. Johnson to Dr. Baldwin, August 21, 1901, United Methodist Archives, Madison, New Jersey (1259-7-2:67). On the transfer of the Cullis mission to the Methodists see *Official Minutes of the Fourth Session of the Bombay Annual Conference of the Methodist Episcopal Church* (Madras: M.E. Publishing House, 1896), 27; "Minutes of the Committee on India, Methodist Episcopal Church Missionary Society, 1893–1898," United Methodist Archives, 80–81; and J. E. Scott, *History of Fifty Years: Comprising the Origin, Establishment, Progress and Expansion of the Methodist Episcopal Church in Southern Asia* (Madras: M.E. Press, 1906), 187, 191.

69. On V. G. and Celia Ferries McMurry see V. G. McMurry to Bishop J. E. Robinson, July 15, 1904, and Rev. and Mrs. V. G. McMurry to Bishop A. B. Leonard, June 15, 1906, United Methodist Archives (1259-7-2:93); and Byron S. Lamson, *Venture! The Frontiers of Free Methodism* (Winona Lake, Ind.: Light and Life, 1960), 76–77, 81.

70. *Minutes of the Annual Conferences of the Methodist Episcopal Church: Spring Conferences 1935* (New York: Methodist Book Concern, [1935]), 270–271; "Minutes of the Executive Committee of the Board of Foreign Missions of the Methodist Episcopal Church," vol. 15 (1935), 129, United Methodist Archives (1307-6-3:02).

71. Mary J. Anderson, "Basim," *Other Sheep* (August 1937), 17.

72. Beals to Morrison, March 6, 1935. See India Council to Department of Foreign Missions, November 28, 1934.

73. Carolyn Myatt, *A Tapestry Called Orpha* (Kansas City, Mo.: Nazarene Publishing House, 1991), 34–57. Compare, on women physicians in India, Singh, *Gender, Religion, and "Heathen Lands,"* 281–312.

74. Chapman, "To the Pastors and People of the Church of the Nazarene in India," [1937] (file 472-22); Chapman, "The Church of the Nazarene in India," *Other Sheep* (April 1938), 24. See also Agnes Gardner, "India Council Meeting," *Other Sheep* (February 1938), 16–17.

75. Beals, *India's*, 173–177. Chapman's ordination sermon is printed in D. Shelby Corlett, *Spirit-Filled: The Life of the Rev. James Blaine Chapman, D.D.* (Kansas City, Mo.: Beacon Hill, n.d.), 132–134.

76. Hinshaw, *Native Torch Bearers*, 87–89; Beals, *India Reborn: The Story of Evangelism in India* (Kansas City, Mo.: Beacon Hill, 1954), 79–81.

77. Hinshaw, *Native Torch Bearers*, 78–105; "Proceedings of the Twenty-Ninth Annual Council" (1938).

78. Beals, *India Reborn*, 80.

79. Beals, *India Reborn*, 80; Samuel Bhujbal, "District Superintendent's Report," [1939]; Ralph Cook, "Touring in India," *Other Sheep* (November 1938), 10–11; Bhujbal, "The India District Superintendent's Report," *Other Sheep* (October 1941), 19–21. See also Hazel C. Lee, *Treasures of Darkness* (Kansas City, Mo.: Beacon Hill, 1954), 13–20.

80. Beals to Jones, February 6, 1940. See H. H. Pagare, "India District Assembly," *Other Sheep* (February 1940), 10; Agnes Gardner, "One Interesting

Day on Tour," *Other Sheep* (September 1940), 22; Mary Anderson, "The N.Y.P.S. Convention," *Other Sheep* (May 1941), 16; Bhujbal, "The India District Superintendent's Report," *Other Sheep* (October 1941), 19–21.

81. Bessie Beals, "Annual Council Meeting, India, 1940," *Other Sheep* (September 1941), 17–18.

82. Orpha Cook, "A Visit at the Boy's School," *Other Sheep* (May 1940), 23–24.

83. John McKay, "Our Bible School," *Other Sheep* (June 1941), 17–18. See Prescott Beals, "A Happy Occasion," *Other Sheep* (November 1939), 16–17, for a history of the school. See also Jones to Beals, December 9, 1942; Bessie Beals, "New Recruits for India," *Other Sheep* (May 1941), 19.

84. Beals to Jones, "General Review—India," June 24, 1942; Beals to Jones, July 22, 1943; Beals to Jones, November 27, 1945.

85. Beals, "India District Assembly, April 1943." See Beals to Jones, August 10, 1942. See also Heideman, *From Mission to Church*, 567, 572.

86. Beals, "Chairman's Report, 1947."

87. Compare similarities in Heideman, *From Mission to Church*, 628, 632, 634–636.

88. Beals, "Chairman's Report, 1947"; Beals to General Superintendents [1944]; Beals to Jones, September 13, 1946; Beals to H. C. Powers, September 25, 1947.

89. Beals, "Chairman's Report, 1947." See Rajah B. Manikam, ed., *Christianity and the Asian Revolution* (New York: Friendship, 1954), 134–136, on the resurgence of Hinduism and its association with nationalism. Contrast Kenneth S. Latourette, *Christianity in a Revolutionary Age: A History of Christianity in the Nineteenth and the Twentieth Centuries*, vol. 5: *The Twentieth Century outside Europe* (Reprint, Grand Rapids, Mich.: Zondervan, 1969), 301–302, 318–331.

90. Beals, "Salient Facts about India," n.d. [1947] (file 1251-29).

91. Beals to Powers, September 25, 1947 (6 pp.); Borde, Bhujbal, [and others] to Miller, n.d. [1947] (file 790-23). See also J. W. Anderson to Miller, n.d. [1947] regarding the Bible Training School (also file 790-23).

92. S. T. Ludwig and Greta Hamsher, eds., *Journal of the Twelfth General Assembly of the Church of the Nazarene* (N.p., [1948]), 214–215, 234f.

93. India Mission Council *Journal* (1954); India Mission Council *Journal* (1955); Indian District Assembly *Journal* (1956); Indian Mission Council *Journal* (1957); D. I. Vanderpool to Powers, April 21, 1959; India Mission Council *Journal* (1960); M. V. Ingle, "Radio Marathi," *World Mission* (May 1985), 6.

94. Mary Anderson, "Daily Diaries," vol. 1 (1953–1954), no pagination. See also India Nazarene Mission Council, *New India and the Gospel* (Kansas City, Mo.: Nazarene Publishing House, 1954), 89–98; Orr, *Evangelical Awakenings in Southern Asia*, 174; Martin, *The Missionary of the Indian Road*, 204.

95. India Mission Council *Journal* (1960), 40; Parker, *Mission*, 234–240.

96. Various issues of the Indian Mission Council and District Assembly journals.

97. India Mission Council, *New India and the Gospel*, 115–118; *Other Sheep* (October 1938), 22; Orpha Speicher, "In India Again," *Other Sheep* (May 1945), 4–5, and "Workers Together," *Other Sheep* (February 1948), 6; India Mission Council *Journal* (1960), 40, India Mission Council *Journal* (1963), 14; Myatt, *A Tapestry Called Orpha*.

98. Earl Lee to Rehfeldt, September 5, 1955; India Mission Council *Journal* (1960), 19; India Mission Council *Journal* (1963), 12, 14; India Mission Council *Journal* (1967), 15; India Mission Council *Journal* (1970), 10–15; Mission Council to [Jerald] Johnson, September 21, 1976.

99. Donald Owens to Coulter, August 4, 1962; Cleo James to Coulter, September 27, 1962; India Mission Council Meeting (1973), 65.

100. (Unsigned), Buldana, to Edward Lawlor, March 3, 1975.

101. Compare Heideman, *From Mission to Church*, 608–609, 613–614.

102. For example, D. Kharat, "Hospital," *Other Sheep* (May 1965), inside back cover.

103. Padu Meshramkar, "The Indian Source," *World Mission* (March 1986), 17; Parker, *Mission*, 235–238.

104. Bronnel Greer, "Nazarene Troika," mimeographed [1969], Part Three, "Evangelism and the Evangelist," 31–32.

105. Greer, "Nazarene Troika," Part Three, "Evangelism and the Evangelist," 33–34. For similar sentiments in another mission see Heideman, *From Mission to Church*, 644–650.

106. Greer, "Nazarene Troika," Part One, "Manual," 47; Part Two, "Missionary Policy," 51, 53, 60, 63–65, 69, 73, 75–76; Part Three, 20–21, 23–24, 25f, 31–34.

107. Edward Lawlor to Orpha Speicher, June 6, 1975. See *World Mission* (September 1989) issue.

# Chapter 3

# Japan

In India, the Church of the Nazarene was built upon missionary dominance, a slow process of local indigenization and institutional work. The work in Japan began in 1905 and, in contrast to India, there was partnership between strong Japanese leaders and missionaries and less concentration upon schools and medical work. The long-serving American missionaries who dominated Japan, Minnie Staples and William Eckel, worked cooperatively with Hiroshi Kitagawa and Nobumi Isayama. Both Kitagawa and Isayama lived and studied in the United States before returning to Japan, as had J. I. Nagamatsu, who became the first Japanese district superintendent. Both Kitagawa and Nagamatsu were graduates of Pasadena College and the church commissioned and paid them as missionaries. A volatile and hurtful struggle between Eckel and Staples, which extended from the 1910s through the 1930s, fueled sentiments within the Japanese church that its own leaders were as capable—indeed were *more* capable—than the missionaries in intellect, diligence and spirit. By the 1930s Eckel himself and many Japanese leaders believed that Eckel would be the last American missionary sent to Japan.

The Japanese church in nearly every way was self-sufficient and was beginning to share responsibility for the Nazarene work in both China and Korea. World War II changed the situation entirely. At the close of the war the church in Japan seemed as debilitated as the country as a whole, and Kitagawa and Isayama seemed like drawn and weary men rather than vigorous leaders. So the church renewed its missionary impetus in Japan and concentrated on the education of both pastors and laypersons, as well as the building and rebuilding of churches. A new generation of Japanese Nazarene leaders emerged, some of whom also had studied at Pasadena and other colleges in America. They were eager to assume leadership of the church and worked toward the level of autonomy promised during the pre-war years.

## Setting the Foundations

The beginning work of the Church of the Nazarene in Japan is tied to other holiness missions. The Salvation Army, with clear holiness teachings, began in 1895 and for many years was led by Gunpei Yamamuro. William Booth himself visited Japan in 1907. The Japan Evangelistic Band, which began in 1903 through the efforts of Barclay Buxton of the Anglican Church Missionary Society, also furthered the message of holiness. It held revivals and conventions in Japan that drew Methodists and Anglicans.[1]

As early as 1899 the *Holiness Banner*, printed in Sunset, Texas, reported on the work of F. L. Smelser, who had been sent out by the Hephzibah Faith Missionary Association, headquartered in Tabor, Iowa (which joined the Church of the Nazarene in 1950). Smelser worked in Yokahama. Charles Cowman and Lettie Cowman, Methodists who also had contacts with the Hephzibah Association, arrived in Japan in 1901. Juji Nakada, a Japanese holiness minister who had been influenced by A. M. Hills while both were attending conferences at Moody Bible Institute, soon joined the Cowmans' ministry. Charles Cowman was ordained by Martin Knapp, Seth Rees and Charles Stalker, and Knapp's Apostolic Holiness Union initially supported the Cowmans' work. In 1910 the Cowmans formed the Oriental Missionary Society. Their work centered in Tokyo, where, within a short time, a holiness Bible institute was thriving. On a deputation tour in 1911 the Cowmans raised support in Nazarene churches in California. The OMS work in Japan was organized as the Japan Holiness Church in 1917. For decades the church held regular Sunday afternoon holiness rallies in Tokyo.[2]

The Holiness Church of Christ had missionaries in Japan when it united with the Pentecostal Church of the Nazarene in 1908. Lulu Williams and Lillian Poole had ventured there on faith and associated themselves with the Cowmans and what was to become the Oriental Missionary Society. They stayed in Tokyo, working in slums, from their arrival in 1905 until late 1907 when they transferred to Kyoto. They established a Sunday School in Kyoto. When the women's home churches joined with the Nazarenes in 1908, they and the Sunday School became part of the denomination.

Other Nazarene missionaries arrived in 1910 and soon Williams and Poole went on furlough. One of the newly arrived missionaries, Minnie Upperman, had previously served in Japan, first arriving in January 1904. Her support at that time came from independent sources in California and she affiliated herself with the work of Charles and

Lettie Cowman. She had served with Williams and Poole in Tokyo for about two years and knew some Japanese. Soon after returning in 1910 she married another of the party, J. A. Chenault, the newly appointed superintendent of the work. They stationed themselves in Kyoto. Mr. Taniguchi assisted the work for a time. When he left, the missionaries tried to carry on with an English Bible class but this was ineffectual. So the Nazarenes had established little by 1912 when the Chenaults returned to the United States.[3]

Shortly before their return, Cora Snider and Minnie Staples, Nazarenes from California, arrived in Japan as emissaries of Phineas Bresee, apparently without the knowledge or consent of his co-general superintendent and Foreign Missions Secretary, H. F. Reynolds. The act portended the freewheeling intervention of Southern California Nazarenes in Japan in this and succeeding decades. Indeed, until Reynolds's trip to Japan in 1914, Bresee rather than Reynolds seemed to be overseeing the Japan work. Staples had worked with Japanese migrants in Upland and Los Angeles and could preach some in the Japanese language. She visited Kumamoto, the hometown of her Japanese protégé, Hiroshi Kitagawa, who was still studying at Pasadena College, and there made some converts among members of his family and others who belonged to the Russian Orthodox faith. Bresee requested that Snider, who had been principal of the academy at the Nazarene University in Pasadena, report to him on prospects she saw for the work in Japan (and, if possible, also on Korea, which had recently come under Japanese political control). When the Chenaults and Staples departed, Snider agreed to remain alone to carry on the mission of the church, although Staples vowed to return. Snider stayed in Kyoto and Bresee appointed her superintendent of the Japan work. He told her to organize a church whenever possible but advised her: "Now do not take upon you the burden of the Japanese Empire, nor of all the heathen you ever can see or hear of, but simply try to do the little that one little mortal can do, and rest at that."[4] Out of necessity as well as philosophy, Snider considered close contacts with the Japanese most advantageous to accomplish the task given her. "To secure and retain the best workers," she wrote, "there must be such constant companionship as will enable the young workers and prospective helpers to take on the burdens, hopes and ideals of the missionaries."[5]

Bresee also commissioned a co laborer for Cora Snider, J. I. Nagamatsu, whom he ordained shortly before his departure for Japan in January 1913. While studying at the Pasadena school in preparation for ministry, Nagamatsu had become well acquainted with both Staples and Leslie Gay, who was chiefly responsible for boosting foreign missions work in the California wing of the church. In fact, Nagamatsu's salary was at first paid by Gay. Both Gay and Bresee recognized that Nagamatsu would need about as much salary as any missionary, and that is what they considered him, a missionary to his own people (in the same way that Banarjee and Biswas had been to theirs in India). Gay believed that Nagamatsu rather than Snider would and should be the true leader of the work. Soon after his arrival in Japan, he and Snider transferred the mission station to Fukuchiyama, in the mountains northwest of Kyoto, where Nagamatsu had contacts. Snider resided there, and Nagamatsu's ministry centered on children.[6]

The prominence of Japanese workers and the close cooperation between strong Japanese leaders and missionaries evident in the Church of the Nazarene were common in Japanese Protestantism. The lives and deeds of Japanese Christian leaders such as Joseph Hardy Neesima were well known to American Protestants. Among holiness groups, Paul Kakihara and T. Kawabe founded the Free Methodist church in the 1890s before the arrival of missionaries. Juji Nakada worked alongside Charles and Lettie Cowman and E. A. Kilbourne in beginning the Oriental Missionary Society. Among Nazarenes, this partnership set the stage for the next series of developments in the Japanese church, many of which involved struggles over leadership.[7]

At the same time, Snider worried that Staples had established such strong ties with Nagamatsu in the United States that it would be she who most influenced the work. Snider and Staples had not parted company on the best of terms. Staples gave Nagamatsu money so as to enable him to marry after his return to Japan, and advised him in letters regarding the mission. Snider felt that Staples was undercutting her authority from afar and she tried to secure a promise from Bresee that Staples would not return as a missionary. Though Bresee told Snider that it was not his intention to appoint Staples to the field, he offered Snider a position at the Pasadena college.[8]

Such was the situation when Hiram F. Reynolds arrived in Japan in January 1914 for a three-week visit, and in a sense for the first time began oversight of the work in Japan. Accompanying him were Rev. and Mrs. L. H. Humphrey, Lillian Poole and Lulu Williams, both returning for second terms. Reynolds had already decided that Humphrey, despite his inexperience, would take over from Snider as superintendent. Reynolds found Snider and Nagamatsu conducting a lively Sunday School program and a Bible Training School in which two were enrolled—Misters Namba and Tanada. Reynolds preached, with Nagamatsu translating, and claimed twenty-five converts. He also recorded that twenty-five others, already Christian, were sanctified wholly. American revival methods seemed to work. The church's site, the caliber of the congregation, which included teachers, merchants and other prominent citizens, and, most of all, Nagamatsu himself impressed Reynolds. He toured several other Japanese cities in the company of Nagamatsu and came to esteem him as a "Christian gentleman, a man of vision, culture and power for good."[9] Reynolds's only reservations about Nagamatsu were that he did not press people hard enough toward conversion or sanctification and that he was too cautious in what Reynolds considered to be normative displays of the "freedom and liberty and unction of the spirit."[10]

Reynolds expected an American rather than Japanese style of leadership and campmeeting-like displays of spiritual commitment. Nevertheless, the personal relationship between Reynolds and Nagamatsu proved important to future events. Reynolds instructed Snider to furlough immediately, and he assigned the Humphreys along with Poole and Williams to Kyoto. He wanted Kyoto to be the headquarters for the mission, and Nagamatsu could carry on in Fukuchiyama quite well by himself. After all of his years directing missions from afar, Reynolds relished his role in the field, and set missionaries in motion here, as he was to do a few weeks later in Calcutta.[11]

Before departing, Reynolds and the workers, including Nagamatsu, drafted a policy to govern the work of the Church of the Nazarene in Japan. Thus preceding by a few months the policy set for India, and dated January 17, 1914, it began by placing the work under the *Manual*. Reynolds conceived of the *Manual* not only as the American church's, but as the international constitution of the Church of the Nazarene. As the policy itself both assumed and asserted, the "manifestations of the Holy Spirit are practically the same in all countries." Basically, Reynolds wrote his own philosophy of the mission of the church into the policy. It indicated, for instance, that the primary role of the missionaries was to "get souls saved and sanctified, and trained for the work of the Kingdom of God on earth." At the same time, entire sanctification was to be "kept to the front." Methods of evangelism were to be virtually the same as in America: visiting house-to-house, organizing Bible classes, establishing Sunday Schools, opening preaching stations, and distributing literature. Upon these presuppositions of similarity between the situations in Japan and America, local churches, whenever Nazarenes established them, should assume as much of the support of the work as possible. A local church reaching self-support could call for and retain a pastor as provided in the *Manual*.

When the district as a whole achieved self-support and (unclearly defined) measures of self-government, "all missionary control [would] be relinquished except such superintendency as is provided in the *Manual*." That is, the work would be both responsible to and a part of the General Assembly and accountable to the general superintendents it elected. Though the policy gave missionaries front-line roles in the beginning, general leaders never questioned that their stay was temporary, not permanent. Until the district achieved self-support, the church gave the appointed missionary district superintendent a firm position of authority over the national church, but instructed him or her to place important decisions before the General Board.[12]

Reynolds preached in Japan with the same sort of messages, methods and seeming successes as he had in America. Given his limited allowance for cultural differences in creating missions strategies, Reynolds assumed that the same sort of means could be used to establish the church in Japan as in America. Reynolds thought highly of Nagamatsu's leadership capabilities. The mission work began with confidence in both national leadership and the universal applicability of Nazarene doctrines, methods and administration.

The policy mentioned no important institutional aspects of the work. At the time, other Protestants were working in Japan's slums and were active in combating prostitution and other social evils. Toyohiko Kagawa, the most famous Asian Christian of the early twentieth century, involved himself in slum work and labor organization. In India, the area of the country where the Church of the Nazarene had responsibility demanded medical and primary school work. Duty required it. But these types of involvement were not on the Church of the Nazarene's agenda in Japan, where the church did not have a defined area in which to work. Like other Protestant missions, the Church of the Nazarene invested more in China than in Japan. It was not just the romance that Americans had with China in the early twentieth century. In comparison to India and China, Japan seemed more advanced, and seemed to require less social concern by Nazarenes. The only educational work envisioned at the beginning was for training ministers. Reynolds wanted to raise up sanctified, "thoroughly equipped" Japanese pastors. In order to accomplish this, the Bible Training School and, later, other schools were to be "hot spiritual centers" from which strong Japanese leaders would emerge and thus serve the ultimate end of evangelism. Since evangelism was the thrust, very importantly, from the beginning, Reynolds saw that maintaining a large force of missionaries was neither necessary nor expedient in Japan.[13]

## Leadership Crises

Isaac and Minnie Staples, along with Hiroshi Kitagawa, arrived in Japan in January 1915; Nobumi Isayama came later the same year, and young William and Florence Eckel early in 1916.

The spiritual mentorship of Minnie Staples toward Hiroshi Kitagawa lasted decades. Staples, born in Tyler, Texas, in 1880, never finished grammar school. She was active as an evangelist for five years in the Friends Church before joining the Church of the Nazarene at Upland, California, in 1906, where W. C. Wilson, a rising leader in the denomination, was pastor. By that time she had married a widower, Isaac B. Staples, 17 years her senior who was a birthright Quaker and railroad telegrapher for the Santa Fe Railroad. During their years in Upland, Minnie Staples became burdened for the Japanese migrant workers on the surrounding farms. Wanting to preach to them, she secured Hiroshi Kitagawa as her translator. Later he became her tutor in Japanese. She won the Japanese workers, including Kitagawa, by her kindness (for instance, making chicken soup for them and distributing it to them during their sicknesses) as well as by her sermons. In January 1910 Kitagawa was converted. Staples and Kitagawa began a Japanese church in Upland, but soon both moved to the Los Angeles area—he to study at the Nazarene college and she to take charge of the Nazarene mission for Japanese in the city. With the support of her friends in California, who included Leslie Gay, Seth Rees and W. C. Wilson, the Foreign Missions Board could scarcely refuse her application for missionary service in Japan. Upon his wife's calling to Japan, Isaac Staples felt it was his duty to follow her, but everyone knew *she* was "the missionary."[14]

Kitagawa also returned as a missionary to his own people. Born in 1988 in Kumamoto, on Kyushu island in southern Japan, he was the son of Russian Orthodox parents. Although there was apparently a sizable community of Russian Orthodox believers in his hometown, it represented a tradition outside of the dominant Shintoism. The first missionaries of the Russian Orthodox faith had emphasized indigenous leadership. Russian Orthodoxy provided a stepping-stone toward Protestantism.[15]

Yet it was Kitagawa's experiences in America that led to his conversion. He went to America at age eighteen to seek his fortune. For a while he worked tending pigs, sheep and cattle, and then as a translator in a camp of Japanese sharecroppers. He suffered under anti-Japanese discrimination, which hardened his attitudes against both his bosses and their religion. His experiences with Americans embittered him. After his conversion in January 1910, he entered the Nazarene college in Pasadena, where he finished both his high school diploma and a bachelor's degree in religion. At the same time he ministered in the Nazarene church's Japanese mission in Los Angeles. He became friends with both Nagamatsu, a fellow student at Pasadena College, and Nobumi Isayama, who was converted at the mission. Before leaving with the Stapleses for Japan he raised support for Nazarene missions by touring churches in America with Reynolds, who ordained him at the Chicago District Assembly in 1914. The church at Kumamoto, which he and Staples organized within a few months after his return to Japan, (and which was the first organized Nazarene church in the country), included his brother Shiro Kitagawa and others with whom Staples had established contact on her earlier visit. Members of the church in Kumamoto included schoolteachers, a post office worker, a banker and college students. As in Japanese Christianity generally, Nazarene converts did not come primarily from the lower classes. The "white-collar" prominence in the Kumamoto church, as in Fukuchiyama, was characteristic of the Japanese response to Christianity in this era. Soon Kitagawa began a Bible school in Kumamoto, a move consistent with Reynolds's ideas about the necessity of education, and also, as Kitagawa saw it, necessary to reach the professional classes.[16]

Staples supported Kitagawa's leadership in education. She devoted her energies to revivalism. Her skills and enthusiasm for evangelism complemented the more pastoral and scholarly Kitagawa. In fact, belying her own lack of formal education, Staples was not eager to establish schools in Japan that she thought would turn out "high collared folks," and "cold, proud preachers."[17] She held many tent meetings over the next years. She could preach in Japanese fairly well and was a curiosity and crowd-drawer. She demanded that converts not only forsake their Shinto idols, but quit smoking and drinking. She required that converts undergo a period of probation to make sure they really were changed before she would either baptize them or receive them into church membership. Nonetheless, within two years she had baptized 130 persons, all converted through her ministry. One striking early convert was an Anglican minister who attended her Bible classes for several months and thereby came into the testimony of entire sanctification.[18]

While his wife busied herself with revivals and Bible studies, Isaac Staples drove the car for her and helped to pitch the tent under which his wife often preached. He tended to the financial records of the mission.[19]

In spite of all of the successes that her ministry showed, almost immediately after the Eckels' arrival, Staples and William Eckel became embroiled in quarrels that affected the Nazarene mission in Japan for decades. Eckel, born in 1892, was the son of Howard Eckel, formerly a Methodist circuit rider in Pennsylvania who had joined the Association of Pentecostal Churches of America and afterwards pastored in Haverhill, Massachusetts. An acquaintance with Reynolds developed during these days before the merger of the APCA with Bresee's Church of the Nazarene in 1907. William Eckel attended both Olivet College in Illinois and Pasadena College, and Bresee ordained him in 1912. In 1915 Howard Eckel accepted the superintendency of the Southern California District. After Staples's departure for Japan, Howard Eckel appointed his son William, who felt a calling to the mission field, to lead the Japanese mission in Los Angeles.[20]

As district superintendent, Howard Eckel played a prominent and controversial role in February 1917, in officially disorganizing the University Church of the Nazarene in Pasadena, then pastored by Seth Rees. The ensuing struggle nearly tore the entire denomination apart. Eckel and other conservative leaders were afraid of the excessive "freedom of the Spirit" in the Pasadena church. Pentecostalism loomed as a danger in their minds. But the real matter of contention became that of the authority and powers of the superintendency to so control local congregations that they could arbitrarily close them—as Eckel, with the approval of General Superintendent E. F. Walker, did. As a result, Rees left the denomination and formed his own church, the Pilgrim Tabernacle, down the street from the Nazarene church. Out of this, Rees later helped to form the Pilgrim Holiness denomination.[21]

Staples was a friend of Rees, who was, like her, a former Quaker. Likewise, both enjoyed freedom of expression in worship, and neither liked episcopal control. Staples was a member of the University Church and the events in Pasadena surrounding Rees disturbed her. Upon a trip to California for an operation in 1917, soon after the split, Staples spoke at the Pilgrim Tabernacle. She also joined Rees in criticizing the actions of both Eckel and Walker. She moved her local Nazarene church membership to Kansas City First Church, where a friend of Rees pastored. But her base of support remained in Southern California. Later Staples transferred her membership to the Los Angeles First Church, where the Eckels also were members.[22]

Throughout her ministry in Japan these experiences and others led Staples both to distrust and to circumvent general church leadership as she felt led by the Spirit. She could not help but instill the same feelings in Kitagawa, although the sources of Kitagawa's feelings toward

American control were personal and nationalistic as well as based on loyalties to her. Eckel, on the other hand, imbibed his father's Methodist heritage of respect for superintendency. Both Staples and Eckel carried across the ocean their attitudes about the issues of authority that the church fought over in these early years.

For more than forty years, Eckel worked side-by-side with Isayama, ten years his senior. In 1898 Isayama found his way across the Pacific to the United States, and stayed for seventeen years. He became a Christian in 1913 after attending some English classes at the Japanese Nazarene mission in Los Angeles. Staples, then still head of the mission, was instrumental in his conversion. When she left for Japan in 1914 Isayama welcomed Eckel and served as his Japanese language teacher. Indeed for a time he lived in the mission hall with the Eckel family. Isayama returned to Japan in 1915 only with the intention of finding a Japanese woman to be his wife, after which he planned to return to America. But Humphrey persuaded him to stay in order to be the key national worker for the Kyoto area, even though he was neither ordained nor prepared for the ministry. Isayama thus was there to greet the Eckel family when they arrived in February 1916.[23]

Eckel and Isayama at first concentrated upon work at Kure. Eckel was determined from the beginning not only to learn Japanese but to think and act Japanese. He was respectful toward the culture and its customs. He also was tenacious. Though other missionaries left Japan for various reasons after short periods during the early years of the Nazarene work, Eckel remained. He also was determined that Staples not hold sway over the affairs of the church.[24]

Following the 1914 Policy, the work in Japan was organized under a District Assembly. In India it made little difference to organize a District Assembly, since no Indian workers were yet eligible for participation in one and, in any case, the foreign missionaries were in control. But in Japan both Nagamatsu and Kitagawa were ordained and thereby were entitled to full participation in the administration and direction of the district. Both Nagamatsu and Kitagawa had their memberships in the University Church at Pasadena until it was disbanded. Like Staples, Kitagawa then transferred to Kansas City First Church. Nagamatsu, Kitagawa and Isayama were paid at a scale about equal to that of the American missionaries—and considerably higher than the other Japanese workers who were beginning to join the ministry force. Isayama was paid by the Missionary Board of the Southern California District and later by the General Missionary Board at a salary about equal to Nagamatsu and Kitagawa, both of whom were paid by the General Missionary Board. Kitagawa received $25 monthly. Kitagawa also received a supplement to his salary from Leslie Gay, and the wives of Nagamatsu, Kitagawa and Isayama were each paid additional amounts through the support of both local Nazarene churches in the United States and the General Missionary Board for their work as teachers in local churches. In addition, these Japanese workers received compensation from the local churches they pastored. The Stapleses, by comparison, each received $35 monthly.[25]

Dissension brewed on the status of Japanese workers, and other animosities among the missionaries caused further polarization. Each of the four mission stations that were operating at this time—Fukuchiyama, Kumamoto, Kyoto and Kure—functioned virtually autonomously after Humphrey left in 1915. For a time there was no successor to Humphrey as mission superintendent. In March 1917, Reynolds appointed Eckel to preside over a District Assembly planned for later that year. But Staples refused to cooperate with his leadership, especially after Reynolds clarified that he had indeed appointed Eckel as "acting" district superintendent for the entire empire of Japan until an assembly could meet. In Eckel, then only 25 and with only one year on the field, Reynolds had a person (like Leighton Tracy in India) in whom to place his trust. Reynolds planned to be present at the next assembly to solve disputes that also had arisen between Staples and Williams, who was ministering in an urban mission work in Kyoto, and between Staples and Paul and Gertrude Thatcher, who had recently arrived on the field. When World War I and other pressing matters delayed Reynolds's scheduled trip that year, the situation among missionaries deteriorated even further.[26]

Eckel held an assembly in July 1918, but Staples refused to attend it. Both Nagamatsu and Kitagawa participated in the Assembly and voiced their opinions on various matters along with the others, as equal partners. But discussion among the other missionaries centered on whether to consider these Japanese workers as full participants in the decision-making body of the mission, which established and set budgets and stationed both missionaries and Japanese workers. The official policy at this time was to so include them, but Williams and several other missionaries strongly opposed this. Eckel recommended that they be called "home missionaries" as distinguished from "foreign missionaries." The participants elected Thatcher, then stationed at Omuta, rather than Eckel, as District Superintendent. However, since the assembly exacerbated, rather than solved, the problems plaguing the field, Reynolds placed each station under the direct control of the General Board and refused to accept the election of Thatcher. Rather, he reappointed Eckel as district superintendent. He agreed, though, that

Eckel would not visit—nor interfere with—Staples's work.[27]

Reynolds arrived, at long last, in May 1919, and convened a District Assembly. Before coming he had asked Nagamatsu to translate the *Manual* into Japanese, an indication both that Reynolds was eager for more national involvement, and, once more, that he saw the *Manual* as an internationally binding church constitution. Reynolds heard the complaints of Lulu Williams and four other missionaries, all stationed in Kyoto, and listened to the arguments against the participation of the Japanese leaders in the decision-making body of the Japanese church. They told Reynolds plainly that either the Japanese leaders must be treated as subordinates or they themselves would leave. Reynolds had, of course, received such a letter before from disgruntled missionaries in India, and he was predisposed to act in the same way as he had with the Woods and Lillian Sprague in India some years before. That is, he forthrightly accepted the resignations. These included those of Williams and four newer missionaries: Ethel McPhearson, Helen Santee and Rev. and Mrs. H. H. Wagner. The latter couple in particular also had opposed the work and leadership of Eckel. They had, Reynolds felt, such deep animosity toward the General Board's policy in promoting the nationalization of districts that he felt that they could no longer work effectively with the Japanese. The Wagners soon joined the Free Methodist mission in Japan. To Reynolds there were two issues precipitating the resignations: (1) that the missionaries would not accept the Japanese as having equal rights and privileges with themselves; and, (2) that they had contempt toward the policy of the church. Their resignations took effect May 19, 1919.[28]

Reynolds moved Eckel from Kure to Kyoto in order to preserve the work there. Before departing on his way to India Reynolds ordained Nobumi Isayama, thus making him also a member of the council. He reappointed Eckel as "acting" district superintendent, but freed him from duties as such, ostensibly so that he could pursue language study. Actually Reynolds saw the necessity of keeping Eckel and Staples from infringing upon one another. Reynolds met separately with the Stapleses while he was in Japan. Unlike his actions with the other missionaries, Reynolds did not move decisively against the Stapleses. Reynolds knew of the deep support that they had in the Southern California District. But he also could not deny her effectiveness. Reynolds appointed Minnie Staples as district evangelist and Isaac Staples district treasurer. Nagamatsu remained in Fukuchiyama. He assigned the Thatchers to Okayama but they returned to America the same year.[29]

Nagamatsu praised Reynolds for saving the work in Japan as a result of these actions, and through letters the Japanese pastor advanced in the esteem of both Reynolds and E. G. Anderson, who now was both general treasurer and foreign missions secretary. Reynolds took a bold yet strategic move on his next visit to Japan in the fall of 1922—he appointed Nagamatsu district superintendent. The Stapleses were on furlough at this time, and the Eckels were due theirs shortly, so the church acutely needed leadership in the district. By this action Reynolds reaffirmed his commitment to the advancement, as quickly as possible, of both national leaders and mission fields as a whole to regular district status. Japan was in some ways an experimental field since its leadership was ahead of most others in educational attainments. At this time only Mexico had a local leader, V. G. Santin, serving as superintendent of a Nazarene district outside of North America, and only because political realities prevented missionaries. In Japan there were unique reasons for Nagamatsu's appointment. Not only was he a graduate of one of the Nazarene colleges in the States, but his appointment was a way of solving the leadership jealousies between Eckel and Staples without alienating either one of them or their constituents in America. Nagamatsu was not as closely allied with Staples and Eckel as were Kitagawa and Isayama. But Reynolds genuinely desired the indigenization of the work and possessed confidence in Nagamatsu.[30]

After this appointment, Anderson proceeded to consult with Nagamatsu on various matters, treating him with the same respect as he would any missionary superintendent. Anderson noted his recommendations regarding the stationing of missionaries, and Nagamatsu charted the course for the district. At one point Nagamatsu listed for Anderson the essential characteristics of missionaries for Japan: that they be (1) good Bible teachers who could preach well in English, for he felt that missionaries lost their "unction" when they tried to preach in Japanese; (2) musicians; (3) "intellectual" rather than "sentimental"; and, (4) ones who are able to pray with and encourage the Japanese.[31] Nagamatsu complained, however, that though he was superintendent the general church left finances out of his control. He was not aware of how much money was available and so was prevented from budgeting accordingly. The recording and distribution of general finances remained with Isaac Staples, although each station had its own benefactors, who, despite policy, supplied money to the field without channeling it through Kansas City.[32]

The handling of finances led to Nagamatsu's downfall. He received funds directly from individuals and local churches in America as well as from the general church for the Fukuchiyama station in order to support the children enrolled in the kindergarten and several Sunday

Schools there, the primary focus of his ministry. For one photograph sent to headquarters he rounded up scores of children who were not actually attending the school. The Stapleses accused him of financial mismanagement in regards to the funds, and forced Nagamatsu to transfer from Fukuchiyama, where he had worked for several years, to Kyoto.[33]

Soon after, with remorse, Nagamatsu sent Anderson notice of his resignation from the superintendency. "Alas! I confess you I have betrayed your confidence on me.... I was entirely fell [sic] in the Devil's trap. I am very sorry that I sinned against God, against Christ and lost your confidence on the money sake.... I pray you would not distrust my countrymen because of me. My heart is broken because I have contaminated the Glory of God." He stated his plans to repay the church and to go to America. Nagamatsu remained in the United States until the Second World War, when he was deported to Japan. He rejoined the Nazarene ministry after the war.[34]

Reynolds proceeded to appoint Kitagawa as superintendent in Nagamatsu's stead. His faith in Japanese leadership was not—as Nagamatsu had hoped it would not be—shattered by the failings of one man. Kitagawa moved from Kumamoto to Kyoto in 1922, since Reynolds wanted to keep the headquarters of the work in Kyoto, and Kitagawa relocated the Bible school there also.[35]

The missionaries suffered accusations as well. When the Stapleses took a furlough in 1924, charges against Minnie Staples on matters relating to her independency circulated in Southern California. These, coupled with financial problems in the general church in the mid-1920s, prevented her return to Japan under regular status. Her supporters nevertheless succeeded both in sending her back and in pressuring the church to remove Eckel from full-time missionary salary.

Against Staples was J. E. Bates, the regional superintendent for the "Orient." (The 1923 General Assembly had set up such positions.) Until being appointed to this office, Bates had served as district superintendent in Southern California for four years. That experience provided a background for his dealings with her. She brought, Bates said, embarrassment to the church. Bates wrote to the general superintendents that Asians would not accept a woman, especially one so brazen as Staples.[36]

Reynolds also initially opposed her return to Japan after her furlough. He believed that there might be some validity not only on this point but in other charges eventually brought against her. These were: (1) that she had made statements to the effect that the church could not afford to return her because it had invested and lost money in business deals with L. Milton Williams, a well-known evangelist in the church; (2) that she had, without permission from the Foreign Missions Department, raised money both in and out of the denomination in order to return to Japan on a "faith" or independent basis, if the church could not or would not send her back; and, (3) that she had some affiliation with the Pentecostal (tongues) movement. The church appointed an investigating committee that included Reynolds, Bates, Leslie Gay, J. I. Hill and E. L. Hawkes (later replaced by J. T. Little). On the first point, if Staples had made such statements they were at least partly true, for the church had lost money by poor investments. The second and third charges were laid to rest as groundless. The exoneration did little good. Reynolds and other members of the Foreign Missions Department still decided that the church was in such financial difficulties that it could not return her. The decision was made in the light of both the controversies in which she had been entangled with Eckel and the needs of the church in Japan, which Reynolds felt did not require missionaries other than Eckel.[37]

Minnie Staples was a strong woman who outshone the evangelistic and church-planting efforts of male missionaries. Her preaching was passionate, and it won converts. Her ministry established churches. The groups that had come to form the church of the Nazarene each had ordained women. It was no problem to Bresee to have Emma Eaton and Sukhoda Banarjee at the head of the work in Calcutta—where the work was primarily among women. But it was equally no problem for him to have Mae McReynolds lead ministries to Spanish-speaking people in the United States, or to have Cora Snider as superintendent of the work in Japan—ministries in which they led men and evangelized both men and women. But, slowly, some in the denomination, affected by rising fundamentalism in the evangelical subculture, or shamed by the success of women, were having doubts about the rightfulness of women in leadership. By the 1920s when the controversies with Staples arose, there were undoubtedly others besides Bates who believed that women—in spite of their successes—should not be so prominent in the work of the church.[38]

Reynolds was less prone to place women in positions of leadership than Bresee had been. Reynolds told some Nazarenes gathered in Nampa in 1917, "There are mighty few men who seem to think [missions] is a big job. What is the matter with our men folks anyway?" To this, one in the congregation responded: "Why it is a man's job and the women have to do it." Reynolds affirmed: "Yes I guess that is so. Why don't we have more men to help in this? Why don't more men go as missionaries? They are so few, and mostly girls and women."[39] In India

Leighton Tracy and later George Franklin were appointed as leaders in eastern India to rule over the single women missionaries; and in Japan he preferred Eckel to Staples. Yet Reynolds was not overt or even deliberate, perhaps, in these appointments. Indeed other factors were equally at work: a preference for better-educated missionaries; for missionaries with their roots in the East; or, more importantly, for missionaries who would be loyal to the church.

It was difficult for Staples to have that loyalty for an equally diverse set of reasons: a Quaker heritage, a personal relation with ousted leaders, and, perhaps, a distrust of Northeasterners. But just as likely a component of her distrust was her attempt to find an untraditional sphere, outside of the home, wherein she could use her gifts and talents. Her reluctance to be bossed by white men led her to empathize, too condescendingly, with Japanese people. This sense of identity with them was part of her success as a missionary. They understood that she stood with them against impersonal forces in Kansas City.

But Staples also had powerful supporters. Leslie Gay, whom Minnie Staples addressed as "Father" Gay, believed a scheme had developed between Eckel and Bates to keep her from returning. Gay stated to the Foreign Missions Department that Staples *would* return to Japan whether or not it was under the official auspices of the church.[40]

Gay, 80 years old, was still an influential and revered figure in the church, having been one of Bresee's founding members in 1895, and having served continuously on the general foreign missions board from 1907 until 1923. Anderson also supported Staples, who occasionally sent him gifts from Japan. He justified her return to Japan on "faith" on grounds that any district in the denomination, including the Japan district, had the right to call for an evangelist. As district superintendent, Anderson said, Kitagawa had made such a call, so Staples really needed no permission from the Foreign Missions Department in order to accept the position of district evangelist. Leslie Gay secured from his own pocket, from pledges among members of the Los Angeles First Church, and from other supporters, enough money both for her passage to Japan and for her needs in the field for a year. Thus circumventing normal channels, and much to Reynolds's chagrin, Staples returned to Japan in late 1925. Thereafter she and her husband resided in a modest apartment fixed for them adjacent to the Honmachi Church in Kyoto, pastored by Hiroshi Kitagawa. The Eckels also lived in Kyoto. Staples worked in one part of the city with Kitagawa and Eckel worked in another with Isayama.[41]

Meanwhile, Anderson, who had encouraged the Stapleses' return, decided that if the department did not have enough money for them, it did not have enough for the Eckels either. In 1925 Anderson sent Eckel a letter of recall, and then cut off his salary. Even while he knew that Staples was on her way, Anderson stated that it was the plan of the board to have *no* missionaries in Japan. This was, he said, not only a policy that the church had previously decided on in regards to Japan, but due to the necessity of worldwide retrenchment. Of course Eckel knew of Anderson's support for Staples, and of her imminent arrival, and would not accept defeat. Eckel rallied his own supporters in America and found a job teaching in a government school in order to remain in Japan with his family.

Anderson himself was involved in a financial scandal that involved church funds investment. He resigned, and in 1926 Reynolds reassumed the position of missions secretary. Reynolds knew of and tacitly approved of the means of support being offered Eckel. The Miami, Florida, church, where Howard Eckel then pastored, sent one thousand dollars to keep William Eckel in Japan. The New York District Missionary Society, under the prodding of Susan Fitkin, Women's Foreign Missionary Society president and another old friend from Association of Pentecostal Churches of America days, agreed to take up regular support for him. Meanwhile, Eckel worked 12 hours a week teaching in a commercial school. His salary for this job alone was greater than what he had been receiving from the Missions Department. Florence Eckel also worked, teaching music and English. But Eckel consistently expressed his desire to return to the regular employment of the church.[42]

Eckel, despite this arrangement, remained the recognized Nazarene missionary in Japan. But from 1925 until 1934, when Eckel was re-employed full-time, the church had no regularly appointed missionaries in Japan.[43]

In apparent harmony during the year that Staples was away, in 1924-1925, Kitagawa toured each of the churches with Eckel. Kitagawa wanted to see Eckel move out of Kyoto to do pioneer work. He believed that as district superintendent he should decide such matters as the stationing of missionaries as well as other workers. He also told Reynolds of his plan to station the Stapleses in Osaka when they returned. Ultimately, however, neither of the missionaries could be unwedged from Kyoto.[44]

Staples and Kitagawa were responsible for almost all of the church growth of the Church of the Nazarene in Japan during the 1920s and early 1930s. When Staples returned from furlough she immediately engaged in a whirlwind of revival activity, holding meetings in every local congregation except the one in Kyoto pastored by Isayama. Staples held 89 tent revival crusades from 1925 to 1937. Seekers testified to becoming born again. Believers testified to being entirely sanctified. Restitution followed. Some even claimed visions. She also initiated an ongoing evangelistic work to lepers living near Kumamoto. Her tent meetings and gospel hymns were pure American revivalism, but somehow it produced converts.[45]

Between 1926 and 1934 Staples personally received and spent over $26,000 for her work in Japan. Some came through contacts she had made while speaking during her furloughs at interdenominational holiness camp meetings, but most came from Nazarene contributors in California. She distributed the money for church buildings and Japanese Nazarene workers' salaries (thus ingratiating herself to them) as well as for her own living. In 1934, against the wishes of the Missions Department, she brought Pearl Wiley, daughter of theologian H. Orton Wiley, to Japan as her co-worker, on "faith."

Pearl Wiley, who had done doctoral work at the University of California (Berkeley), had been rejected by the Nazarene Missions Department because of a chronic physical condition. After three weeks in Japan, she suffered a heart attack. Minnie anointed her and prayed for her healing. Within a short time, Wiley had recovered not only from the heart problem but from her chronic physical problem, and was able to teach in Kitagawa's school in Kyoto. She remained a "faith" missionary until 1939, when she finally was appointed by the Nazarene board.[46]

As church growth continued, so did aspirations among both the Japanese leaders and Staples for greater autonomy from the general church. Tent evangelism produced churches. So did contacts made in various localities by laypersons or Bible school students.[47]

Yet by 1928 there were only eight organized churches: two in Kyoto—at Kamikyo, where Isayama pastored, and at Honmachi, where Kitagawa pastored; a church at Yamashina, near Kyoto, also pastored by Kitagawa; still a church in Fukuchiyama, pastored by S. Oura; one in Okayama under E. Ichihara; one in Kure and another in Kegoya, near Kure, both pastored by K. Kaku; and the church in Kumamoto under Shiro Kitagawa. From the beginning these local churches aimed toward self-support and so were somewhat prepared when the general church drastically cut financial support and greatly reduced pastors' and workers' salaries late in 1925. (Though reduced, the salaries of Kitagawa and Isayama remained significantly higher than those of the other Japanese workers.) Although money continued to come into the district through Staples's sources, independently of Kansas City, the church's leaders still tried to maintain control. Knowing this, the Japanese church petitioned the 1928 General Assembly to allow it full, regular district status, by which it hoped to gain complete autonomy from decision-makers in Kansas City. The Assembly referred the matter back to J. G. Morrison, by this time foreign missions secretary, and the Department of Foreign Missions of the General Board. The Department then recommended that Japan be listed along with other fully organized districts, but at the same time it recognized Japan's need for continued financial assistance.[48]

Kitagawa's position as superintendent was strong in the district, though there were occasional difficulties relating to Eckel. There was ambiguity because there were few foreign fields with national district superintendents and the lines of authority between Kitagawa and Eckel were not always clear. For the most part Kitagawa corresponded directly with the succession of foreign missions secretaries—Anderson, Reynolds, Morrison, and, after 1936, C. Warren Jones. Accompanied by Staples, Kitagawa represented Japan at the 1928 General Assembly. (Eckel also attended.) Isayama, meanwhile, remained as pastor of his strong church in Kyoto, where the Eckels worshipped. Isayama had difficulties submitting even his annual reports to Kitagawa and refrained from most district activities.[49]

The general superintendents and the department remained convinced that Japan needed neither missionaries nor money as much as other fields. In 1935, from afar, J. Glenn Gould saw the indigenous character of the Japanese work: "The future of our Nazarene work in Japan, in common with every other similar undertaking, is in the hands of these Japanese leaders. . . . And the missionary and the native leaders must labor on side-by-side if this vast land is to be evangelized and won for Christ. But the missionary who succeeds in Japan today must be the self-effacing, John-the-Baptist type, who is willing to decrease that Christ and the Japanese servants of Christ may increase."[50] The Japanese leaders themselves of course acknowledged this. They understood that the Eckels would be the last missionaries sent to them.[51]

Kitagawa meanwhile attempted to achieve unity among Japanese holiness leaders. Pastors transferred back and forth among the Nazarene, Free Methodist and Oriental Missionary Society (Japan Holiness Church) denominations. When the Nazarene Bible School was closed, 1923–1930, Nazarenes attended either the Free Methodist school in Osaka or the OMS school in Tokyo. The Nazarenes helped to sponsor a holiness convention in Kyoto in 1929, with Isayama uniting with Kitagawa for once in an effort to reach the entire city. Another revival in Kyoto took place with General Superintendents John Goodwin and R. T. Williams in October of the same year. The visit of the two general leaders, incidentally, did not change the status of either Staples or

Eckel, though they met separately with both.[52]

Kitagawa was friendly with both Bishop Juji Nakada of the Holiness Church of Japan (affiliated with the Oriental Missionary Society) and Bishop Tetsuji Tsuchiyama of the Free Methodist Church. Nakada had helped arrange Kitagawa's marriage soon after his arrival in Japan. The Holiness Church that Nakada headed was among the fastest growing denominations in the country at this time. It followed A. B. Simpson's "fourfold" emphasis upon justification, sanctification, divine healing, and the second coming, rather than, as the Nazarenes did, emphasizing entire sanctification. In late 1930 these three men drew up a creed of faith and resolutions of union that would bring together the Nazarene, Free Methodist and Holiness groups. Although nothing came of this, another meeting was held in Osaka in January 1933 to form a federation of holiness denominations and independent churches. But by this time Nakada was teaching a particular doctrine of the second coming that related Japan's rise to power to biblical prophecies. The Free Methodists were closer to the Nazarenes. Tsuchiyama was formerly a Nazarene and had attended the Nazarene school in Pasadena. Staples favored the plan of union, perhaps because she retained contacts with supporters of the Oriental Missionary Society work. But most of the Japanese Nazarene pastors were not in favor of union, and neither, of course, was Eckel nor the general church.[53]

The importance of education grew in the minds of missionaries in the 1930s. Other missions in Japan had launched liberal arts—not just Bible training—colleges. Eckel laid plans for a Japan extension of Pasadena College. He envisioned a four-year liberal arts college, with no less than twelve departments, and corresponded with school administrators at Pasadena College who decided that finances for the Japanese school should be shouldered by the Japan branch, and that Pasadena, in order to ensure sufficient theological fidelity, would appoint the religion professor. Takeshi Ban, a Japanese lecturer in religion and oriental history at Pasadena College since 1933 and a member of the Pasadena Nazarene Church, was the prospective president of the school mentioned in the late 1930s. The requirements for other faculty members were that they be evangelical Christians and that they have master's degrees. Morrison favored the idea of having a college in Japan, but because of financial constraints the project remained in planning stages throughout the 1930s.[54]

Another crisis in leadership developed in relation to Kitagawa in 1934 and 1935. The Bible school had not operated for several years when Frank B. Smith, formerly a district superintendent in Northern California, volunteered his services to the mission and arrived in Japan in 1931. He was appalled to discover the divisions in the Nazarene Church between the Eckel and Staples factions and was especially perturbed with Staples's "irregular" means of support. What embroiled Kitagawa with Smith was a simple $20 money order, payable to Smith, which Kitagawa cashed following Smith's return to America in May 1933. Kitagawa used the money to pay rent for the Southern Mission Hall in Kyoto (where one of the translators whom Smith had used worked), and to pay Smith's translator. Kitagawa wrote Smith regarding these actions and did not receive any complaints from Smith about it until February 1934. Very quickly Kitagawa wrote Smith a letter of apology and explanation. Nevertheless, Smith threatened to sue Kitagawa over the issue. What Smith really wanted was the Japanese superintendent's immediate resignation. Smith brought the matter to the attention of Morrison.[55]

Morrison polled General Board members in early 1935 as to whether Kitagawa should be asked to resign from office. All but two responded that he should. In a sense it was the opening some in the church had been waiting for, to be rid of Staples and her influence. On June 13, 1935, Morrison telegrammed both Kitagawa and Isayama, demanding Kitagawa's resignation and appointing Isayama as district superintendent. Immediately Japanese pastors on the District Advisory Board wrote to the general superintendents, expressing both their dismay at the demand for Kitagawa's resignation and their support of him. With such backing, Kitagawa refused to resign.

Actually Morrison did not consider the charges against Kitagawa serious enough to warrant his removal from office. Nonetheless, Morrison saw this as an excuse to change the district leadership. He believed that Kitagawa had too long been dominated by Staples. A former Methodist, Morrison was much like Reynolds in wanting order and strict accountability to Kansas City. He also realized that the church's move against Kitagawa might cause schism.[56]

In fact, he told Isayama, "we will let it split." As far as Morrison was concerned, the Staples faction could form its own organization separate from the Church of the Nazarene. The General Board would continue to support those loyal to it. Morrison put it bluntly: "We want someone who will conduct our work hereafter in full harmony with the church and yet entirely free from any contact with the influence, activity and the personal and financial relations of Sister Staples." Since he could do little, however, until Kitagawa resigned, Morrison laid plans to deal with the matter at the next District Assembly, at which General Superintendent Chapman would preside.[57]

The situation was tense, then, when Chapman led the Japan District Assembly in October 1935. Politically, the United States and Japan were nearing confrontation, and it was likewise at this District Assembly. The Japanese leaders were already upset that Kansas City was interfering in the business of their district. Chapman told them plainly that until the district was fully self-supporting it should expect to be guided by the foreign missions secretary. On the matter of the election of a district superintendent the assembly delegates refused to follow the dictates of the general leadership, and instead exercised the rights they believed the *Manual* gave them, and reelected Kitagawa superintendent. After the election, Chapman met privately with the pastors to explain that the legal situation regarding the money order of Frank Smith made Kitagawa an absolutely unacceptable choice. However, Kitagawa had enough supporters to prevent the election of Isayama. After further consultation with Chapman, both Kitagawa and Isayama announced their unwillingness to serve as superintendent.

The delegates then elected the only other ordained minister among them, Shiro Kitagawa, who like his brother had been converted under Staples's ministry. He had attended a vocational school and, later, his brother's Bible school. He had pastored at Kure briefly before being transferred to Kumamoto, where he remained for many years. Goodwin and Williams had ordained him in 1929. He could neither read nor speak English. After Shiro Kitagawa's election as district superintendent, Hiroshi Kitagawa remained head of the Bible school and pastor of the Honmachi church in Kyoto. The assembly also elected him rather than his brother to represent Japan at the 1936 General Assembly. He translated letters from Kansas City for his brother. In effect, if not in name, Hiroshi Kitagawa remained as district superintendent. Little changed.

There were thirty-three organized churches at this time, a significant increase since 1928, with about 1,600 members. Thirteen of the churches were fully self-supporting. But only in four cases did the churches own property, and the deeds of these were in the name of Hiroshi Kitagawa, as per Japanese law, which prevented land being held in the name of a church. Chapman's hands, therefore, were tied. Before leaving, he ordained nine ministers and declared the 1935 Assembly as Japan's first as a regular district. Almost immediately after Chapman's departure, with desires to assert nationalist prerogatives that mirrored the political aspirations of their fellow citizens, the Japanese pastors drew up notification to Kansas City that as of January 1, 1936, the district would be fully self-supporting.[58]

In January 1936, the General Board officially granted the Japan District regular status while at the same time, and without the prior consent of the Japan District, it created a second, "missionary" district to the northeast, centered in Tokyo. Morrison, who was greatly disappointed at the way the District Assembly had turned out, appointed Eckel to lead the work in Tokyo, assisted by Isayama. He expected those pastors discontented with the leadership of Kitagawa and Staples to transfer to the Tokyo area. Isayama moved to Tokyo in August and Eckel joined him when he returned from furlough later that year. There was but one church in Tokyo, having begun in 1933 through contacts made by one of Isayama's former church members. There was another independent church, pastored by Mr. Tomiki, a graduate of Pasadena College, which affiliated with the Nazarenes when the district began. According to the General Board action, the Western or Kwansai District would be the regular district, with all the rights and privileges of any of the American districts, subject to the *Manual* and the General Assembly. The general church would support the undeveloped local churches on the regular district for five years, with support diminishing proportionately each year, and it would continue to finance the Bible school. Bertie Karns was transferred from China to Japan (where she had worked briefly many years before) in order both to handle the funds sent by the general church to the Kwansai District and to teach in the Bible school. But it was clear to Morrison that after May 1, 1936, the church no longer considered the Kwansai District a "mission field."[59]

Minnie Staples's years in Japan came to a close. Frank Smith published a pamphlet lambasting her work in Japan. Though he did not specifically mention Staples, the implications were clear enough to anyone in the Church of the Nazarene. What is more, Isaac Staples, past 70, was in failing health. Then, in 1937, as part of the Japanese government's increased control over religion and all areas of public and private life, the government placed restrictions on the holding of tent meetings. Revivals could still be held in churches, but the use of tents had been Staples's main means of evangelism. Finally, she resigned her commission as district evangelist and returned with her husband to California late in 1937. She fully expected to return some day. In sending her off Kitagawa remarked that only God knew what the Stapleses had meant to the work in his country. "Sister Staples is needed in evangelistic work and [as a] mother to our workers."[60] She continued to correspond with Kitagawa after her return to California and in so doing remained influential. Her husband lingered in ill health until his death in 1940. By that time the political situation prevented her return to Japan.[61]

Under Isayama and Eckel the work in the new district grew rapidly and reached into Korea. In part this growth was due to the tensions of the social and political environment. Within one year ten churches were planted and by the end of two there were over five hundred members in the new district. There were problems in sending prospective ministers to Kyoto to attend Bible school (Eckel complained that they tried to keep them there to work in that district), so they began another Bible school in Tokyo. As the result of contacts with Koreans in the city, Eckel and Isayama strengthened the work in Korea, which had begun in 1932. By 1938 there were two Nazarene churches in Korea under the superintendence of Eckel and Isayama.[62]

## The Social Crisis and the Church

The expansion of the Japanese Empire into other areas of Asia brought both opportunities and hardships for Nazarenes. Japan invaded Manchuria in 1931. In 1932 Bishop Nakada attempted to persuade the Nazarenes and the Free Methodists to go along with the Holiness Church in taking a stand together against the government's invasion and colonial policy. But the Nazarenes refrained from doing so. As in other countries, Nazarenes in Japan were unaccustomed to taking stands on political issues. Yet in Japan, the "otherworldly" holiness churches of Nakada stood against the government.[63]

In July 1937, war between China and Japan began full-scale in northern China. An editorial in "The Heavenly Way," edited by Hiroshi Kitagawa, soon affirmed: "We pray for our imperial army, for its perpetual victory. We also pray that Japan may pursue our mission in the Orient. We pray that Asian people may be saved from darkness and anti-religious power, and serve God in peace, receiving the favor of the emperor. Our prayer is 'Thy Kingdom come, thy will be done on earth as it is in heaven.'"[64] Within a few months the Japanese army took control of the area that was the center of Nazarene work in China in the southern part of Hebei Province. Insofar as the Japanese were concerned, they desired to rid Asia of Western dominance—to liberate China and eventually the Philippines and other countries from foreign control. They believed that they would be hailed as liberators by fellow Asians. The goal of their conquest and colonial domination was to create a "co-prosperity sphere" and to assimilate subjected people. For that reason the Japanese government encouraged Japanese Christians to allay the fears of Christians in China and elsewhere by visiting conquered territories. When it became necessary for Americans and other Western missionaries to leave the sphere of Japanese influence in Asia, the Japanese church was ready to maintain and expand further Christian work.[65]

During the late 1930s the government drafted several Japanese

Nazarene pastors to serve on the front lines. Nazarene pastors were killed or wounded. One pastor sent back this testimony: "Even in muddy trenches God's grace is in my heart, and between battles my soul communes with God and I seek after spiritual blessings found in his Word."[66] Other pastors were forced into factories or other work in the homeland. This prevented much work from being carried on in local congregations, of course, but the war itself opened Japanese Nazarene minds to their responsibilities both at home and abroad.

Nonetheless, Japanese Nazarenes supported their country's invasion of China and the war effort. Their loyalties to their country far outweighed loyalties to their denomination. "We are Christians but at the same time we are Japanese," went an article in "The Heavenly Way" in 1937. "When the peace is achieved, we Japanese Christians intend to lead and guide the Asian peoples and cooperate with them. Any Japanese who does not love Japan cannot be a true Christian."[67] The Salvation Army as well as other denominations likewise supported the nationalist agenda.[68]

Kitagawa became eager to spread the work among Japanese in Taiwan, China, Korea and Manchuria. Mr. Hada, pastor of one of the churches in Kyoto, and a graduate of Pasadena College, served in China, as did Mr. Nagasaka, the pastor of the Kurumi church. Another Nazarene pastor, K. Kaku, formerly the pastor at Kure, began church services among the Japanese army while recuperating from his own injuries in Tianjin, China. He returned there to pastor after the army discharged him. The church in Tianjin became fully self-supporting and began to reach out to Chinese. This encouraged Kitagawa to take an offering for the entire Nazarene church in China. Japanese Sunday School children as well as others contributed sacrificially. Afterward, in 1939, Hiroshi and Shiro Kitagawa traveled to China to personally present the money and to meet the Chinese Nazarenes. They saw Kaku's work in Tianjin and met Japanese Nazarenes in different stops along their route. Though the trip to Daming was dangerous—Chinese were fighting Japanese in the area—the brothers arrived with their donation of three hundred yen. Missionary Leon C. Osborn translated from Hiroshi Kitagawa's English into Chinese. As instructed, Kitagawa said nothing of a political nature, but simply gave his testimony. The brothers stayed only one day in Daming and visited the Nazarene church in Handan, the site of the nearest railway station, on their way south. They assured both Chinese and Japanese Christians wherever they went that the church in Japan was praying for them. Later, upon learning that Japanese bombs had destroyed the Chao-cheng Nazarene church in China, Japanese Nazarenes took an offering for its rebuilding. Such charity evidenced both a sense of Japanese responsibility for the repercussions of the war in China, and a willingness to assume leadership for mission work in Eastern Asia.[69]

Shiro Kitagawa himself became eager to go as a missionary. He applied for such service through the East Asia Christian Mission, a Japanese mission organization, which sent him to Soochow, near Shanghai, in mid-1939. Three other pastors served with him: Takeshi Uematsu, Tadashi Fujiwara and Asao Miyata. Japanese Nazarenes celebrated this event. Hiroshi Kitagawa explained the missionary call of his brother and the other Japanese Nazarenes: "We are yet weak but we must have a missionary spirit and we felt that we must begin missionary work while we are yet weak. Japanese preachers can help solving problems between Chinese and Japanese officers, besides preaching to them both this wonderful gospel of salvation."[70]

Naturally with Shiro Kitagawa in China it became necessary for the church to choose another district superintendent. C. W. Jones, now missions secretary, asked that Eckel preside over a specially called District Assembly. But when Eckel notified Hiroshi Kitagawa that he was too ill to come to Kyoto for the assembly, Kitagawa proceeded in August 1939 with the assembly anyway—and found himself, unsurprisingly, elected district superintendent on the first ballot. In a sense Kitagawa became what he had been in fact during his brother's four-year tenure. Upon learning of the assembly and of Kitagawa's election, Jones was not at all happy; but, as with missions secretaries before him, there was little he could do.[71]

The social and political situation heightened the sense of urgency in preaching the gospel. Eckel himself interpreted Japan's rise to world power apocalyptically: "Yes, out of the very armies of the Kings of the east, the Church of the Nazarene of the Orient is to gather that number to hasten the coming of the Lord!"[72] The Korean work was especially heartening. Both Eckel and Isayama spent several weeks there in 1939 and, according to Eckel, "found the door wide open to us."[73] "With a little encouragement," Eckel prophesied, "that field would outgrow all of Japan."[74] In fact he thought that throughout East Asia the times were fortuitous for the gospel. He hoped for the early entrance of the Church of the Nazarene into both Hong Kong and the Philippines.[75]

But the "thrill" of watching the supposed last days of the world soon turned to deep anxiety. Eckel found himself watched at every corner. Mail was read. Basic rights were denied to Japanese citizens. "The strain," confessed Eckel, "has been hard."[76] Of more pressing concern to the Japanese church was a religious question as to whether a

Nazarene might bow before a state shrine. It became necessary for Christians to assure the government that they would not oppose this practice, a sign of loyalty to the state and, in government annals, a civil rather than religious function. The common people, however, associated the shrine with the Shinto religion. In a letter to C. W. Jones, Eckel asked, "Could we as Christians go there and take off our hat and bow because we are told to do so, but in our heart we resent it and have no spirit of worship and yet be a Christian?"[77] Jones passed the question on to the general superintendents. J. G. Morrison responded: "The question of whether Nazarene nationals in Japan shall worship shrines shall be left to the individual conscience of the ones affected." The question could not be answered for them in Kansas City.[78]

"Over-internalizing" their faith and fearing persecution, as a later Japanese pastor was to put it, Japanese Nazarenes followed social dictates.[79] They were unlike members of other Japanese holiness groups, who were imprisoned and tortured for refusing to bow at shrines. The Holiness Church of Japan was known as one of the chief resistance forces to Japanese imperialism.[80]

Restrictions on religious freedom increased. In late 1939 the Japanese government pressed each denomination to have a single representative or leader to represent it in a kind of Christian parliament being set up under civil control. Kitagawa interpreted this as meaning that the government would never recognize two Nazarene districts or superintendents. He requested that Kansas City move to once more consolidate the work into one district. He was not subtle in nominating himself to Jones for the position of superintendent—especially as the government would never allow a foreigner to serve as such. The Kyoto District, he also reminded Jones, still had several times the membership of the Tokyo District. Jones clearly preferred Isayama, but he wondered if Kitagawa would cooperate with him should he appoint Isayama to the office. Pearl Wiley, though she originally had gone to Japan to assist Staples, was now disillusioned with Kitagawa's leadership. She urged Jones to appoint Isayama as district superintendent, even if that meant a major schism in the church. In the long run she thought the church would be better rid of the "irregular elements" and the continued "dominance of Mrs. Staples."[81] Jones appointed Isayama as district superintendent in March 1940, and he ordered the districts to be reunited. Likely it was a union only in name. Kitagawa initially accepted the decision but he began to fear that Isayama would rule over him with an "iron hand." Soon he urged the general church to call for a District Assembly so that the Japanese themselves could once more have the *Manual*-given privilege of electing their own superintendent. Clearly he thought he would be chosen.[82]

Kitagawa, Eckel and Isayama attended the 1940 General Assembly, where they had meetings with church leaders. Jones and the general superintendents realized that the political tension might very soon rend the church in Japan apart from America. They decided to place responsibility for whatever accommodations might be necessary in the future upon the shoulders of both Kitagawa and Isayama.[83]

Immediately upon returning to Japan after the General Assembly, Isayama and Kitagawa found that the religious situation had indeed changed drastically. The government now demanded that various denominations combine into several blocks or minor unions within the Christian Church of Japan. Each group needed to have at least 5,000 members and 50 churches. This was more than the Church of the Nazarene had. The Free Methodists were in the same predicament. Even before the arrival of the two Nazarene leaders, Free Methodist Bishop Tsuchiyama had consulted with the Nazarene church's pastors and had made preliminary plans toward union. Certainly the close friendship between the Free Methodist and Nazarene leaders as well as the union talk of previous years helped in this situation. The Nazarenes held a District Assembly in September 1940 (meeting for the first time as a united district since 1935). Isayama presided. A district missionary convention held in conjunction with the assembly evidenced the burden of the Japanese church for China. Delegates also agreed on the necessity of joining the Free Methodists—and saw the move as a constructive way of following the government's policies. "We do have hope in this change," wrote Isayama to the Nazarenes: "We also must cooperate in order to extend our work to the continent."[84]

The general church kept in contact as long as possible with Japanese leaders. The Eckels remained in America after the Assembly for their scheduled furlough in 1940 and Pearl Wiley and Bertie Karns left Japan in early 1941. Jones was able to send in one lump sum a portion of the money designated from the general budget for Japan to cover the next two years. In one of his last letters before the outbreak of war Isayama wrote: "Whatever may be the developments in the future, [the missionaries] have laid the foundation, and it is my prayer that we may be enabled to build thereon a superstructure that will stand the test of fire."[85]

Though under dire circumstances, the Church of the Nazarene in Japan was completely in Japanese hands. The leadership crises across the years had brought to the fore strong-willed and forceful leaders. With both Staples and Eckel gone, and with the social condition as it was, the leaders evidenced cooperation. For a time the social and political situation even furthered the growth of the church. In a sense there was no crisis of loyalty among the Japanese leaders between their American supporters and the Japanese cause. While ardent defenders of Christ and his church, the leaders at the same time were as always deeply and fervently Japanese. Certainly there was no trauma about having no missionaries among them. They were ready not only to carry on the work in Japan proper, but to expand the work of the church wherever the Empire might extend.

The Nazarene churches in Korea continued under the care of Japanese pastors. Tei Ki-sho, a Nazarene pastor stationed by the Japanese government in Korea, made contacts with one of the churches in Pyongyang and even opened an outstation at Tonsanri. In 1940 he began yet another work at Shinri. He maintained contact with the Seoul church as well, and urged the Japanese to help in construction projects for the congregations in Korea.[86]

A union assembly met in April 1941. The Church of the Nazarene in Japan joined the Free Methodists and two other small holiness groups, the Scandinavian Missionary Alliance and the World Missionary Society, to form the Nihon Seika Kirisuto Kyodan (Japan Holiness Church of Christ). This was the eighth of eleven blocs derived from theological traditions. The union assembly chose Tsuchiyama as leader, and he proceeded to ordain thirty ministers, most of whom were Nazarenes. There was certainly pride in this—not having to have an American general superintendent do the ordaining. Persons of all denominations long had been dissatisfied with having to have Japanese ministers appointed or ordained by North American or European church leaders.[87] The Japanese delegates chose Kitagawa to lead a united Bible college at Osaka, where the Free Methodists had their school and compound. Nazarenes planned to finance a building on the Osaka campus and to station a teacher there. Isayama remained in charge of the Nazarene segment and continued to strengthen the churches in Tokyo. He also maintained contact with the Korean and Chinese work.

At least publicly, Tsuchiyama and other leaders of the Nihon Seika Kirisuto Kyodan bloc welcomed steps toward broader unification under strict government control. In November 1942 the bloc system was abolished in favor of a unified church order. Both Tsuchiyama and Isayama served on the Executive Council of the Nihon Kirisuto Kyodan, the Christian Church of Japan.[88]

The loyalty to Japan among Nazarenes at this time of crisis is seen in the story of one Japanese man, Shiro Kano, who was studying at Boston University at the beginning of the hostilities. He had preached in various churches while attending Eastern Nazarene College in the late 1930s and had become a favorite of the school's students, teachers and administrators. After his graduation from ENC, he continued studies in philosophy of religion at Boston University. The church's leaders, including J. B. Chapman, viewed him as a potential leader for Japan, and even offered to finance his doctoral work. However, he was incarcerated soon after Pearl Harbor. He was given the choice of working for the U.S. government in translating communiques, or repatriation. His American friends urged him to stay. But Kano knew that returning to Japan was the only way in which he could effectively minister to his own people after the war. So he chose repatriation. However, after he reached Japan in 1942, he found that the war situation made it impossible for him to preach. About September 1943 he joined the Japanese navy as a translator, and set out for the South Seas. Although escaping one bombing, aboard a second ship he did not, and Kano died in the area of the Solomon Islands in January 1944.[89]

## The War and Post-War Years

During the war the church in Japan faced increasing problems. The government continued to conscript those under sixty years of age, including pastors. Government informants visited churches in order to make sure that religious leaders did not criticize the war effort. Some in other holiness churches had put so much emphasis on the Second Coming of Christ as king that the government took this as either some veiled reference to America or as a sign of disloyalty toward the Emperor. Officials told Kitagawa that he must not preach about the Second Coming at all. They suspected he and Isayama of being spies because of their close American contacts. Nazarenes were willing to bow toward the East, in the direction of the Emperor, but assured themselves that this was only out of respect and not worship.[90]

Even so, increasingly it became impossible to carry on as normal. Members scattered away from the cities to the provinces. The Allied bombing of Japan late in the war destroyed churches as well as factories and homes. Pastors subsisted along with others on sweet potatoes or pumpkins. Kitagawa's family bartered clothing for food. They also dug a bomb shelter between their home and the church in Kyoto. Isayama remained under the scrutiny of the Japanese government. His church in Tokyo remarkably escaped harm from a fire that destroyed nearby buildings, but part of it was then taken over by the military for offices. After a bombing raid it was used as a place to treat the wounded, and the church floor became stained with blood. The church in Hiroshima was left standing after the nuclear attack there, but the pastor, Rev. Kikuo Nagase, soon succumbed to the bomb's radiation.[91]

Nazarene chaplains with the U.S. armed services were the first to make contact with the church in Japan after the war. After a long search through the rubble of Tokyo, Joseph S. Pitts and Orval J. Nease, Jr., finally found Isayama. Mrs. Isayama had the young men take off their muddy boots before entering the home. Only with reluctance did Pitts comply with this request or to the customary bowing that accompanied his greetings toward Isayama. Not only were the actions signs of deference to Japanese custom, but to the dignity that the Japanese leaders still required. After Pitts and Nease made their report to Kansas City, the church undertook financial support for the Japanese leader. In addition, Pitts brought much-needed food and arranged for Isayama's employment as a translator. In Kyoto, after difficulty, Nazarene Clinton Mayhew found Kitagawa's church, which was still open. Soon food, clothing and other supplies came to Kitagawa's family and neighbors through this and subsequent contacts with Nazarenes serving in the military.[92]

Eckel, who had served as district superintendent in the Rocky Mountains during the war, returned to Japan in January 1947. He found only two of the ten Tokyo churches still functioning, and only three others nationwide. Two Nazarene pastors, Kawaguchi and Ohashi, along with their congregations, already had decided to join the Immanuel Gospel Mission, led by David Tsutada, formerly affiliated with the Holiness Church.[93]

In the spring of 1947 Eckel conducted a preachers' meeting in the Honmachi church in Kyoto, and twenty-six pastors attended. At Eckel's prodding the pastors agreed, though not all with enthusiasm, to withdraw from the Kyodan. On a trip to Kansas City to report to the General Board in early 1948, Eckel expressed great optimism and suggested that the church seize the moment, as other denominations were doing, and pour its energy and resources into the evangelization of Japan. Indeed the church began to send missionaries to Japan in greater numbers than ever before.[94]

But it was not until 1949, when General Superintendent Orval J. Nease visited Japan, that the district was officially reorganized. There was no desire among either the Japanese or the general church to return to the division of the district. The Japanese themselves, after several ballots in which the chief contender was Kitagawa, elected Eckel as district superintendent. Japan reverted to the status of a "missionary district." Isayama and Kitagawa were simply members of the District

Advisory Board. By this time Eckel had secured, through the American occupation forces, property for churches. (Other denominations were doing the same.) Eventually he secured 45 such sites and each became the location of a Nazarene church. For a time it appeared that the unexpected benevolence of the American forces coupled with the Emperor's denial of his own divinity at the close of the war would induce Japanese to more readily accept Christianity, but this optimism soon faded.[95]

Regarding the church's leaders, in 1950 Eckel persuaded Kitagawa to move from his Kyoto church, which he had pastored since 1922, to open a work in Yokohama, near Tokyo. Isayama also transferred to a different church in the same city, to Oyamadai, where Eckel planned for the denomination to construct its national headquarters. Both Isayama and Kitagawa began kindergartens in their churches, which seemed somewhat below their dignity, but many other Protestant churches in Japan were doing the same in order to meet financial expenses.[96]

Eckel began to set up an educational work that would attempt to reach Japanese effectively in the post-war era. He believed that education was the most important means of evangelism. He passionately desired that the church buy and take over operations of a school run by Ugo Nakada, the son of the late Holiness Church bishop and a friend of the Nazarenes, in Chiba, near Tokyo. Eight hundred students, including some Nazarenes, already were enrolled in the high school, which rested on 250 acres. Eckel initially received authorization from the General Board in 1947 for $10,000 for this. The total cost of the property was $80,000, but airplane hangers located on the property could be sold. By 1948, however, the general superintendents had changed their mind. The church had quickly overextended itself financially in the heady post-war years, and the leaders felt the church could not afford such a major investment in Japan. But Eckel would not accept the general superintendents' decision and proceeded to write about the lost opportunity to his lay supporters in Southern California—to the ire of General Superintendent Orval Nease, who resided in the area, and other general church leaders. Because of the delay and rising costs in Japan, Eckel now estimated that the final cost to the church would be about $25,000 for the same project. But it was not to be. Instead of the purchase of the Chiba property, the church approved that of only two acres near the Oyamadai church for a Bible college.[97]

Nease also opposed the return of Pearl Wiley Hanson to the field. During the war, Wiley had married a former Salvation Army missionary. Nease feared that her return would stir up the Eckel–Staples feud "just when things were looking up." Hanson returned anyway, without a commission from the church, and she and her husband worked with the Young Men's Christian Association. Susan Fitkin lent personal financial support. Later the Hansons were supported by the International Gospel League, headed by Nazarenes Basil Miller and E. G. Anderson.[98]

The educational work began in earnest nonetheless. Nazarenes were not alone in seeing the importance of education in post-war Japan. The Free Methodists reorganized their Bible college as Osaka Christian College. The Southern Baptists, building upon their earlier high school work, established a four-year liberal arts college in 1949.[99]

The Nazarene Bible College reopened in 1951. Eckel served as president, with both Kitagawa and Isayama among the teachers. They devised a four-year curriculum. Then, after a visit of General Superintendent Hugh C. Benner to Japan in 1959, leaders in Kansas City decided after all to take over the Chiba school, which now occupied only seventeen acres but included both a high school and a junior college. It was a momentous decision—the culmination, at least partly, of the long-held vision of Eckel and others to establish in Japan a liberal arts college—the type of school that had so effectively served the Church of the Nazarene in the United States. The junior college was made up of only two departments, English and religion. The government approved graduates of the English program to teach in public schools at the junior high level. Graduates of the religion program were able to enter the Bible College. As a result, leaders revamped the curriculum of the Bible College, reducing it to three years but requiring the junior college religion program as prerequisite for entrance.[100]

Harrison Davis, who began a long career in education in Japan in 1950, taught at the Bible College before taking leadership at the junior college. He articulated the ideals of both schools in 1960: "We feel that the preparation of Christian teachers as well as ministers is basic in the evangelization of cultured and education-conscious Japan."[101] Many who entered the college were not Christian. A Japanese teacher, Terry Yoda, desired to see graduates of the junior college "walk out of their own commencement with a diploma in one hand and a genuine Christian experience [in the other]."[102]

Mildred Bangs Wynkoop was instrumental in reorganizing the Bible College during the six years, 1960–1966, she and her husband were assigned to Japan. A former student of H. Orton Wiley at Pasadena College, and an ordained minister, Wynkoop had received a doctor of theology degree from the Northern Baptist Theological Seminary in Chicago and had been teaching at Western Evangelical Theological Seminary in Portland, Oregon, before accepting the assignment in Japan. There she, along with other leaders, quickly sensed the high priority to be placed on education. As she put it in a 1963 report, Japanese schools must undertake "the tedious rebuilding of the foundations of thinking." She reminded the American church of its own compulsion to build schools and thus preserve its Christian heritage. The "evangelistic arm" of the church had to be supported by "educational muscles and bones." The context, however, made it necessary in theological education in Japan to understand the religious and even psychological makeup of the people. "God" had little meaning to them, she thought, and "sin" was a foreign concept. Their emphasis upon conformity to social mores also disinclined them toward Christianity and kept them tied to Shintoism. Meanwhile, Japanese stressed education and where possible the attainment of a degree from a reputable school. On this basis, Wynkoop believed that Nazarene schools should seek government approval and standing in order to attract high-caliber students. She envisioned, as had leaders in 1930s, a strong liberal arts college with various majors, and also a graduate-level seminary built upon a humanities and social science-based core. Until these goals were realizable, she worked at developing the religion major in the junior college. Under her curriculum revisions, the school required more courses than could possibly be taken in two years, so as to elevate the prerequisites for the Japan Nazarene Theological Seminary, as the Bible College was now called.[103]

Wynkoop began to realize, by the end of her term, how much the highly developed theological education system she saw as necessary depended upon the church's securing missionaries with doctorates in theologically related fields. The goal, she knew, was Japanese professors with the same qualifications, but she thought that to be far in the future. Some Japanese were studying at masters' or even higher levels abroad, including Germany. But she felt that the young Japanese scholars and pastors were being influenced too much by the existentialism of Soren Kierkegaard and by the neo-orthodox biblical theology and methodology of Rudolph Bultmann. Some Japanese pastors had studied at Pasadena College in the 1950s when that school was undergoing great unrest in the religion department over some of these issues, and had come to neo-orthodox conclusions. So she believed the continued missionary presence in the theological seminary in Japan to be essential. However, when Wynkoop went on furlough in 1966, thinking that she and her husband would return to Japan, the church could not even find a one-year replacement for her. The general church, it seemed to her, did not seem committed to advanced theological education on mission fields, even in Japan. It seemed futile. So instead of returning to Japan, she accepted a position at Trevecca Nazarene College teaching theology and missions.[104]

In their interest in existentialism and neo-orthodox theology, Nazarene scholars and pastors were like other post-war Japanese Protestants. Existentialism's philosophy of despair fit the post-war mood. Neo-orthodoxy stripped away worldviews and culture from the Bible in order to find its essential meaning at a time when the Church of the Nazarene in Japan was uncomfortable with the American-ness of its orientation. Both Kierkegaard and Bultmann de-emphasized the church and its structures. Their non-churchism appealed to a strain in Japanese thought that had sought nondenominationalism and loyalties to Christ rather than to organizations. These impulses reverberated among those still stung by the heavy-handedness of missionaries and Kansas City figures earlier in the century, and, perhaps, especially among those of Minnie Staples's and Hiroshi Kitagawa's lineage.[105]

During these theological developments, the Japanese church resumed its pre-war relationship with the general church. Membership in 1952 stood at 4,129 members with 40 full-time pastors and 33 fully organized churches. Under Eckel's guidance the church broke ties with the ecumenical National Christian Council in 1954. Leaders set a five-year program of self-support in 1959, and General Superintendent Benner ordained 12 that year, including Rika Nagase, who had continued to pastor the church in Hiroshima after her husband's death. She was the first Japanese woman ordained in the Church of the Nazarene. Aside from the case of Rika Nagase, support for Japanese women in ordained leadership positions in the Church of the Nazarene was minimal. The number of ordained Japanese in 1959 was 35. The number of churches grew from 52 in 1962 to 68 in 1970. The number of pastors grew to fill the number of organized churches, but overall membership stagnated at about 5,000 after 1970.[106]

The Church of the Nazarene in Japan grew less rapidly in the post-war years than the Japan Holiness Church and the Immanuel Gospel Mission, which broke away from the latter in 1946. Indeed there were many splits in the Japan Holiness Church both before and after the war. The Free Methodist Church in Japan also suffered schisms. Despite occasional wishes from Kansas City that there would be a split in the Nazarene church in Japan, the Church of the Nazarene in Japan suffered no divisions.[107]

Perhaps there were a few who could remember the days before the war when the Japanese had established themselves through many years of trial as ingenious leaders and faithful laypersons taking responsibility not only for their own churches in Japan but for other areas of Asia as well. However, not until 1964, when Eckel retired, did a Japanese again, for the first time since 1941, become district superintendent. The assembly elected Aishin Kida, educated in the United States and a leader in the church since the 1930s, to this position. Kida was known to the Japanese as a close associate of Eckel and Isayama, and as one in whom the missionaries had great confidence. Some of the younger pastors who elected him saw Kida as a transitional, even symbolic figure, rather than as one who would wield power. Though they were happy that finally a Japanese was district superintendent, they were still resentful at the way in which Eckel had usurped, in their eyes, the leadership position over Kitagawa in the post-war years. Furthermore, there was still a division among the Japanese pastors between those loyal to Kitagawa and those still loyal to Isayama and Eckel. They considered Kida "Eckel's man." Under Kida's leadership the Oyamadai headquarters property was sold for $750,000 in 1964. The money eventually was used to construct a new headquarters building in Tokyo. In 1970 the church also relocated the seminary, which had been on the Chiba campus, to Tokyo. Kida served as district superintendent until 1966, when he was replaced by Takichi Funagoshi, a close associate of Kitagawa. Kida served as president of the theological seminary from 1966, when Wynkoop departed, to 1976.[108]

The Christian churches in Japan recognized and respected the older Nazarene leaders in later years. Isayama continued to serve the Oyamadai church in Tokyo until retiring in 1957. He died in 1969. Kitagawa served as chairman of the Evangelical Fellowship of Japan, an organization of holiness denominations initiated by the Nazarenes in 1951. This served as the focal point of Nazarene ecumenical relations after the denomination broke with the National Christian Council. Kitagawa's position in this led to his attendance at the World Evangelical Fellowship Conference in Switzerland in 1953. On his return trip to Japan he somewhat triumphantly toured Nazarene churches in the United States. Kitagawa replaced Eckel as chairman of the board of regents when the latter retired. He also served as chairman of the New Century Crusade in Japan and as both the representative from Japan and vice-chairman of the Fellowship of Asian Evangelicals, organized in 1965. He died in 1975.[109]

An era ended when Eckel retired in 1964. There was some apprehension among younger missionaries that Eckel would retire in Japan. He had stayed on at the request of the Foreign Missions Department for several years past retirement age. He felt that he had become what he had aspired to be as a young missionary, at one with the Japanese.[110]

Following his departure, the young Japanese became more assertive. The shock of the immediate post-war years was over, and they felt it time to re-assert their claims for autonomy. The post-war missionaries, with Eckel gone, believed that they could move closer to Japanese leaders, but found that they could give little supervision. The Japanese expected a lot of missionary oversight to depart along with Eckel. Missionaries continued to be active in new congregations and a succession of missionaries were stationed in Nagoya, an area in which there were few Nazarene churches. The younger Japanese pastors, not interested in being dominated from abroad, minimized missionary involvement on district boards, and improvised upon the *Manual*. For instance, their ways of choosing leaders and reaching decisions by consensus fit perfectly the Japanese context, but it was not the way the *Manual* outlined. To all of which the younger missionaries, such as Bartlett McKay, had mixed feelings. He was glad for decreased missionary leadership, but saddened over moves away from denominational structures.[111]

In the Church of the Nazarene as in other dimensions of culture, the Japanese had a way of "preserving the essence of their own ways while taking on the appearance and manner of another."[112] Social and personal factors, much more than missiological ones, produced an independent-minded church. This frustrated Nazarene leaders, but from the beginning Japan's leaders were unique in the annals of Nazarene history, and the church afforded Japan greater freedom than other fields to develop in its own way. The independency of Minnie Staples as well as the missionary-like standing of both Kitagawa and Isayama at several junctures led the general church to frustration. Eckel himself was not always in the good graces of church leaders either, but generally he promoted cooperation with the general church.

In the case of Japan, by design as well as gifts, Japanese leaders were from the beginning in the forefront. The policies, and conflicts, as well as the economic situation, allowed for the Japanese to have great measures of self-government. Though difficult to manage from Kansas City, the early years of close cooperation between national leaders and missionaries was optimal for the establishment of a self-directing church.

The Japanese remembered better than the post-war administrators in Kansas City the progress and promises of the 1930s. Out of necessity as well as planning, the Nazarene work in Japan reverted to the status of a mission field in the late 1940s, but the longing for independency remained within the Japanese. When the general church set new standards and procedures for achieving regular district status in the 1970s, Japan was among the first around the world to attain this distinction.

Hiroshi Kitagawa's son Shin Kitagawa was district superintendent at the time. As William L. Sachs concluded for the Protestant Episcopal mission in Japan, "Self-support finally meant the inability of the West to ensure its own continued influence"—so it was for the Church of the Nazarene as well.[113]

# Notes

1. Paget Wilkes, *Missionary Joys in Japan, or Leaves from My Journal* (London: Morgan and Scott, 1913), 35, 86, 97, 111–112, 193; Otis Cary, *A History of Christianity in Japan: Roman Catholic, Greek Orthodox, and Protestant Missions*, 2 vols. (Reprint, Rutland, Vt.: Charles E. Tuttle, 1976), 2: 344; R. David Rightmire, *Salvationist Samurai: Gunpei Yamamuro and the Rise of the Salvation Army in Japan* (Lanham, Md.: Scarecrow Press, 1997), 13, 37–41.

2. *Holiness Banner* (November 1899), 1; Lettie Cowman, *Charles E. Cowman: Missionary, Warrior* (Los Angeles: Oriental Missionary Society, [1928]), 89, 114, 130; Paul W. Worcester, *The Master Key: The Story of the Hephzibah Faith Missionary Association* (Kansas City, Mo.: Nazarene Publishing House, 1966), 38; Robert D. Wood, *In These Mortal Hands: The Story of the Oriental Missionary Society: The First Fifty Years* (Greenwood, Ind.: OMS, 1983), 67, 70, 102–103, 181; John J. Merwin, "The Oriental Missionary Society Holiness Church in Japan, 1901–1983," D.Miss. thesis, Fuller Theological Seminary, 1983, 105.

3. *The Christian Movement in its Relation to the New Life in Japan*, third issue (Tokyo: Methodist Publishing House, 1905), 257; *The Christian Movement in Japan*, 6th ed., eds. Ernest W. Clement and Galen M. Fisher (Tokyo: Methodist Publishing House, 1908), 484, 489–490; J. A. Chenault to H. F. Reynolds, August 3, 1911, and September 6, 1911; Chenault, "Annual Report" [1912]; Cora Snider, "Annual Report" [1912]; [Minnie] Chenault to [Maurice] Rhoden, July 21, 1954 (file 1314-34); W. A. Eckel, *When the Pendulum Swings* (Kansas City, Mo.: Beacon Hill, 1957), 74–75; Wood, *In These Mortal Hands*, 68; J. Fred Parker, *Mission to the World: A History of Missions in the Church of the Nazarene through 1985* (Kansas City, Mo.: Nazarene, 1988), 290. For Taniguchi also compare E. A. Girvin, *Phineas F. Bresee: A Prince in Israel, A Biography* (Kansas City, Mo.: Nazarene Publishing House, 1916), 256; Cowman, *Charles E. Cowman*, 143.

4. Bresee to Snider, January 1, 1913, Bresee papers.

5. Snider, "Annual Report," August 19, 1913. See Bresee, letter of commission, March 13, 1912; Bresee to Chenault, March 23, 1912; Bresee to Cora Snider, December 4, 1912; Snider to Bresee, April 20, 1913, Bresee papers; James P. Knott, *History of Pasadena College* (Pasadena, Calif.: Pasadena College, 1960), 18, 20.

6. Bresee to Snider, January 1 and January 21, 1913; Snider to Bresee, August 28, 1913, and September 16, 1913; M[aria] E. Bresee to Snider, December 14, 1913. Previous to going to America, Nagamatsu had graduated from the government university at Kumamento. See Reynolds, *World-Wide*, 58. On the long-range effects of the children's work, see Eckel, *Pendulum*, 76; and Ross Kida, *The Many Faces of Japan* (Kansas City, Mo.: Nazarene Publishing House, 1964), 49.

7. Arthur S. Hardy, *Life and Letters of Joseph Hardy Neesima* (Boston: Houghton, Mifflin, 1893); J. D. Davis, *Rev. Joseph Hardy Neesima* (New York: Fleming H. Revell, 1894); Byron S. Lamson, *Venture! The Frontiers of Free Methodism* (Winona Lake, Ind.: Light and Life Press, 1960), 90-94; John J. Merwin, "The Oriental Missionary Society Holiness Church in Japan, 1901-1983."

8. Snider to Bresee May 23, 1913, August 13, 1913, February 3, 1914; Bresee to Snider, December 30, 1913, Bresee papers.

9. Reynolds, *World-Wide*, 63.

10. Reynolds, China, to members of the General Missionary Board, February 17, 1914.

11. Reynolds, "Supplement," February 25, 1914; Reynolds, China, to members of the General Missionary Board, February 17, 1914; Reynolds, *World-Wide*, 20-64.

12. "The Policy of the General Missionary Board of the Pentecostal Church of the Nazarene, to govern the work in Japan" (Fukuchiyama, Japan, January 17, 1914), (files 305-14 and 241-47).

13. Reynolds, "The Annual Report of 1914 to the General Missionary Board of the Pentecostal Church of the Nazarene." On the social ministries of Christians see, e.g., Richard H. Drummond, *A History of Christianity in Japan* (Grand Rapids, Mich.: Eerdmans, 1971), 220-241; Robert Schildgen, *Toyohiko Kagawa: Apostle of Love and Social Justice* (Berkeley, Calif.: Centenary Books), 47-72. Comparing American missions boards' preferences for China as compared to Japan, James Reed, *The Missionary Mind and American East Asia Policy 1911-1915* (Cambridge, Mass.: Harvard University Press, 1983), 26-34, and throughout.

14. W. C. Wilson, President, District Missionary Board, to General Missionary Board, September 8, 1913; "Missionary's Application: Minnie L. Staples," and "Missionary's Application: Isaac B. Staples," both received November 20, 1914. Four daughters from the previous marriage were college-age or beyond, so remained in America. Note the similarities between Staples and Emma Eaton, both of whose husbands played supporting roles to their wives' missionary careers. See also Amy N. Hinshaw, *Messengers of the Cross in Palestine, Japan and Other Islands* (Kansas City, Mo.: Woman's Foreign Missionary Society, Church of the Nazarene, n.d.), 45-48, 53-58; and Basil W. Miller, *Twenty-Two Missionary Stories from Japan* (Kansas City, Mo.: Beacon Hill, 1949), 99-104, which is a positive reflection on her ministry in Japan.

Miller says Staples never attended school. His account is based on an interview with her second husband, C. P. Frazier. See also Mallalieu Wilson, *William C. Wilson: The Fifth General Superintendent* (Kansas City, Mo.: Nazarene Publishing House, 1995), 55.

15. Cary, *A History of Christianity in Japan*, 1: 375–404; Kenneth S. Latourette, *Christianity in a Revolutionary Age: A History of Christianity in the Nineteenth and Twentieth Centuries*, vol. 3: *The Nineteenth Century Outside Europe: The Americas, the Pacific, Asia and Africa* (Reprint, Grand Rapids, Mich.: Zondervan, 1969), 453.

16. "Missionary Application: Hiroshi Kitagawa," August 8, 1914; Hiroshi Kitagawa to General Missionary Board, August 30, 1916; Hiroshi Kitagawa, *The Guiding Hand*, trans. Jun Ooka (for History of Nazarene Missions class, Asia-Pacific Nazarene Theological Seminary, Manila, Philippines, March 1987), 11–17; Catherine P. Eckel, *Kitagawa of Japan* (Kansas City, Mo.: Nazarene, 1966), 11–28; Amy N. Hinshaw, *Messengers [in] . . . Japan*, 53–58; Hinshaw, *Native Torch Bearers*, 62–67. See Tetsunao Yamamori, *Church Growth in Japan: A Study in the Development of Eight Denominations, 1859–1939* (South Pasadena, Calif.: William Carey, 1974), 101–104.

17. Staples to Gay, April 25, 1916.

18. "The Japan Letter," April 1916 and June 1916. See Wilkes, *Missionary Joys in Japan*, 112, regarding Methodists and Anglicans participating in holiness revivals.

19. Kitagawa, "From Southern Japan," *Other Sheep* (September 1915), 5; Kitagawa, "Farewell Meeting for Mrs. Staples" [1916] (file 402-3); Staples to E. G. Anderson, April 8, 1916; Reynolds to E. J. Fleming, April 1, 1925.

20. Juliatte Tyner and Catherine Eckel, *God's Samurai: The Life and Work of Dr. William A. Eckel* (Kansas City, Mo.: Nazarene Publishing House, 1979), 18–20.

21. Timothy L. Smith, *Called Unto Holiness: The Story of the Nazarenes: The Formative Years* (Kansas City, Mo.: Nazarene Publishing House, 1962), 275–281. See also Paul Rees, *Seth Cook Rees: The Warrior-Saint* (Indianapolis: Pilgrim, 1934), 86–92.

22. Staples to Anderson, January 29, 1917; April 2, 1917, April 17, 1917, May 6, 1917; Anderson to Staples, April 23, 1917; Reynolds to Staples, April 16, 1917. Staples asked Gay, rather than Reynolds, for permission to return to America for her operation. Staples to Gay, October 16, 1916, Staples papers. See "Annual Field Report: Kumamoto," 1922. For Gay's continuing financial support for Staples, Kitagawa and their work, see Kitagawa to "Father and Mother and Sister Clemie Gay," January 9, 1925. On Seth Rees's theology of the church, which influenced Staples, see Melvin Dieter, "Primitivism in the American Holiness Tradition," *Wesleyan Theological Journal* 30 (Spring 1995), 88–91.

23. Eckel, *Pendulum*, 79–80; Isayama, *Consider Nippon: Incidents from My Life* (Kansas City, Mo.: Beacon Hill, 1957), 17–23.

24. Eckel, *Pendulum*, 82; Tyner and Eckel, *God's Samurai*, 33.

25. Eckel to Reynolds, June 13, 1917; Cora Santee (Kyoto) to Reynolds, May 3, 1918, and various station reports.

26. Reynolds to Kitagawa, January 17, 1918; Reynolds to Staples, January 24, 1918; Anderson to Eckel, May 14, 1918. Comparable problems among Southern Baptist missionaries in Japan are described in F. Calvin Parker, *The Southern Baptist Mission in Japan, 1889–1989* (Lanham, Md.: University Press of America, 1991), 115–121.

27. "Proceedings of the Second Annual District Assembly," July 1918; Nagamatsu to [Anderson], August 28, 1918; Reynolds to Eckel, March 20, 1917; Eckel to Reynolds, August 30, 1918; Reynolds to Staples, October 12, 1918. See Eckel to Anderson, September 28, 1918, for long criticisms of both Lulu Williams and Minnie Staples. Yet compare the positive evaluation of Williams in Eckel, *Pendulum*, 80–81. Similar questions about Japanese leadership had arisen in regards to the YMCA in Japan. See Jon T. Davidann, "The American YMCA in Meiji Japan: God's Work Gone Awry," *Journal of World History* 6 (Spring 1995): 107–125.

28. Eckel to Anderson, January 31, 1919; Eckel to Wagner, January 31, 1919; General Board, untitled, unsigned typescript [1919] (file 262-47); *Herald of Holiness* (June 25, 1919); Reynolds, "To Whom It May Concern," April 7, 1919, concerning Santee, and May 6, 1919. The Wagners joined the Free Methodist mission. See Lamson, *Venture*, 99, 255.

29. Nagamatsu to Anderson, February 3, 1919; "Annual Meeting of the Japan District," (n.d.); "Annual Meeting of the Missionaries and Invited Workers of the Missionary District of Japan," (n.d.).

30. Nagamatsu to Anderson, July 5, 1919; Tyner and Eckel, *Samurai*, 42; Catherine Eckel, *Kitagawa*, 47. Santin was named district superintendent in 1919. See Smith, *Called*, 344; Parker, *Mission*, 403.

31. Nagamatsu to Anderson, July 17, 1923.

32. Nagamatsu to Anderson, July 17, 1923; Anderson to Nagamatsu, August 15, 1923.

33. I. B. Staples to Anderson, February 13, 1923, April 4, 1923, and July, 1923; Minnie Staples to Anderson and Reynolds, August 14, 1923. See various notices of the Fukuchiyama work in *Other Sheep* (January 1915), 2–3, 6; *Other Sheep* (March 1916), 5; *Other Sheep* (April 1917), 5; *Other Sheep* (August 1917) 3; *Other Sheep* (November 1917), 7.

34. Nagamatsu to Anderson, August 13, 1923. The work in Fukuchiyama eventually closed. According to Aishin Kida, after the Second World War the people in the city invited Nagamatsu to return there in order to reorganize the church. Instead he started a church in Yamoto in Miyagi-ken. See Kida, *Faces*, 49; Yoshiaki Aoki, et al., eds., [*The Ninety Year History of the Japan Church of the Nazarene*] (Tokyo: Japan Nazarene District, 1999), 17, 38.

35. Eckel, *Pendulum*, 99; Catherine Eckel, *Kitagawa*, 47.

36. Bates to Board of General Superintendents, July 28, 1925; Bates to Department of Foreign Missions, [1925] (file 453-4).

37. Reynolds to Fleming, April 1, 1925 (file 453-11); "Report of Staples Committee," Reynolds to Fleming, April 1, 1925; Staples, "Honmachi Nazarene Church and Bible School, Kyoto, Japan," August 11, 1933. The first point had to do with a North Dakota land scheme with which Anderson was involved. Anderson was also accused of not taking careful enough watch over the funds previously sent to Nagamatsu. Anderson resigned as church treasurer in 1925 and as foreign missions secretary in 1926. Reynolds took over again in the latter capacity in order to restore confidence to the missions program, serving until 1928. See "Outline of Investigation" (unsigned, n.d.); Anderson to Board of General Superintendents, February 19, 1925, (file 239-21); *Herald of Holiness* (February 10, 1926); Smith, *Called*, 339.

38. On the concern about women dominating missions see Ruth Tucker, "Women in Missions: Reaching Sisters in 'Heathen Darkness'," in *Earthen Vessels: American Evangelicals and Foreign Missions, 1880–1980*, ed. Joel A. Carpenter and Wilbert R. Shenk (Grand Rapids, Mich.: Eerdmans, 1990), 269–270; and Margaret L. Bendroth, *Fundamentalism and Gender, 1875 to the Present* (New Haven, Conn.: Yale University Press, 1993), 88–90.

39. Reynolds, "Missionary Service," June 10, 1917.

40. Staples to Anderson, April 2, 1923; Gay to Staples, December 7, 1925.

41. Staples to General Board, July 28, 1925; Anderson to Eckel, December 18, 1925; Reynolds to E. J. Fleming, April 1, 1925, which includes a quotation from a letter from Kitagawa to Bates, mention of Anderson's favorable stand toward Staples, and the report that Gay would take care of her fare (file 646-9). See also Kitagawa to Anderson, April 23, 1925; Kitagawa to members of the Missions Board, September 1, 1925; Anderson to Kitagawa, October 6, 1925; Kitagawa to Gay, November 16, 1925; and Kitagawa to Staples, November 14, 1925.

42. Eckel to Morrison, December 9, 1930; Morrison to Emma Word, April 27, 1934, Morrison correspondence.

43. Anderson to Eckel, October 7, 1925, November 17, 1925, and December 18, 1925; Eckel to Bates, November 14, 1925; Eckel to Anderson, December 22, 1925; District Advisory Board of the Japan Church of the Nazarene, "Resolution," January 2, 1926; Eckel to Reynolds, January 27, 1926, March 31, 1926, and November 2, 1926; Reynolds to Howard Eckel, February 27, 1926; Bates to General Superintendents, November 14, 1925; Morrison to Eckel, August 1, 1928; Morrison "Minutes, 1931," Department of Foreign Missions, 14–16; E. J. Fleming and M. A. Wilson, ed., *Journal of the Seventh General Assembly of the Church of the Nazarene* (Kansas City, Mo.: Nazarene, 1928), 174; Tyner and Eckel, *Samurai*, 49–50.

44. Kitagawa to Reynolds, May 25, 1925; Kitagawa to Anderson, June 29, 1925.

45. Frank B. Smith, *The Dual System in Nazarene Missionary Activity on Japan District: Unparalleled, Unbelievable, True* (N.p., n.d.), 8 (file 452-4); Frank B. Smith, notarized statement, November 12, 1934 (file 646-18); Pearl Wiley, "Japan," in Maud F. Widmeyer, Everette D. Howard and Pearl Wiley,

*Our Island Kingdoms* (Kansas City, Mo.: Nazarene, 1939), 131–134, 137; Miller, *Twenty-Two*, 102.

46. Miller, *Twenty-Two*, 59–64; Basil Miller, *Standing on the Promises in Japan: The Story of Pearl Wiley Hanson* (Pasadena, Calif.: International Gospel League, n.d.).

47. I. B. and Minnie Staples, "The Japan Letter," March 1926; Kitagawa to Reynolds, April, 1926; *Other Sheep* (May 1926); Minnie Staples, "Brother and Sister Staples Return from Japan," *Other Sheep* 25 (February 1938), 12.

48. Kitagawa to Anderson, September 30 and November 17, 1925; Emma Word to Eckel, April 13, 1928; Morrison, "Minutes, 1931, Department of Foreign Missions," 14 (file 451-35); *Journal of the Seventh General Assembly*, 179–180; *Proceedings of the General Board of the Church of the Nazarene*, Special Sessions (Kansas City, Mo.: General Board of the Church of the Nazarene, [1929]), 11. The churches and pastors are listed in Mary E. Cove, *Friends on the Islands* (Kansas City, Mo.: Nazarene, n.d.), 14.

49. Kitagawa to Anderson [received January 5, 1926]; Reynolds to Kitagawa, January 11 and July 27, 1926; Kitagawa to Reynolds, July 6, 1926.

50. J. Glenn Gould, *Missionary Pioneers and Our Debt to Them* (Kansas City, Mo.: Nazarene Publishing House, [1935]), 71.

51. Eckel to Morrison, June 22, 1933; "Annual Report of the General Stewardship Committee to the General Board," January 1931. The proposed expenditures amounted to $5,512 for Japan as compared to $33,067 for India and $24,236 for China for 1931–32. See *Journal of the Seventh General Assembly*, 4, 37, 89.

52. Roy T. Williams, "Notes on the Missionary Trip Round the World" (file 544-1); Kitagawa, *The Guiding Hand*, 35, 37.

53. Eckel to Morrison, December 9, 1930, and January 31, 1931; Kitagawa, *The Guiding Hand*, 28, 37; Catherine Eckel, *Kitagawa*, 35. See also Cowman, *Charles E. Cowman*, 241–242; and Rees, *Warrior*, 105. On Nakada and the growth and then division of the Holiness Church see Merwin, "The Oriental Missionary Society," 355f., and Yamamori, *Church Growth*, 116–120, 128–133. On Tsuchiyama's early contacts with the Church of the Nazarene and Pasadena College, see Tsuchiyama, *From Darkness to Light (My Testimony)* (New York: n.p., 1917), 31–32, 50.

54. "Preliminary Draft of Policy for Proposed Japan Branch of Pasadena College, Osaka, Japan," October 6, 1930 (file 452-4); Eckel to Morrison, April 10, 1931; Morrison to Eckel, April 22, 1931; "Vitae of Takeshi Ban," [1941] (file 282-46). See also Kirkemo, *For Zion's Sake*, 159.

55. Staples to General Superintendents and General Board of Foreign Missions, July 5, 1934, and July 10, 1934; notarized statement of Frank B. Smith regarding Kitagawa and Mrs. Staples, July 12, 1934 (file 646-18); Smith to Morrison, October 23, 1934; Kitagawa to General Board of Foreign Missions, December 6, 1934; Morrison to Department of Foreign Missions members, April 9, 1935 (and, generally, file 453-54); Smith, *The Dual System*, throughout; Kitagawa, "Explanatory Statement" [1935]; Isayama to Morrison, July 10, 1935.

56. Morrison to Isayama, January 15, 1935; Isayama to Morrison, June 27, 1935; Eckel to Morrison, August 2, 1935; Morrison to Eckel, August 28, 1935; Morrison to Emma Word, December 11, 1935, Morrison papers.

57. Morrison to Isayama, August 2, 1935. The Free Methodist Japanese had declared themselves free of mission support in December 1932. See Lamson, *Venture*, 98–99.

58. Shiro Kitagawa and Takichi Funagoshi, "Notification from Headquarters," October 15, 1935; Isayama to Morrison, November 12, 1935; Chapman to General Superintendents, the Department of Foreign Missions and the General Board, December 31, 1935 (file 453-6). Compare the issue in the Episcopal Church: William L. Sachs, "'Self-Support': The Episcopal Mission and Nationalism in Japan," *Church History* 58 (December 1989), 489–501.

59. Morrison to Isayama, January 17, 1936; Morrison to Shiro Kitagawa, January 13, 1936; Pearl Wiley, "Japan," in *Our Island Kingdoms*, 123; R. V. DeLong and Mendell Taylor, *Fifty Years of Nazarene Missions*, vol. 2, *History of the Fields* (Kansas City, Mo.: Beacon Hill, 1955), 60; Isayama, *Consider*, 67; Eckel, *Pendulum*, 90.

60. Kitagawa to C. Warren Jones, October 15, 1935; "Brother and Sister Staples Return from Japan," *Other Sheep* (February 1938), 12.

61. Eckel to Word, August 6, 1935; Kitagawa to Word, May 3, 1940; Miller, *Twenty Two*, 100–101; Susan Fitkin and Emma B. Word, *Nazarene Missions in the Orient* (Kansas City, Mo.: Nazarene Publishing House, n.d.), 30, 39–40, 46; Swim, *History*, 117.

62. Eckel to Jones, August 4, 1937; November 22, 1937; March 22, 1938; and November 17, 1938; Eckel, "The Other Sheep in Japan," *Other Sheep* 24 (March 1937), 9; Eckel, "One of Our Nazarene Sunday Schools in Korea," *Other Sheep* 27 (September 1939), 15.

63. Merwin, "The Oriental Missionary Society," 340–341. Compare Schildgen, *Toyohiko Kagawa*, 214–217, 227–241; Ishida Manabu, "Live Peace! A Commentary on the Confession of Responsibility of the Church of the Nazarene in Japan During the Second World War," English version manuscript published by the Department of Social Affairs of the Church of the Nazarene in Japan (Oyama-shi, July 1994), 55.

64. Quoted in Manabu, "Live Peace," 47–48.

65. John Toland, *The Rising Sun: The Decline and Fall of the Japanese Empire* (New York: Bantam, 1971), 507–519; Mark A. Peattie, "Japanese Attitudes Toward Colonialism, 1895–1945," in *The Japanese Colonial Empire, 1895–1945*, eds. Ramon H. Myers and Mark R. Peattie (Princeton, N.J.: Princeton University Press, 1984), 96–127.

66. S[usan] N. Fitkin, *Holiness and Mission*, second ed. (Kansas City, Mo.: Nazarene Publishing House, 1940), 25.

67. Quoted in Manabu, "Live Peace," 49. See also p. 13.

68. Rightmire, *Salvationist Samurai*, 132, 140–150.

69. Kitagawa to Jones, December 6, 1938, and June 6, 1939; Wiley, "Japan," 111, 115, 140; Kitagawa, "Trip to China" (5 pp.), June 9, 1939; Kita-

gawa, "Japanese Ministers Visit China," *Other Sheep* (August 1939), 13, and *Other Sheep* (September 1939), 12; Fitkin, *Holiness and Mission*, 25–26; Geoffrey W. Royall, "Walking in the Shadows: Japanese Nazarenes," *Other Sheep* (June 1942), 19.

70. Kitagawa to Jones, October 25, 1939. See also Manabu, "Live Peace," 51; Aoki et al., ed. [*The Ninety Year History of the Japan Church of the Nazarene*], 27.

71. Kitagawa to Jones, December 6, 1938, and August 15, 1939; Kitagawa to General Board of Foreign Missions, December 6, 1938; Eckel to Jones, September 10, 1939; Jones to Kitagawa, September 27, 1939; Kida, *Faces*, 72–73.

72. Eckel to Jones, March 22, 1938.

73. Eckel to Jones, September 10, 1939.

74. Eckel to Jones, November 17, 1938.

75. Eckel to Jones, November 17, 1938; Eckel to "Our Homeland Friends," April 26, 1939.

76. Eckel to Jones, December 5, 1939. See Eckel to Jones, March 21, 1938; and the long letter of Eckel to Jones, March 11, 1939.

77. Eckel to Jones, March 11, 1939. But note Alice Spangenberg, *Oriental Pilgrim: Story of Shiro Kano* (Kansas City, Mo.: Beacon Hill, 1948), 41–43.

78. Morrison to Jones, April 20, 1939 (file 540-25).

79. Manabu, "Live Peace," 7. On March 15, 1993, the Church of the Nazarene in Japan issued a "Confession" in which it stated its "regret" that it "did not resist the aggression, but rather cooperated with it." See *Asia Pacific Ambassador* (October 1995), 5; and John P. Bowen, "Japanese Church Seeks Reconciliation with Nazarenes in Korea," *World Mission* (February 1996), 2.

80. Richard T. Baker, *Darkness of the Sun: The Story of Christianity in the Japanese Empire* (New York: Abingdon-Cokesbury, 1947), 133–144; Charles W. Iglehart, *A Century of Protestant Christianity in Japan* (Rutland, Vt.: Charles E. Tuttle, 1959), 255–256.

81. Pearl Wiley to Jones, February 10, 1940.

82. Jones to Kitagawa, January 11, and April 8, 1940; Kitagawa to Jones, February 5, February 15, April 2, and June 25, 1940; Jones, telegram to Kitagawa [March 1940].

83. Jones to Kitagawa, July 3, 1940; Kitagawa to Jones, August 22, 1940; Kitagawa to Nazarene friends, September 5, 1940.

84. Quoted in Manabu, "Live Peace," 42. See also p. 50.

85. Isayama to Jones, August 24, 1941.

86. Emma Word to Ross Kida, May 9, 1941; Kida to Word, July 10, 1941, and August 4, 1941; Tei Ki-sho, "A Letter from Korea," trans. R. A. Kida, *Other Sheep* (January 1942), 13–14.

87. Cary, *A History of Christianity in Japan*, 2: 332.

88. Jones to Isayama, February 5, 1941, and July 7, 1941. See Isayama to Jones, October 10, 1940, December 3, 1940, and July 7, 1941; Kitagawa to Jones, October 21, 1940, and September 17, 1941; Jones to Isayama, October

25, 1940; William D. Eckel, *Japan Now* (Kansas City, Mo.: Nazarene Publishing House, 1949), 94–96; Pearl Wiley, "Two Historic Assemblies," *Other Sheep* (December, 1941), 9–10; Tei Ki-Sho, "A Letter from Korea," trans. R. A. Kida, *Other Sheep* (January 1942), 13–14; Manabu, "Live Peace," 41–46. For the broader context of developments see Drummond, *A History of Christianity in Japan*, 257–265.

89. Spangenberg, *Oriental*, throughout.

90. Isayama, *Consider*, 69–71; Catherine Eckel, *Kitagawa*, 60; Kida, *Faces*, 73.

91. Isayama to Jones, December 10, 1945; Joseph S. Pitts, "The Road to Tokyo," in Lauriston J. Du Bois, ed., *The Chaplains See World Missions* (Kansas City, Mo.: Nazarene Publishing House, 1946), 21–25; William D. Eckel, *Japan*, 128; Catherine Eckel, *Kitagawa*, 61, 63; Isayama, *Consider*, 71–72, 80–81.

92. Isayama, *Consider*, 82–84; Catherine Eckel, *Kitagawa*, 69–71; Pitts, "Road," 19; Pitts to Jones, September 20, 1945; J. B. Chapman to H. V. Miller, October 17, 1945 (file 772-3).

93. Merwin, "The Oriental Missionary Society," 431.

94. Japan "Council Minutes," March 29, 1954; Kida, *Faces*, 79; W. D. Eckel, *Japan*, 109–112, 116–117. The Free Methodists stayed within the Christian Church of Japan until 1952. See *Japan Christian Yearbook 1957*, ed. Kiyoshi Hirai (Tokyo: Christian Literature Society, [1957]), 177, 181–182.

95. Orval J. Nease, "Foreign Visitation, 1948," n.d.; Nease, "Closing Service in Tokyo," n.d., Board of General Superintendents; Eckel, *Pendulum*, 121, 124; Bartlett McKay to George Coulter, March 6, 1965; Catherine Eckel, *Kitagawa*, 73.

96. Isayama, *Consider*, 89; Catherine Eckel, *Kitagawa*, 76–79. Compare James M. Phillips, *From the Rising of the Sun: Christians and Society in Contemporary Japan* (Maryknoll, N.Y.: Orbis, 1981), 60.

97. Eckel to Jones, March 11, 1947; Eckel to Powers, July 15, 1948; Eckel to Nease, June 2, 1949; Nease, "Foreign Visitation, 1948"; G. B. Williamson to Ruby Apple, July 29, 1949; Nease to Remiss Rehfeldt, October 8, 1949, October 20, 1949, and October 24, 1949. On Ugo Nakada see Merwin, "The Oriental Missionary Society," 312.

98. Nease to Rehfeldt, February 27, 1950; Miller, *Standing on the Promises*.

99. Lamson, *Venture*, 256; Parker, *The Southern Baptist Mission*, 181.

100. Harrison Davis, "Educational Policy Recommendations," n.d., and Mildred Bangs Wynkoop, "Missionary Report," August 31, 1962 (both in file 412-5); Kida, *Faces*, 95–99; Parker, *Mission*, 301–302.

101. Harrison Davis and Doris Davis to "Dear Ones at Home," July 20, 1960, Davis papers. See also Ross Kida to Samuel Young, November 6, 1964; Davis, "Educational Report," n.d. (file 1360-26), and "Interim College Report," March 16, 1967, Coulter papers.

102. Terry Yoda, Christmas letter, 1961.

103. Mildred Wynkoop, "Educational Problems in Japan," April 1963 (22 pp.) (file 1387-74); and see Wynkoop, "The Educational Situation in Japan as It Relates to Japan Christian Junior College, April 1963, Young papers (file 1387-74).

104. Wynkoop, "Educational Problems in Japan"; Wynkoop to E. S. Phillips, June 14, 1965; Japan Mission Council Minutes, October 29–30, 1965; Wynkoop, "Annual Report of the Ministerial Training Program," October 1965; Wynkoop to Coulter, December 20, 1965. On the controversies at Pasadena see Kirkemo, *For Zion's Sake*, 218–227.

105. John P. Howes, "The Marunouchi Lectures of Uchimura Kanzo (1861–1930)," *Fides et Historia* 24 (Winter/Spring 1992), 25–32; Miura Hiroshi, *The Life and Thought of Kanzo Uchimura, 1861–1930* (Grand Rapids, Mich.: Eerdmans, 1996), 105–113; Seiichi Yagi, "The Third Generation," in *A History of Japanese Theology*, ed. Yasuo Furuya (Grand Rapids, Mich.: Eerdmans, 1997), 85, 101–102. On the German theological influence upon the Church of the Nazarene in Japan see Makoto Sakamoto, "The Challenge of Articulating the Doctrine of Holiness in Japanese Culture," paper presented at the Asia-Pacific Theological Conference, Chongju, South Korea, October 9, 2001, 7.

106. Merrill Bennett, "A Prosperous Journey," *Other Sheep* (May 1957), 4–6; Harrison Davis, "Silver Anniversary at Hiroshima," *Other Sheep* (February 1960), 4. Compare Hugh Trevor, *Japan's Post-War Protestant Churches* (Monrovia, Calif.: MARC, 1995), 102.

107. Trevor, *Japan's Post-War Protestant Churches* (N.p., 1995), 45–54. The Bible Missionary Church, which split from the Church of the Nazarene in the United States in 1956, began work in Japan in 1970. See also Izuta Akira, "Evangelical Churches," in *Christianity in Japan, 1971–90*, ed. Kumazawa Yoshinobu and David L. Swain (Tokyo: Kyo Bun Kwan, 1991), 298–309.

108. Eckel, "To the Fall Mission Council 1962 Meeting in Tokyo"; "Report of Local Churches April–December 1962"; Eckel to Samuel Young, July 3, 1963; Ross Kida to Young, April 8, 1964; Bartlett McKay to George Coulter, May 12, 1964, March 6, 1965, March 22, 1965; Hubert Helling to Coulter, December 22, 1965, and June 20, 1966; Helling to E. S. Phillips, June 20, 1966; Davis, "Silver Anniversary at Hiroshima," *Other Sheep* (February 1960), 4; Donald Owens, *Sing Ye Islands: Nazarene Missions in the Pacific Islands* (Kansas City, Mo.: Nazarene Publishing House, 1979), 27–29.

109. Remiss Rehfeldt to Kitagawa, August 27, 1953, World Mission Division, Church of the Nazarene, microfilm number 92; *The Japan Christian Yearbook, 1957*, 177, 181–182; *Other Sheep* (May 1969), 23; Catherine Eckel, *Kitagawa*, 82–84; *Nazarene Biography Index* (Nampa, Idaho: Northwest Nazarene College, 1984), 33, 65, 90.

110. Eckel, "To the Fall Mission Council 1962 Meeting in Tokyo"; Eckel, "Notice of Withdrawal," August 30, 1962; Tyner and Eckel, *Samurai*, 73, 86, 97.

111. Japan Mission Council Minutes (August 30–31, 1962), 8; McKay to Coulter, May 12, 1964; Coulter to McKay, May 20, 1964; Bartlett McKay to Coulter, March 6, 1965; Coulter, "Recap of Activities in Japan," November 8, 1965; Hubert Helling to E. S. Phillips, January 27, 1966; T. Uematsu to Samuel Young, n.d. (file 1386-9); Shin Kitagawa, "Becoming an Independent (Full) District," n.d. [February 1976], trans. Hubert Helling (file 1360-25). See also Jerald Johnson to Charles Strickland, July 27, 1978, Coulter papers.

112. James Thomson, Peter Stanley and John Perry, *Sentimental Imperialists: The American Experience in East Asia* (New York: Harper, 1981), 213.

113. Sachs, "'Self-Support'," 501.

# Chapter 4

# China

Beginning in 1914, the Church of the Nazarene worked by comity arrangements in North China among Mandarin-speaking rural peasants in northwestern Shandong and southern Hebei Provinces. This was an area plagued by natural and man-made problems. Across the three decades of work in this area of China, the ministry of the church was well balanced. Without hesitancy the church conformed to the patterns and expectations of other missions in China. In addition to energetic village evangelism, the church undertook famine and flood relief projects, educated boys and even girls and old women as well as ministerial students, and established a hospital. These enterprises flowed as much out of compassionate as out of evangelistic concerns, though the missionaries rarely, if ever, separated the two. The spiritual needs were acute, as the missionaries perceived them. Education and medicine as much as the Bible could dispel the superstitious customs and ancient traditions that, as the missionaries saw it, kept the people in spiritual bondage. In China, it is evident how much outside events affected the missionaries both in spirit and in behavior. Social and political changes swirling around the mission field made an impact on missionaries' actions. In very concrete ways the attempt of the mission to meet immediate needs often outweighed other considerations of philosophy and policy.

In some respects the mission lagged behind other fields such as Japan and even India in the development of a district. In spite of the fact that Chinese leaders had been pressing missionaries for several years to allow them a louder voice in the affairs of the church, there were only three ordained Chinese ministers when the missionaries left North China in 1942, and all three fled to the south during or after the war. Actually having no Chinese district organization may have benefited the church in some ways as a loose but effective band of Chinese lay pastors and itinerants pressed the work forward for decades without contact with or support from the general church. Future events seemed to bear true what one Chinese told a departing missionary in 1940: "You do not need to be ashamed to go back to America; you have lots of 'face' as you return home. . . . You can say that you left behind you in China a self-governing, self-supporting church."[1] Because the church in North China was markedly evangelistic, it was able both to maintain itself and convert thousands to the Christian faith.

There was a fleeting contact with the field in 1947, but by then Mao Ze-dong's Seventh Army was in control of the area. So the Nazarene Church turned its attention to the South, where both missionaries and national leaders concerted an effort in Jiangxi Province for about twenty months, 1947 to 1949. Then that area also fell to the Communist government. In the middle of the 1950s Nazarenes officially entered Taiwan, and in the 1970s Hong Kong, but in neither of these locations was there much connection with the original work in North China.

## Before the Nazarene Work

Being at the crossroads of Shandong, Hebei, Henan and Shanxi Provinces, political and criminal activity surrounded the area assumed by the Nazarenes. Natural disasters related to the Yellow River's frequent flooding combined with antagonism toward both the imperial rule in Beijing and foreign intervention in Chinese affairs to produce political and social rebels in the area by the late nineteenth century. The imposition of textile manufacturing by foreign concerns misdirected labor and further worsened the economic situation. So young men turned against order and law. These included the Boxers, who arose in this region, and others who engaged in banditry. Those seeking to escape from the law could easily do so by crossing provincial borders.[2]

Roman Catholic mission activity in the area that became Nazarene preceded the Protestant work. The Catholic mission was represented by mostly German and Belgian friars of the Society of the Divine Word and Jesuits who had been active around Daming as early as the seventeenth century. They protected converts, some of whom were suspected criminals, from local officials. In eastern Shandong in the late 1890s the friars called in the German militia to protect themselves, their property and churches, and their converts. Protestant missionaries, who began to arrive in eastern Shandong Province in the mid-1860s, likewise advocated foreign intervention to protect their interests. Some local Chinese embraced Christianity in the desire both to reap financial rewards and to escape from government authorities. The missionaries faced hostile political forces. Numerous sects had arisen in the area. The Chinese gentry resented intrusion upon their established Confucian-based order. The alliance between the imperial state and foreign powers in the late nineteenth century caused discontent on local levels with Christian churches. The reputation of Christianity in the region was abysmal at the end of the century.[3]

The inevitable outbreak against foreign control came in 1900 following a great drought. The Boxer Rebellion saw 200 missionaries and 30,000 converts killed. The Boxers, who believed themselves to be possessed by spirits, attacked both Roman Catholics and Protestants. Shandong and Hebei Provinces were centers of violence against missionaries. Many missionaries welcomed not only foreign intervention to end the rebellion, but also the humiliating concessions from the Chinese that followed.[4]

The establishment of a republic under Sun Yat-sen reinforced confidence among missionaries. Protestants in America had great hopes for China becoming a Christian nation. After decades of working for the end of opium addiction in China, by 1911 missionaries began to see local Chinese officials enforce an end to opium trade with India and reduce local production. Until the next wave of antiforeignism in 1927, calmness toward Christianity dominated Chinese society.[5]

Into this relatively beneficent political and religious climate, Horace Houlding, his wife, and a group of young missionaries established the "South Chili Gospel Mission" in southern Hebei Province. The Houldings had first arrived in Tianjin in 1896 and had worked unconnected with any society. Fleeing to the United States after the Boxer Rebellion, the Houldings found that news of the rebellion and its martyrs had piqued interest among American Christians toward China missions. The Houldings had little problem recruiting a group of young missionaries, whom they took with them when they returned to China in late 1901. After language study in Tianjin, the band established a headquarters near Daming. They were among the first missionaries to enter the area after the Boxer Rebellion. The missionaries claimed that though there were Moslems in Daming, who in fact warmly greeted them, there were only two known Chinese Christians in the city. French Jesuits entered Daming in the same year. The Gospel Mission band eventually numbered as many as 76 persons living in nine cities within a radius of 60 miles from Daming. Their work included three "higher" primary schools.[6]

Among the first missionaries in the Houlding group were some with holiness movement affiliations. For instance, Jacob Kohl and Mary A. Hill were members of Phineas Bresee's Church of the Nazarene in Los Angeles. Houlding stationed Kohl, who arrived in China in 1903, in a crude house two miles from Daming, where he labored, with only one three-month furlough, until his death at age 52 in Shanghai in 1919.[7]

Hill, who had served for a year as principal of the Nazarene school in Los Angeles, eventually served in China for over thirty years under the National Holiness Association (later renamed the World Gospel Mission). Other early arrivals affiliated with the Houlding mission included Catherine Flagler and Leon and Emma Osborn, all of whom eventually joined the Nazarene mission.[8]

A rift occurred in the South Chili Gospel Mission in 1909. Though the work bustled with activity, many of the young missionaries failed to adjust to either the culture of China or the captain of the mission. Houlding did not teach holiness as clearly or as strongly as some of those whom he recruited. Furthermore, policy disagreements developed over both the "Americanization" that some missionaries saw being forced upon Chinese converts and undemocratic procedures within the mission itself. In January 1909 two strong young leaders, Cecil Troxel, the treasurer and deputy director of the mission, and Woodford Taylor, withdrew from the Houlding work. The two men quickly traveled to Lintsing and met with the American Congregationalist Mission there. They apparently attended a conference that was being held regarding comity arrangements in the area. The conference included representatives from the London Missionary Society and the Northern Presbyterian and Methodist Episcopal Missions. Houlding's South Chili Gospel Mission was accounted for only by letter, which, perhaps, Troxel and Taylor bore themselves. As a result, the American Board ceded ten counties from its own field to Troxel and Taylor, who must have given the conference representatives some assurance that they would find a sponsoring agency. Apparently these counties transferred from the American Board included at least some of the area in which Houlding's work was already established.[9]

Troxel, Taylor, and their families returned to America in 1909 and undertook fund-raising within the holiness movement for the China work. With this prodding, the National Holiness Association, successor to the National Campmeeting Association for the Promotion of Holiness, formed its own Missionary Society in 1910, with C. J. Fowler, a Methodist who was also president of the National Holiness Association, as Missionary Society president. With this backing, the missionary couples twenty-five miles northeast of Daming, and recruited two Chinese workers, Hang Hung-yu and Chang Hung-en. The 1911 Republican Revolution forced the missionaries to evacuate briefly to Tianjin, but otherwise the work grew rapidly.[10]

Troxel and Taylor had well established the National Holiness Association mission when talks began concerning the possible incorporation of it with the Church of the Nazarene. The Nazarene church included many who felt deep kinship with all holiness people, no matter their affiliation. Some dreamed of a united holiness denomination encompassing all the dynamics of the movement. C. W. Ruth, one of the best-loved evangelists of the National Holiness Association who served on its Missionary Society Committee, was both a keen booster of the young denomination and one who retained close ties to the holiness movement as a whole. As such, it was natural for him to try to bring the National Holiness Association work in China together with the Church of the Nazarene. The NHA board, in fact, advised the missionaries in China to seek affiliation with a denomination, since the NHA had no intention of forming a separate one. The board approved of the Church of the Nazarene's taking over the work if matters could be arranged satisfactorily. By 1913 there were nine American missionaries working under the NHA, along with ten Chinese preachers and ten Bible women. Bible women visited homes around the field, shared the gospel, exhorted and did a variety of other tasks. A small school operated for training pastors. Ruth advised patience so that a transition could be amicably effected in order to bring the work under the Church of the Nazarene.[11]

Meanwhile, General Superintendent and Foreign Missions Secretary H. F. Reynolds saw an opportunity for the denomination in a young couple, Peter and Anna Kiehn, both of whom were former missionaries to China. Peter Kiehn had been raised Mennonite and was a member of a holiness congregation in Hutchinson, Kansas (which became Nazarene in 1908). Kiehn had attended the holiness Bible school there before sailing to China in 1906 at the age of twenty-one. He worked in the Shanhsian district in Shandong Province under the Light and Hope Mission of the Mennonite Missionary Society, which had begun work in 1905. The Mennonite Mission included one lower and three higher primary schools, two middle schools, an orphanage and industrial work. Henry C. Bartel, the organizer of the Mennonite work, was a friend of Kiehn's family and an uncle of Anna Schmidt. Like Peter Kiehn, Anna Schmidt had been raised a Mennonite. She arrived in China in 1906 and also worked in Shandong Province. She and Peter Kiehn were married in China in 1908. For a time they helped to establish a station in Tsaochoufu, working there in cooperation with the South Chili Gospel Mission. They furloughed in 1912 and then officially united with the Church of the Nazarene while attending the Nazarene college in Bethany, Oklahoma. Kiehn was ordained by Reynolds in 1913. Both Peter and Anna Kiehn were eager to return to China as Nazarene missionaries.[12]

Reynolds learned through Ruth that though there was a good possibility of the NHA work affiliating with the Nazarenes, in no way would their missionaries accept Kiehn as leader. They knew him from his previous term. Ruth warned that a premature departure for China by Kiehn might cause the negotiations between the Church of the Nazarene and the NHA to fail. He thought that Kiehn should wait until matters were decided.[13]

Nevertheless, Reynolds took Kiehn and his wife, along with Glennie Sims, on his worldwide trip (1913–1914) as the officially appointed Nazarene workers to China. Reynolds's eagerness for the Church of the Nazarene to enter China must have been fueled by the news pouring into America about the opportunities that awaited Christianity under China's new Republican government. The 1911 Revolution was prominently and positively portrayed in small- and large-town American newspapers. Yuan Shi-kai, China's President, had appealed for a day of Christian prayer for the nation on April 27, 1913. Warm to missionary endeavors as well as democratic ideals, in the early days of his administration, to the chagrin of European powers, President Woodrow Wilson recognized the legitimacy of the Republican government. He made the United States' protection of China a prominent part of his foreign policy. There was great optimism that China would become a Christian country. Just as in East Asian foreign policy, among American missions, to the relative neglect of Japan, China occupied the center of concern.[14]

The young Church of the Nazarene absorbed this great passion of the American church for China. Reynolds, with the Kiehns and Sims, arrived in Shanghai in January 1914. They made their way to the NHA headquarters in Nankwantao. The NHA work impressed Reynolds. Amiable and frank talks ensued between Reynolds and the NHA missionaries.

In a letter that soon followed to the General Missionary Board of the Church of the Nazarene, the NHA missionaries expressed their desire to give their converts the privileges of a church home. They understood that the National Holiness Association refused to take denominational form even in its mission work, and found it acceptable for the NHA mission in China to be taken over by the Nazarene church, and governed according to its *Manual*. They presented themselves as candidates for missionary appointment. Their only stipulation was that the Nazarenes assume full financial responsibility by November 1916.[15]

At the time Reynolds recognized it as a "splendid opportunity," though a great financial undertaking. He considered Woodford Taylor a good superintendent ("until such time as the work had developed into a district and had its assembly, when it would elect its own superintendent").[16]

While waiting for the matter to be fully decided, the NHA gave about one-half of the area assigned to it by comity to the Church of the Nazarene. This partition would become unnecessary if and when union took place. The Kiehns took a station in the area apportioned to the Nazarenes, at Chaocheng, on the northern side of the Yellow River in Shandong Province. Reynolds visited the place and he as well as the NHA workers felt that the area held strong possibilities. NHA missionaries regularly itinerated there and had recently begun Sunday worship services in the city. The first ones to attend were Moslems. While the NHA missionaries waited for the Nazarenes to decide on the merger, they assigned Kiehn a Chinese evangelist, Li Ching-ho, as his co-worker.[17]

Before going on his way to India (to meet a host of crises in Calcutta), Reynolds, Peter and Anna Kiehn and Glennie Sims established the first policy statement for the Nazarene work in China. The policy followed closely a similar one drawn for Japan a few weeks earlier, but sanctioned more institutional work in the case of China. The primary impetus remained evangelism, which was to be accomplished through touring from village to village, visiting house-to-house, opening new stations and preaching at fairs and markets. Then the church would nurture converts in local congregations. In addition, the group in China saw the necessity of medical work, literature work (translating and selling holiness books), schools, and even industrial training so that students could support themselves. The policy stated that the missionaries must encourage Chinese Christians to tithe. The policy was more explicit than the one in Japan in stating that when a local church achieved one-half self-support in paying the pastor's salary and property rental it would be entitled to elect its own board members. When a local church became fully self-supporting, missionary control over it was to be relinquished, except as provided for in the *Manual*. That Reynolds and the church in general had not thought through the ultimate goals of church government was clear in one statement Reynolds made: that the Chinese would eventually have their own general as well as district superintendents, along with evangelists and college presidents.[18]

Reynolds returned to America optimistic that union with the NHA work would be effected. He was hopeful that its present supporters would not cease financial contributions should the work become denominational, and he was prayerful that the Nazarenes would be able to fully support it by 1916. But it was not to be. The Pentecostal Mission headquartered in Nashville, Tennessee, united with the Church of the

Nazarene. The Pentecostal Mission had extensive missionary work and heavy financial obligations around the world. The Great War also created many uncertainties. Accessioning the NHA work and workers seemed too great an undertaking for the young denomination at the time. Nevertheless, some Nazarenes independently continued to support the NHA work in China.[19]

## Evangelistic and Institutional Work

Peter Kiehn built the church in Chaocheng upon the contacts of the NHA work and extended evangelistic activities to the north. By 1915 nine Chinese workers were in the employment of the church, including three Bible women, Li Ching-ho, the evangelist, and Chang Hua-hsin, who had assisted Kiehn during his earlier term in China. The paid workers lived at the mission station established in Chaocheng and itinerated from this base. The first Nazarene church to be organized in China, in May 1915, was thus at Chaocheng. Twelve Chinese, including some but not all of the workers, joined. Kiehn bound himself closely to the Chinese workers. In the absence of other missionaries, he found that "no place is left for lonesomeness, but Jesus and the Chinese have taken the place of home and loved ones."[20]

By this time missionaries had decided that the Nazarene church in China would be called the Hsuan Sheng Hui, meaning, loosely, "The Preaching [or Proclaiming] Holiness Church." This was the same name as the NHA. This was by intention so that the Chinese would recognize that the Church of the Nazarene and the NHA were alike. Across the years missionaries and Chinese workers from one side preached for the other. Following along the lines that Reynolds had initiated, the Nazarenes in China abided by comity arrangement. They worked harmoniously—particularly with Free Methodists, headquartered in Kaifeng, 125 miles south of the Nazarene field. Nazarenes used Sunday School literature published interdenominationally by the China Sunday School Association.[21]

The missionaries continued to gather Chinese workers for the various ministries they initiated, which included primary schools for both boys and girls. Sims in particular worked among children, and persuaded some families to unbind their daughters' feet. The missionaries paid teachers and other workers from contributions from laypersons and from Sunday School classes and churches in America, rather than through the church's general budget for China. This forged close bonds among American contributors for the work in China.[22]

By the time of the first so-called district assembly, held June 4, 1917, there were four missionaries (Ida Vieg had transferred from the NHA to the Nazarene work), and nine Chinese workers ranging in age from their twenties to their forties. Among them, Chang Hua-huw, Jen Chin-ya, Chang Hsi-tien and Chang Chien-hsun toured and preached at fairs and tent meetings, and Li Ching-i pastored an outstation at Puchow. Kiehn prepared a Chinese course of study for educating the workers and used winters for conducting daily Bible studies with them. He sent a few to the NHA training school. Other workers joined, including several Bible women past sixty years old. Among the emerging leaders, Chang Chien-hsun had been converted at Chaocheng after earlier contacts with the National Holiness work. Eventually Chang served as preacher in Chaocheng, Fanhsien, Puchow, and other locations. Li Ching-i was converted from Confucianism in 1914 at the NHA station at Nankwantao under the preaching of Chang Hua-hsin. Kiehn later visited his village and persuaded him to attend the daily Bible studies for workers, and then sent him out. National workers such as Chang Chien-hsun and Li Ching-i pioneered outstations, which the missionaries visited from time to time.[23]

The converts were mostly poor farmers and they often came into the church as families. In choosing to become Christians, they cut themselves off from other family clans. Christians formed their own social groups within villages.[24]

When new missionaries joined the mission in the late 1910s, including Otis and Zella Deale and Leon and Emma Osborn, the missionaries decided to enter Daming and to make it the center of the Nazarene mission. They apparently decided this with the permission of Houlding, who still had the base of his mission just outside the city walls. Both the Mennonites and the Jesuits were active as well in Daming. Nonetheless, the Nazarene missionaries planned for Daming to be the site of a Bible school, a hospital, and missionary residences. The Osborns, former Methodists who had served in China under the Houlding mission before being commissioned as Nazarene missionaries, took the Kiehns' place at Chaocheng, and the Kiehns moved to Daming.[25]

Though the Nazarene compound in Daming grew and developed, unlike many earlier missionaries to China, Nazarenes did not isolate themselves from Chinese people. Missionaries of all types traveled frequently into the villages and towns and became acquainted with Chinese people on personal levels.

During the 1920s the Chinese church grew stronger as a result of the expectations placed upon it by missionaries. A requirement for membership in the church was the ability to read one of the New Testament Gospels. As this was imposed upon women as well as men, it necessitated that more education be given to women than normally available in Chinese society—especially its rural areas. The requirements of literacy indicated the desire of the church that members know what they believed. Prospective members were also made to answer a list of questions of a doctrinal and ethical nature, a kind of catechism. This, missionaries hoped, guarded against individuals affiliating with the mission for any but spiritual reasons. Nazarene efforts to uplift rural peasants by offering them literacy, medicine and improved living conditions corresponded to a national push in China called the Mass Education Movement.[26]

The expectations that missionaries had for converts demonstrated a certain respect among them for Chinese. An early description of the Chinese written by Amy Hinshaw, a Nazarene missions publicist who had never been to China, relied upon Arthur Smith's disparaging late nineteenth-century book *Chinese Characteristics*. She described the Chinese as being inscrutable, indirect, insincere, and mutually suspicious, as lacking in sympathy and as having disregard for accuracy. Later missionary books were fairer in their descriptions of Chinese life and culture, and letters and reports from missionaries to headquarters were relatively free of prejudice. Francis Sutherland, after spending many years in China, described positively the people's family values, cheerfulness, organizational talents, ability to suffer, capacity for friendship and desire for education. Missionary presentations in local churches presented China as a field of great challenge and potential harvest.[27]

As for organization, each evangelist and worker reported to the district assembly, which they also divided into committees in order to discuss various facets of the work. By 1922, when Reynolds returned to China and presided over a district assembly composed only of missionaries, there were three established local churches, including those in Daming and Chengan as well as Chaocheng, and 207 members. No Chinese workers were ready yet for ordination. Stella Reynolds, who accompanied her husband on this trip, initiated the first missions auxiliary among the Chinese women. The church employed 70 Chinese workers by the beginning of 1923. In spite of the strict scrutiny of members, the church grew to 625 members by 1925. Two hundred ninety-two of these were members of the Daming church. There were about 1,500 "probationary" members awaiting baptism. The Chinese also contributed to the district's expenses, giving over $1,200 in 1925.[28]

Part of the reason for the growth of the denomination in these years was the social concern evidenced by the church and its missionaries. To missionaries, it seemed a natural and inevitable part of the mission of the church, especially as educational, medical, and industrial work also had been part of the Houlding and Mennonite missions out of which several of the missionaries came. From the beginning, the Kiehns and Sims dispensed medicine. The mission extended direct help to poor women at Daming. At Chaocheng the missionaries distributed used clothing to the poor. As in India, across the years, Nazarenes maintained primary schools in rural towns. By 1924, for instance, the Morning Light School for boys in Chengan had 110 students.[29]

During the severe 1920-1921 famine, Nazarenes in North America raised $25,000 for "China Famine Relief." In order to distribute this amount, the missionaries employed Chinese workers to construct a large brick church, missionary residences, and a wall around the compound at Daming. At the same time, Kiehn was responsible for Red Cross funds, which he used to pay workers to construct a 45-mile road from Daming to Handan, where there was a railroad station. While the men worked on the road, their wives were enrolled in Bible and literacy classes. Meanwhile, parents desperate for food sent their children to Nazarene primary schools, where they not only were fed, but received a stipend to help their families. French Jesuits in Daming were doing the same at their schools. At Chaocheng, Osborn used money from the International Famine Relief Commission to initiate a straw-braiding industry. Workers also constructed a large Nazarene church in Chaocheng at this time. And at Puchow, missionary Otis Deale distributed corn and black grain bread. Then, in 1922 the Yellow River once more overflowed. In this case the International Famine Relief asked missionary Harry Wiese to distribute 30,000 bags of grain and to oversee a crew of 10,000 workers in the rebuilding of a dam near the Nazarene mission station at Puhsein. Osborn supervised another crew of 5,000 in the southeastern part of the field.[30]

To the missionaries, medical and social ministries demonstrated the perfect love that holiness of heart was supposed to create, and fulfilled the church's responsibilities and duties to the poor. Nazarene missionaries such as Kiehn and Wiese took for granted that these were appropriate for a holiness mission. They also liked the idea that these projects were not mere handouts, but required something from the Chinese themselves. Neither the American value of self-reliance nor the missiological goal of self-support was put aside. Nazarene missionaries in China never thought of these deeds in terms of the "Social Gospel," which, like other evangelicals in the 1920s, Nazarenes associated with Modernism.[31]

From the Chinese perspective, these same ministries provided incentives and inducements for them to become Christians. The Chinese could be pragmatic when it came to looking for benefits that would improve their material as well as spiritual lives. Christianity offered affiliation with a prosperous people. They saw the large houses Nazarene missionaries built on the compound in Daming for their boisterous families. Possibly not all of the Chinese converts saw immediately the necessity of jettisoning household gods and other spiritual influences from their lives—but Nazarenes insisted that these must go if they were to be Christian.[32]

Ida Vieg developed an interest in the education and conversion of elderly women. Raised among Swedish Lutherans in Iowa, Vieg had studied at Augustana Business College. She was converted in a Methodist church while teaching in Washington State. While working in an urban mission in Portland, Oregon, she attended a holiness camp meeting. She became a Nazarene shortly before going to China in 1911. She transferred from the NHA to the Nazarene mission in 1916. Her assignment was to keep the mission's financial records. Once settled in Chaocheng, where she was stationed at first, she became burdened for the elderly women. No one seemed to be caring for them. In the protocol of society, such care would have to come from another woman. The Chinese did not like the idea of men and women studying together. Vieg began to teach the old women to read the Bible. Mr. Yu, who was business manager at the Bresee Hospital in Daming, remarked regarding her work: "For sixty or even seventy years their brains had hardly ever been used. . . . But Miss Vieg did not seem to mind it. She had love and patience in helping old women."

As with previous generations of women missionaries in China, Vieg's approach was intensely personal. After working with old women in Chaocheng for four years, and a furlough (1920–21), Vieg expanded her ministry to women throughout the Nazarene field. The next six years were productive and endeared her to the Chinese church. She furloughed again in 1927, but this time headquarters was unable for financial reasons to send her back to China. So she involved herself in a rescue mission in Oakland, California. The old Chinese women kept asking the missionaries on the field when Vieg would return. Being informed, eventually, that the reasons were financial, the Chinese women through their own Woman's Foreign Missionary Society took up a collection for her among the Chinese churches and outstations. The missionaries then forwarded the money to Kansas City.

Finally, in 1932, Vieg returned and continued her work among the old women. Then in 1934 she developed cancer. She refused to return home for treatment and seemed to recover. The cancer recurred in 1936, but again she decided to stay in China. She died in Daming in

1937 at age 55, and was buried on the compound. Mr. Yu eulogized about her: "She comes to this land, a foreign land to her, and adopts these old women as hers; she does not consider them too dirty or uncouth to associate with. . . . Just to think of such love for our people, ready to die out here away from relatives and native land, she certainly considered us her people." Her gravesite became a favorite prayer spot for Bible school students. Even at night, awakened missionaries could hear students praying at her tomb.[33]

Like other Christian groups, the Church of the Nazarene gave Chinese women opportunities beyond what was available to them in society—especially the rural peasant society in which the Church of the Nazarene worked. Through the church, some women achieved leadership roles that otherwise would have been impossible. In Chaocheng, Mrs. Chao enrolled in Bible study classes for women, became a leading Bible woman, and then discovered a gift for healing the sick and casting out demons. Another woman in Chaocheng, Mrs. Ma, was determined to send her younger daughter to school. Though the family was not yet Christian, the daughter enrolled in the Nazarene school, and became "an active little missionary" in her home, urging her grandparents and parents to discard their idols. The young girl even threw away the idols herself, to her grandfather's ire. She won her mother and grandmother and eventually even her grandfather became a Christian. The mother, in turn, became an "ardent evangelist" and successful Bible woman, itinerating from village to village, telling thousands of women and children of Christ. Another Chaocheng worker, Mrs. Kao, bore 13 children (five of whom lived to maturity) before her husband died and she was reduced to begging. She became a Christian, and soon thereafter a Bible woman. She served as the Wieses' language assistant during their early days, and became close personally to Katherine Wiese. Kao was called to preach and was stationed in a variety of localities. Another woman, Hsu Kweipin's wife, was educated in a Christian home for girls in the South Chili Mission, and, confessed her husband, was "a truer, hotter-hearted Christian than I am."[34] She taught in the school for girls at Daming.[35]

Not only did the mission refuse to enroll girls in their primary schools if their feet were bound, but in the Bible school women were educated alongside men (even if they had to enter their classrooms by separate doors). They served as Bible women, which meant not only teaching and praying with other women, but preaching and evangelizing entire families. If their spouses were pastors, the Bible women worked alongside them as partners in ministry, and often spearheaded local missionary societies.

The example of strong women among the missionaries, both those married and those single, such as Vieg, provided an alternative model of being a woman in Chinese society. Unlike other missions, a Nazarene woman missionary, whether married or single, was never merely an "associate missionary." She was expected to and did have a significant ministry role. If they were not nurses or doctors, many missionary women preached and taught.

Other social ministries included the expanding medical work, which provided contacts with potential converts. The NHA maintained dispensaries. Both the Southern Baptists and Presbyterians had hospitals in Shandong Province. In 1926 American Presbyterians were supporting 49 hospitals in China, including a School of Medicine at the Christian University in Jinan, Shandong—not far from the Nazarene field.[36]

For the Nazarenes, Bresee Memorial Hospital in Daming became an important ministry. The Woman's Foreign Missionary Society and California laypersons undertook the building project. C. J. Kinne, a Nazarene publisher who had spearheaded the fund-raising, and who late in life married Susan Bresee, the daughter of Phineas Bresee, went to China to oversee the building's construction. When completed in 1925, the hospital accommodated one hundred beds. A nurses' training school began soon after, with missionary nurses as instructors. The hospital was designed, as Kinne wrote, to be both a "'Good Samaritan' to relieve the sufferings of the people and an evangel of mercy to lead them to Christ."[37] Both motives were there, both paradigms represented: that of ministering to people simply out of love, and that of evangelizing them through medicine. The social and evangelical components of the work were held in balance, though the hospital seemed to need to justify its existence in the years ahead by appealing to its evangelistic role. Despite fundamentalist pressures, the Nazarenes kept their medical, educational and other social work through the years in China.[38]

Medical doctor R. G. Fitz arrived in 1920. He was in charge of the medical work for several years. But Fitz felt called to evangelism, and the mission secured other doctors, both Chinese and missionaries, to help him in the hospital.[39]

The hospital's workers were helpful in initiating a revival that swept through the Nazarene mission in 1926–1927—right on the eve of a nationalist rebellion that swept the country. Antiforeign feeling in China had been rising since 1919, when the Treaty of Versailles sanctioned spheres of influence in China. The Treaty, which China refused to sign, gave to Japan the German sphere of influence in Shandong Province, close to the Nazarene field. Chinese realized and were discontent with the realization that missionaries gained from the unequal treaties that Western powers forced China to accept. In early 1926 some Nazarene church workers were dismissed for making antiforeign statements.[40]

Dr. C. E. West, in charge of the hospital during Fitz's furlough, began to pray for revival while recuperating from smallpox. Missionaries at the Daming compound set a daily prayer time, 11:30–12:00 noon, which was later extended. Soon the Chinese workers and students petitioned to have their own prayer meeting. Missionaries themselves felt spiritually transformed.[41]

Aaron J. Smith, the Nazarene field superintendent at this time (while Kiehn was on furlough), became convinced that not only was he himself as yet unsanctified, but unsaved. Smith (originally Schmidt) was the brother of Anna Kiehn and had Mennonite background. He had attended both Central Holiness College in Iowa and Chicago Theological Seminary. He pastored Congregationalist and Evangelical churches in America while applying to become a Nazarene missionary. He had little direct acquaintance with the Church of the Nazarene before he arrived in China in 1920. He became so burdened with guilt, during the 1926 revival, that he confessed his faults to his Chinese houseboy and to a mason on the compound, both of whom he believed he had offended. Further confessions impressed certain Chinese with Smith's humility. Smith prayed, studied, and read of John Wesley's *A Plain Account of Christian Perfection*. Then, Smith testified, "The Holy Spirit came upon me like an electric current and vibrated through my whole soul and body." Perhaps, upon reading this, Reynolds wondered whether this China revival would be like the similar one in India about fifteen years before, which produced dubious results, and whether Smith would turn out to be someone like M. D. Wood. Smith pointedly assured Reynolds that though he felt himself baptized with the Holy Ghost and fire he did not speak in unknown tongues, but only praised God with a loud voice in English.[42]

To the worry of holiness missionaries, Pentecostalism was growing in China. One of the missionaries formerly affiliated with the Houlding mission had returned to China in 1908 after receiving the "Pentecostal blessing" of speaking in tongues at Azusa Street in Los Angeles. He and others established a Pentecostal mission in Zhengding, about half way between Handan and Beijing.[43]

Spiritual deepening experiences like Smith's, though not so extreme, took place among other Nazarene missionaries and soon the revival touched the Chinese. The revival helped to convince the missionaries that the Chinese were spiritually capable of both maintaining and advancing the church. In the missionaries' minds, signs of spiritual maturity were related to spiritual crisis experiences and external manifestations. When Chinese asked forgiveness from one another, testified to receiving the Holy Spirit, and voiced loud "hallelujahs" and "amens," the missionaries concluded, as the mission policy statement said, that men and women demonstrated spiritual victory in the same way across cultures. Smith typified this sentiment: "When the Holy Ghost gets hold of a man, I care not of what nation or tribe or language he may be, there will be the same manifestation of the Holy Spirit which has been peculiar to all the holy people of all ages."[44] Osborn realized that he had been mistaken as to how the Chinese would react once they "got through." He felt that he had limited God and by his pessimism had been a stumbling block to some.[45]

Now Osborn saw Chinese tithing voluntarily, witnessing spontaneously, and catching a vision for the work. West even stated that it was time for the missionaries to stand aside to let God work through the Chinese. Before, West now realized, some Chinese had been so dependent on missionaries that they had neither sought spiritual victory for themselves, nor thought themselves even so worthy. Similarly, Smith, after the revival crested, believed that God was able to carry on his "own work in his own way among the Chinese . . . perhaps even better than the foreigners."[46]

Leaders in Kansas City did not return Smith to China after his furlough in 1927, but they could not help his speaking widely of his experiences throughout the denomination. His book on the China revival, *Jesus Lifting Chinese*, was not published by the Church of the Nazarene, its leaders understandably embarrassed. Had they sent out a missionary who, as he now confessed, had not even been saved when he had arrived on the field?

Smith became superintendent of the Manitoba–Saskatchewan District in 1930. After some years, he left the Church of the Nazarene and became quite critical of it. Later he served as president of a college in Highpoint, North Carolina, associated with the People's Methodist Church. Against the mainstream of holiness theology, Smith associated the baptism with the Holy Spirit and Pentecost with new birth rather than entire sanctification, a view for which he was dismissed from the presidency of the college. Smith also was actively involved in later years in the search for Noah's Ark.[47]

The revival at the Bible Training School in Daming affirmed both the spiritual character of the educational work and the capabilities of the students. The school began in 1923 with a two-year course. Thirty students of varying educational backgrounds enrolled. The Nazarene school trained ministers and emphasized evangelistic goals. Unlike the colleges being established by larger denominations, the Nazarene school had no lofty goals toward transforming society or educating the gentry. Its call was to the rural peasants. Though students were required to pay their own way, there were always more applicants for admission than the school was able to care for. The Nazarene school was open to anyone, man or woman, as long as the person was a Christian and professed a call to ministry.[48]

The school was led by Francis Sutherland, a Canadian educated at Montreal Theological College (M.A. and S.T.L.). He had worked with the Student Volunteer Movement before venturing as a Nazarene missionary to China in 1920. When the revival came upon the mission compound in 1926, Sutherland dismissed the school sessions and Chinese teachers and students scattered to their hometowns. In this way the revival spread throughout the Nazarene field. This was a very different student activity than what had transpired some time earlier, when the same Bible school students had taken to the streets of Daming making speeches against foreigners.[49]

Although mostly abated in the Nazarene mission by the revival, antiforeign feeling in China rampaged in 1926–1927. While for the most part missionaries opposed the "extraterritoriality" privileges being demanded by foreign governments of the Chinese, new restrictions imposed by the Guomindang government of Chiang Kai-shek forced many primary schools run by missions, including those of the Church of the Nazarene, to close. The government required not only that schools register, but that each day students stand three minutes in silence and bow in reverence to a picture of Sun Yat-sen. By 1927 antiforeignism was so strong that about 50 percent of all missionaries in China left their fields. In March of that year Nazarene missionaries took refuge in Tianjin, where the NHA maintained a mission station and Bible school and stayed there until June, when many of the missionaries, including Smith, returned to North America for furloughs. Some never returned to China. Their consolation was their newly found confidence in the Chinese to carry on the work.[50]

The political situation reified in their minds, and in the minds of their missionary colleagues in other missions, the urgency of firmly establishing the Chinese church. Beyond this, and what the insurgency meant for the continuation of their ministries, Nazarene missionaries expressed little interest in Chinese politics. To a degree, it may have been the German Mennonite background of many of the Nazarene missions in China that created ambivalence toward wider political concerns—but holiness people in general in the 1920s, including those in the United States, drew away from social responsibilities.[51]

## A Sense of Urgency

Chiang Kai-shek stabilized matters somewhat by establishing a national government under the Guomindang in Beijing, and missionaries returned to the field in mid-1928. Under the pressures of nationalism, like other Protestant missionaries at the same time Nazarenes returned under greater antiforeign fervor and violent civil turmoil, but with renewed commitments toward establishing a self-reliant church. Unlike some Presbyterian, American Board, Methodist and other missionaries, Nazarenes did not envision even in these tumultuous times joining the wider Christian community in a united Protestant church. The strong denominational distinctions of the church kept Nazarenes apart from such possibilities.[52]

Peter Kiehn resumed his role as mission director after returning from furlough in 1928. Like other successful pioneer missionaries, Kiehn remained "self-confident, temperamentally certain, and occasionally self-assertive."[53] He favored a complete organization of the China district. Especially given the political and social situation, it was necessary, said Kiehn, for missionaries to stay in the background and to serve as advisers while training Chinese workers. He had full confidence in the Chinese people's spiritual readiness. Kiehn found that they received and experienced entire sanctification in the "old fashioned" holiness way. He believed that Chinese pastors possessed a sense of belongingness to the church, and that Chinese laypersons would support it. With the aim of eventually ending all foreign support, Kiehn believed that the mission's money should be used to open new work rather than to support already established churches and their pastors. But Kiehn found that his ideas and his methods were not always acceptable to fellow missionaries.[54]

There was greater urgency toward self-support and self-government during the lean years preceding and during the Great Depression. The sharp decline in giving for missions limited the general church's expenditures overseas. J. G. Morrison, foreign missions secretary, sent a letter in 1930 to the Chinese church that plainly related the problem. He stated that the Chinese should cooperate with the missionaries, while each congregation should support its own pastor by tithing, fasting and praying. If they were able to do so, Morrison wrote, the general church could open new fields among the unreached in other parts of China, as well as in the Philippines and portions of Europe. He appealed to the Chinese church's own sense of mission. Morrison knew as well that for either political or economic reasons missionaries might at any time be forced out of China and he wanted the Chinese church's own leaders to be ready.[55]

In preparation for this, in 1931 the missionaries allowed the Chinese to choose eight Chinese pastors to compose a district board, one step toward greater self-government. Among the pastors on the board was Hsu Kwei-pin, the only Chinese elder, who had been ordained in 1929 by General Superintendents Roy T. Williams and John Goodwin. Formerly affiliated with both the Presbyterian Church and Houlding's South Chili Gospel Mission, Hsu pastored Nazarene churches in Chaocheng and Daming, where he also served as a teacher in the Bible school. Another leader on the board was Wu Tung-tai, who worked in the bandit-plagued area of Peikao before transferring to Chichei. He and his wife evangelized through tent meetings.[56]

By early 1933 six Chinese workers felt bold enough to ask for a say and a vote in mission council proceedings, on equal footing with missionaries. There was still no officially organized district assembly in China. What had formerly been called such were really mission council meetings that extended certain privileges to the Chinese—sponsoring annual meetings with representatives from the churches and outstations. But the composition and purpose of these meetings were not defined in Nazarene polity. The Chinese workers felt criticism from outsiders about the work being run totally by foreigners. They also questioned whether the missionaries who routinely assigned workers to various jobs and locations were following policy, which they knew emphasized the training and education of Chinese workers. The request signaled the desire of Chinese leaders for more self-determination.[57]

Actually there may have been an additional, hidden agenda in the request of the Chinese, if, as missionaries surmised, Peter Kiehn prompted them toward this action. The autocratic leadership of Kiehn came to a point of exasperation for the other missionaries, who forced Kiehn from the superintendency of the mission in January 1933. Earlier the missionaries had voiced their complaints to headquarters officials about Kiehn not adhering to policies, including that of holding an election for the superintendency. They wondered if Kansas City had given him some "extraordinary powers" that placed both him and the field outside of mission policies and *Manual* requirements. They were, they said, distressed and confused. Morrison sent Kiehn a telegram in October 1932 instructing him to hold a council meeting and to retain the superintendency—*if* elected. Policies were in force in China, Morrison instructed Kiehn. Though Kiehn held the meeting, he did not call for an election. There followed another spate of telegrams back and forth between the missionaries and Morrison. Finally, Kiehn resigned. Morrison then appointed Harry Wiese to convene a council meeting, which was held in February 1933. At the meeting the Kiehns protested nearly every proposal generated by the other missionaries, especially the one that transferred them from Daming to Chaocheng. They walked out of the meeting in protest. The Kiehns proposed that they be stationed at Kwangping, to the north, if they must leave. Then, after this seemed to be agreed upon by all, they changed their minds and requested to move to Chaocheng after all, where, they hoped, they might have charge of the surrounding area and be accountable directly to Morrison rather than to the other missionaries.[58]

In the meantime Kiehn raised some Chinese leaders' ire against Wiese, who the missionaries had elected superintendent. Morrison (who at the same time was trying to work through the situation with Staples and Kitagawa in Japan) accused Kiehn of plotting against the mission and chastised him for raising up a pro-Kiehn faction among the Chinese. When Morrison sought advice on the problems in China from members of the Foreign Missions Department of the General Board and the general superintendents, most admonished Morrison to recall Kiehn from the field. Nevertheless, since J. B. Chapman planned to visit China as well as Japan in 1935, Morrison postponed action. He hoped that the general superintendent could solve some of the problems.[59]

Before Chapman's arrival, the General Board received remarkable letters from Chinese leaders seemingly in support of Kiehn. But the letters expressed more than that, a longing for autonomy. The Chinese leaders stated that they realized that Kiehn had faults. They wished that he would confess them to the Lord. Nevertheless they wanted Kiehn to remain. Many older Chinese, they reminded the General Board, had been converted under his ministry. The Chinese leaders criticized Wiese for being a "typewriter missionary." But they thought the factionalism that was wrecking the field even worse than the faults of either Kiehn or Wiese. Though they were grateful for the money given from America for the Chinese church, the leaders stated: "We do not hope to receive such help financially, also we hope that the time will come when we will not need people of other countries to preach for us. We sincerely hope that we can be free, that is self-supporting and propagating . . . that we may help the poor and needy in our land." The sentiments of the Chinese leaders demonstrated a certain nationalism as well as sense of spiritual equality in the face of the wrangles among the missionaries. By this time, they seemed to say, after twenty years of

Nazarene missions work in the area, the financial commitments of the church were about all the justification left for retaining any of the missionaries.[60]

Wiese was already moving toward transferring responsibilities to the Chinese church, but the Chinese misunderstood his intentions. He thought of self-support as "a means to increase the spiritual vitality of the churches." Wiese believed that the incentive for self-support was greater self-government, wherein a pastor would be, as he should be, held accountable to the local congregation. One of his other concerns was that the local churches have the titles to their own property. But he felt that simply giving it to them outright would not generate either a sense of stewardship or ownership. The land had been purchased, of course, by the mission, but the mission never intended to hold the property permanently. Wiese suggested that local churches buy the land from the mission at one-twentieth of its cost each year for twenty years. After the final payment the property would be turned over to a proposed central church organization under the Chinese. But the Chinese leaders argued that the property already purchased did not rightly belong to the mission, but to the church—and they were the church as much as anyone. They wanted the property transferred to them without any payments on their part.[61]

Thus when Chapman arrived in October 1935, high on his agenda were the clarification of the relationship between the Chinese churches and the mission council, and the placement of the Kiehns. Chapman saw that policy concerning the maintenance of strict separation between the mission council and the Chinese church was not being followed. This led to confusion on the part of the Chinese leaders, who wanted to control the stationing of national workers and to have a say in how money was spent. The problem was compounded by there being no real district assembly.

In response, Chapman reminded both the missionaries and the Chinese leaders that the aim of the church was to develop "self-directing and self-supporting" churches. Problems commonly arose, Chapman told them, when the indigenous church clamored for self-direction before it achieved self-support. He assured the Chinese that the missionaries would stay only as long as necessary, meaning, until the churches were able financially to carry on for themselves. "And just as we hope that the indigenous church may become self-directing and self-supporting, the mission must remain so itself, and when this is impossible or unnecessary, the mission should be definitely withdrawn and the field left to the indigenous church." The Chinese church was to have full control over all the finances it raised, Chapman reminded everyone, and the missionaries were to serve only as advisers regarding such. In the same way the finances from the general church channeled through the mission council were to be used totally at the missionaries' discretion. This meant, Chapman further explained, that when mission money was used to support a worker, he or she would be stationed wherever the missionaries deemed best.

Chapman allowed the Chinese Annual Meeting to continue in the place of full district organization, despite the fact that there were no provisions in policy for such. Chapman also told the missionaries and Chinese workers, "There is the strongest bond in the world that binds us together, and that is our love for the Lord Jesus Christ. This bond is stronger than blood or race or language . . . and it is sufficient to make us one in both purpose and effort. We want to spread his Kingdom everywhere because of our love for him."[62]

Apparently there were enough tensions between Chinese leaders and missionaries to warrant both the admonitions that Chapman gave and his cautiousness toward the Chinese government of the church. No Chinese workers were ordained by Chapman at this time.[63]

Chapman then tackled the problem with the Kiehns. Chapman felt that much of the turmoil resulted from having too many missionaries stationed in Daming and from their having too little supervision from the general church. He realistically noted that the strain between the Kiehns and the other missionaries was "practically unbearable," and concurred with the plan to send the Kiehns to Kwangping, where they might have charge of four counties in Hebei Province, in the northwestern reaches of the field. But he also believed that Wiese, whom the missionaries again elected superintendent of the field while Chapman was present, should be stationed in Chaocheng, to spearhead the work in the southeastern end. Osborn would have temporary charge of the Bible school and Fitz the hospital, so that both could remain in Daming. Chapman hoped that by separating these leaders the talents of all would be maximized. He genuinely believed that the decentralization of the missionaries was best for the fullest evangelization of the field. The Kiehns seemed reconciled at the council meeting. With Chapman there, they apologized to the other missionaries on several counts.[64]

Regarding the hospital work, Chapman was impressed with both Dr. Henry Wesche, a NHA missionary who was giving part-time service to the Nazarene work, and Dr. Feng Lan-xin, who was proving to be a "true Christian and a good surgeon, and a tireless worker." Chapman hoped that Feng, a graduate of Shandong Christian University and School of Medicine, who spoke English well and who was paid a higher salary than other Chinese workers, would stay permanently at

Bresee Hospital. But within a short time the doctor left the Nazarene work and joined the Jesus Family Movement. This was an indigenous sect that emphasized spiritual gifts and the imminent return of Jesus.[65]

Other doctors—both Chinese and missionary—followed for brief periods. Hester Hayne worked at the hospital as a nurse from 1921 to 1926. Following her evacuation in 1926 and furlough, she finished a medical degree at the University of Kansas. Returning to China in 1934, she continued studies at the Peking Union Medical Center and served at Bresee Hospital from 1936 to 1941. In the meantime, Wesche had become full-time with the Nazarene mission.[66]

The Bible school reopened in the fall of 1935 under Osborn. While operating from 1923 to 1928 as a two-year course, only one class had graduated. During the interim years missionaries sent the most promising pastors elsewhere, such as to the NHA school in Tianjin, for their education. After several years on furlough, Francis Sutherland returned in 1936 to resume charge of the school. The structured and regimented life of the students, along with the tuition they paid (which made the school self-supporting) neither dampened the spiritual ardor of the students nor hindered numbers from applying. Many were turned away for lack of housing on the compound. About 130 were enrolled in the late 1930s. Among the teachers was Hsu Kwei-pin who was made vice-president in 1939. He and other teachers emphasized evangelism and the school regularly sent bands of students into the field to evangelize. One group sent into Daming County in 1939, for instance, included 68 workers who visited 133 villages and preached to more than 22,000 people. One large class was prepared for graduation in 1940, and another smaller one for 1941.[67]

Among the Chinese educators beside Hsu Kwei-pin was Lu Yu-cheng, dean of men. Sutherland noted that Lu gave all his spare time to preaching and giving personal advice to students. When Lu was killed in a Japanese attack on Chengan in 1938, Sutherland remarked: "I feel personally that I have lost one of my best friends."[68]

By all accounts the most outstanding student, frequently employed as an evangelist even while studying, was Chang Chin. He came from a Christian family of modest means and was converted during a revival in Daming in 1927, when he was about 13 years old. However, unable to get the education he desired, he joined the army of General Feng Yu-hsiang, a warlord with ties to the Soviet Union, and became a Communist. He became the leader of the Communists in his village of Yuchachai. During a revival that the renowned Dr. Song Shang-jie (John Sung) held at Daming in 1935, Chang decided to leave politics. Soon he entered the Bible school. A zealous worker, his success in making converts even during these early years was greater than more experienced pastors.[69]

The work of Chang typified the evangelistic fervor of the field in the late 1930s. Missionaries such as John Pattee were involved in village evangelism. He trained a succession of students at the Bible school in preaching and soul winning by traveling with them from town to town. Protégés of Pattee included Kao E-feng, who was an atheist before his conversion; Chi Yuew-han (John Chi), who was raised by zealous Buddhists, but who also had a Presbyterian background; Li Sui-chung, who was from a poor family and was influenced to become a Christian through the relief work undertaken by the church during famine times; Shang Chih-rung, whose father had been a worker with the Houlding mission; and Yuan Hsuan-ch'un (Allen Yuan), whom Pattee met while undertaking language study in Beijing. Yuan also worked in the late 1930s with Song Shang-jie (John Sung). The evangelistic teams attracted crowds of five or six hundred at village fairs and market days.[70]

The sound of artillery punctuated the evangelistic services, however, when the Japanese moved to conquer northern China in 1937. This followed episodes with Chinese bandits, and a time of famine, flooding and even earthquake. When the Japanese invaded, missionaries hung a large American flag prominently in the center of the mission compound. As the Japanese still did not want to widen the war, this protected the missionaries and Chinese workers for a time. The compound thus served as a refuge for Chinese workers. In 1938 Japanese ground troops reached Daming. By this time, following the warnings of American Secretary of State Cordell Hull, most American missionaries had already evacuated their fields. Except for Wiese, the Nazarene missionaries fled again to Tianjin, on the coast. Indeed the Chinese deemed Wiese's willingness to stay and suffer with them during the siege of their city heroic. The war destroyed the large church at Chaocheng, along with missionary residences there. The Japanese allowed missionaries to return to the field in 1939. The missionaries, themselves deeply disturbed by the Japanese and empathetic to the plight of the Chinese, sensed that the Chinese people were now open to the gospel more than ever. Prayer meetings and even evangelistic bands continued to meet and spread the message of salvation under the eyes of the Japanese occupation forces.[71]

Even though Wiese was a cautious leader in this regard, the church made identifiable progress toward the indigenization of leadership. Wiese realized that as long as money from the United States supplied the various needs of the field there was little incentive for self-support.

Like other missionaries, he worried that if the Chinese were Christian only for material benefit—if they were only "rice Christians"—the church was not really the church. When churches erected their own buildings, as did the congregation in Pei-i-ko in Puchow County, and when they sponsored their own evangelistic campaigns, it pleased Wiese. Even whether the mission should provide a thin soup to all who attended various district meetings seemed to Wiese a matter of self-support, and the mission stopped the practice.

Wiese also believed that the second generation of Christians more than the first would be ready to carry on the church. Only in the second generation were certain Christian moral and ethical standards able to replace the cultural, he said. Whereas the first generation of converts often was only "nominal," succeeding generations were truly "evangelical." [72]

Wiese's assessments regarding the spiritual nature of the Chinese Christians were more pessimistic than Kiehn's and others' had been, especially during the previous revival. By the 1930s the older leaders had been Christians for nearly a generation, and a new, strong band of young leaders was emerging that naturally desired more independence. Wiese's attitudes reflected the hesitancies of missionaries to sufficiently trust the local church that they themselves nurtured—or, a hesitancy to relinquish their own positions as church leaders.

In 1939 the foreign missions secretary, C. W. Jones, set a policy for all of the fields by which all general church money would be used for starting new work, rather than supporting the existing. This plan would be phased in slowly. Indeed in China the church still had not reached 4,000 villages in the Nazarene field. The local Chinese churches, so challenged, agreed to cover immediately 10 to 40 percent of their pastors' salaries and other expenses. When a change of pastors at the Daming church was necessary in 1940 due to the increased responsibilities of Hsu Kwei-pin in district affairs, the mission required the church's deacons to provide a full salary to the man they chose as their new pastor—Yu Wan-ch'ien. [73]

In turn, Chinese leaders in September 1940 pressed for a "Committee of Twenty-Four," which might have the right to hold the annual meetings when sanctioned by the General Board, and to both hire and dismiss workers if war forced the missionaries again to leave the field. The committee was to include ten lay persons and have a five-member executive committee with a chairman, Hsu Kwei-pin, who was still the only ordained pastor. In fact the Chinese promised to care for the missionaries in case their salaries and other support from America should be cut off due to the war. No formal action was taken on this plan, which had no justification in either the Nazarene *Manual* or mission policy. But at this point, with war looming closer, the missionaries felt that they could not yet anticipate what course of action might be necessary. In the meantime they prepared to nominate several others for ordination.[74]

In early 1941 missionaries further strengthened Chinese leadership by placing Hsu Kwei-pin in charge of the Bible school and designating him to become "chairman" of the district if the missionaries left. They had faith in Hsu, who had worked closely together with Wiese for years. Indeed, as Katherine Wiese later described it, Wiese and Hsu "worked together like one man; they loved each other and had faith in the other. Truly Hsu was co-superintendent as Brother Wiese always consulted him on Chinese problems. . . . These two men had worked together constantly for nearly eleven years. Sometimes Hsu was head, sometimes Brother Wiese, but I don't believe either thought of who was boss. They were workers together and loved each other like David and Jonathan."[75]

On personal levels, perhaps even more than on formal ones, missionaries did see their roles as supporters and fellow workers. Indeed, the relation of missionaries to national workers, said Wiese, should be one of friends, partners and comrades. As for other leaders, missionaries appointed Wong Pao-hsi vice-president of the school and Dr. S. E. Liu, from Fujian Province who had recently graduated from Peking Union Medical College, as head of the hospital. Most missionaries looked upon the increased leadership of the Chinese favorably, while a few, including Osborn, believed that such fifteen more years of Bible school graduates and saying, "For us to go soon would be losing much that has been invested."[76]

Tensions still remained between Kiehn and the other missionaries. During the Kiehns' last term in China, 1928–1938, they had planted several new churches in the northwestern section of the field—from Chengan, where they ultimately stationed themselves, to Handan, the site of the main railroad station, where they established a thriving congregation. By 1938 the Japanese made missionary work in the area impossible, and the Kiehns somewhat suddenly decided to furlough. During their following deputations tour, American congregations received them gloriously as the pioneer missionaries that they were. But in China missionaries unanimously asked the department not to return the Kiehns to the field. The Kiehns had caused too many tensions with other missionaries across the years. Jones and other leaders agreed with the missionaries on the field and decided not to send the Kiehns back to China. As their furlough extended, the Kiehns became aware of the church's desire to retire them although they were only in their mid-fifties. They then approached the National Holiness Association with the idea of going back to their old field. C. W. Ruth, by this time president of the NHA mission board, was not sympathetic to the idea. Kiehn then advised the Nazarene Department to divide the China field into two districts—he would take the northwest district. Neither Jones nor the missionaries on the field wanted this, but how could Jones explain to loyal Nazarenes in the States why the Kiehns were not being sent back?

By 1940 Jones had decided to try to send Kiehn to begin a work—far from Daming—in what was then called "Free China," in Yunnan Province. However, the church needed permission from the U.S. State Department for this and it was the government's policy to allow missionaries there, through the Burma Road, only if either they or their denomination had a previously established work. Though Jones attempted to secure a visa for Kiehn on grounds that it was likely that Nazarenes from the northern field had fled there, the State Department rejected the reasoning. Finally, the declaration of war with Japan made the question entirely moot, and nothing came of the attempt to open a new field in Free China.[77]

This is where the church stood, then, when the war situation forced the missionaries to evacuate North China for virtually the last time. At the time there were 130 enrolled in the Bible school, with a fully Chinese faculty of 8; 134 workers, including the medical staff, Bible women, and 75 pastors; 54 organized churches; 2,120 full and 3,412 probationary members; and 8 elementary schools enrolling 260 students. The Chinese church also was contributing well to the overall expenses.[78]

The Japanese incarcerated the Nazarene missionaries on the field at the time of Pearl Harbor, Leon and Emma Osborn, John Pattee, Arthur Moses, who had recently arrived to help administer the hospital, and Mary Scott, who also had but recently come to China. When the Japanese took over the mission compound they also jailed Hsu and Yu for forty days. While the missionaries remained interred in the area for six months they deeded the Bible school to the Chinese and handed over a complete record of all other property held by the church, including the hospital, which by this time the Japanese military had confiscated. The Japanese eventually repatriated all except Scott, who expressed her preference to stay in China rather than seek repatriation and remained imprisoned through the duration of the war.[79]

While interred, Osborn, then serving as superintendent, irregularly authorized the Chinese church to ordain several Chinese pastors, including Yu Wan-ch'ien and Ma Hsueh-wen.[80] The Committee of Twenty-Four Chinese leaders met and planned the next annual meeting. As if to prove to the missionaries that the church would go on without them, by the time the interred missionaries left the country the Chinese had already built four new churches.[81]

The persecution of the church during the war with Japan only seemed to increase the number of preaching places, and churches assumed full support of their pastors. Hsu Kwei-pin continued the Bible school until 1942 or 1943 and significant workers were added to those who had graduated previously.

The situation "by one stroke made the Chinese church entirely independent and self-supporting."[82] The irony was that the Chinese church would not have been as able to carry on later, under communism, if it had not first had to endure the "second imperialism" of the Japanese.[83] The achievement of self-support, self-government and self-propagation came not at the end of the slow processes of missions strategy and planning, but because of social and political realities. Only a few workers left the mission. At least two young leaders, Kao E-feng, whom the missionaries had tried unsuccessfully to send to Pasadena College, and Shang Chih-rung fled to northwestern China.[84]

There were no further contacts with the field until the end of the war. When the Japanese evacuated at the close of the war, the Communist army of Mao Ze-dong quickly moved in. Like other missionaries, the Nazarenes recalled the execution of missionaries John and Mary Stam by Chinese Communists in 1934.[85] Nevertheless Wiese and Pattee returned to Beijing in 1946 and had conversations with Yuan Hsuan-ch'un and others from the Daming area. Yuan had preached in Chengan during the war and had recently transferred to Beijing, where he, along with Chao, who had graduated from the Bible school in 1942 or 1943, worked with a Norwegian missionary. Yuan and others advised Wiese and Pattee that it was best for them not to attempt a trip to the Daming area but to send word to the field that they were in the country and to wait for some of the workers to come to Beijing. Wiese and Pattee also received a report from Yu Wan-ch'ien, who along with Hsu Kwei-pin had remained in Daming for the duration, that only about six pastors remained engaged in full-time ministry. Two pastors had been killed outright during the civil war. As Communists criticized pastors for taking money from the poor, some had begun businesses or taken second jobs to support themselves and their families. In turn, local congregations reduced support to them. Wiese lamented this.

Unwilling to wait in Beijing, Pattee secured permission to visit Handan with a United Nations worker distributing medicine there, and clandestinely traveled to Daming at the same time. He found the large church building on the compound completely destroyed and the other buildings taken over by the county government. The county magistrate himself was living in one of the missionary residences. Both Wiese and Pattee realized that though it was still theoretically possible for missionaries to work in the area, the Communist government would severely curtail their activities. They would not be able to visit other stations, the chief buildings of which were also now in government hands. It was hard for Christians in general. Authorities constantly questioned Christians and their worship activities. But Wiese and Pattee were heartened that laypersons were carrying on the faith.[86]

Meanwhile, at the close of the war Peter and Anna Kiehn, who had become involved with the Chinese Nazarene work in Los Angeles during the war, returned to China. They believed that they had the blessings of the church, but they financed themselves—supported by friends and relatives. They opened a mission in Beijing assisted by Mr. and Mrs. Kuan, who had previously ministered with the Salvation Army. Kiehn began to organize the work along Nazarene lines and initiated measures of self-support before being forced to flee the city in late 1948. The Kiehns made their way first to Shanghai (where they met General Superintendent Orval Nease who was visiting the field in Jiangxi that the Nazarenes by this time had begun), then to Hong Kong, and finally to Taiwan. Indeed they said later that Nease at the time had given his approval for their opening the work of the Church of the Nazarene in Taiwan.[87]

In succeeding years, in spite of periods of repression by the government, Christian workers advanced the church in the old field. As the result of migrations during the post-war years, no ordained Nazarene pastors remained on the field after 1947. Many buildings either had been destroyed or were being used for other purposes. If the church had been rigidly attached to these forms of churchly structure, there may have been less freedom to carry on in whatever ways were necessary and possible. In effect, the Gospel Mission and Mennonite work merged with the Nazarene in the area to form a loose but practical structure. As it turned out, committed leaders, graduates or former students of the Bible school, emerged on the basis of both gifts and preparation for ministry. They placed at least one Bible school graduate in each of the counties in which the Nazarenes had work. These maintained the respect of the people apart from any ecclesiastical sanctions.

That meant that when the support and control of the world church was cut off, the church not only survived, it flourished. The Nazarene churches registered with the government in the 1950s, and became part of the Three Selfs Patriotic Movement. Though the hospital and schools could not continue, pastors continued to preach the message of holiness as they had been taught it and to evangelize the unconverted.[88]

During the Cultural Revolution, which began in 1966, all churches were closed. Christians were persecuted. The church moved underground—into houses. After the Revolution, in 1982, the government issued "Document 19," which promised religious toleration and allowed churches to reopen. Once again, those churches that had been Nazarene registered with the government, and the workers affiliated again with the Three Selfs Patriotic Movement. Within it, situations varied; but pastors in the old Nazarene field—though forbidden to address political issues—continued to itinerate on county circuits, preach and teach. The former Nazarenes were able to maintain theological distinctions while participating in the Three Selfs church. Several graduates of the Bible school, including Chang Chin, continued to work as evangelists and pastors through the 1990s, until they were well past seventy and eighty years old. Many pastored while farming. Almost all of the leaders of the large church in Handan had roots in the Nazarene mission. The church remained strong in Chengan. In several places Bible women continued the work. One maintained work at the site of the Houlding mission outside of Daming. In 1992 the government allowed the reopening of a church inside the city itself. About the same time, a Bible school led by former Nazarenes was opened in Handan. Eventually, as the former Bible school graduates began to pass away, the children and grandchildren of these leaders continued and extended the ministry. They served as itinerant evangelists and Bible women, preaching and teaching holiness just as their fathers and mothers had done. A conservative estimate was that by that time there were 75,000 believers in the five Hebei Province counties in which the Church of the Nazarene had worked.[89]

## The Southern Field

Wiese and Pattee, certain, though mistakenly, that the Nationalist government would soon defeat the Communists and open up the old field again, turned their attention toward the possibility of the church entering a new area. They contacted the National Christian Council in Shanghai about which sections of the country might be open for work.

Upon the suggestion of the council, the Nazarenes chose a field in southern Jiangxi Province around the cities of Ji'an and Kanhsien. One strong factor in choosing this field was that Mandarin, the dialect the missionaries had learned in the North, was spoken in the area.

Even before the war, Chiang Kai-shek had been eager for Christian missions to establish themselves in this area, to form a bulwark against communism. Though both the Methodists and the China Inland Mission had been at work in the Ji'an and Kanhsien area, they were willing to give way to the Nazarenes. The Methodists, in fact, already had turned over their work to the Episcopalians, who did not prove to be evangelistic. The Roman Catholic Church was strong in the area, and the Seventh-day Adventists were present in Ji'an, but it still seemed to Wiese a "virgin territory" for the gospel. As yet there was little political unrest and the people seemed to welcome the church.[90]

Nazarenes began work in 1947. Katherine Wiese and Lillian Pattee soon joined their husbands. Others who arrived were R. G. and Lura Fitz and Mary Scott, from the old field, and newly appointed missionaries Michael and Elizabeth Varro (daughter of the Fitzes) and Ruth Brickman. Both Hsu Kwei-pin, whom the missionaries had feared was dead, and Yu Wan-ch'ien fled south from the Communists and found the Nazarene work. Yu became pastor of the church in Kanhsien. Contacts with Christians in the city easily persuaded them to join the Nazarene church. Hsu aided the Bible school, which began in October 1948. The mission quickly erected buildings in Ji'an and established a compound. In comparison to the work in the North, in which most of the converts were poor farmers, the members in the southern field were from the business and professional classes. As the months wore on the missionaries sensed the political reality that the Communists would take over the entire country. Just as they had in north China before the war with Japan, the missionaries intensified their efforts to raise a self-supporting church and promoted indigenous leadership.[91]

The work quickly came to a close. When General Superintendent Orval Nease toured eastern Asia in 1948 and visited Jiangxi, he officially recognized the earlier, irregular ordinations of Yu and Ma Hsueh-wen, who also had fled south. In addition, Nease ordained Chi Yuew-han. Chi had been taken into the church by Peter Kiehn in 1938 and had worked with John Pattee in Chengan before the war. From 1940 to 1944 he studied at North China Theological Seminary. Following his graduation he returned to Shandong Province to preach. With the spread of the Red Army in 1946, Chi fled south and made contact with the Nazarene missionaries in Jiangxi. Nease was impressed with both the Chinese leaders and the solid beginnings of the work, but he knew that evacuation of the missionaries was imminent. Even while he was there the American consul gave advice on this regard and several missionaries returned home. By 1949, after 21 months of work, all were forced out. At that time there were three organized churches and 70 members, plus 200 probationers. After the missionaries left, the Bible school continued under Hsu Kwei-pin for at least one year. Though the missionaries held some optimism about returning, it was the Chinese who carried on the work.[92]

Wiese became involved in promoting the Chinese work in California, hoping that he was training workers for the day when China would again be open. The Missions Department sent John and Lillian Pattee to the Philippines. The Kiehns and the Osborns turned to Taiwan, but did so independently. R. G. Fitz pioneered the Nazarene work in Alaska. Francis Sutherland found a position teaching history at Northwest Nazarene College. In 1950 Scott became general secretary of the denomination's Women's Foreign Missionary Society.

Meanwhile, a Chinese pastor in California, Mary Li, gained the attention of the church. She had been raised in mission schools and had been a member of a holiness church in Tianjin, perhaps affiliated with the NHA, and so was acquainted with the Church of the Nazarene. She went to the United States in 1947 under Youth for Christ auspices, leaving her husband, a medical doctor, in China. She joined the Church of the Nazarene in 1948 after becoming unhappy with the Youth for Christ program, and attended Pasadena College, studying theology under H. Orton Wiley. She received a master of arts degree in 1950. She then attended the Presbyterian Theological Seminary in San Anselmo and started a Chinese church in San Francisco. She was ordained a Nazarene minister on the Northern California District in 1952. Upset over the United States' involvement in the Korean War and feeling called to return to her homeland, she left for China in November 1954. She and her husband settled in Shanghai, where she taught Bible, English and music for seven years in the only theological seminary remaining open in China. Then the government forced its closing. Not until a letter from her reached World Mission Secretary Jerald Johnson in 1979 did the Church of the Nazarene resume contact with her.[93]

## Conclusion

In retrospect, though Nazarene missionaries worked both closely and congenially with Chinese workers, the development of national leadership as a whole was slow. Missionaries held on to positions of leadership. In old China pastors had to petition for positions of responsibility in the field even after revivals and evangelistic fervor proved their spiritual worthiness and equality with the North American workers. Their advancement and the eventual indigenization of the entire work in mainland China was prompted by political and social necessities, not by deliberate action on the part of either the mission council or the general church.

Though the church was by policy committed to the development of a district along the "episcopal" lines of Nazarene polity, rather than locally autonomous congregations, district organization lagged far behind the evangelistic aspect of the work. This proved advantageous. Were it not for the self-propagating part of the work, it would not have survived under changes of the government's policy toward Christianity. The Chinese, convinced of the necessity of self-direction, were independently heading toward this as well as toward self-support when political crises hastened the process. Part of the reason for the delay in both the advancement of Chinese leaders and the full organization of a district was related to the sporadic attention given to ministerial education. Not until the last years of work there did the church give concerted attention to this, but through intensive effort it developed a highly motivated, second generation of workers that carried on the church long after the missionaries left. Rather than attempting to resurrect an episcopal form of government, a "circuit" system, with Bible school graduates assigned to specific counties, was put into effect by common consent. The circuit system fit political realities.[94]

As important as were the evangelistic and social ministries of the church, the future depended largely upon a capable leadership. By the 1980s, "shouting" and other heresies developed in Shandong. Chinese leaders believed that their theological grounding had prevented more of these sorts of heterodox phenomena. But leaders still craved theological books and instruction through which a new generation of leaders might be indoctrinated in holiness.[95]

The evangelistic ministry of the church was tied somewhat to shifting political and economic realities, but the educational component, the passing on of tradition as well as practice, was necessary for the fullest development of the indigenous church. Without the Bible school graduates, both men and women, the work would have been much less. This is not to say that the Church of the Nazarene's work in China was laggard. The enthusiasm for spreading the faith by lay members and lay pastors kept the church on the mainland strong and growing. Indeed, if there had been a more hierarchical structure in place there, the evangelistic movement may have been more constrained.

# Taiwan

The entry of the Church of the Nazarene into Taiwan is only tenuously related to the story of the church in mainland China. Not many of the rural farmers from the Daming area migrated to Taiwan. Compared to other denominations that entered Taiwan soon after the closing of China to missionaries, the Church of the Nazarene was late in going to Taiwan—even though it entered other Asian and Pacific countries in the decade following the close of China. It missed the decade of greatest growth for Protestantism in Taiwan: 1948 to 1958. Unlike other denominations that transferred "old China hands" from the mainland to either Hong Kong or Taiwan, the Church of the Nazarene did not. For a while, leaders were afraid that the same thing would happen as had happened in Jiangxi, that the Communists would take over Taiwan. In spite of Taiwan appearing to many other denominations as a "missionary heaven,"[96] Nazarenes did not want to waste time and resources in what might amount to a short-term project. Leaders might also have been aware that the holiness movement-related Oriental Missionary Society already had a strong work on the island.[97]

When the church officially entered Taiwan in 1956 it chose not to use its former missionaries to mainland China. This was partly because many of them were already at work in other areas of the world and partly because the church saw the old missionaries as unprepared for the challenges of pioneering a new field. There could have been more direct ties to the work on the mainland, however, through Peter Kiehn and the work he and his wife established in Taiwan shortly after the Second World War. The church did not take over Kiehn's Taiwan Gospel Mission and its Chinese leaders, including one of the pastors ordained on the mainland, for reasons having to do with Kiehn's attitudes toward church structure and policies.

The Kiehns entered Taiwan after fleeing from Beijing in 1948. While officially retired and on pension by the Church of the Nazarene, they began a work called the Formosa (later Taiwan) Gospel Mission. Kiehn established a board of trustees for the Mission in Taiwan made up of strong Chinese leaders. Kiehn planted five churches and opened a Bible school. Kiehn used the Nazarene *Manual* and *Christian Theology* by Nazarene theologian H. Orton Wiley, part of which had been translated into Chinese by one of Kiehn's co-workers, Chung Lin-ching (Samuel Chung), as bases for polity and doctrine. C. B. Widmeyer, a prominent Nazarene educator, taught for some months at the school. Family and friends of Kiehn as well as former supporters of his work in China supported the Gospel Mission.

For a time the Gospel Mission also garnered financial support from the Voice of China, a radio program and mission organization based in Pasadena, California, led by Robert Hammond, a sometime Nazarene minister and formerly a missionary to Hong Kong under the South China Peniel Holiness Mission. Hammond solicited funds over his radio broadcast for used clothing for Taiwan and shipped these to Kiehn. With the millions of refugees fleeing the mainland in order to escape communism, Christians in the United States proved sympathetic, and tons of used clothing arrived in Taiwan.[98]

The Kiehns' co-workers were strong Chinese leaders. These included the ordained Nazarene minister Chi Yuew-han, who had fled from Jiangxi to Taiwan shortly after the Nazarene missionaries left in 1949. He taught in the Gospel Mission Bible Institute and served as its academic dean. Chung Lin-ching, a retired general in the Kuo Ming Tang army, had been a member of the Friends Church. A third associate of Kiehn was Ding Hsin, who opened a mission in Dahsi using rented facilities. Another was Pan Ming-ding, also a former army officer, who served as business manager for the mission. Eventually Kiehn persuaded Pan to attend the Bible school and enter the pastorate and he started a church at Yang Mei. Congregations in the Taiwan Gospel Mission, once established, had more autonomy than was provided for in Nazarene polity and boards of deacons rather than trustees. But apparently from the inception of the work Kiehn told his board, the workers and the churches of his hope to transfer the Mission to the Church of the Nazarene.[99]

Although the Nazarene Department of Foreign Missions was aware of Kiehn's work, in 1956 it asked L. C. Osborn to prepare a report in regard to the church's officially opening work in Taiwan. Osborn had returned to mainland China in 1947 under the sponsorship of Inter-Varsity and had held evangelistic meetings in the South. He thought this better than attempting to plant a work, since the Communist takeover seemed to him inevitable. He returned to the United States in 1948 and pastored Nazarene churches in Ohio for several years. In 1954 the Osborns went to Taiwan with Worldwide Evangelization Crusade. While there they became active in the Taiwan Leprosy Relief Association. In his report, Osborn advised Nazarene leaders not to affiliate with

Kiehn and Hammond. Based on his strained experiences with him in mainland China as much as his observations in Taiwan, Osborn thought Kiehn too domineering to allow for much cooperation with other missionaries.[100]

Nonetheless, the Church sent two missionary couples to Taiwan—Ray and Ruth Miller, and John and Natalie Holstead—with the possibility of building upon Kiehn's work very much in mind. The Millers had long missionary experience. They had been Pilgrim Holiness missionaries in Africa before joining the Church of the Nazarene and then had served the Nazarene Church in the Caribbean for seven years. They arrived in Taiwan in December 1956 and the Holsteads arrived the following month. The Kiehns greeted and entertained the Millers and then the Holsteads, then in their twenties, for whom Taiwan was their first assignment. Miller, whom the general superintendents had appointed to head the mission, found the Kiehns in financial difficulty. So immediately Miller started providing the Taiwan Gospel Mission $600 per month. The Holsteads moved into the Gospel Mission's Bible school and began studying Mandarin.

Miller found that there had been a recent rift and an ongoing lawsuit between Kiehn and Hammond, who had begun sending his own retinue of missionaries to Taiwan. These included Michael and Elizabeth Varro, former Nazarene missionaries in Jiangxi Province. Kiehn and Hammond were fighting each other in Taiwanese courts over property titles, which were held in Kiehn's name but which had been purchased with money donated through the Voice of China. Hammond threatened to stop sending to Kiehn the used clothing his broadcasts were generating. Miller told the Chinese government's relief association that the Church of the Nazarene itself would continue such efforts, even without Hammond. This seemed to have some bearing on the Taiwan court's final decision in favor of Kiehn. The Taiwanese courts gave Kiehn clear title to the properties. In turn, Kiehn assured Miller that when all was settled he would, as he put it, be able to hang "Church of the Nazarene" on the five Taiwan Gospel Mission churches and the Bible school.[101]

Michael and Elizabeth Varro helped to establish nine churches and various other programs under the Voice of China. Michael Varro, who remained a Nazarene minister, thought that Hammond would agree to turn over the work to the Church of the Nazarene. But Hammond made too many conditions for this to be effected. Varro's continued presence in Taiwan with another agency discomforted Nazarene missionaries in Taiwan. Eventually Varro left the Voice of China and worked in film evangelism and literature ministry and taught in several denominations' schools.[102]

With Kiehn's approval, by 1957 both Pan Ming-ding and Ding Hsin, and the Taiwan Gospel Mission churches they had initiated, had become Nazarene. In spite of this and the settlement with Hammond in favor of Kiehn, and Miller's help in solving the case, it was becoming clear that there were serious problems in bringing Kiehn's work into the Church of the Nazarene. Chung Lin-ching, who was both a pastor and prominent member of the Gospel Mission Board, had been divorced and remarried in a way out of harmony with the Nazarene *Manual*. There was also the matter of local church polity. More importantly, Kiehn and his board made certain demands to safeguard Kiehn's permanent leadership over the Nazarene work in Taiwan. He gave Miller five ultimatums in order for affiliation to be consummated: (1) that the Church of the Nazarene would erect new buildings on each of the three sites where the Taiwan Gospel Mission still had work, to be paid for entirely by the general church and started within six months; (2) that Chinese workers' salaries be increased; (3) that no worker would be dismissed except by the decision of local boards of deacons; (4) that Kiehn would be district superintendent of the Church of the Nazarene in Taiwan so long as he chose to remain there, with full salary as an active missionary and all other rights and privileges; and, (5) that if and when the Kiehns returned to the United States they would not be pensioned, but receive full missionary salary for life. Peter and Anna Kiehn were already past seventy years old.[103]

Though it is difficult to believe that Kiehn could have thought that the church would agree to all this—as it contradicted established policies—the Millers and the Holsteads met with Kiehn and the Gospel Mission Board to go over the demands point by point. The meeting was explosive. Miller referred to the mission policy then in effect (though often violated) that church buildings be at least half paid for with indigenous support. The request for the Chinese workers to receive more money reflected a "mercenary spirit," said Miller, since they already received more than other holiness denominations paid. The third point was not in keeping with the Nazarene *Manual*. The requests regarding Kiehn were beyond the possible, Miller was sure. As Miller stated these responses, the meeting, he later reported, "became increasingly violent." Gospel Mission Board members hurled insults at the Church of the Nazarene and stated their preference to remain independent. Chung Lin-ching especially opposed the idea of affiliation, and may have been behind much of the resistance to it, but Miller concluded that Kiehn himself may have never really intended to transfer the work to the

Nazarenes. To Miller his demands indicated a continuing vendetta against the church for what Kiehn perceived to be its wrong treatment of him in China. Chi Yuew-han wrote to the general superintendents on behalf of the Gospel Mission, complaining to them about Miller's intransigence. Holstead had tender feelings toward Kiehn and believed that the situation had been handled badly on both sides. But he agreed with Miller that the Nazarenes should be pleased to be rid of the Taiwan Gospel Mission. It had proven only to "hamper" and "hamstring" the program and advancement of the work on the island. By this time Holstead believed that nothing could be done to effect the merger. Thus the Church of the Nazarene lost Kiehn and Chi Yuew-han as well as the other workers and the three remaining Gospel Mission churches, but was free to build its own foundations.[104]

Kiehn retired from Taiwan in 1960 at age seventy-five. His personality patterns were productive when it came to relating to Chinese, but detrimental toward his relations with fellow missionaries and leaders in Kansas City. Kiehn turned over supervision of the six churches that then composed the Taiwan Gospel Mission to the International Gospel League, the Pasadena-based missions organization that had been founded by Nazarene ministers E. G. Anderson and Basil Miller. But the property deeds remained in Kiehn's name. Kiehn worked with Chinese Nazarene churches in Southern California almost until his death in 1974—a ministry to Chinese people that spanned nearly sixty-eight years.[105]

Chi Yuew-han left Kiehn after the split with the Church of the Nazarene and held revival services for a variety of denominations, including the Church of the Nazarene. Chi continued to call himself a Nazarene and to refer to his ordination by Nease. He pastored an independent church located in a factory that employed 3,000 workers.[106]

The matter with Kiehn had been settled. But the Nazarene Church in Taiwan continued to suffer grave leadership crises before progressing toward self-support, self-propagation and self-direction. Miller kept leadership positions tightly under his own control. He appointed himself president of the Nazarene Bible school (which began in 1958), district superintendent, missionary council president, and titular pastor of all of the local churches.

In 1958 the Church of the Nazarene offered a one-year contract, later extended, to the Osborns. This brought them once more into the work. They occasionally met people from the Daming area in Taiwan. One graduate of the Bible school in Daming became a successful banker in Taiwan but did not attend church. Another graduate, Kao E-feng, worked with the Baptists. Osborn pastored the church in Taipei, which had been started by Ruth Miller and Adam Lin through Sunday School evangelism some time before. Osborn was especially effective as an evangelist.[107]

Miller discouraged the Holsteads, George and Donna Rench, who arrived in 1959, and, later, other newly appointed missionaries from learning Chinese. Neither did he learn it himself. He believed Chinese to be a "heathen" language incapable of bearing the gospel.[108]

Though Miller agreed in 1962 to making Rench the principal of the college, he remained as "superintendent" of the school "system," which, in addition to the college, included a pre-school under Ruth Miller. This kind of action increasingly frustrated the younger missionaries. As Rench put it, "Brother Miller is a one man missionary team."[109] Under Miller the mission council became a kind of employer toward national workers. Responsibility for finances, church ownership and long-range planning rested with the missionaries. The general church typically paid for all church building costs in Taiwan. At Miller's request, Holstead, the mission treasurer, would pay pastors and other workers monthly. They were to submit all receipts and they would go over with Holstead the details of their expense reports. None of this seemed to promote progress within the church toward its stated goals or trust between Chinese pastors and missionaries.[110]

Miller kept overspending the yearly budget the church allotted to Taiwan. He frequently cabled Kansas City about some emergency need for money, and the church's missions secretary, George Coulter, would complain and then, often, send the amount Miller requested. But as "emergency" situations continued year after year, despite increases in its budget, Coulter began to wonder why the field could not stay within its allotment. Furthermore, the money that Miller asked for and spent often went unaccounted for. Miller simply asked Holstead for cash for undesignated expenses.[111]

In March 1962 General Superintendent V. H. Lewis visited Taiwan and convened a missionary council, which had never officially been organized. By this time the missionaries were completely frustrated with Miller but could not convince Lewis or Coulter to take immediate action.

The missionaries began to take the situation in their own hands. In a missionary council meeting in October that year the missionaries elected Harry Wiese, at the time serving in the Philippines but under consideration for reappointment to Taiwan, as chairman. Although this action required approval from the Department of Missions, Lewis and Coulter agreed to Wiese's appointment, effective January 1963. Coulter warned Wiese to avoid controversies and to maintain peace with the

Millers, but Wiese agreed to take up the responsibilities in Taiwan only with assurances from headquarters that he would have a sweeping enough authority to do whatever might be necessary. He had spent the previous five years in the Philippines trying to solve leadership and legal problems there that revolved around actions of another pioneering missionary, Joseph Pitts. The situation he faced in Taiwan was similar.[112]

The Osborns, who had been promoting their friends the Wieses for this position, retired later in 1963, the same year that the Wieses arrived. Osborn had reached the age of 70, but still wondered if he had been forcibly retired because of his opposition to Miller. The Osborns won permission from the general church to stay in Taiwan after retirement to resume work with the Taiwan Leprosy Relief Association.[113]

The Millers remained with the mission for almost a year after Wiese arrived. Miller refused an assignment south of Taipei (which he considered an "insult") and refused to leave the Shihlin church that he pastored. The Millers caused commotion in council meetings and tried to block various actions, especially those pertaining to themselves. (This must have reminded Wiese of the Kiehns' behavior toward fellow missionaries in mainland China decades earlier.) Meanwhile, without the knowledge and consent of the Missions Department, both Millers secured positions teaching at the American School in Taipei, which served primarily children of United States military personnel.[114]

Tense conditions remained between the Millers and the other missionaries. They suspected Miller of indiscretions with a Chinese woman, and were frustrated that Kansas City did not take seriously enough the embarrassment and shame his actions were causing. Ruth Miller suspected her husband's behavior in this regard but continued to defend him. Wiese and the other missionaries finally forced Kansas City to act. First, in May, Wiese offered his own resignation as superintendent. He complained that leaders in Kansas City were not following his recommendations to recall the Millers. He mentioned Miller's widely assumed relations with a Chinese woman. Coulter responded by promising to strengthen Wiese's authority but did not take immediate action regarding the Millers. The missionaries then wrote to Coulter and V. H. Lewis, the general superintendent in jurisdiction: "We have come to the conclusion to ask the Board to either take the undersigned missionaries home or the Millers." Their method, an ultimatum, "shocked and disappointed" Coulter, yet their action produced the desired effect. In November 1963 Coulter finally forced Miller out, not because of the charges of immorality, but for breach of contract—for teaching and earning a salary at the American School without permission from the department.[115]

After their dismissal, effective December 31, 1963, the Millers remained in Taiwan. They complained to Coulter that they had been condemned without a hearing. They began an independent work called the "Spring of Living Water," splitting in half the Shihlin congregation. Ruth Miller also led a congregation in Pei Tou that had been built while they were under the Church of the Nazarene, but with money that had been given to her personally. Five Nazarene workers left the church and joined the Millers' independent work. The Millers supported them financially with money raised by Ruth Miller and given to them directly by Nazarenes in the States. Miller tried to undercut Wiese and distorted the reasons for their dismissal both in Taiwan and to supporters at home. Eventually Lewis reported Miller's independency to his home district in Oklahoma. Starting an independent work without the permission of the general church was grounds for the discipline of a minister under the church's *Manual*. By 1967, however, the issue was moot. The Millers divorced, and R. R. Miller married a 22-year-old Chinese woman. Ruth Miller remained in Taiwan, teaching in the American School and at the University of Taipei. R. R. Miller died in Okinawa in 1968.[116]

Wiese served as council chairman until January 1966. As he had in mainland China, Wiese initiated some measures intended to reduce the financial dependency of the Chinese upon the mission. He disagreed with the way in which the mission supplied so completely all of the needs of the churches and Bible school students. Decades earlier, the Chinese on the mainland had had a hard time with Wiese's ideas of self-support when he had opposed the mission's providing soup at church gatherings and wanted the local congregations to start paying the mission back for their church property. Now in Taiwan Wiese increased the amount of money or work that students were to provide for their own education. Although Bible school students even under Miller had worked on campus in return for scholarship assistance, they opposed Wiese's attempts to raise the amount for which they were responsible, and several students said that they were unable to return to school. This angered preachers, other students and laypersons, who wrote a report to V. H. Lewis in which they called Wiese "unhumanitarian." Some of the students filed a case against the mission in Taipei courts. Nothing came of the case, however. The Chinese courts favored those in positions of authority.[117]

Wiese attempted to build a holy church by carefully screening those who joined the Church of the Nazarene. He promoted revivals and brought in evangelists, including Chi Yuew-han, and preachers from other holiness denominations such as John Trachsel of the old NHA work and James Taylor of the Free Methodist Church. Wiese personally interviewed each candidate for baptism and membership. "I am convinced," Wiese said, "that if we are to have a clean church the place to make a close check is when they come in at the door." Wiese required baptism for membership even though this was not in the Nazarene *Manual*. Just as he had in the Philippines while mission director there, he interviewed each prospective member about his or her beliefs, reading habits, vices, Sabbath keeping, debts, enemies, and tithing. Wiese inquired into their religious experiences of new birth and entire sanctification, both of which he required for membership, even though entire sanctification was not required for church membership according to the *Manual*. He was stricter than many North American churches on these matters because he believed that the Chinese concept of the significance of baptism was greater than that of Westerners.[118]

Other denominations also hesitated to baptize too quickly. Like many of them, for baptism the Church of the Nazarene required that more than one person in a family be baptized or already be baptized. This was a contextual response to the reality that family pressures in Chinese society would be too great for a person to remain a Christian unless there was a fellow believer in the family. The Chinese understood that a person was not fully saved until he or she was baptized, and only after being baptized were persons allowed to take the Lord's Supper. Wiese did not challenge these assumptions even though, again, they were not particularly in keeping with the understandings of baptism prevalent in the holiness movement, but reflected the practices of Presbyterians in Taiwan.[119]

In another attempt to ensure purity within the church, Wiese kept potential members on "probationary" status for six to twelve months. During this period they would be able to prove whether they had really overcome vices such as smoking, which was not tolerated among members. Clearly Wiese was not concerned with church growth statistics. He would rather have a pure church than a large one. He pruned the membership rolls of those who were not attending church, thus reducing the membership of the entire Church of the Nazarene in Taiwan in 1965 to only 190 persons. In a sense, Wiese's measures that intentionally restricted growth reflected both holiness and Chinese mentalities. He wanted to make sure that those brought into the faith would be able to remain Christians not only on the basis of their own strength, but with the support of significant persons in their families.[120]

Not all of this strictness sat well with the other missionaries. Like the younger missionaries in Japan who were wondering about the same time whether William Eckel would ever retire, the missionaries in Taiwan feared that the church would keep Wiese on past the age of seventy. They were relieved when Coulter announced Wiese's retirement. The missionaries then elected Holstead as field superintendent.[121]

Holstead and the other missionaries developed plans toward building a national church, particularly by reducing the missions subsidy to each church, using a 10-step plan. Some of the city churches were able to become self-supporting quite quickly, while the rural and mountain churches remained more dependent. As the 10-step plan took effect under Holstead, the general church subsidy went to local churches rather than to pastors, with the idea that churches would take responsibility for their own finances, including their pastor's salaries. However, pastors still had recourse to the mission and even could borrow money from the mission for children's marriages and the like. The 10-step plan was not rigidly imposed on all of the churches until the 1970s.[122]

Like other denominations in Taiwan, the Church of the Nazarene had difficulty with self-support. On another matter, at this time the official missions policy still advised, wherever possible, for deeds and property titles on mission fields to be held in the name of the general church, headquartered in Kansas City, with mission councils as legally responsible parties. While this guarded against independency and schism, it also prevented congregations from taking any real sense of ownership over their own churches. It was also a long-standing general missions policy for local churches to raise 50 percent of the funds for their own buildings. However, there were many ways of getting around this policy. Money given to missions through the church's "Alabaster" offering, taken throughout the denomination and divided among the fields, was exempt. Likewise, money donated for "memorial" churches was exempt from having to be matched by the local congregation. So it was not unusual in Taiwan as on other mission fields for the local congregation to pay very little if anything for their church building. For these reasons the general church appeared to the Chinese as a landlord and they remained dependent upon it for years to come. They were prone to turn to missionaries even for routine building repairs.[123]

In Taiwan, having an organized Bible college from the beginning went without question. The school had been established in 1958, soon after the controversy with Kiehn. In 1960 Holstead secured an eight-acre campus overlooking Taipei. Though both John and Natalie Holstead taught in the Bible College, for years it was under the leadership of George Rench. Both Holstead and Rench were graduates of Nazarene Theological Seminary, and, after becoming superintendent, Holstead requested that the church send only seminary graduates to Taiwan as missionaries. This helped to assure that the missionaries were united in their emphasis upon ministerial education. Yet, in 1965, due to the controversies that had wracked the mission for years, of the 23 persons who had graduated from the school since it began, only 14 remained in the Church of the Nazarene. Eight of these were pastoring, and, of these eight, five were pastoring in the mountain area in the South. Other graduates were working in kindergartens or still attending school. Nevertheless, the school raised entrance and other requirements and produced capable Chinese leaders. Meanwhile, the value of the college property rose markedly. The sale of portions of it over the next decades helped to finance the district.[124]

The Church of the Nazarene cooperated with other denominations in Taiwan, especially those related to the holiness movement. The holiness churches in Taiwan were comparatively stronger than the Methodist Church itself. With the Free Methodists and the Oriental Missionary Society-affiliated Taiwan Holiness Church, Nazarenes formed a consortium that granted bachelor of theology degrees. The Friends Church in Taiwan was strongly influenced by the holiness movement and often joined with these denominations, as it did in helping to sponsor "Wesley Graduate Theological Seminars," which began in July 1965. Rench was elected to positions with interdenominational agencies, serving as chairperson of the Taiwan Missionary Fellowship and as treasurer of the Taiwan Leprosy Relief Association.[125]

In spite of the early association of the Church of the Nazarene with immigrants from the mainland and the fact that the missionaries were Mandarin-speaking, and unlike some other denominations that worked predominantly with one group or another, the church developed almost equally among mainlanders, indigenous Taiwanese, and mountain tribes.[126]

Work among the Paiwan people of the mountains came through contacts in Taipei and through contacts with an independent preacher in the village of Gu Lou, Timothy Dzau. In 1962 the missionaries sent a worker, himself from the mountain area, Phillip Dzau, to explain to the people more completely about the Church of the Nazarene. Even though Phillip Dzua died soon after, the work in the South among these indigenous people proved strong. They possessed an identity that separated them from the Nazarene churches in the Taipei area. Phillip and Darlene Kellerman, who began service as missionaries to Taiwan in

1962, were stationed in Kaohsiung to be nearer the Paiwan work. The Free Methodists also had strong work among the Paiwanese.[127]

Chinese leaders emerged in the 1960s. Some potential key leaders, including Chi, the one ordained Chinese Nazarene pastor who had made his way to Taiwan from the mainland, remained outside of the church. Some graduates of the Nazarene school in Taiwan joined other denominations. One even got into trouble with the law. Tragically, the church lost one of its brightest potential leaders, Betty Lin, in an airplane crash in 1969 that also killed a missionary, Pat Burgess. Lin had been educated at the Nazarene college in Bethany, Oklahoma. But there were bright spots as well. The church sent Gloria Chen to study at Nazarene Theological Seminary in Kansas City and she returned to take leadership of the Christian education program for local churches in the district. Paul Hwang, who had been born on the mainland and had been converted under Osborn in Taipei, emerged as a pastor and educator. In 1972 he became the first Chinese president of the theological college.[128]

The general church allowed missionaries to conduct unofficial district assemblies, and then allowed the election of an assistant district superintendent. To the missionaries' surprise, the delegates elected Dai Chun-de to this position. Dai had been an independent worker, had been affiliated at one time with the Little Flock of "Watchman" Nee, and remained something of a mystic. He had attended Kiehn's school for one year before transferring to the Nazarene Bible College. He started a church near Taipei.[129]

Inevitably, however, another of the early Chinese pastors, Pan Ming-ding, proved to be the more outstanding leader. He was born in 1917 and had studied law on the mainland before joining the army and serving in the war against Japan. He retired as a full colonel. By 1951 he was working as business manager for Kiehn's Gospel Mission. Kiehn persuaded him to consider the ministry and he attended the Gospel Mission Bible school. In 1954, while still affiliated with Kiehn's Formosa Gospel Mission, he began the church at Yangmei, 30 kilometers from Taipei. Kiehn allowed it to be transferred into the Church of the Nazarene and in 1956 it became the first congregation in Taiwan to call itself a "Church of the Nazarene." Though other missions in Taiwan offered him opportunities for leadership, he stayed with the Church of the Nazarene, testifying that his spiritual life had begun with the Nazarenes. The building at Yang Mei was built by offerings from the Nazarene Missionary Society, but operated on faith. After Miller's departure from the church, Pan became pastor of the Shihlin church, which became the first Nazarene congregation to be fully self-supporting. Pan had weathered the storms of missionary leaders. He was ordained by Coulter, by then a general superintendent, in 1965. In 1975 General Superintendent Eugene Stowe appointed him district superintendent. He was, thus, the first Chinese district superintendent in the Church of the Nazarene. He served until 1980. Pan died in 1989, living to see the district achieve regular status under his successor, Kuo Min-hua, in 1987.[130]

A report on Taiwan undertaken on behalf of the World Missions Department in the late 1960s by Howard Conrad, a missionary serving in the Caribbean and Peru, greatly disturbed the missionaries. Conrad gathered information on various Nazarene fields. He reported from the data that the Church of the Nazarene in Taiwan was composed mostly of young people who could not financially support the church. He said that the church was not growing as rapidly as it had in the early years under the leadership of Miller. Conrad believed that the church had been mistaken to center itself in Taipei rather than in rural areas, where, he believed, people were more ready to accept the gospel. Conrad advised that the Church of the Nazarene pull out of Taiwan completely.

Conrad's conclusions paralleled other assessments of why some churches grew faster than others in Taiwan. Denominations that entered after the peak years were at a disadvantage. Urbanization and materialism made it increasingly difficult to evangelize, especially using old methods. Groups that divided their attention among ethnic groups rather than concentrating on one tended to lessen their impact. The reticence to allow an indigenous church to emerge was a weakness of almost every denomination.[131]

But George Rench responded strongly to such pessimism. He believed that Conrad had gotten it wrong. The church in Taiwan included military leaders and professionals. The rapid growth under Miller was spurious. Wiese had had to prune the rolls. Rench thought it "suicide" to surrender the strategic city for the countryside.[132]

After all that the mission in Taiwan had gone through, with all kinds of problems with missionary leadership and mistaken policies in the early years, it had survived and was maturing. Its constituency was more like that of Jiangxi than Daming in mainland China. In 1974 church leaders transferred John and Natalie Holstead from Taiwan to begin the work of the denomination in Hong Kong. By then self-supporting congregations and strong national leaders were emerging in Taiwan and the ways in which the sale of some Bible college property was supporting the district and various projects enhanced the church's financial situation. Yet the size of the church in Taiwan remained small compared to the work in mainland China. There were few advantages in the political situation in Taiwan, even though Chiang Kai-shek himself once attended a Nazarene church and was known to be a Christian. In spite of the social disruptions affecting not only the immigrants from China, but also the Taiwanese people already inhabiting the country, Chinese people in Taiwan did not seek Christianity. Just as in Japan after the Second World War, the churches were not able to capitalize to any great extent upon the social upheaval. In both countries people sought material rather than spiritual comforts. The Nazarenes in Taiwan remained a small minority within a small minority. They located themselves with other holiness people and attempted, after many early crises in missionary leadership, to build a church that would be reflective of the holiness lifestyle and beliefs.

# Notes

1. John W. Pattee, "Effect of the War on the Churches of Chengan County," *Other Sheep* (October 1942), 12; and Pattee, *Hazardous Days in China* (Pasadena, Calif.: the author, n.d.), 103.

2. Joseph E. Esherick, *The Origins of the Boxer Uprising* (Berkeley: University of California Press, 1987), 68–95. See also Diana Preston, *The Boxer Rebellion: The Dramatic Story of China's War on Foreigners that Shook the World in the Summer of 1900* (New York: Walker, 1999), 22–32, 275–282.

3. Esherick, *Boxer Uprising*, 88; Paul A. Cohen, *China and Christianity: The Missionary Movement and the Growth of Chiense Antiforeignism, 1860–1870* (Cambridge, Mass.: Harvard University Press, 1963), 4, 17, 33, 77–109. On Roman Catholic relations with Protestants see Sidney A. Forsythe, *An American Missionary Community in China, 1895–1905* (Cambridge, Mass.: Harvard University. Press, 1971), 72–74. On Roman Catholic work in this area see Edward J. Malatesta, "China and the Society of Jesus: An Historical-theological Essay," paper presented at the Symposium on the History of Christianity in China, Hong Kong, October 2–4, 1996, pp. 40–43 (cited with the permission of the late author).

4. See John L. Nevius, *Demon Possession and Allied Things*, third ed. (New York: Fleming H. Revell, n.d. [1st ed., 1894]), 17–40; Isaac Ketler, *The Tragedy of Paotingfu*, second ed. (New York: Fleming H. Revell, 1902); Geraldine Taylor, *Pastor Hsi (of North China): One of China's Christians* (London: Morgan Scott, 1903), xiii-xiv; Paul A. Cohen, *History in Three Keys: The Boxers as Event, Experience, and Myth* (New York: Columbia University Press, 1997), especially 96–118, "Mass Spirit Possession."

5. Paul A. Varg, *Missionaries, Chinese, and Diplomats: The American Protestant Missionary Movement in China, 1890–1950* (Princeton, N.J.: Princeton University Press, 1958), 31–50, 86–87; Forsythe, *An American Missionary Community in China*, 2, 77, 89; Stuart C. Miller, "Ends and Means:

Missionary Justification for Force in Nineteenth Century China," in *The Missionary Enterprise in China and America*, ed. John K. Fairbank (Cambridge, Mass.: Harvard University Press, 1974), 273–282; Kuang-sheng Liao, *Anti-Foreignism and Modernization in China: 1860–1980*, second ed. (Hong Kong: Chinese University Press, 1986), 39–52; Murray Rubinstein, "Witness to the Chinese Millenium: Southern Baptist Perceptions of the Chinese Revolution, 1911–1921," in *United States Attitudes and Policies Toward China: The Impact of American Missionaries*, ed. Patricia Neils (Armonk, NY: M. E. Sharpe, 1990), 154, 166–167; Kathleen L. Lodwick, *Crusaders Against Opium: Protestant Missionaries in China, 1874–1917* (Lexington: University Press of Kentucky, 1996), 166–167, 171–172, 182–185.

6. Thomas Cochrane, *Survey of the Missionary Occupation of China* (Shanghai: Christian Literature Society for China, 1913), 312; Kenneth S. Latourette, *A History of Christian Missions in China* (New York: Macmillan, 1929), 402; Mrs. Cecil Troxel and Mrs. John J. Trachsel, *Cecil Troxel: The Man and the Work* (Chicago: National Holiness Missionary Society, 1948), 23–52. See Malatesta, "China and the Society of Jesus," 40.

7. *China Mission Year Book*, ed. E. C. Lobenstine and A. L. Warnshuis (Shanghai: Kwang Hsueh, 1920), 339; L. C. Osborn, *Hitherto! 1914–1939* (Tientsin: Peiyang Press, [1939]), 1–2; Osborn, *The China Story: The Church of the Nazarene in North China, South China, and Taiwan* (Kansas City, Mo.: Nazarene Publishing House, 1969), 9–14.

8. Osborn to Reynolds, September 14, 1918; W. W. Cary, *Story of the National Holiness Missionary Society* (Chicago: National Holiness Missionary Society, 1940), 7–12, 77, 135; E. A. Girvin, *Phineas F. Bresee: A Prince in Israel; A Biography* (Kansas City, Mo.: Nazarene Publishing House, 1916), 237; "In Memoriam: Catherine Flagler, 1874–1956," *Other Sheep* (January 1957), inside front cover; Timothy L. Smith, *Called Unto Holiness: The Story of the Nazarenes: The Formative Years* (Kansas City, Mo.: Nazarene Publishing House, 1962), 138, 250–251; Ronald Kirkemo, *For Zion's Sake: A History of Pasadena/Point Loma College* (San Diego: Point Loma, 1992), 8.

9. *China Mission Year Book*, fourth issue, ed. D. MacGillvray (Shanghai: Christian Literature Society for China, 1913), 279; Ida Vieg, "A Brief History of the Nazarene Mission in China," April 20, 1921 (file 262-56); Troxel and Trachsel, *Troxel*, 52, 88–91; Cary, *Story*, 7–8. Compare R. Pierce Beaver, *Ecumenical Beginnings in Protestant World Mission: A History of Comity* (New York: Thomas Nelson, 1962), 119.

10. Troxel and Trachsel, *Troxel*, 93–113; Cary, *Story*, 9–10, 15.

11. *Holiness Unto the Lord* (N.p., [1913]), 16 pp. (file 451-45); H. F. Reynolds, "Around the World Trip," to the General Missionary Board of the Pentecostal Church of the Nazarene, n.d. (file 262-19); C. W. Ruth to Reynolds, November 8, 1913, in [H.F. Reynolds], "China," n.d. (File 453-3); Cary, *Story*, 293–294. On Ruth see Smith, *Called*, 129–130, 206–207, 230, and C. T. Corbett, *Our Pioneer Nazarenes* (Kansas City, Mo.: Nazarene Publishing House, 1958), 26–32.

12. Cochrane, *Survey of the Missionary Occupation*, 289; Latourette, *Christian Missions in China*, 600; Amy N. Hinshaw, *Messengers of the Cross in China* (Kansas City, Mo.: Woman's Foreign Missionary Society, n.d.), 7–13; R. R. Hodges in *Herald of Holiness* (October 15, 1930), typescript (file 759-1); Osborn, *China*, 15; Kiehn, "The Legacy of Peter and Anna Kiehn," received January 15, 1970, Nazarene Archives, 10, 23, 29–30, 39–40, 48–50, 52.

13. [Reynolds], "China," 1–4; Reynolds, "Around the World Trip"; Reynolds, *World-Wide Missions* (Kansas City, Mo.: Nazarene Publishing House, 1915), 66–67, 88–97.

14. James Reed, *The Missionary Mind and American East Asia Policy, 1911–1915* (Cambridge, Mass.: Harvard University Press, 1983), 34–39, 127–129, 140–144.

15. National Holiness Association, China, to General Missionary Board, Pentecostal Church of the Nazarene, February 11, 1914 (file 453-3).

16. [Reynolds], "China," 4.

17. [Reynolds], "China," 4; *Holiness Unto the Lord*, 11; "Third Annual Report of the National Holiness Mission in China," April 1, 1914, 5; Reynolds, *World-Wide*, 94; Glennie Sims to Fifth General Assembly, Kansas City, Mo. [1919] (file 214-45); Cary, *Story*, 126–129; Kiehn, "Legacy," 52. For later World Gospel Mission work see also Laura Trachsel, *Kindled Fires in Asia* (N.p., 1960).

18. [Fragment of] "China Policy" (file 305-15); Reynolds, "China," 7; "The Policy of the General Missionary Board of the Pentecostal Church of the Nazarene to Govern the Work in China," n.d. [1919?] (file 305-14).

19. Reynolds, "China," 11–13; Reynolds to A. J. Smith, March 5, 1927. See also John T. Benson, *Holiness Organized or Unorganized? A History 1898–1915 of the Pentecostal Mission* (Nashville, Tenn.: Trevecca, 1977), 181–182. Compare Smith, *Called*, 197–199.

20. Kiehn, "Annual Station Report: Chaocheng," August 12, 1916.

21. Kiehn, "Chang Hua-hsin," *Other Sheep* (August 1914), 2; Kiehn, "Annual Report, May 24, 1915, "First District Assembly," June 4, 1917; Glennie Sims, "An Interesting Letter from China," *Other Sheep* (July 1915), 3; *Other Sheep* (November 1917), 6; Anna Kiehn, "Death of Chang Hua-hsin," *Other Sheep* (February 1918), 2, 5; Roy E. Swim, *A History of Nazarene Missions* (Kansas City, Mo.: Nazarene Publishing House, n.d.), 92–94; Pattee, *Hazardous Days*, 57–58; Osborn to Samuel Young, November 30, 1964; Kiehn, "Legacy," 54.

22. Sims, "China's Open Door Your Opportunity," *Other Sheep* (January 1915), 3–4.

23. Kiehn, "Annual Station Report: Chaocheng," August 12, 1916; "First District Assembly"; "Annual Station Report: Chaocheng," 1917; "Annual Station Report: Chaocheng," 1919; "Li Ching-i's Testimony," *Other Sheep* (June 1918), 5; [Reynolds, comp.], *History of the Foreign Work of the Church of the Nazarene* (Kansas City, Mo.: General Board of Foreign Missions, 1921),

25; Amy N. Hinshaw, *Native Torch Bearers* (Kansas City, Mo.: Nazarene Publishing House, 1934), 50–51.

24. Hinshaw, *Native Torch Bearers*, 42–60; Martin C. Yang, *A Chinese Village: Taitou, Shantung Province* (New York: Columbia University Press, 1945), 211, 241.

25. *China Mission Year Book*, sixth issue, ed. D. MacGillvray (Shanghai: Christian Literature Society for China, 1915), 82, 84; Swim, *History*, 95–96; Osborn, *China*, 19–21; Kiehn, "Legacy," 68. See James Thomson, Peter Stanley and John Perry, *Sentimental Imperialists: The American Experience in East Asia* (New York: Harper, 1981), 184–185.

26. "Proceedings of the Fifth Annual Assembly," November 1921; "Annual Station Report: Daming," 1923.

27. Amy Hinshaw's *Pictures of Chinese Life*, published along with C. J. Kinne, *Our Field in China: The Field and the Mission of the Church of the Nazarene in China Briefly Described and Illustrated*, second ed. (Kansas City, Mo.: Nazarene Publishing House, n.d.), 19–26, briefly summarized chapters from Arthur H. Smith, *Chinese Characteristics*, second ed. (New York: Fleming H. Revell, 1894). Compare Sutherland, *China Crisis* (Kansas City, Mo.: Nazarene Publishing House, 1948), 23–26. See also L. A. Reed and H. A. Wiese, *The Challenge of China* (Kansas City, Mo.: Nazarene Publishing House, 1937).

28. "Proceedings of the Sixth Annual Assembly," December 1922–January 1923; "Proceedings of the Third Annual Council, China District," October 1924; "Proceedings of the Fourth Annual Council, China District," September 1925; Swim, *History*, 98–99.

29. Sims, "China's Open Door," 3–4; "China," *Other Sheep* (March 1916), 5; "Proceedings of the Fourth Annual Council"; *The China Nazarene* (March 1924), 8 (file 628-8).

30. "Proceedings of the Fifth Annual Council, China District, September 1926"; Swim, *History*, 96–98; Osborn, *China*, 29–34. Rarely did the Nazarene missionaries reflect on broader political currents in China. Similarly, see Rubinstein, "Witness to the Chinese Millennium," in *United States Attitudes*, 161, and, in the same volume, Arline T. Golkin, "Missionaries and Famine Relief to China," 196–201. Also, though it deals with conditions in the South and somewhat later, see James C. Thomson, Jr., *While China Faced West: American Reformers in Nationalist China, 1928–1937* (Cambridge, Mass.: Harvard University Press, 1969), 43–50. On Jesuit relief activities in Daming see Malatesta, "China and the Society of Jesus," 41–42.

31. For similar views toward medical and other social ministries see Wayne Flynt and Gerald W. Berkley, *Taking Christianity to China: Alabama Missionaries to the Middle Kingdom, 1850–1950* (Tuscaloosa: University of Alabama Press, 1997), 169–170, 180. See also Frank Wilson Price, *The Rural Church in China: A Survey* (New York: Agricultural Missions, 1948), which concentrated on the 1930s and included, among the 73 churches it studied, one National Holiness Church congregation in Houtsun; and William A. Brown, "The Prot-

estant Rural Movement in China (1920–1937)," in *American Missionaries in China: Papers from Harvard Seminars* (Cambridge, Mass.: Harvard University Press, 1966), 217–248.

32. Hinshaw, *Native Torch Bearers*, 57. On conversion see Alan Hunter and Kim-Kwong Chan, *Protestantism in Contemporary China* (Cambridge: Cambridge University Press, 1993), 163–168. Perspectives on the larger issues are contrasted in various articles in Jessie G. Lutz, ed., *Christian Missions in China: Evangelists of What?* (Boston: D. C. Heath, 1965).

33. Edith P. Goodnow, *Hazarded Lives* (Kansas City, Mo.: Nazarene Publishing House, 1942), 127–147. See also Hinshaw, *Messengers of the Cross in China*, 23–27; *Other Sheep* (June 1937), 2–3; Anne Sutherland, "Under the Locust Trees," *Other Sheep* (August 1937), 24–25.

34. Hinshaw, *Native Torch Bearers*, 52.

35. Hinshaw, *Native Torch Bearers*, 42–60. Compare Yang, *A Chinese Village*, 188–189; Jane Hunter, *The Gospel of Gentility: American Women Missionaries in Turn-of-the-Century China* (New Haven, Conn.: Yale University Press, 1984), xiv, 15–22; Marjorie King, "Exporting Femininity, Not Feminism: Nineteenth-Century U.S. Missionary Women's Efforts to Emancipate Chinese Women," in *Women's Work for Women: Missionaries and Social Change in Asia*, ed. Leslie A. Flemming (Boulder, Colo.: Westview, 1989), 117–135; Kwok Pui-lan, *Chinese Women and Christianity, 1860–1927* (Atlanta: Scholars Press, 1991), 70–86; Kwok Pui-lan, "Chinese Women and Protestant Christianity at the Turn of the Twentieth Century," in *Christianity in China from the Eighteenth Century to the Present*, ed. Daniel H. Bays (Stanford: Stanford University Press, 1996), 200–203; and Flynt and Berkley, *Taking Christianity*, chapter 9, "Woman Consciousness among Alabama Missionaries."

36. Cary, *Story of the National Holiness Missionary Society*, 171–176; Flynt and Berkley, *Taking Christianity*, 181–189; G. Thompson Brown, *Earthen Vessels and Transcendent Power: American Presbyterians in China, 1837–1952* (Maryknoll, N.Y.: Orbis, 1997), 221–225, 232.

37. C. J. Kinne, *Our Field in China: The Field and the Mission of the Church of the Nazarene in China Briefly Described and Illustrated* (Kansas City, Mo.: Nazarene Publishing House, n.d.), 13. See also C. J. Kinne, *The Modern Samaritan: A Presentation of the Claims of Medical Missions* (Kansas City, Mo.: Nazarene Publishing House, n.d.); Swim, *History*, 99–100; Osborn, *Hitherto!*, 15–21.

38. See, for example, "P. F. Bresee Memorial Hospital for Ta Ming Fu, China," pamphlet published by Nazarene Medical Missionary Union (file 451 14); Henry C. Wesche, *Medical Missions: What? Why? How?* (Kansas City, Mo.: General Board, Church of the Nazarene, n.d.); Sutherland, *China Crisis*, 86–94. On the financing of the hospital see Swim, *History*, 99–100. The Nazarene Medical Missionary Union was organized in California in 1921 to promote medical missions. See also Hinshaw, *Messengers*, 117. On the broader debate see William R. Hutchison, *Errand to the World: American Protestant Thought and Foreign Missions* (Chicago: University of Chicago Press, 1987),

ch. 5; and Philip L. Wickeri, *Seeking the Common Ground: Protestant Christianity, the Three-Self Movement, and China's United Front* (Maryknoll, N.Y.: Orbis, 1988), 32–36.

39. Smith to Reynolds, November 26, 1926; Zella W. Deale, "Hospital Work and Workers," [1931] (file 213-13); Hinshaw, *Messengers of the Cross in China*, 51–56; Maxine F. Fritz, *But God Gives a Song: The Story of Dr. and Mrs. R. G. Fitz, Pioneer Missionaries to China and Alaska* (Kansas City, Mo.: Nazarene Publishing House, 1973), 46–47, and throughout. Similarly, medical doctor T. W. Ayers of the Southern Baptist Hospital in Shandong Province preferred evangelism to medicine. See Flynt and Berkley, *Taking Christianity*, 186.

40. A. J. Smith, "A Word with the Supporters of Native Workers," *The China Nazarene* (March 1926), 8 (file 628-8). See also Smith, "Report," Proceedings of the Fifth Annual Council, China District, September 1926 (file 406-22).

41. A. J. Smith, *Jesus Lifting Chinese: Marvelous Spiritual Awakenings in China* (Cincinnati: God's Bible School and Revivalist, n.d.), 18–37, and throughout. Some of the more radical statements about the revival were downplayed in the *Other Sheep*. See Hinshaw, *Messengers*, 72–74. See also Smith to Reynolds, December 16, 1926; January 10, [1927]; February 1, 1927; Osborn to Smith, n.d. (file 214-52); Reynolds to Smith, March 5, 1927.

42. Smith to Reynolds, April 22, 1926. See Hinshaw, *Messengers*, 67–74.

43. On Pentecostalism see Daniel H. Bays, "Indigenous Protestant Churches in China, 1900–1937: A Pentecostal Case Study," in *Indigenous Responses to Western Christianity*, ed. Steven Kaplan (New York: New York University Press, 1995), 130; and Bays, "The Protestant Missionary Establishment and the Pentecostal Movement," in *Pentecostal Currents in American Protestantism*, ed. Edith L. Blumhofer, Russell P. Spittler and Grant A. Wacker (Urbana: University of Illinois Press, 1999), 55, and regarding the influence of Pentecostalism upon other holiness missions in China see pp. 55–61.

44. Smith, *Jesus Lifting*, 26.

45. Smith, *Jesus Lifting*, 36.

46. Smith to Reynolds, April 12, 1927. See Smith, *Jesus Lifting*, 42, 55, 69, 110.The widespread nature of the revival is evident in Smith, *Jesus Lifting*, 213–234; Mary K. Crawford, *The Shandong Revival* (Shanghai: Baptist Publication Society, 1933); Carey, *Story*, 210–215; and Daniel Bays, "Christian Revival in China," in *Modern Christian Revivals*, eds. Edith Blumhofer and Randall Balmer (Urbana: University of Illinois Press, 1993), 168–169, 172–174. See also Leslie T. Lyall, *John Sung* (London: China Inland Mission, 1954), and John Sung, *My Testimony: The Autobiography of Dr. John Sung* (Reprint, Hong Kong: Living Books for All, 1977).

47. Smith, *Jesus Lifting*, 18–19, 36, 70–88, 109. See Smith, *Bible Holiness and the Modern, Popular, Spurious* (N.p., [1953]), 92–95; Victor P. Reasoner, "The American Holiness Movement's Paradigm Shift Concerning Holiness," *Wesleyan Theological Journal* 31 (Fall 1996), 139–140.

48. "Annual Station Report: Daming," 1923; Hinshaw, *Messengers*, 75–81; Sutherland, *China Crisis*, 77–78. See also Robert Sutherland and John Sutherland, *Behind the Silence: The Story of Frank and Ann Sutherland* (Kansas City, Mo.: Nazarene Publishing House, 1999). Compare Jessie Lutz, *China and the Christian College, 1850–1950* (Ithaca, N.Y.: Cornell University Press, 1971), 17–24.

49. Smith, *Jesus Lifting*, 27–33, 55, 107; Smith to Reynolds, December 16, 1926, and January 10, [1927].

50. Reed and Wiese, *The Challenge of China*, 60–64; Dorothy Borg, *American Policy and the Chinese Revolution, 1925–1928* (Reprint, New York: Octagon, 1968), 361; Thomson, *While China Faced West*, 35–40.

51. "Proceedings of the Fifth Annual Council," September 1927; Smith, "China's Future Yet Hopeful," June 1927; Latourette, *Christian Missions in China*, 699; Borg, *American Policy*, 363. On what was happening in China politically and socially see Jonathan Spence, *The Gate of Heavenly Peace: The Chinese and Their Revolution, 1895–1980* (New York: Viking, 1981), 207–236. Sidney Forsythe similarly found missionaries little aware of the political and social situation in China. Forsythe, *An American Missionary Community in China*, 3–4. 87. Contrast, however, Borg, *American Policy*, 68–94, 194, 429; Shirley Sone Garrett, "Why They Stayed: American Church Politics and Chinese Nationalism in the Twenties," in *The Missionary Enterprise*, ed. Fairbank, 295–302, 308–310; Flynt and Berkley, *Taking Christianity*, 300–308.

52. See Lian Xi, *The Conversion of Missionaries: Liberalism in American Protestant Missions in China, 1907–1932* (University Park: Pennsylvania State University Press, 1997), 165–167.

53. See the general personality profile in Valentin Rabe, "Evangelical Logistics: Mission Support and Resources to 1920," in Fairbank, ed., *The Missionary Enterprise*, 75.

54. Kiehn, "The Past, Present and Future of the Church of the Nazarene," [1926] (file 604-15); "Council Minutes," May 1, 1930; Kiehn, "Legacy," 75.

55. J. G. Morrison to "Our Chinese Church Members and Converts," June 28, 1930, and Morrison's report in the "Minutes," 1931. See also Osborn, *China*, 52–53.

56. "Minutes of the China Council," 1931; Hinshaw, *Native Torch Bearers*, 42–44, 51–53.

57. Minutes of the Nazarene China District Council," February 8–10, 1933.

58. "Minutes of the Nazarene China District Council," February 8–10, 1933; telegram to Kiehn, October 11, 1932; [China missionaries] to General Board, October 28, 1932; Morrison to Kiehn, November 26, 1932; telegrams to Kiehn, January 13 and 26, 1933. Various conflicts between other missionaries in China are described in Flynt and Berkley, *Taking Christianity*, 242–246.

59. L. C. Osborn, E. Osborn, R. G. Fitz, Mrs. R. G. Fitz, H. Wiese, C. Wiese and Catherine Flagler to General Board, Department of Foreign Missions, October 28, 1932 (file 453-28); "Minutes of the Council Meeting," 1934; Wiese to Morrison, July 25, 1934, and February 23, 1935; Morrison to Wiese,

January 11, 1935; Kiehn to Morrison, February 22, 1935; Morrison to Kiehn, July 19, 1935.

60. Translations of the Chinese letters (undated) are in file 453-29.

61. Wiese, "Question of Organizing District Assembly," and "The Subject of Self-support: China," to Morrison and Chapman, December 1, 1934 (file 453-28).

62. Chapman, "To the China Mission Council," in a report to the General Superintendents, Department of Foreign Mission and General Board, Church of the Nazarene, with a cover letter to [Emma] Word, December 31 [1935].

63. Chapman, "To the China Mission Council," and Chapman, "To the pastors and people of the Chinese section of the Church of the Nazarene," contained in the same report; "Minutes of the China Council, Church of the Nazarene," [1935] (file 604-15).

64. Chapman, report to the General Superintendents, 1935; "Minutes of the China Council," [1935].

65. Chapman, report to the General Superintendents; "Minutes of the China Council" [1935]; Wiese to Jones, July 16, 1946; Susan N. Fitkin and Emma B. Word, *Nazarene Missions in the Orient* (Kansas City, Mo.: Nazarene Publishing House, n.d.), 87; and conversations with John W. Pattee and the son of Feng, Feng Ke-yi, Beijing, China, May 23, 1989. The elder Dr. Feng served as a surgeon throughout the years of war with Japan, and then he served as a medical doctor with the Red Army. On the Jesus Family Movement see D. Vaughan Rees, *The "Jesus Family" in Communist China* (Chicago: Moody, 1956), especially p. 58; Wickeri, *Seeking the Common Ground*, 160–162; and Daniel Bays, "The Growth of Independent Christianity," in Bays, ed., *Christianity in China*, 312. Eventually Feng left the Jesus Family and his leanings, and those of his family, returned to those teachings he had learned while working with the Church of the Nazarene. See Maxine F. Fritz, "By Faith Alone," *World Mission* (May 1986), 12–13; Feng Ke-ye, "Perseverance through Persecution," *World Mission* (April 1992), 4–5, 14–15. On Wesche see "Minutes of the Council Meeting," 1934.

66. Hinshaw, *Messengers of the Cross in China*, 86–91; Zella Deale, "Hospital Work and Workers"; *World Mission* (September 1984), 16.

67. "Report of Committee on Memorials" (n.d. [received at headquarters December 16, 1938]); Wiese, "The Bible School Our Life Line," *Other Sheep* (April 1939): 24–25; Wiese, "Bible School Evangelistic Bands," *Other Sheep* (June 1939), 16–17; Sutherland, *China Crisis*, 77–81; J. Fred Parker, *Mission to the World: A History of Missions in the Church of the Nazarene through 1985* (Kansas City, Mo.: Nazarene Publishing House, 1988), 257–258. For a sense of the importance of education see also Yu-ming Shaw, *An American Missionary in China: John Leighton Stuart and Chinese-American Relations* (Cambridge, Mass.: Harvard University Press, 1992), 40–44.

68. Sutherland to C. W. Jones, February 2, 1938. See also Pattee, "Late News from China," *Other Sheep* (May 1938), 24.

69. Katherine Wiese, "Chang Chin," *Other Sheep* (February 1942), 23–24. Other accounts of Chang's ministry are Pattee, "Pressing the Battle," *Other Sheep* (February 1941), 21; Pattee, "The Chengan Revival," *Other Sheep* (August 1940), 15–16; Osborn, "Revivals in China," *Other Sheep* (August 1940), 16; Wiese, "Bible School Turns Out an Evangelist," *Other Sheep* (January 1939), 24; Sutherland, "Chin T'an Chen," *Other Sheep* (November 1937), 23; Osborn, *Hitherto*, 28; Pattee, *Hazardous Days*, 45–46; conversations between Wang Yu-xian and Pattee, May 29, 1989, at Daming; between Shang Chih-rung and Pattee, May 31, 1989, at Chengan; and between Li Bae-ch'in and Pattee, June 1, 1989, at Handan. On the evangelist John Sung's ties to the holiness movement churches see Lyall, *John Sung*, 55, 59, 67, 95, 106, 108, 112, 150. Daming is mentioned on p. 106. See also Fritz, *But God Gives a Song*, 62.

70. Pattee, *Hazardous Days*, 39–43; Lillian Pattee, "Three Hour Testimony Meeting," *Other Sheep* (February 1941), 24; Osborn to Remiss Rehfeldt, February 5, 1955; and, regarding the last two named, conversations in China, May 16, 19 and 31, 1989. See the report on this trip on file in the Nazarene Archives. See also C. Ellen Watts, *John Pattee of China and the Philippines* (Kansas City, Mo.: Beacon Hill, 1984), 51–66.

71. Sutherland to Jones, August 25, 1937, November 4, 1937, and February 2, 1938; Wiese, telegram to Kansas City, Mo., September 15, 1937; Cordell Hull, telegram to Church of the Nazarene, January 14, 1938; Wiese, "When Duty Calls," *Other Sheep* (December 1937), 21–22; "Preparing for War," *Other Sheep* (December 1937), 24–25; Pattee, "Seeing Our China Field," *Other Sheep* (June 1938), 20–21; Pattee, *Hazardous Days*, 40–41; Sutherland, *China Crisis*, 95–98; Osborn, *Hitherto*, 8–9, 41–46. See also Dorothy Borg, *The United States and the Far Eastern Crisis of 1933–1938: From the Manchurian Incident through the Initial Stage of the Undeclared Sino-Japanese War* (Cambridge, Mass.: Harvard University Press, 1964), 328–329; Donald J. Friedman, *The Road from Isolation: The Campaign of the American Committee for Non-Participation in Japanese Aggression, 1938–1941* (Cambridge, Mass.: Harvard University Press, 1968), 70–73.

72. Reed and Wiese, *The Challenge of China*, 71–75; Wiese, "Chinese Hire Three Men to Preach," *Other Sheep* (July 1937), 21; Wiese, "More Self-Support," *Other Sheep* (May 1937), 13. Compare Flynt and Berkley, *Taking Christianity*, 262–263, 273.

73. Katherine Wiese, "Phenomenal Growth of the China N.F.M.S.," *Other Sheep* (December 1940), 12–13; Osborn, "Self-Support in the Church of the Nazarene in China," *Other Sheep* (February 1941), 24. See Pattee, "Notes from Chengan," *Other Sheep* (July 1941), 11.

74. "China District of the Church of the Nazarene Council Minutes," September–October 1940; Osborn to Jones, November 6, 1940.

75. Katherine Wiese to Jones, November 28, 1946, World Mission office (reel 49).

76. Osborn, "Self-Support in the Church of the Nazarene in China," *Other Sheep* (February 1941), 24. Similarly, Osborn, *Hitherto*, 48. Also see Reed and Wiese, *Challenge*, 128; [Lillian] Pattee, "Forty Dollars Paid Back," *Other Sheep* (October 1941), 14; Kiehn, "Our Native Workers," *Other Sheep* (April 1939), 25–26; Kiehn to Jones, November 12, 1940. Osborn, "News from the China Field," *Other Sheep* (November 1941), 14–15; Henry Wesche, "Bresee Memorial Hospital Notes," *Other Sheep* (January 1942), 16–18; Arthur Moses, "Bresee Memorial Hospital Report," *Other Sheep* (April 1942), 7; "Council Minutes," 1941.

77. Kiehn to Jones, May 26, 1938, March 15, 1939, April 4, 1939, November 12, 1940, December 9, 1940; [Anna] Kiehn to Emma Word, July 15, 1938; Kiehn, "My Last Term of Service, 1928–1938," n.d. (file 214-3); Sutherland to Jones, October 21, 1938, and July 15, 1941; Jones to Kiehn, July 15, 1940, December 10, 1940, December 11, 1940, February 7, 1941, November 7, 1941, December 30, 1941; Peter and Anna Kiehn to Foreign Missionary Department, n.d. [January 1941]; "Resolution," unsigned, n.d. (file 214-6); R. B. Shipley to Jones, February 8, 1941, and March 3, 1941; Jones to Shipley, February 11, 1941, and letters regarding the Kiehns' tours throughout the United States (file 214-4).

78. "Field Statistics, 1941"; "China District Church of the Nazarene Council Minutes," September 1941; "Latest News from China," *Other Sheep* (April 1942), 7. By comparison, the Jesuits had only one Chinese priest in the area of Daming in 1940, and 16 seminarians, but about 40,000 adherents. See Malatesta, "China and the Society of Jesus," 43.

79. Pattee, *Hazardous Days*, 72–82; Mary L. Scott, *Kept in Safeguard* (Kansas City, Mo.: Nazarene Publishing House, 1977), 30–47.

80. Orval Nease, "Foreign Visitation: 1948," 9; conversations with Liu Wan-cheng, Lee Ling-en and others, Handan and Daming, March 14–15, 1999.

81. (Ed.), "Our Work in China," *Other Sheep* (April 1942), 11, quoting a letter from Osborn; Osborn to Swiss Consul General, June 25, 1942, which details the property holdings, assessed to be about $600,000 (file 453-29); Wiese, "Chinese Facts," n.d., in the papers of Orval Nease (file 784-61).

82. Pattee, "Effect of the War on the Churches of Chengan County," *Other Sheep* (October 1942), 11–12.

83. Timothy Brook, "Toward Independence: Christianity in China Under the Japanese Occupation, 1937–1945," in *Christianity in China*, ed. Bays, 318, 337.

84. Osborn to Jones, May 30, 1940, and March 24, 1942; Osborn to General Superintendents and Department of Foreign Missions, July 3, 1940; Scott, Peking, to Jones, October 22, 1945; conversation with Shang Chih-rung, May 31, 1989; and conversations with Liu Wan-cheng and others, Handan and Daming, March 14–15, 1999.

85. [Geraldine] Taylor, *The Triumph of John and Betty Stam* (Philadelphia: China Inland Mission, 1935), 100–125; Borg, *The United States and the Far Eastern Crisis*, 596.

86. Wiese, "Conditions on Our Field"; Wiese to Wesche, September 10, 1946; Wiese, "Report of Our China Field" (received July 1946); Wiese, "What the Bible School Meant to Our Work During the Recent Years of Stress," *Other Sheep* (July 1947), 7–8; Wiese, "The Peril of the Church in Our Old Field in China," n.d., World Mission office (reel 53); Sutherland, *China Crisis*, 106–107, 132–133; conversations with Yuan Hsuan-ch'un, Beijing, May 19, 1989.

87. Kiehn, "Legacy," 80–83.

88. Compare the similar account of Yunnan province Christians at this time in T'ien Ju-K'ang, *Peaks of Faith: Protestant Mission in Revolutionary China* (Leiden: E. J. Brill, 1993), 69–71, 129–132, and throughout.

89. On the basis of my trips to Daming, Chengan and Handan, May 29–June 1, 1989; and conversations with Liu Wan-cheng and others, Handan and Daming, March 14–15, 1999. See John Pattee to Rev. and Mrs. Chi Yuew-han, May 3, 1988; my report in the Nazarene archives; and Floyd T. Cunningham, "The Church Is Not the Buildings but the People," *World Mission* (November 1989): 12–13. See also the May 1986 issue of *World Mission*. For Document 19 see appendix I, in *Christianity in China: Foundations for Dialogue*, ed. Beatrice Leung and John D. Young (Hong Kong: University of Hong Kong, 1993), 286–309. See also Wickeri, *Seeking the Common Ground*, 185–195; Tony Lambert, *The Resurrection of the Chinese Church* (Wheaton, Ill.: OMF, 1994), 72–77, and throughout; Hunter and Chan, *Protestantism in Contemporary China*, 66–104.

90. Wiese, "Why We Chose Kiangsi for a New Field," n.d.; Wiese, "The City of Ki'an Where We Open the First Station." On Jiangxi see Thomson, Jr., *While China Faced West*, 85–90, and, especially on the Roman Catholic presence, Alan R. Sweeten, *Christianity in Rural China: Conflict and Accommodation in Jiangxi Province, 1860–1900* (Ann Arbor, Mich.: University of Michigan, 2001).

91. Nease, "Foreign Visitation," 8–12; Wiese to Jones, January 8, 1947, and March 27, 1947; Osborn, n.d. (file 1257-20); Sutherland, *China Crisis*, 108–112, 123–124.

92. Nease, "Foreign Visitation"; Wiese, "Chinese Feasts"; Nease, "Chinese Feasts," *Other Sheep* 36 (July 1949); "Testimony of John Ch'i," trans. R. G. Fitz, *Other Sheep* (August 1949), 12; Wiese, "Southern California Convention," May 11, 1950 (file 2069-26); Russell V. DeLong and Mendell Taylor, *Fifty Years of Nazarene Missions*, vol. 2: *History of the Fields* (Kansas City, Mo.: Beacon Hill, 1955), 88–92; Osborn, *China*, 63–69; Osborn, *Christ at the Bamboo Curtain* (Kansas City, Mo.: Beacon Hill, 1956), 117–120. Hsu died in the mid-1970s. See John Pattee to Rev. and Mrs. Chi Yuew-han, May 3, 1988.

93. Notebook of H. A. Wiese (file 2069-25); Wiese to Board of Foreign Missions, December 1, 1951; Wiese to Remiss Rehfeldt, December 18, 1951; Wiese to D. I. Vanderpool, December 17, 1951, May 23, 1952, September 1952, and "Chinese Budget," Vanderpool papers; Wiese to Friends, June 1, 1955, quoting from a letter from Mary Li (file 2069-29); Mendell Taylor, *Fifty Years of Nazarene Missions*, vol. 3: *World Outreach through Home Missions*

(Kansas City, Mo.: Beacon Hill, 1958), 146–147; Jerald Johnson, "'Great Things' in China," *World Mission* (April 1980); Mary Li, address at the Asia-Pacific Regional Conference, Church of the Nazarene, Manila, June 14, 1987; Mary Li, "Autobiographical Statement," November 4, 1990 (file 1269-27); "Mary Li," *World Mission* (July 1991), 19.

94. Conversations with Shang Chih-rung, May 31, 1989, and Li Bae-Ch'in, June 1989. Compare Brown, "The Protestant Rural Movement," 231–232, on systems of leadership at rural levels.

95. See also Wickeri, *Seeking the Common Ground*, 237; Hunter and Chan, *Protestantism in Contemporary China*, 152–155; Brown, *Earthen Vessels*, 308.

96. Peter Chen-main wang, "Christianity in Modern Taiwan: Struggling over the Path of Contextualization," in *China and Christianity: Burdened Past, Hopeful Future*, ed. Stephen Uhalley and Xiaoxin Wu (Armonk, N.Y.: M. E. Sharpe, 2001),

97. Hollington K. Tong, *Christianity in Taiwan: A History* (Taipei, Taiwan: China Post, 1961), 97; Dorothy A. Raber, *Protestantism in Changing Taiwan: A Call to Creative Response* (Pasadena, Calif.: William Carey, 1978), 72; Murray A. Rubinstein, *The Protestant Community on Modern Taiwan: Mission, Seminary and Church* (Armonk, N.Y.: M. E. Sharpe, 1991), 41, 43, 56.

98. Hammond had worked in Kowloon, Hong Kong, with the South China Peniel Holiness Mission before the war, and had been interred by the Japanese. For this account see his *Bond Servants of the Japanese* (San Pedro, Calif.: Sheffield, 1943), 3–11. See also Charles E. Jones, *A Guide to the Study of the Holiness Movement* (Metuchen, N.J.: Scarecrow, 1974), 412.

99. Osborn to Remiss Rehfeldt, February 5, 1955; R. R. Miller to Foreign Missionary Committee, December 22, 1956, World Mission office; Osborn, *Bamboo*, 117–120; "Nazarenes in Taiwan," *Other Sheep* (October 1957), 7; Holstead to Coulter, February 1, 1966; Holstead to Cunningham, May 7, 1991; Holstead to Cunningham, May 7, 1991.

100. Osborn to Remiss Rehfeldt, February 5, 1955, and August 18, 1958; Osborn to Rehfeldt, n.d. [1957] (reel 110), World Mission office; Osborn, "Leon and Emma Osborn's Years of Service in the Church of the Nazarene," [1971] (file 809-69); Osborn, *Bamboo*, 120–122; Osborn, *China*, 72–74.

101. Miller to Foreign Missionary Committee, December 22, 1956; Miller to G. B. Williamson and Rehfeldt, March 4, 1957; Benner to Rehfeldt, April 9, 1957; Rehfeldt to Miller, April 12, 1957, World Mission office; Miller to Rehfeldt, September 14, 1957; Holstead to Cunningham, May 7, 1991.

102. Michael and Elizabeth Varro to Coulter, December 1, 1966; Michael and Elizabeth Varro to Phillips, December 1, 1966; Varro to Coulter, July 16, 1967, and March 20, 1979.

103. L. C. Osborn to Rehfeldt, February 5, 1955, World Mission office; Miller to Rehfeldt, October 4, 1957 (file 908-11).

104. "Nazarenes in Taiwan," *Other Sheep* (June 1957), 7; Miller to Rehfeldt, September 14, 1957; John Chi [Chi Yuew Han] and workers to General Superintendents, September 26, 1957; Rehfeldt to Miller, September 27, 1957, World Mission office; Miller to Rehfeldt, October 4, 1957; Holstead to Cunningham, May 7, 1991. Kiehn does not describe any of the controversies in his "Legacy," 88–89.

105. Wiese to Lewis, November 27, 1964.

106. Wiese to Lewis, November 27, 1964.

107. Rehfeldt to Osborn, October 28, 1958, World Mission office; Leon and Emma Osborn to Mary Scott and Helen Temple, December 4, 1959, and February 16, 1961, Osborn file (Box 829); Holstead to Cunningham, May 7, 1991.

108. Rench to Coulter, November 27, 1962.

109. Rench to Coulter, November 27, 1962.

110. Miller to Lewis, September 13, 1962; interview with John Holstead, February 11, 1997.

111. Summary of "Taiwan Emergency Funds," 1960–1961; Wiese to Lewis and Coulter, June 28, 1963; Missionaries (signed) to Lewis, August 12, 1963; Wiese to Coulter, August 13, 1963; Wiese to Lewis, June 22, 1965.

112. Taiwan Missionary Council Meeting, March 21, 1962; Coulter to Miller, January 8, 1963; Coulter to Wiese, February 14, 1963; Wiese to Lewis, May 30, 1963; Lewis to Wiese, June 10, 1963; Coulter to Wiese, June 14, 1963; Taiwan Field—Council Meeting Minutes, November 8, 1965, Coulter papers.

113. Coulter to Osborn, January 21, 1963; Coulter to Rev. and Mrs. Osborn, February 14, 1963.

114. Coulter to Miller, February 14, 1963; Wiese to Coulter and Lewis, June 28, 1963; Miller to Lewis, November 11, 1963; Wiese to Lewis, June 22, 1965.

115. Rench to Lewis, October 24, 1962; Rench to Coulter, November 10, 1962, and November 27, 1962; Wiese to Coulter, March 12, 1963, and November 12, 1963; Wiese to Lewis, May 30, 1963, and July 2, 1963; [Missionaries] to Lewis, August 12, 1963; Ruth Miller to Lewis, August 20, 1963; Coulter to Wiese, August 21, 1963; Coulter to Rev. and Mrs. R. R. Miller, August 21 and November 5, 1963; Lewis to Rev. and Mrs. R. R. Miller, September 19, 1963; Wiese to Lewis, January 2, 1965; Coulter, "Report on Trip to Taiwan" [1967]; Rench to Phillips, January 8, 1969, Coulter papers.

116. Wiese to Lewis, April 30, 1964; Wiese to Ministry of Foreign Affairs, May 16, 1964; Miller to Lewis, n.d. [1965] (file 1361-18); Wiese to Lewis, January 12, 1965; Wiese to Lewis, April 12, 1965; Lewis to Wiese, April 15, 1965; Wiese to Lewis, July 7, 1965; Wiese to Lewis, July 31, 1965. See also *Manual of the Church of the Nazarene: History, Constitution, Government, Ritual 1960*, John Riley et al., editing committee (Kansas City, Mo.: Nazarene Publishing House, 1960), 134–135; "In Memoriam: Mrs. Ruth Andrews Miller (1903–1981)," *World Mission* (August 1981), 15.

117. Chinese Nazarene Preachers, All Nazarene Seminary Students, and Taipei Nazarene Church Members to [V. H.] Lewis, August 9, 1963 (file 1361-16); Coulter to National Pastors and Bible School Students of Taiwan, August 21, 1963.

118. Wiese, "Report to Council," November 8, 1965.

119. Wiese, "Report to Council," November 8, 1965; Allen Swanson, *Mending the Nets: Taiwan Church Growth and Loss in the 1980s* (Pasadena, Calif.: William Carey, 1986), 37; Rubinstein, *The Protestant Community*, 21, 25, 29, 36.

120. Wiese, "Report to Council," November 8, 1965.

121. Katherine Wiese to Lewis, June 7, 1965; Wiese, "Report to Council," November 8, 1965, Coulter papers. See also "A Veteran of the Cross Has Gone Home," *World Mission* (October 1977), 16.

122. Miller to Rehfeldt, December 4, 1957; Rehfeldt to Miller, June 2, 1958; "Minutes of Taiwan Council Meeting," October 25, 1960; Miller to Missionaries and National Workers, February 19, 1963; Holstead to Cunningham, May 7, 1991. Compare Allen Swanson, *Taiwan: Mainline Versus Independent Church Growth: A Study in Contrasts* (Pasadena, Calif.: William Carey, [1970]), 117–121; Wang, "Christianity in Modern Taiwan," 326.

123. *Church of the Nazarene Taiwan Field Annual Report—1966*, 46, cited in Jim Williams: "The Long-Lasting Impact of Early Financial Policy and Practices of the Taiwan Nazarene Church," Asia Pacific Nazarene Theological Seminary, 1986; Holstead to Coulter, April 3, 1967.

124. Wiese to Lewis, July 7, 1965; Holstead to Coulter, May 23, 1966; Rench to Phillips, January 8, 1969, and August 18, 1969; interview with Holstead, February 11, 1997.

125. Wiese, "Report to Council," November 8, 1965; Rench to Phillips, January 8, 1969. See also Allen J. Swanson, *The Church in Taiwan: Profile 1980: A Review of the Past; A Projection for the Future* (Pasadena, Calif.: William Carey, 1981), 429–431.

126. Interview with Holstead, February 11, 1997. On ethnicity and other factors, Swanson, *The Church in Taiwan: Profile 1980*, chapter 7, "The Local Church"; Rubinstein, *The Protestant Community on Modern Taiwan*, 38–40.

127. Executive Committee Meeting Minutes, July 7, 1962; Holstead, "Once They Were Headhunters," *Other Sheep* (July 1965), 8–9; George Rench, "Among the Mountain People," *Other Sheep* (May 1968), 19; Parker, *Mission to the World*, 279–282. Compare Ralph Covell, *Pentecost of the Hills in Taiwan: The Christian Faith Among the Original Inhabitants* (Pasadena, Calif.: Hope, 1998), 224–229.

128. Executive Committee Meeting Minutes, June 8, 1962; Wiese to Lewis, December 9, 1964; Katherine Wiese to Lewis, June 7, 1965; Coulter, "Taiwan," n.d. [1967].

129. Holstead to Coulter, December 13, 1965, February 1, 1966, and May 23, 1966; interview with John Holstead, February 11, 1997.

130. Ruth A. Miller, *The Darkest Side of the Road* (Kansas City, Mo.: Nazarene Publishing House, 1962), 59–61; Wiese to Lewis, March 8, 1965; Holstead to Coulter, December 13, 1965; Holstead to Coulter, February 1, 1966; Pan Ming-ding to Coulter, September 28, 1975; R. Franklin Cook, *Water From Deep Wells: A Survey to the Church of the Nazarene in India, Korea, Taiwan, Hong Kong, Australia, New Zealand* (Kansas City, Mo.: Nazarene Publishing House, 1977), 101–103; Jirair Tashjian, *Taiwan in Transition* (Kansas City, Mo.: Nazarene Publishing House, 1977), 38–40, 42–43, 50–54; "Taiwan Assembly," *Asia Pacific Ambassador* (April 1987), 1; *Asia Pacific Ambassador* (April/May 1989), 6. See also Jim Williams, "Accurate Contextualization: Prerequisite to Church Growth in Taiwan," M.A. religion thesis, Asia Pacific Nazarene Theological Seminary, 1987.

131. Raber, *Protestants in Changing Taiwan*, 80–82; Swanson, *Taiwan: Mainline Versus Independent*, 117–121.

132. Rench to Phillips, January 8, 1969.

# Chapter 5

# Korea

When China closed its doors to missionaries in 1949 Nazarenes keenly felt the urgency of missions in Asia. The threat of "godless communism" in the world meant that churchly and political aims coincided, and there was no place where this was more clearly the case than in Korea.

Elsewhere in Asia the church's expansion included the opening of new fields in the Philippines, Australia, New Zealand, Papua New Guinea, Taiwan and, in 1960, Samoa. The work that the church began in these countries during the post-war era represents the "second generation" of Nazarene efforts in this part of the world.

There were three stages of beginning for the work of the Church of the Nazarene in Korea. Abrupt political changes in the country necessitated these shifts. In the first stage, in the 1930s, Koreans trained in Japan, and under leadership from Japan, began work in both Pyongyang and Seoul. Little of that, however, survived World War II. Following this, in the second beginning, the church linked itself to a forceful leader of the holiness movement in the country, Chung Nam Soo. Many who came into the Nazarene church during this time had been converted under his ministry. Chung suddenly retired soon after young missionaries Donald and Adeline Owens arrived in 1954. Owens started the Bible College and dealt with a host of problems in the third beginning. Owens was dependent, nonetheless, on strong Korean leaders throughout his years in Korea, which extended to 1966. Indeed, one common characteristic of the Nazarene church in Korea, evident in each of the beginning stages, was that there were strong national leaders. Unlike Japan, where the missionaries and national leaders were on a nearly equal footing at the start, in Korea missionaries always played largely supportive roles, and this proved successful. In terms of membership, Korea became the most successful Nazarene work in Asia.

The holiness movement was already present in Korea before the coming of the Church of the Nazarene. A revival broke out in 1903, emanating from the Methodist Episcopal Church, South, mission. It was related to the revival that was sweeping the world, starting with Evan Roberts in Wales, and was part of the same movement that affected the Pentecostal Association mission in Buldana, India, at about the same time. As in much of the world, the revival in Korea spoke the language of holiness Wesleyanism. A medical doctor, R. A. Hardie, claimed the gift of the Holy Spirit, confessed his hardness of heart, and repented of his pride. Others spoke of receiving the "fire" of the Holy Spirit, not only empowering them for witnessing, but "burning sin out of their lives."[1] In spite of the Pentecostal language used, the revival in Korea was noted, said one Methodist bishop, for its "almost entire absence of fanaticism." Similarly, another Methodist missionary wrote that: "This work is genuine. There has been no false fire." As another revival was to do in the Nazarene mission in China about twenty years later, this revival in Korea convinced missionaries of the spiritual capacities of Asians. The revival crested in 1907.[2]

Very soon after this revival, the Oriental Missionary Society, which had begun in Japan and represented the holiness movement, entered Korea. Among OMS's first workers in Korea were John and Emily Thomas. The Thomases were supported by Star Hall in Manchester, England, and by other holiness missions in Great Britain. Several of these missions became part of the International Holiness Mission directed by John Thomas's older brother, David Thomas. (The International Holiness Mission united with the Church of the Nazarene in 1952.) John and Emily Thomas served in Korea from 1910 to 1920 and were instrumental in the founding of the OMS Bible School in Seoul. Some Nazarenes served under the OMS in Korea. These included William and Norah Heslop, also from England, who were friends of the Thomases. While serving the OMS from 1916 to 1921, the Heslops planted churches outside of Seoul. Such connections with the OMS were among the reasons that the Church of the Nazarene did not consider it imperative to enter Korea as a denomination in the early decades of the century.[3]

## The First Beginning

The Church of the Nazarene did not intend to enter Korea. Japanese and Korean workers were principally responsible for beginning the Church of the Nazarene there. The Church of the Nazarene in America knew little of the mission in Korea while it was under Japanese political control because leaders placed Korea on the Japan District. Before entering Korea, the Japanese church already had established two Korean congregations in Japan, one at Osaka and the other at Kyoto. These were the first Korean Nazarene congregations. They consisted of Koreans conscripted for work in Japan, and their families. In 1932 the Korean pastor of the Osaka church, Chang Sung Oak (whose Japanese name was Seigyoku Cho) volunteered to open the Church of the Nazarene in his own country. While in Japan he worked for the police as a Korean language translator and had studied at the OMS-affiliated Holiness Bible School in Tokyo. But he left the Japan Holiness Church of the OMS out of discontent with its various schisms. In 1932 he returned to Korea under the auspices of the Japan Nazarene district. He proceeded to Pyongyang, where Christianity was strong, and planted a Nazarene church there. He served as its pastor. As the church remained a part of the Japan District, Chang expected to be ordained by Nazarene General Superintendent J. B. Chapman at the 1935 District Assembly and felt himself discriminated against by Japanese leaders who rejected his suitability for ordination that year. In 1936 Chang was joined by Cho Jung Hwan, who had pastored the Korean Nazarene Church in Kyoto before city officials forced its closing. Cho began a second church in Pyongyang. After establishing this church, Cho also established work in Heijo, to the north of Pyongyang. Two hundred attended the Christmas 1937 service there. Like many Korean pastors, Cho conducted daily 5:00 a.m. prayer meetings.[4]

In the meantime, Nazarene leaders made other contacts. In 1931 Chung Nam Soo, who was then on a trip to the United States and contemplating leaving the Methodist Church, contacted J. G. Morrison, the Nazarene foreign missions director, about the possibility of his helping to begin the Church of the Nazarene in Korea. At that point, however, the church lacked funds to enter new fields. Chung then joined the OMS. Susan N. Fitkin, Woman's Foreign Missionary Society president, and Emma Word, its treasurer, visited Korea in 1936, toured some of the OMS work, and also met with Chung Nam Soo. Chung again expressed his desire to help in beginning the Church of the Nazarene in Korea. In 1937, while in the States, Chung again contacted Morrison. Chung told him that the OMS work lacked cohesion and was ready to disintegrate, and that the Nazarenes should be prepared to "save the pieces." (Although the Holiness Church suffered leadership problems and schisms, Chung was wrong in his estimation of its impending demise.) Morrison asked Eckel, the Nazarene missionary in Japan, to investigate the situation and make some specific recommendations.

When the General Board divided the Japan District in early 1936 it placed Korea on the Eastern Japan (Kwansai) District under William Eckel and Nobumi Isayama. Eckel went to Korea and contacted ten or twelve congregations, each with thirty or forty members. According to him, each stated its desire to be reorganized as a Church of the Nazarene. If these congregations were formerly associated with the OMS, as was probably the case, it would explain why Eckel hesitated to take them in, and did not do so. In spite of this, Eckel thought that the prospects for the Church of the Nazarene in Korea were even brighter than in Japan, where the church was growing rapidly in the 1930s.[5]

In 1938 Isayama visited Korea. An independent "Gospel" church in Youngchun, Seoul, which had been started by a Japanese pastor and had about forty members, approached Isayama about becoming Nazarene. Isayama agreed to take it in. In October 1938 the congregation was organized as the fourth Nazarene church in Korea. Chang Sung Oak attempted to pastor this church in Seoul as well as the one he had established in Pyongyang. He met with the Seoul congregation once a month, leaving some of the work in Pyongyang to Son Shin Gu, a Bible woman. In late 1939, when the Japanese increased their persecution of Christians in Pyongyang, Chang moved to Seoul. Though the Japanese ordered both of the Nazarene churches in Pyongyang to close, they continued secretly, led by lay leaders.[6]

The Korean leaders eventually found it impossible to continue their ministries. Chang Sung Oak continued to pastor the Seoul congregation until June 1941, when his refusal to obey Japanese demands for him to bow toward the emperor's shrine forced him to temporarily retire. He turned to farming for the duration of the war. At the same time the Japanese military government sent Pastor Cho Jung Hwan to a mining camp where, apparently, he died. The churches in Korea fell completely under the care of Japanese pastors. Tei Ki-sho, a Nazarene pastor stationed in Korea by his government, made contacts with one of the churches in Pyongyang and even opened an outstation at Tonsanri. In 1940 he began yet another church at Shinri. He maintained contact with the Seoul church as well, which was then under lay leadership. Tei encouraged the Nazarene church in Japan to help in church construction projects in Korea.[7]

During the war the Protestant churches in Korea suffered just as they did in Japan itself and other countries under Japanese control. The Japanese government strictly controlled religious activities.

After the war, the Protestant churches in Korea no longer wanted or needed their connections with Japan and Japanese churches. Koreans shunned connections with Japanese churches and attempted to forget any roots that their churches might have had in Japanese Protestantism. The Church of the Nazarene did not attempt to place Korea once more under the Japan District. Chang Sung Oak wrote to General Superintendent Chapman soon after the war ended, asking the church to send missionary Eckel to reorganize the work in Korea.[8]

Meanwhile, Chung Nam Soo pursued talks with C. Warren Jones, then foreign missions secretary, in order to persuade him that the Church of the Nazarene should enter Korea and sponsor him as its first missionary. The Korea Holiness Church, he said, could not cope with the needs of the millions. He told Jones that he knew of several independent holiness congregations that would join him immediately, should he be allowed to "begin" the Church of the Nazarene in Korea. Chung solicited Jones's help in starting a Workers Training School by sending a "blessed, strong and outstanding holiness brother to teach us."[9] Chung impressed Jones, who urged General Superintendent Orval J. Nease to visit Korea on his scheduled trip to Asia in 1948.[10]

## The Second Beginning

Kansas City leaders envisioned Chung Nam Soo as the church's key leader in post-war Korea. Chung was born near Pyongyang in 1895. One of his grandfathers converted from shamanism to Christianity through the efforts of a Presbyterian missionary, and burned the family's idols. Chung himself became a Christian at age thirteen, and was soon exhorting and preaching. Desiring more education than his family could give him, he found a sponsor in An [Ahn] Chang Ho. An was a leading anti-Japanese nationalist leader in the Pyongyang area and a teacher at Taesong College. A Presbyterian, An helped to found the Independence Club, but he favored personal renewal rather than armed resistance as the way to reform the nation. When the Japanese arrested An in 1910, Chung took care of him in prison. When An escaped from prison and fled to mainland China, he took Chung with him. The pair made their way through Russia, to Europe and England, and finally to New York, where they arrived in 1911. There An and Chung parted company, but Chung retained strongly nationalist sentiments. An resumed his leadership in the nationalist movement from abroad and later returned to Korea.[11]

Chung, still only sixteen years old, settled in Los Angeles, where he found a job as a dishwasher in a hotel and studied English. He also worked for a time in a hospital, all the while donating money from his earnings to the Korean nationalist cause. He became active in the Korean Presbyterian Church in Los Angeles. In 1916, he and a friend decided to attend college in order to prepare for the ministry, and they decided upon a Presbyterian school, Berea College in Kentucky. Aboard the train from California to Kentucky, Chung met Henry C. Morrison, the president of Asbury College, a Methodist-related and strongly holiness school in Wilmore, Kentucky. Morrison persuaded Chung to attend Asbury rather than Berea.

At Asbury, Chung learned the revival techniques as well as the Wesleyan holiness theology of conservative Methodism, and professed that he was entirely sanctified. He became a member of and was ordained in the Kentucky Conference of the Methodist Episcopal Church (South). His classmates included Nazarenes. Morrison took Chung to various holiness camp meetings and holiness Bible colleges around the country, where, as at Asbury, he became acquainted with Nazarenes. Chung himself became a popular camp meeting speaker. E. Stanley Jones, missionary to India and himself a graduate of Asbury, met Chung and persuaded him that Korea needed him more than America. After Chung graduated from Asbury in 1925 he applied for missionary service in the Methodist Church. They refused him. Chung thought it was because of his holiness leanings. He decided to go to Korea anyway, and, after raising money for his support from camp meetings and individual donors, set sail for Korea. He arrived in Pusan in 1926.

He struggled to regain mastery of his own language and made contacts with Korean Methodist leaders. Soon he was holding revivals throughout the country and even among Koreans in Manchuria. He used the same style of revivalist evangelism that he had learned in America. He invited seekers to bow at an altar rail in the front to confess their sins and be born again. For several years, Chung retained his ministerial credentials in the Kentucky Methodist Conference and did not join the Methodist Church in Korea. Chung went back to the United States to generate financial support for his ministry in 1928, 1931 and 1937.

In 1931 Chung joined the Oriental Missionary Society, which by this time had established a strong Holiness Church in Korea. Chung became a key evangelist and a leading light in the holiness movement in Korea. He held "come-and-go" tent revivals, organized a nationwide circuit, and traveled with a band of young evangelists. Chung was best in large, city- or town-wide crusades. His associates would hand out tracts during the day, and he would hold mass revival meetings in the evenings. Thousands attended his crusades. Churches were planted throughout the country as his revivals won seekers and adherents. Chung's successes greatly impressed OMS missionaries. One called Chung "God's mouthpiece through which silver tones of an unadulterated gospel swept in musical rhythm over the souls of men," and declared that Chung "made souls tremble as he preached 'Hell fire'."[12] In 1933 the First General Assembly of the Korea Holiness Church appointed Chung director of its evangelism committee.[13]

But Chung was party to a division in the Korea Holiness Church. A large faction in the Holiness Church favored the OMS model emerging from Japan. Most of this faction ministered in the central part of the country. Chung, however, was part of a faction that favored American holiness movement ties. This group had most of its supporters in the northwestern part of the country. In 1935 the Holiness Church's General Assembly elected one of Chung's protégés, Pyun Nam Sung, superintendent. However, the opposing faction nullified the election. Chung and his followers harshly criticized the central faction for this and other actions, including some financial dealings, and began its own paper, *Holy Fire*, which forged a network among converts and followers in several denominations. In 1936 Chung's northwestern faction withdrew from the Holiness Church. Chung hoped that the Church of the Nazarene would take interest in organizing these as Nazarene churches. Chung became acquainted with Chang Sung Oak, the Nazarene pastor. When Eckel proved reluctant, however, to accession these churches, Chung established ties with the Church of God (Anderson). A Church of God missionary stationed in Japan visited Korea in 1937.[14]

By 1940 Japan forbade any foreign money from entering Korea, and secret police began following Chung everywhere. Eventually they confiscated his tent. The Japanese suspected him of being a spy because of his numerous foreign contacts and arrested him that September. They imprisoned him for three months, during which time they tortured him. He lost the sight in one eye as a result. Afterward Chung moved outside of Seoul and ceased activities. Literally, he tended his garden. After the war, Chung returned to America. In 1947 he again approached the Church of the Nazarene about his affiliating with it. This time he persuaded Jones that the Nazarenes should enter Korea in earnest.[15]

The time also was ripe from the perspective of the general church. The situation in Korea was on the minds of Americans. The United States had pushed for an election in South Korea, which took place in May 1948. Syngman Rhee, an ardent anti-Communist and Protestant loyal to United States interests in Korea, was elected president of the country. Other Korean Christians held top government positions. Korean Christians in general and Protestants in particular were pro-American.[16]

At the same time, Nazarene general superintendents challenged the church to broaden its vision and responsibility toward the post-war world. So Orval Nease traveled to Korea in October 1948—two months after the founding of the Republic of Korea—with a mandate to establish the church in the country.

Nease held an organizational meeting, later considered the birth date of the Church of the Nazarene in Korea. Nease talked at length with Chung and other pastors whom Chung brought in for the meeting about the Nazarene church. Chang Sung Oak and Seung Hak Su, the Nazarene pastors, also were present. Nease transferred the ministerial credentials of Chung Nam Soo, Quak Chae Kun, Suh Jae Chul and Ahn Hyung Chu to the Church of the Nazarene. Apparently Quak, Suh and Ahn had been ordained in the Church of God (Anderson) and believed that the Church of God was not going to return to Korea following the war. It was a strong group of pastors.

Seung and Chang represented threads connecting the new group with what the Church of the Nazarene had done before the war. Seung Hak Su was a graduate of both the Nazarene and the Free Methodist schools in Japan. Right after the war Seung had returned to Korea and had taken up the pastorate of the Seoul Youngchun church. Both Chang Sung Oak and Seung Hak Su had been ordained during the war, though it is not clear under what auspices. From them Nease received reports of three previously established Nazarene congregations functioning north of the thirty-eighth parallel, which by then separated North from South Korea.

Nease ordained one other minister, Park Ki Suh, who also had been affiliated with the Church of God. Nease also issued ministers licenses to at least three others. He preached in a Church of God (Anderson) church in Pildong, Seoul.[17]

There may have been misunderstandings on both sides. To the Korean leaders, the 1948 meeting represented the union of the Church of the Nazarene in Korea and the Church of God (Anderson). But Nease was under the impression that the pastors were OMS men (as they may have been originally). Nease related nothing whatsoever in his report about the Church of God.[18]

That most were Bible school graduates pleased Nease. He found them to be "seasoned" and "clear in their message and experience of second blessing holiness with the Wesleyan emphasis." He also called them "an intelligent, earnest, loyal group of men." Nease accepted into the Church of the Nazarene nine fully organized churches: Mokpo, Pyongtaek, Inkwangri, Anjung, and five churches in Seoul. The only previously existing Church of the Nazarene included in the group was the Youngchun Church in Seoul, still pastored by Seung Hak Su. The rest had been affiliated with the Church of God. In all there were about eight hundred members. Nease seemed wholly pleased with the start. He preached holiness in the American evangelistic style and seekers crowded to the front in "altar calls" that followed.[19]

Nease proceeded to organize what he called a "Native Missionary Council," which elected Chung as chairman. There were no provisions in the *Manual* or in missions policy for this type of set-up. He believed that the situation in Korea was unique because it could and should be led by Koreans from the start. The recommendations that Nease gave to the Foreign Missions Department included: (1) giving financial support to the Korean pastors; (2) providing additional money in order to secure worship places; (3) implementing an evangelistic campaign; and, (4) establishing a Bible Training School. He also advised that the church invite Chung to the States to raise the support and consciousness of the church regarding the Korean work. Significantly, Nease did *not* recommend that the church send missionaries to Korea, and implied to the Koreans that it was not the church's intention ever to send missionaries to Korea.[20]

Chang Sung Oak left the denomination soon after Nease's departure, to take up a prison chaplain ministry. In fact, it seemed to him that he and Seung were not given recognition for their pioneering efforts, or significant leadership in the reorganization.[21]

The church paid and treated Chung Nam Soo as a missionary. Leaders in Kansas City had full confidence in him, since he could speak not only English but the holiness language as well, and could preach in the American revivalist fashion. The Missions Department deposited his salary in a bank account he maintained in Wilmore. As advised by church leaders, Chung toured Nazarene churches in America in 1949 in order to raise both interest in and financial support for the "new" mission of the church in Korea. At the Nazarene college in Bethany, Oklahoma, for instance, he raised $6,200 in cash and pledges from students and faculty members. Chung captivated the attention of young Bethany students, including Donald Owens. However, when it was time for Chung's return to Korea, the political situation in Korea had worsened and the possibility of war with China loomed in the minds of many. Nease worried about sending him back. He feared that if war should occur Chung would be a "marked man" by the Communists.[22]

Chung returned to Korea, nonetheless, in the spring 1950 and met in Suwon with the band of Nazarene pastors. He conducted prayer meetings and a revival in conjunction with the workers' meeting. But war began in June, shortly after Chung's return. The Communist army quickly invaded from the North. Chung feared for his life and that of his family. Thousands of Koreans fled from Seoul every way they could, the Chung family among them. Chung drove a 1947 Chevrolet that had been donated to him in the States across the rough, muddy roads going south, and the family made their way as quickly as possible in front of the fast-advancing Communist army. Tires kept going flat. But they finally reached Pusan safely. At the same time, Seung Hak Su and his family also fled south from Seoul. But Seung and all of his family except one son were killed by the United Nations air forces, which mistook their band fleeing south for advancing Chinese Communists. Upon reaching Pusan, the Chungs secured passage to America, mostly on the basis of his passport, which recorded his previous trips. He returned to Korea briefly in late 1950, and then went back to the United States again, where he resumed his preaching. He and his family remained in America until November 1952.[23]

During this interval in the States, Chung and Nazarene general leaders decided on post-war plans. Nease died in 1950, and with him any promises that might have been made that missionaries would not be sent. Not only that, the political and social situation in Korea altered the scenario, and Chung himself now favored the appointment of a missionary. He and Remiss Rehfeldt, foreign missions secretary, agreed that it would be in the best interests of the work to send a missionary to Korea when it was possible, primarily to teach in the proposed Bible school. However, there was confusion in leaders' minds as to what this missionary's relation would be to Chung. General Superintendent Hardy C. Powers, for instance, believed that the missionary would assume the "top spot" in Korea, but Rehfeldt seemed willing for Chung to maintain the highest position.[24]

Chung and Rehfeldt did nothing to dissolve the council that Nease had established, of which Chung was still chairman, and it remained intact. Rehfeldt and the general superintendents, on advice from Chung, also decided that it would be well for the church to undertake some unstated "rehabilitation" projects in Korea. On some occasions between 1950 and 1952, Chung spoke to churches in America about opening an orphanage in Korea, even though the general church was opposed to this, at least over the long term. Rehfeldt wanted little to do with commitments such as this, which he feared might absorb funds needed elsewhere and dilute the evangelistic thrust of the church in Korea. By late 1952 the general church had set aside $10,000 for the Korean work in addition to what Chung himself had raised during his two-year stay in America.[25]

Chung established himself in Pusan while the war continued in the North. He made contacts with some Korean Nazarenes who had fled there, and established a temporary headquarters. Nine preachers and four Bible women had survived the war, he found. With the permission of Kansas City, Chung gave money set aside for other purposes directly to the remaining pastors for their immediate relief.[26]

He proceeded, despite the general church's disapproval, with the orphanage project and channeled money that he had raised into a Methodist-affiliated work called the "Miss Choe Orphanage." He also furnished money for a sewing school associated with the Nazarene church in Pyungtaek.[27]

Despite his attempts to reorganize the work of the Church of the Nazarene, Chung sensed discontent among some of the Korean pastors. For some, Chung's credibility as a leader had been lost when he had fled to the United States during the war. He had not suffered with them. When Chung attempted to assert superintendency of the work, they resented it.

At the same time, a Church of God (Anderson) missionary stationed in Japan went to Korea to gather the remnants of his denomination's work. The Church of God had built the churches that the Nazarenes then used in Pildong and Suwon (though the Church of the Nazarene had helped to rebuild these churches). Quak Chae Kun of the Mokpo church, Ahn Hyung Chu of the Pildong church, Kim Yung Chin, a minister licensed by Nease in 1948 who was pastoring the Suwon church, and, later, Lee Byung He, returned to the Church of God. The issue was not only the arrival of the Church of God missionary. These Korean pastors chaffed under Chung and the kind of church structure he represented. They preferred the congregational polity of the Church of God. In April 1954, the Nazarenes went so far as to "excommunicate" Quak, Ahn and Kim, accusing them of denying holiness and of disagreeing with the Nazarene church's form of government.[28]

The work was in disarray, then, when Chung wrote to the general leaders in 1953 about the plans for sending a missionary: "Have you find [*sic*] the blessed brother, the missionary who will come to Korea? We have to have a missionary."[29] Chung needed to return to the States for an eye operation. After pursuing several other possibilities, Rehfeldt and the general superintendents decided upon Donald and Adeline Owens to become missionaries to Korea. They were recent graduates of Bethany, where Donald Owens had earned both a bachelor of arts and bachelor of theology degree, and were pastoring in Nebraska while waiting for a missionary appointment. (This was the pattern set by Rehfeldt in these years, to send very young missionaries—recently graduated, newly married, and just ordained.) Yet Rehfeldt could have done what he had done in Taiwan and transfer some middle-aged and experienced missionaries to Korea. Rehfeldt certainly could have found a similar couple for Korea if he had so chosen. But in the case of Korea, Rehfeldt understood that Chung would be remaining and that he would be the senior missionary in charge. Korea was a unique case. In Rehfeldt's estimation Korea did not need a heavy-handed or authoritarian American missionary. It was not like Japan, where early missionary and national leaders were about the same age. In Korea, someone younger and inexperienced would be more likely to get along with and follow the leadership of Chung. Owens had heard Chung speak at Bethany and warmed to the prospects of working with him. Chung wrote Owens encouraging, fatherly letters after hearing of his appointment to Korea. He was eager for him to come as soon as possible, especially to get the Bible school started, and Chung dissuaded the church from stationing the Owenses in Japan for a few months to learn the Korean language before coming.

The Owenses arrived in Korea in May 1954. The Koreans called them *oh un-soo*—"recipients of many blessings." However, their youthfulness did not impress them. Several of the pastors who remained loyal to Chung were uncertain about Owens. The Owenses immediately began laying plans for the Bible school and plunged into language study. The church had decided to buy the house in Seoul and surrounding land on which the Chungs lived. The Owenses stayed with the Chungs for about two months, until the upper story of one of the Bible school buildings under construction on the property was habitable.[30]

## The Third Beginning

Owens faced several divisive issues from the very beginning. Quak, Ahn and Kim Yung Chin had just been "excommunicated" and were ready to take their congregations with them back into the Church of God. In several other places where there was a church, legal titles to the property were unclear. In some cases the local pastors held the deeds in their own names. Chung and Owens oversaw the registration of the properties under the "Corporate Board" of the "Church of the Nazarene in Korea," of which Chung was still chairman. They completed this by August 1954.

In the same month Chung abruptly left for America. His eye operation could not wait. But he expressed his expectation to return to Korea as soon as possible in order to continue his leadership. He appointed Park Ki Suh, the only other ordained minister remaining in the church whom Nease had taken in in 1948, to act in his stead as board chairman. This made it difficult for Owens to assume any leadership role, since, without a functioning District Assembly and District Board, the corporate board was the highest administrative as well as legally recognized entity of the church in Korea. Owens found the pastors outwardly cooperative, but still independent-minded. They hesitated to act on Owens's recommendations while waiting Chung's return.

Chung attempted to control the church from America through letters to the pastors and instructions to Park, bypassing Owens. Chung even elicited Rehfeldt's support to keep the church from Owens's control by explaining that he fully intended to return. Acting upon this, Rehfeldt told Owens that Korea was not a mission field like other countries, since national leadership prevailed, and that Owens's position, therefore, was different. He admonished Owens simply to hold the pastors steady until Chung returned. All of this frustrated Owens. He was uncertain as to who should make the daily decisions necessary for the church—should it be he or Park, Chung's appointed representative? The Korean pastors told Owens that he should refrain from interfering with the work of the church and Rehfeldt, for the most part, agreed. Even after Chung had been in America for eight months, Rehfeldt told Owens to work together with Park before disbursing funds for the ongoing program of the church.[31]

Although frustrated and uncertain as to his role, Owens proceeded in his assigned tasks. He had taken few missions courses while a student at Bethany. What he adopted as a missionary were the philosophies that had worked so well in other missions in Korea. Since the beginning of Protestantism in the country, missionaries had modified and implemented the ideas of John Nevius, a late-nineteenth-century missionary to China who had held conferences with Presbyterian and Methodist missionaries in Korea when their missions were just beginning. Nevius stressed the "three-selfs" of mission theorists such as Henry Venn and Rufus Anderson and, like them, Nevius emphasized evangelism over institutional and educational work. He put emphasis upon the true indigenization of the churches. Owens learned from Nevius and the older missions the importance of allowing Koreans to build their own church. Of course, in a sense, Owens had little choice.

Pastors were ready to build the Church of the Nazarene in Korea with or without the help of Owens or any other missionaries. Owens also preferred that the Church of the Nazarene work where there was less competition with other Protestant groups—which meant away from the cities, in rural localities.[32]

Owens's first tasks were to learn the Korean language and begin the Bible Training School that would train Korean leaders and educate them in the theology and polity of the Church of the Nazarene. Owens developed a three-year curriculum. The school began in September 1954, with twenty-three students, eight of whom were already pastoring. Owens set up the school's board of trustees, which consisted of two missionaries (Donald and Adeline Owens initially), two pastors and two lay persons. From the beginning, thus, the school was led by a predominantly Korean board. During the next school year Park Ki Suh and Cho Moon Kyung joined the faculty. As some educated pastors from Presbyterian and other denominations expressed interest in joining the Church of the Nazarene, it became policy that all wishing to be Nazarene ministers must attend the Bible school for at least one year. This signified Owens's desire to maintain the doctrinal distinctives of the church. The first commencement, April 1, 1958, marked the graduation of five: Kim Hwan Sun, Park Nah Won, Oh Jung Hwan, Lee Bong Hwan and Lee Young Jun. In late 1958, Owens helped to secure a 21-acre tract in the Kimpo area of Seoul, and the school transferred there the following year. The previously purchased property was sold to help in this move. By 1960 a high school diploma became necessary for admittance.[33]

In an attempt to move toward measures of self-government, Owens and the Korean pastors laid plans in mid-1955 to hold a District Assembly. Owens oversaw the translation of the *Manual*. Rehfeldt gave his approval for the Assembly as long as Chung received notification in time to return, should he want to be considered for the district superintendency. Since Chung was still the chairman of the corporate board, both he and the pastors considered this position to be higher than the district superintendent anyway, as only the corporate board had legal standing and could hold property. Rehfeldt discouraged Owens from considering himself for the district superintendency. The Department of Foreign Missions, said Rehfeldt, would even allow the election of an unordained minister, in this case, should the Korean church decide that this was best. (In India in 1937, Bhujbal had been ordained one day and elected superintendent the next.) Owens agreed that he should not be considered for district superintendent, even though he felt that Park, the most likely candidate, who did not speak English, did not yet fully comprehend Nazarene district organization. Some pastors told Owens that they preferred him over Park. Factions were developing. Chung reported to Rehfeldt that Owens was turning the pastors against him and that Owens was posturing himself for election to the superintendency. Rehfeldt assured Chung that the general church had no desire to take leadership positions away from the Koreans, and again warned Owens not to accept the position. More importantly, Rehfeldt told Chung that as far as he was concerned the Korean district would enjoy the same status as a United States district once a Korean superintendent was elected. Rehfeldt still hoped Chung himself would return but could not envision his serving as district superintendent unless he got back to Korea in time for the District Assembly.[34]

Chung did not return, however, and Owens presided over the assembly that took place in August 1955. Pastors and delegates from eleven churches comprised the assembly. Owens spent two days going over the organization and agenda of the assembly before proceedings actually began. He preached holiness sermons in the evenings. Revival seemed to settle upon the national workers. In the business sessions Owens explained that while an ordained minister was the preferable choice for election as district superintendent, the general church was permitting them to consider ones not yet ordained. Owens told them, also, that he himself was not a candidate and that Chung had withdrawn himself from consideration by his failure to return by this time. Apparently Chung had told the pastors over whom he had influence to vote for Park. As required by the Nazarene *Manual*, a two-thirds vote was necessary for election. The first ballot gave Park twelve votes and Owens ten. Some thought that Owens should have withdrawn from the election, but he did not. On the third ballot Park had thirteen votes, and Owens nine. When, after the fourth ballot, there still was no two-thirds majority for either, Owens referred the matter to Kansas City for an appointment to be made by the general superintendents.[35]

Owens wrote to Rehfeldt: "Personally, we have no desire to be superintendent here, and recommend to the department . . . that Brother Park be appointed to this position. You can be sure we will do our best to support him."[36]

In January 1956 the general superintendents appointed Park as district superintendent. In the intervening months, between the assembly and the appointment, Owens consulted with Park on pastoral arrangements and other matters that arose, and a solid working relationship between them developed. Administrative problems remained, however. After the appointment of Park, with Chung out of the picture, the general superintendents now looked upon Owens as "the missionary in charge of all of our work in Korea." As such they also saw that the Korean work was not after all very different from other countries around the world in which there were national superintendents as well as missionaries. Park was to present all of his problems to Owens, rather than directly to headquarters.[37]

A complication remained in that Chung was still chairman of the corporate board. As such he still attempted to control events in Korea from America. The church owed Chung several thousand dollars for his house in Seoul, which he had sold to the mission. In fact, while in America, Chung started legal procedures against the general church in order to secure the money. The final arrangement was this: that if Chung resigned as chairman of the corporate board the church would expedite its remaining financial obligations to him. It worked. Chung resigned as of October 1, 1956, and the church paid what it owed him.[38]

In addition to setting up the Bible College and the district, Owens helped to settle matters pertaining to the Church of God. The Church of the Nazarene accepted $2,000 from the Church of God (Anderson) for what it had invested in the Pildong and Suwon churches and used this money toward the purchase of the Kimpo property, where the Bible College and headquarters relocated. With these issues finally resolved, Owens wrote to Rehfeldt late in 1956: "The difficulties we have faced in our first two years here are all but over."[39] He looked forward to revival while stressing self-support measures.[40]

The district organization proceeded efficiently in helping the church to expand and grow. From the earliest days there was a push from the Koreans as well as from Owens for self-support. A district advisory committee in November 1956 established a plan for reaching self-support within ten years. Korean Nazarene pastors and laypersons alike accepted the challenge to move as quickly as possible toward self-support. Local churches evidenced faithful tithing among members. By 1962 each of the organized churches was paying all of its local expenses, with the exception that some were still receiving support for their pastor's salary. Five were completely self-supporting: Chung Nong Dong, An Jung, In Kwang, Nai-Gieli and Youngchun. There was a schedule in place to increase pastoral support in all of the remaining churches so that all would be self-supporting within ten years.[41]

Churches and pastors accepted Nazarene polity. The Anjong church sponsored a short-lived Bible school, but it failed to receive either recognition or support from the district (as it would have seemed to compete with the Bible Training School in Seoul). At the 1959 District Assembly, General Superintendent Benner ordained or recognized the ordination credentials of fifteen. It was the first ordination service since 1948. The same assembly unanimously (but for one abstention) reelected Park as superintendent, yet expressed thanks for the continuing support of Chung Nam Soo, belying his continuing influence. Park reported 822 full and 1,066 probationary members, a 42 percent increase over the previous year, but about the same number of members as the church had had in 1948.[42]

New leaders emerged in the late 1950s and 1960s. Among them, Cho Moon Kyung was converted in 1951 and united with the Church of the Nazarene in 1952 in Pusan. There he served as an assistant to Chung Nam Soo, who advised him to attend an interdenominational seminary. This education enabled him to join the faculty of the Nazarene Bible Training School in 1955. Benner ordained him in 1959. While he pastored the Wonjung church about 65 miles from Seoul he helped to start other churches. He eventually pastored what was then the largest church, the Seoul Sajikdong church. He became superintendent of the Central District in 1973 (when the country was divided into two districts) and served until 1979.[43]

Another leader, Oh Jung Hwan, was a teacher in Anjung when he came into contact with holiness preaching. Chung Nam Soo sent him to start a church in Youngdeungpo, Seoul. He was among the first to enroll in and graduate from the Bible Training School. He served as district treasurer for nine years. While later pastoring the Taehong congregation, he continued to plant churches. He became superintendent of the South District in 1973 and served until 1982.[44]

Kim Young Baek was another young pastor with ties to Chung. Kim had belonged to the Hongjaedong Church of God in Seoul, which a bomb destroyed during the war. While a refugee in Pusan he made contact with Chung, who urged him to continue his education at the Methodist Seminary in the same city. Later Kim studied at Central Theological College, Nazarene Bible Training School and Seoul Theological Seminary. While enrolled in the Nazarene school he pastored the Younsuchun church. General Superintendent Samuel Young ordained Kim (and two others) in 1962. Eventually Kim joined the Bible school faculty and served for a time as academic dean. Over the years Kim held a variety of church offices, including district secretary, district treasurer, Nazarene Young People's Society president and, while still pastoring the South Seoul church, superintendent of the Central District.[45]

But leadership and other struggles emerged within the church in the 1960s. At the 1960 Assembly, Park received 17 "no" votes out of 74 ballots cast, showing some discontent with his leadership. As the balloting began at the 1961 Assembly, Park failed to receive the two-thirds vote necessary for reelection. As a leader, Park seemed to the younger pastors provincial, strict, and a difficult person with whom to converse. The second ballot included all of the ordained ministers, with Cho Moon Kyung the second-highest, garnering 28 votes compared to Park's 46, out of 92 cast. In succeeding ballots it became clear that neither Park nor Cho would receive the necessary votes, and Kim Chong Soo emerged, surprisingly, as the winner.[46]

After leaving the superintendency, Park Ki Suh became pastor of the Chung Nong Dong church, which at the time was the largest in the district. Later he pastored in Anjung. In 1981, Park became district superintendent again, this time of the newly organized East District, where he served until his retirement in 1983.[47]

Kim Chong Soo, a businessman before he became a minister, had been converted at age sixteen while living in Japan and had become acquainted with the Church of the Nazarene there. Business ventures continued to call him back and forth to Japan after the Second World War, until he felt called to preach. He began pastoring the Pyungtaek Church of the Nazarene in 1949 and later studied at both the Nazarene Bible Training School and the Hanyang Bible Training School. He served as district treasurer under Park Ki Suh. Koreans considered him close to the missionaries and, indeed, Donald Owens called him "a marvelous leader and a holiness preacher."[48]

The district grew markedly under Kim: from 30 congregations, 1,698 members and 14 ordained ministers in 1960 to 70 congregations, 6,155 members and 58 ordained ministers in 1970. This was the result of continued aggressive expansion. Kim emphasized evangelism and outreach, especially in rural localities. The distribution of thousands of tracts each year was one evangelism tool.[49]

During the 1970s Nazarene membership in Korea grew by more than 450 percent. In one year, 1974, the church gained 9,406 members. By 1980 there were 29,000 members worshipping in 148 Nazarene congregations. The growth followed the strategy of church planting, but a lot of it during this decade was related to the general upsurge in conversions in the country. The number of Protestants in the country rose dramatically from 1970 to 1980. The growth accompanied industrialization, urbanization and economic growth. Nazarenes participated in mass meetings, including a Billy Graham crusade in 1973 and "Explo '74." Dawn prayer meetings and cell groups preserved converts. Like other Koreans, they attributed the growth of the church not to sociological factors, but to Bible study and prayer, including daily "dawn prayer meetings."[50]

While there were a few strong city churches, most of the congregations were located on the outskirts of cities or in rural areas. The emphasis on rural areas reflected Owens's philosophy. But in rural areas Kim sensed more opposition from Roman Catholicism than from non-Christian religions. In many areas in the early 1960s the people remained poor and so pastors also suffered financially. Nine out of about 35 organized churches in 1964 supported their own pastors. The following year the number of organized churches had risen to 49, of which 11 were fully self-supporting. As in Taiwan, missionaries and leaders in the 1960s set step-by-step goals for each local congregation to reach self-support. In Korea, because of both the economic progress of the country and the long Protestant tradition that stressed self-support, urban congregations reached their goals earlier than ten years. Leaders then could use district money to open new work rather than maintain existing ones.[51]

The church saw progress in other areas as well. A missionary society developed among the Korean churches. In 1965, for instance, it undertook box work for Africa. In 1967 the church set up a ministerial retirement plan for Korea based on bags of rice, or the equivalent, for so many years of service.[52]

Kim Chong Soo's leadership, however, did not go smoothly, and he was challenged at annual District Assemblies. There were two factions, one representing the Seoul area and the other the more rural areas. At the 1965 assembly Kim was reelected, but not until the sixth ballot. (The former superintendent, Park Ki Suh, was second in the balloting.) Owens sensed, however, that all had been done in a "good spirit" and that Kim had been "gracious" throughout.[53]

The Owenses finished their service in Korea in 1966. This marked the end of the "third beginning." Though in a sense Owens was the "pioneer missionary" in Korea, he preferred to give that honor to Chung. Owens's influence and style of leadership was far different than that of earlier missionaries such as M. D. Wood, Minnie Staples and Peter Kiehn. In his youth, his loyalty to the denomination and its political structure, and his attempt to establish the church along accepted missiological principles, Owens was more like Leighton Tracy, William Eckel and Harry Wiese. From the beginning, the Korean church possessed strong-willed and capable leaders who did not always agree with missionaries and who competed among themselves for positions, but who nonetheless zealously expanded the church. The missionaries served in advisory capacities, except at the college, where they maintained control. A missionary never served as district superintendent, and missionaries left the church's government to the greatest extent possible under the church's *Manual* in Korean hands. The nature of the missionaries as well as the maturity of the pastors created a more indigenous situation in Korea than in other countries where older missionaries were likely to dominate younger workers. The Korean church pushed the Nazarene leaders to recognize the wisdom as well as the necessity of allowing Koreans to lead the way.[54]

Following the Owenses' departure, rifts between missionaries spilled over into issues dividing Koreans. Part of the problem among the missionaries was that they lived and worked together on the same compound in Seoul where the Bible College was located. Even Korean faculty members teaching at the Bible College lived on the same compound. It became difficult to separate life issues such as the distribution of the mail and the use of the mission car, from work, or to separate control over the school from the mission. Eldon Cornett, who had been in Korea since 1957 and who served as mission director after Owens, saw good in building residences for missionaries outside of Seoul. But he admitted that it would not be for the purpose of evangelizing, since that was going along well enough in the hands of Koreans. He also saw several reasons for relocating the school outside of Seoul. One of them would be to separate the functions of the school from that of the mission.[55]

Amid the conflicts among missionaries who lived on the same compound, there was dissension among the school's faculty members that came to a climax in 1968. In 1965 the salary of Korean faculty members was the equivalent of $45 per month (compared to the $50 a month missionaries were receiving).[56] In mid-1968 the Korean professors issued a list of demands that included higher salaries, medical benefits, and vacation bonuses. They insisted that the district superintendent, who was on the college's control board, be present at all meetings pertaining to the school and its policies. They believed that the missionaries rather than the college's board were controlling the school, especially its finances, and insisted that one of the Korean professors rather than a missionary serve as the school's treasurer. The missionaries would not concede to these demands, except that the district superintendent could participate in major policy decisions related to the school. The other issues remained unresolved.[57]

Meanwhile, opposition continued to Kim Chong Soo's superintendency. At the 1970 District Assembly a group of pastors and their lay followers, calling themselves the "Protectors of the Manual," opposed Kim. This opposition group remained loyal to Chung Nam Soo and Park Ki Suh, and included the professors at the Bible College, including Cho Moon Kyung, who had lobbied for reforms in the administration of the school. The college students rallied behind this faction. The group decried breaches in church polity, particularly in Kim Chong Soo's "stacking" of the assembly with his supporters by transferring into the church pastors and local congregations from other denominations. To them, the party of Kim Chong Soo represented acquiescence to American control. The opposition group pledged to cooperate with missionaries but not to be dominated by them. They did not like the fact that one of the missionaries seemed blatantly to be on Kim's side, that this same missionary was chairing the assembly in the absence of a general superintendent.[58]

After seven ballots, when it became obvious that Kim would prevail over Cho and win the two-thirds vote necessary for reelection to the district superintendency, the reformists walked out of the District Assembly. Ten churches separated from the district and held an "independent assembly," in which they elected Cho district superintendent. The college board then dismissed Cho and three other professors. This action led the aggrieved group to file legal charges against the church. They accused it not only of illegally dismissing the college professors, but of conducting an illegal assembly. In response, Kim Chong Soo dismissed disloyal pastors from local congregations. But their churches refused to accept those he appointed in their stead. Echoing student demonstrations in the country as well as around the world, twenty-six students who supported the reformers took over the school, forcing the cancellation of classes, their own suspension from the college, and forfeiture of dormitory privileges. The school's missionary and Korean leaders brought in police to evacuate the students from the campus dormitory. The students continued classes outside with their dismissed teachers. The Korean courts dismissed the case against the district in September 1970. The following month the school reopened and administrators allowed the expelled students to reenroll.

At the next District Assembly, in 1971, both General Superintendent Orville Jenkins and Missions Director E. S. Phillips attended. They were instrumental in persuading the schismatics to return. They also persuaded Donald Owens, then teaching missions at Bethany Nazarene College, to return to Korea for a year in order to try to heal the wounds. Indeed, like Leighton Tracy in 1932 at a Preachers Convention in Budana, India, Owens successfully brought disagreeing factions in the church back together. As part of the solution, Eldon Cornett left Korea in 1972. Discontent remained with Kim's leadership, however, and he was forced to resign in 1973, following the General Assembly. Kim accepted the pastorate of a Korean Nazarene congregation in Chicago.[59]

As in Japan, the Korean leaders preferred greater autonomy from Nazarene headquarters than missionaries allowed. Some interpreted the promise of self-government once self-support had been reached to mean independence from Kansas City.[60]

The near-schism of the Church of the Nazarene in Korea was like the problem affecting other Protestant churches in Korea. Beginning in the 1950s there were a number of major divisions in the Presbyterian Church in Korea. The Methodist and Holiness Churches were among the other denominations to suffer division.[61]

The volatile situations in the District Assemblies also mirrored political tensions in Korean society as a whole. President Park Chung Hee began movements to curb criticism of his government in early 1973. Much of the dissent came from Protestants affiliated with the more liberal denominations that were members of the National Council of Churches of Korea. Students protested against the government in the late 1970s. Park was assassinated in October 1979. Markedly anti-American demonstrations took place in the early and mid-1980s.[62]

The Church of the Nazarene faced peculiarly Korean problems in these years. For instance, the District Assembly urged conformity among the congregations in the name of the church on signboards. This was difficult because "Church of the Nazarene" did not translate well or easily into Korean, and the result made the church sound like a sect or cult. Often churches found the parenthetical description "Holiness Church" necessary, since the Holiness Church of Korea was so well known. Some wanted to delete "Church of the Nazarene" altogether from the signboards.

Another problem involved the designation of church leaders. The Presbyterian custom, which permeated nearly all of Protestantism in Korea, was to ordain "deacons" (*changno*) for life. These were prominent laypersons. The Nazarene church, however, did not use this term and elected lay "trustees" and "stewards" for specified terms of office to local church boards. Though the Church of the Nazarene always had had "deaconesses," at the time it recognized no other order of ordained ministry than that of the "elder." There was no place for a "deacon" in Nazarene church polity until the 1985 General Assembly provided for ordained deacons. Even then, the general church's understanding of a deacon was that of someone who had gone through a course of study and usually was full-time in a ministry assignment in a local church.[63]

The problem in Korea arose when "deacons" from other denominations joined the Church of the Nazarene. They continued to be designated as "deacon." This was a title of honor and respect. Many of the pastors who had transferred to the Church of the Nazarene from the Presbyterian and other denominations saw no reason not to go by the customs prevailing in Korean Protestantism. They saw it as a cultural issue, even though the office was strongly tied to the Presbyterian dominance of Korean Protestantism. Missionaries saw it as a denominational issue. They also believed it dangerous to elevate lay leaders who had attained prestige in other denominations and who often had little understanding of the Church of the Nazarene to positions of power in local churches. The missionaries tried to steer the district away from allowing "deacons" and to enforce the *Manual* on this issue. The 1964 District Assembly decided not to use the word *changno*, but to retain the use of *eesa* (trustee). Yet with more and more deacons transferring into the Church of the Nazarene, the issue remained heated in the years ahead.[64]

Just as the practices of other Protestant churches in Korea influenced the Church of the Nazarene's polity, it also influenced its worship. By the 1960s the Church of the Nazarene in Korea was moving away from American revivalist practices such as the "altar call" that had been a part of Chung Nam Soo's ministry. Also, unlike the American church in the 1960s and 1970s, evening worship services in Korea did not often include times for personal testimonies. Other rituals did not always follow the Nazarene *Manual* and the Korean Nazarenes used a hymnal common to all Protestants. It contained few hymns from the holiness movement. The worship services in Korea were more structured and formal than in American Nazarene churches and were more like the Presbyterian type of services common among most Korean Protestants. For instance, as was the custom among Korean Protestants, Nazarene pastors often read the names of contributors following the reception of tithes and offerings, which were commonly collected after the sermon. Many Nazarene pastors and laypersons in Korea also accepted and tolerated the use of tongues in private devotions and sometimes even in public worship. Korean Nazarenes accepted this custom because it was so prevalent in other denominations and they seemed not to know that the Church of the Nazarene had taken a strong stand against speaking in tongues since its inception. Though missionaries and some Korean leaders tried to persuade the churches to follow not only the *Manual*, but American evangelical customs, Koreans conformed more closely to fellow Korean Protestants.[65]

Regarding other practices, the Nazarene District Assembly urged its members not to sponsor lavish weddings, as was the traditional custom. Likewise, funerals should be as simple as possible, without the use of full traditional dress. And the church reminded members in both instances that Nazarenes should not serve wine or use tobacco. The missionaries in the 1960s encouraged the Koreans to follow then-held prohibitions against women wearing make-up and gold rings; and all members should refrain from attending theaters and from dancing. If a member was found either drinking or smoking, he or she would be warned two or three times, then "punished," presumably by being expelled from the church's membership. However, movie attendance was not much of an issue to the members. Unlike America, the Korean government strictly censored movies it allowed to be shown in the country.[66]

Like other parts of Asia (with the exception of the Philippines), women in Korea were not welcomed in ordained ministry roles. Though they were active in prayer meetings and other local church functions, not until 1994 was the first Korean woman ordained. Song Jung Mahn pastored for nine years on the Central District before her ordination.[67]

Though the church strengthened the academic program of Nazarene Theological College across the years, it remained unrecognized by the Korean government until 1992. The issue of gaining recognition arose in District Assembly debates as early as the mid-1960s and was approved at the 1968 District Assembly, but remained unattained. The lack of government status meant that graduates could not easily pursue graduate degrees that would, in turn, qualify them to teach at the Nazarene college. This prolonged the years in which missionary leadership at the college was necessary. Doctrinally, in spite of well-qualified professors, holiness proved a difficult concept to teach. Presbyterian and Calvinist modes of thought pervaded the church. This was the result of the number of pastors, deacons and laypersons who transferred into the church. In theology as well as practice the Church of the Nazarene in Korea conformed to prevailing customs. Theological controversies were less prominent in the Nazarene church in Korea than in Japan.

The government made it clear that it would not accredit the school unless it moved out of Seoul. The government was attempting to decongest Seoul, decentralize education and move schools into the provinces. In 1978 the mission and district church decided to sell the compound on which the school and missionary residences were located. Most of the property was sold in 1979 for the equivalent of $4.5 million, and the remainder in 1982 for an additional $1.4 million. Most of the proceeds went toward the school's relocation and the remainder to the district and to the mission for missionary residences. The church purchased 32 acres in Chonan, an hour south of Seoul by train, on which to erect a school.[68]

## Conclusion

Even though the growth of the church disappointed Koreans who compared themselves to other Protestants in Korea, other Nazarene leaders were impressed with the growth of the church in Korea. It exceeded the growth of the church in other countries in Asia, and, indeed, in any other part of the world, with the exception of Haiti. Reasons for the growth of the Church of the Nazarene in Korea were similar to the reasons for the growth of other denominations in the country. Like earlier denominations, Nazarenes had kept faith with the Nevius plan that stressed self-support and local leadership. Chung Nam Soo's anti-Japanese activities and suffering was similar to other nationalist Protestants. The missionaries of the Church of the Nazarene in Korea kept a relatively low profile. Koreans themselves were in district leadership positions from the beginning. Relations between the Korean church and the mission were for the most part harmonious. Finally, the Church of the Nazarene in Korea was more "Korean" than typically "Nazarene" in practice.[69]

The Church of the Nazarene in Korea was unique. Its beginning is closely tied to Chung Nam Soo and earlier Korean leaders. Its development rested on the shoulders of experienced pastors. Throughout the decades, pastors, deacons and laypersons who transferred to the Church of the Nazarene from other denominations shaped the practices, theology and ethos of the church. In comparison to other countries, missionaries had little influence. Nonetheless, Korean leaders still complained of missionaries' dominance.[70]

The Korean values of self-reliance and independence more than Nazarene missions strategies encouraged self-support and self-governance, and prevented dependency upon the mission. The Korean church identified itself more with Korean Protestantism and reflected more closely Korean denominations than it did the North American

Church of the Nazarene. As the Church of the Nazarene in Korea continued to develop self-support and self-government, it wondered, as did the church in Japan, why close ties to the Church of the Nazarene in North America were necessary. It felt constrained by the internal and international structure of the church. Just as the American church increasingly acculturated itself to American ways of life and thought, so did the Church of the Nazarene in Korea toward its surrounding society. Even though missionaries tried to encourage conformity to American practices, it could not impose these upon a church that, from its inception, was independent-minded.

# Notes

1. Allen D. Clark, *History of the Korean Church* (Seoul: n.p., [1961]), 130–138; Lak Geoon George Paik, *The History of Protestant Missions in Korea, 1832–1910*, second ed. (Seoul: Yonsei University Press, 1971), 367–378; Martha Huntley, *Caring, Growing, Changing: A History of the Protestant Mission in Korea* (New York: Friendship, 1984), 131–139. The earlier history of missions in Korea also is told in Everett N. Hunt, Jr., *Protestant Pioneers in Korea* (Maryknoll, N.Y.: Orbis, 1980), and Myung Keun Choi, *Changes in Korean Society Between 1884–1910 as a Result of the Introduction of Christianity* (New York: Peter Lang, 1997).

2. Quotations from Yoo Boo Woong, *Korean Pentecostalism: Its History and Theology* (Frankfurt am Main: Verlag Peter Lang, 1987), 84. Yoo calls this revival "Pentecostal," but his evidence mentions no speaking in tongues, and, rather, suggests that the missionaries were afraid, if anything, that such "fanaticism" would break out. See also Myung Keun Choi, *Changes in Korean Society*, 261–287; and Lee Young Hoon, "Korean Pentecost: The Great Revival of 1907," *Asian Journal of Pentecostal Studies* 4 (January 2001), 78, fn. 13. The language of the revival was related to the holiness movement. See Yoo, pp. 74–89. See also George T. Ladd, *In Korea with Marquis Ito* (London: Longmans, Green, 1908), 393, 407–412; Lillias H. Underwood, *Underwood of Korea* (New York: Fleming H. Revell, 1918), 223–225; J. Edwin Orr, *Evangelical Awakenings, 1900–*, rev. ed. (Chicago: Moody, 1975), 164–171; William N. Blair and Bruce F. Hunt, *The Korean Pentecost and the Sufferings Which Followed* (Edinburgh: Banner of Truth Trust, 1977), 64–75.

3. Emily Thomas, "What God Hath Wrought in Korea," *The Way of Holiness* (November 1915), 8; "Interview with Mr. John Thomas, Superintendent of the Oriental Missionary Society in Korea," *The Way of Holiness* (February 1916), 3; John Thomas and Emily Thomas, "Our Call to Korea," *The Way of Holiness* (March 1916), 135; Lettie Cowman, *Charles E. Cowman: Missionary, Warrior* (Los Angeles: Oriental Missionary Society, [1928]), 2-5-214; Robert D. Wood, *In These Mortal Hands: The Story of the Oriental Missionary Society; The First Fifty Years* (Greenwood, Ind.: OMS, 1983), 70, 78–86; Park

Kwang Su, "The History of the Missions of the Jesus Holiness Church in Korea," term paper, Asia Pacific Nazarene Theological Seminary (based on Korean sources); Paul Young Pyo Hong, "Spreading the Holiness Fire: A History of the OMS Korea Holiness Church, 1904–1957," D.Miss. thesis, Fuller Theological Seminary, 1996, 39f. See also O. C. Mingledorff profile file in Nazarene Archives.

4. Cho Seigyku [Chang Sung Oak] to J. B. Chapman, October 13, 1935; Kim Sung Kap, "The Nationals," 1–4; Eckel to Jones, August 4, 1937; Eckel, "Nazarenes in Korea," *Other Sheep* (September 1938), 19; Eckel, "One of Our Nazarene Sunday Schools in Korea," *Other Sheep* (September 1939), 15; Eckel to Jones, March 11, 1939; Pearl Wiley, "Japan," in Maude F. Widmeyer, Everette D. Howard and Pearl Wiley, *Our Island Kingdoms* (Kansas City, Mo.: Nazarene Publishing House, 1939), 125–126, 140–141.

5. Eckel to J. G. Morrison, August 31, 1936; Morrison to Eckel, September 3, 1936; Susan N. Fitkin and Emma B. Word, *Nazarene Missions in the Orient* (Kansas City, Mo.: Nazarene Publishing House, [1936]), 96–106; Eckel to C. Warren Jones, November 22, 1937; "Korea," *Other Sheep* (January 1939), 20; Kong Chang Sul, "[The Historical Research of the Church of the Nazarene in Korea]," M.A. thesis, United Graduate School of Theology, Yonsei University, 1970, portions of which are paraphrased in Kim Sung-kap, "The Nationals in Early Church of the Nazarene in Korea before 1948," term paper, Asia Pacific Nazarene Theological Seminary, March 1987," 1–4.

6. Kim Byung Gi, "A History of Nazarene Missions, APNTS, February 14, 1989, taken from Kong Chang Sul, "Historical Research," 36–37, 42, which is, in turn, based on conversations between Kong and Chang in September 1969; Kang Sam Young, *A History of the Church of the Nazarene in Korea* (N.p., n.d.), translated by Lee So Young, Asia Pacific Nazarene Theological Seminary, 1997.

7. Tei Ki-sho, "A Letter from Korea," trans. R. A. Kida, *Other Sheep* (January 1942), 13–14.

8. Chang Sung Oak to Bishop Japbuman [*sic*], December 29, 1945. See also Clark, *History of the Korean Church*, 154–157; Richard T. Baker, *Darkness of the Sun: The History of Christianity in the Japanese Empire* (New York: Abingdon-Cokesbury, 1947), 191–196.

9. Chung to Jones, May 22, 1948 (file 920-62).

10. Nease, "Foreign Visitation, 1948," 1–2.

11. Choy Bong Young, *Korea: A History* (Rutland, Vt.: Charles E. Tuttle, 1971), 168–171. See also Kenneth M. Wells, *New God, New Nation: Protestants and Self-Reconstruction Nationalism in Korea, 1896–1937* (Honolulu: University of Hawaii Press, 1990), 13–14, 40–41, 61, 65–66, 68, 83, 90.

12. Wood, *In These Mortal Hands*, 257–258.

13. Paul Hong, "Spreading the Holiness Fire," 194, 200.

14. Lester A. Crose, *Passport for a Reformation* (Anderson, Ind.: Warner Press, 1981), 88; Paul Hong, "Spreading the Holiness Fire," 212–213.

15. *Other Sheep* (June 1947), 4; Donald Owens, *Challenge in Korea* (Kansas City, Mo.: Beacon Hill, 1957); Floyd N. Bradley, *Red Terror; or, Robert Chung's Escape* (Louisville, Ky.: Pentecostal Publishing House, 1951).

16. Kang Wi Jo, *Christ and Caesar in Modern Korea: A History of Christianity and Politics* (Albany: State University of New York, 1997), 73–76.

17. "Word from Seoul, Korea," *Other Sheep* (June 1947), 4; Nease, "Foreign Visitation," 1–5; Chang to Rehfeldt, April 5, 1954; Donald Owens to Rehfeldt, November 11, 1954. The 1955 *District Assembly Journal* listed two licensed in 1948.

18. Kang Sam Young, *A History*. Kang and other Korean historians write of this event as a union of the Church of God with the Church of the Nazarene.

19. Nease, "Foreign Visitation," 2–3.

20. Rehfeldt to Nease, May 25, 1949, May 28, 1949, and December 12, 1949; Nease to Rehfeldt, May 28, 1949, and October 31, 1949; Samuel Young to Rehfeldt, February 15, 1950; F. N. Bradley, "More Facts About Korea" [1950], 4.

21. Kim Byung Gi, "A History of Nazarene Missions," Kang Sam-young, *A History*, 20.

22. Nease to Rehfeldt, December 12, 1949.

23. Bradley, *Red Terror*; Donald Owens, "Sung Wun-sung," *Other Sheep* (January 1959), 11; Kang Young Sam, *A History*.

24. Hardy C. Powers to Rehfeldt, October 20, 1952, World Mission office.

25. Rehfeldt to Powers, September 24, 1952; Rehfeldt to Chung, October 28, 1952; Rehfeldt to Mrs. J. D. Irwin, December 9, 1953.

26. Chung to Gerald Berglund, November 29, 1952; Chung to Rehfeldt, December 15, 1952, and February 5, 1953; Rehfeldt to Powers, February 5, 1953.

27. Mrs. J. D. Irwin to Mary Scott, November 28, 1953; Rehfeldt to Mrs. J. D. Irwin, December 9, 1953; E. Alta Clark to Rehfeldt [received January 26, 1954], including a clipping from the *Oakland Tribune*, April 19, 1953, of Chung receiving a check for orphans from the Montclair unit of the American Legion auxiliary; Rehfeldt to Oakland, California, police, January 30, 1956.

28. Rehfeldt to G. B. Williamson, July 31, 1953; Chung to Rehfeldt, April 5, 1954; Owens to Rehfeldt, September 13, 1954; Kong, "Historical," 3; Crose, *Passport for a Reformation*, 127, 178; Kang Young Sam, *A History*; Donald Owens to Hong Ki Young, April 16, 1996. See Robert Chung, "Our Korean Nazarenes," *Other Sheep* (September 1953), 8–9, for pictures of the churches and congregations at Pyingtak, Mokpo, Pusan, and Syntan in 1953.

29. Chung to Rehfeldt, December 4, 1953, and April 5, 1954.

30. Owens to Rehfeldt, December 26, 1953, and July 30, 1954.

31. Owens to Rehfeldt, November 11, 1954, February 10, 1955, and December 5, 1955; Rehfeldt to Owens, October 1954, January 25, 1955, and April 15, 1955.

32. Underwood, *Underwood of Korea*, 99–101; Charles A. Clark, *The Nevius Plan of Mission Work in Korea* (Seoul: Christian Literature Society,

[1937]), 23–43; Paik, *The History of Protestant Missions in Korea*; Roy E. Shearer, *Wildfire: Church Growth in Korea* (Grand Rapids, Mich.: Eerdmans, 1966).

33. 1957 *District Assembly Journal*, 15–17, 35; 1958 *District Assembly Journal*, 8, 13; reports, 4; Owens, "Commencement Day in Korea," *Other Sheep* (May 1959), 6; 1961 *District Assembly Journal*; Kang Young Sam, *A History*.

34. Rehfeldt to Owens, June 16, 1955, August 5, 1955, and August 30, 1955; Owens to Rehfeldt, July 14, 1955, August 9, 1955, and August 15, 1955, and December 19, 1955.

35. August 1955 *District Assembly Journal* (translated by Kim Byung Gi); Owens to Rehfeldt, September 3, 1955; Kang Sam Young, *A History*; (on school moving to Seoul): Jerald Johnson to Charles Strickland, July 27, 1978.

36. Owens to Rehfeldt, November 9, 1955. Likewise, Owens to Cunningham, March 1, 1992.

37. Rehfeldt to Owens, December 22, 1955, January 17, 1956, and February 7, 1956; Owens to Rehfeldt, March 16, 1956.

38. Paul Chung to Rehfeldt, July 5, 1956; Rehfeldt to Chung, May 17, 1956, and June 29, 1956; Chung to Rehfeldt, October 1, 1956. Rehfeldt, to Owens, December 22, 1955, January 17, 1956, and February 7, 1956; Owens to Rehfeldt, March 16, 1956; Paul Chung to Rehfeldt, July 5, 1956; Rehfeldt to Chung, May 17, 1956, and June 29, 1956; Chung to Rehfeldt, October 1, 1956.

39. Owens to Rehfeldt, November 5, 1956.

40. Lester A. Grose to Rehfeldt, April 27, 1956; Rehfeldt to Grose, May 31, 1956; Owens to Rehfeldt, October 8, 1956; Owens, "Korean Bible School Moves Out," *Other Sheep* (April 1959), 6.

41. Owens to Coulter, July 31, 1962, and August 4, 1962.

42. Owens, "A Red-Letter Day in Korea," *Other Sheep* (June 1957), 3.

43. A. Brent Cobb, *Tried and Triumphant: Testimonies of Twelve Korean Nazarenes* (Kansas City, Mo.: Beacon Hill, 1984), 68–73. Compare Jong Sung Rhee, "Types of Church Leaders Today: A Brief Sketch of Church Leaders After the Korean War," in *Korea Struggles for Christ: Memorial Symposium for the Eightieth Anniversary of Protestantism in Korea*, second ed., ed. Harold S. Hong, Won Young Ji, and Chung Choon Kim (Seoul: Christian Literature Society of Korea, 1973), 133–147.

44. Cobb, *Tried and Triumphant*, 11–16.

45. Cobb, *Tried and Triumphant*, 59–64.

46. 1960, 1965, 1966 and 1970 *District Assembly Journal*(s); Owens, *Revival Fires in Korea* (Kansas City, Mo.: Nazarene Publishing House, 1977), 57; Kang Sam-young, *A History*.

47. George Coulter, "Report of Trip to Korea" [1967] (file 1360-28); *District Assembly Journal*(s).

48. Owens to E. S. Phillips, April 2, 1965. See "Introducing Rev. Kim Chong Soo, District Superintendent of Korea," *Other Sheep* (May 1969).

49. Owens, "Church Growth in Korea," 71–108; Hong Ki Young, "Planting an Indigenous Nazarene Church in Korea as a Basis for Church Growth," *The Mediator* (January 1996), 37–63.

50. Owens, *Revival Fires*, 65–75; Parker, *Mission*, 319–320; Kenneth Schubert, "Korea Districts Statistical Information," [1986]. See also *Korean Church Growth Explosion*, ed. Bong Rin Ro and Marlin L. Nelson (Seoul: Word of Life Press, 1983); Kim Byong Suh, "The Explosive Growth of the Korean Church Today: A Sociological Analysis," *International Review of Mission* 74 (1985), 70; Cho Eun Sik, "Korean Church Growth in 1970s: Its Factors and Problems," *Asia Journal of Theology* 10 (1996), 348; John T. Kim, *Protestant Church Growth in Korea* (Belleville, Ontario: Essence, 1996), 120–124, 174–195.

51. Eldon Cornett to Phillips, March 23, 1967, January 30, 1968, and February 12, 1969; Coulter, "Korea Trip" [1967] (file 1360-28); Phillips to Coulter, July 25, 1968; Coulter to Phillips, August 9, 1968; Charles Stroud to Phillips, July 29, 1968, and November 14, 1968. Compare Kim Sung Won, "A Critical Reflection on the History of the Church of the Nazarene in Korea," presented at Global Theology Conference, Guatemala City, April 4–7, 2001, 3–4.

52. Coulter to Phillips, December 2, 1965.

53. Owens to E. S. Phillips, April 2, 1965. See Charles Stroud to Phillips, July 20, 1968.

54. Owens, "Church Growth in Korea," in *Ministering to the Millions*, comp. Department of World Missions (Kansas City, Mo.: Nazarene Publishing House, 1971), 71–108; Hong Ki Young, "Planting an Indigenous Nazarene Church," 37–63.

55. Eldon Cornett to Phillips, March 23, 1967, January 30, 1968, and February 12, 1969; Coulter, "Korea Trip" [1967] (file 1360-28); Phillips to Coulter, July 25, 1968; Coulter to Phillips, August 9, 1968; Charles Stroud to Phillips, July 29, 1968, and November 14, 1968.

56. George Coulter, "Report of Trip to Korea" [1967].

57. Charles Stroud to Phillips, July 20, 1968.

58. Samuel Young, [Report on Overseas Travel, (1962)] (file 1385-14).

59. Owens, *Revival Fires*, 57–59; R. Franklin Cook, *Water from Deep Wells: A Survey to the Church of the Nazarene in India, Korea, Taiwan, Hong Kong, Australia, New Zealand* (Kansas City, Mo.: Nazarene Publishing House, 1977), 76; Kenneth Schubert, "Korea Nazarenes Make History," *World Mission* 7 (October 1981), 4–6; Kang Sam Young, "[A Historical Study of the Denominational Event that Brought Crisis in the Korean Church of the Nazarene]," *Bokyum Gwa Shinhak* [Gospel and Culture] 4 (1992), translated for me by Hwang Ho Sang. See also Nazarene News Service Weekly Summary (February 4, 1994), 2.

60. Kang Sam Young, *A History*.

61. Shearer, *Wildfire*, 212–215; John Kim, *Protestant Church Growth in Korea*, 119, 124, 129.

62. George E. Ogle, *Liberty to the Captives: The Struggle Against Oppression in South Korea* (Atlanta, Ga.: John Knox, 1977); Kang Wi Jo, *Christ and Caesar*, 99–108, 121–126; Bruce Cummings, *Korea's Place in the Sun: A Modern History* (New York: W. W. Norton, 1997), 371–372, 384–386.

63. *Manual/1985 Church of the Nazarene: History, Constitution, Government, Ritual* (Kansas City, Mo.: Nazarene Publishing House, 1985), 161–162.

64. 1963 *District Assembly Journal*, 41; 1964 *District Assembly Journal*, 19, 29; 1968 *District Assembly Journal*.

65. Hong Ki Young, "Planting an Indigenous Nazarene Church," 37–63. See also Kim Sung Won, "A Critical Reflection on the History of the Church of the Nazarene in Korea." Compare Harvey Cox, *Fire from Heaven: The Rise of Pentecostal Spirituality and the Reshaping of Religion in the Twenty-first Century* (Reading, Mass.: Addison-Wesley, 1995), chapter 11, "Shamans and Entrepreneurs: Primal Spirituality on the Asian Rim," 215–241.

66. Owens to Philips, August 27, 1965; Coulter to Phillips, December 2, 1965; Coulter, "Report of Trip to Korea" [1967]; 1968 *District Assembly Journal*; Cook, *Water*, 70.

67. *World Mission* (August 1994), 10. See also Cobb, *Tried and Triumphant*, 37–42.

68. 1968 District Assembly Journal; Mary Mercer, "The College That Miracles Built," *World Mission* (February 1982), 12–14; Shin Min Gyoo, "An Analysis of the Variable[s] That Affect the Financial Support of Korea Nazarene Theological College by the Korean Church," in [*The Gospel and Theology*] (Chonan, Korea: Nazarene Theological College, n.d.), 110–113; Kenneth Schubert to J. Fred Parker, October 24, 1985; Parker, *Mission*, 320–321; Owens to Hong, April 16, 1996.

69. Compare Owens, "Church Growth in Korea," and Owens, "Church Planting and Growth the Nevius Way," *Holiness Today* (May 1999), 30–31, to G. Thompson Brown, "Why Has Christianity Grown Faster in Korea than in China?" *Missiology* 22 (January 1994), 77–88. See also Bong Rin Ro and Marlin L. Nelson, eds., *Korean Church Growth Explosion*, especially part two.

70. Hong Ki Young, "Planting an Indigenous Nazarene Church"; Kim Sung Won, "A Critical Reflection on the History of the Church of the Nazarene in Korea." See Owens to Hong, April 16, 1996.

# Chapter 6

# The Philippines

Along with many other evangelical groups, the Church of the Nazarene began work in the Philippines shortly after the Second World War. After several years when entering new fields had been impossible, in the mid-1940s the Church of the Nazarene's leaders sought to expand its missions rapidly around the world, and the Philippines was a fruitful-looking field to enter. Though no longer an American colony, the Philippines remained tied to the United States economically. English was widely spoken. Unintentionally, American Protestant groups that entered after the war represented a kind of American neocolonial influence.[1]

Here comity arrangements, which had preserved some semblance of Protestant order from the time of the American occupation until the war with Japan, came apart in the mid-1940s. This occurred not only because myriad sects, each with its own brand of the gospel, began to enter the Philippines in a kind of second American invasion, but because the Methodist Church and the United Church of Christ, lynchpins in the comity system, themselves began to invade each other's territory.[2]

## Early Leaders

Though the Church of the Nazarene felt the special responsibility of many American Protestants to "Christianize" the Philippines,[3] and despite contacts that the church had with Filipinos before the war, it delayed entrance into the Philippines until after World War II. Several Filipinos attended the denomination's college in remote Nampa, Idaho. The first, apparently, was Marciano Encarnacion, a native of Cabanatuan, Nueva Ecija, raised in a family that was one of the first in the area to accept Protestantism and join the Methodist Church (which held comity in the area). The Methodist work in Cabanatuan had begun in 1904. In the 1910s Encarnacion migrated to the States. In 1919 he arrived in Seattle, Washington, where he had relatives. Within a short time he became acquainted with the local Church of the Nazarene.

Encarnacion professed to be "saved" and later "sanctified" through the ministry of that church. In 1920, an evangelist persuaded him to attend Northwest Nazarene College at Nampa, where he entered the Academy or high school department. Several Filipino friends also from Cabanatuan joined him. NNC students began a Philippine mission band that included these Filipinos as well as others who wanted to promote missionary work in the country. After one year at Nampa, Encarnacion took other jobs, including a stint working on railroad construction in Montana. Then he returned to Seattle and completed a pharmacy course at the University of Washington.

In 1926 Encarnacion returned to the Philippines. He worked in a pharmacy in Baguio and witnessed about his faith to his family and friends there, in Cabanatuan, and elsewhere. His wife, Epifania, whom he married in 1928, became a teacher and eventually a supervisor in the public school system in and around Baguio. She became active in the United Evangelical Church in Baguio.[4]

One holiness group very similar to the Church of the Nazarene, the Pilgrim Holiness Church, began work in the Philippines in 1932 when Miguel Zambrano, a Filipino converted in California, returned to the country.[5]

Along with R. K. Storey, the first Pilgrim Holiness missionary in the Philippines, Encarnacion helped to establish the Pilgrim Holiness Church in Cabanatuan. It was made up of several persons dissatisfied with the Methodist Church in the city. The Pilgrims purchased a lot and opened a Bible school in Cabanatuan in 1939. Encarnacion also made contacts for the Pilgrim Holiness Church in other localities in the lowlands.[6]

The Methodist Church in the Philippines also included a faction strongly influenced by holiness teachings. Its first Filipino bishop was a graduate of Asbury College. The Methodists retained codes against smoking, drinking alcohol, dancing and other vices through the 1950s.[7]

In the 1930s, Fred Fetters ministered among Filipinos in Pasadena, California, and opened a work associated with the Central Church of the Nazarene in the city. Lack of money prevented the denomination from dispatching them to the Philippines. Missionaries had to return from fields already opened, and there was no budget for entry into new fields.[8]

William Eckel visited the Philippines in 1939 and encouraged the church to enter the field, in particular to minister among the more than 25,000 Japanese living in Manila. He made contacts with two small Japanese evangelical churches. But, again, the church would not rush into this, and the war prevented further discussion of the possibility.[9]

The attention of church leaders turned again to the Philippines through Nazarene chaplains stationed in the country during the closing days of the Second World War. One, J. E. Moore, Jr., purposely sought Encarnacion and found him where he worked in the pharmacy in Baguio. Encarnacion expressed his desire to see the Church of the Nazarene planted in the Philippines and his willingness to help it do so. Moore sought and secured permission from General Superintendent Hardy C. Powers to begin organizing the Church of the Nazarene in the Philippines, but he soon transferred to Japan. Another Nazarene chaplain, A. Bond Woodruff, followed up the contact with Encarnacion and the plan to organize a church. Woodruff helped Encarnacion to organize a church among his relatives and neighbors in Cabanatuan, which already was a center of Methodist and Pilgrim Holiness work. Woodruff officially organized it on May 19, 1946, with twenty-nine members, and appointed Encarnacion as pastor. This can be marked as the founding date of the Church of the Nazarene in the country. The military transferred Woodruff elsewhere, so he left the work entirely to Encarnacion.[10]

Joseph S. Pitts was a Nazarene chaplain who had been stationed in both Japan and the Philippines. After the war he accepted a pastorate in the United States but he felt burdened that the Church of the Nazarene enter the Philippines. In 1947, when he advocated this to General Superintendent Powers, Powers suggested that Pitts himself be the one to go. After prayer and deliberation, Pitts agreed. Encarnacion met him in Manila when he and his family arrived in February 1948.[11]

In the 1940s, Nazarene pastors and evangelists preached about God's demands for holy living. Pitts represented an extreme on matters pertaining to dress and behavior. At the time of his departure to the Philippines he was living in Wilmore, Kentucky, and had other strong contacts in Louisiana and Alabama, where his brother had been district superintendent. Remiss Rehfeldt, then director of foreign missions for the denomination, was equally conservative.[12]

Pitts and his family settled in Cabanatuan and began work immediately. He also had information from the Filipino Nazarene pastor in Pasadena, Rev. Catalina, regarding an independent congregation in Iloilo, on the Visayan island of Panay. Catalina also had sent word about the Church of the Nazarene to the lay pastor there, Elijah Lasam. Pitts organized this group as the second Church of the Nazarene in the country in July 1948.[13]

In late 1948 Nazarene General Superintendent Powers and John Stockton, general treasurer, visited the Philippines and advised Pitts to move his family to Baguio in order to make this the headquarters of the work. They felt that Baguio, in the cool mountains, offered the missionaries a better climate in which to live and work.[14]

Pitts and Encarnacion soon began a church in Baguio among more of Encarnacion's acquaintances, and Epifania Encarnacion, who had been teaching Sunday School in the United Church, joined the Church of the Nazarene at this time. Pitts pastored the Baguio congregation while Marciano Encarnacion remained as pastor of the Cabanatuan church until 1953, when he was appointed the first Filipino pastor of the Baguio church.[15]

Pitts soon contacted some of the many converts and friends that Encarnacion had made across the years. These were good years for American missionaries in the Philippines. Americans were still, for the most part, revered. All things American appealed to common Filipinos. Association with Americans brought status—especially in the provincial barrios where the Church of the Nazarene had most of its work. The post-war years were ones in which Filipinos were willing to try new things, even new denominations. The Church of the Nazarene built upon Encarnacion's and other early leaders' webs of family relations as well as friends and converts. Unlike Japan or Korea, the Philippines was a highly segmented society. American denominationalism fit the ethnic, linguistic and social pluralism already existing in the Philippines.[16]

From a growing web of contacts made by Encarnacion and Pitts, other Filipino leaders emerged. For instance, Encarnacion introduced Pitts to some of his acquaintances in Aringay, La Union, and Pitts conducted a revival there. Pitts did the same at Binday, Pangasinan, where a small independent congregation, in which Gil Sevidal was the associate pastor, invited him to preach. Sevidal had been converted under the holiness ministry of Ciriaco Jamandre, a Pilgrim Holiness preacher and former Methodist, whom Sevidal in turn brought into the Nazarene church. Jamandre and his son, Edison, soon became leaders. The meeting at Binday extended to the village of Balacag, where former affiliates of La Iglesia Evangelica Metodista en las Islas Filipinas (IEMELIF) started a Nazarene congregation after a visit by Pitts. The Fontanilla family principally carried on the work at Balacag. The elder Fontanilla had been a local preacher in the IEMELIF church. General Superintendent Orval Nease organized the church in Balacag with thirty charter members on his visit to the Philippines in November 1948. The church also expanded to Oriental Mindoro at Pinamalayan when nine members of the Carpio family, who had been attending the Baguio church, moved there in 1949. The church remained in Pinamalayan until the assigned student pastor, Ricardo Carpio, was killed in 1956; "the victim," Nazarenes surmised, "of foul play."[17]

The Church of the Nazarene sent a second missionary couple to the Philippines in 1950, John and Lillian Pattee. Having served for several years in mainland China both before and after World War II, they were seasoned missionaries with expertise in evangelism among Chinese peasants. Both were ordained elders and able preachers and evangelists. Lillian Pattee was a registered nurse. John Pattee had earned a master of arts degree in religion at Pasadena College after the war. Pitts stationed them in Baguio, where they had charge of beginning a Bible college for the training of Filipino pastors.[18]

Actually Manila had been Pitts's first choice for the site of the school. But when an initial attempt to buy property in the city failed, the missionaries looked elsewhere. The decision to locate in Baguio, following Powers's advice, meant that the Church of the Nazarene in the Philippines remained rural and provincial in both outlook and leadership.

Pattee began a Christian Worker's Institute in Baguio in 1950 and conducted a Preacher's Institute the following year. Both were intended to indoctrinate and enable emerging Filipino leaders, several of whom were already experienced pastors. In 1952 the missionaries bought property just outside of Baguio on a site overlooking Trinidad Valley. Part of the finances for this came through funds redirected to the Philippines from China, since that field was now closed. Money for a Bible college in China had been donated in honor of former Foreign Missionary Society president Susan N. Fitkin, so the church named the Bible college in La Trinidad the "Fitkin Memorial Bible College." Thirty-five students enrolled during the first year, 1952–53.

From the start the church planned a solid four-year baccalaureate-level curriculum, at the conclusion of which students were granted the bachelor of theology degree. Between the third and last year the school required a one-year field assignment. Pattee had seen the tremendous importance of a well-educated leadership in China during the closing years of the Nazarene field there. In the Philippines during these days there was some likelihood in missionaries' minds that the same situation would occur as in China—that Communists would take over the country. Pattee worked as rapidly as possible to have an organized and motivated church in place if that should happen and missionaries be forced to leave the Philippines, as they had China. English was the language of instruction at the college, as it was, indeed, in all colleges in the Philippines.[19]

The first students had varied backgrounds. At least three had been associated with the Hukbalahap, a Communist movement active among lowland rural peasants. Other students came from Philippine Independent Church or Roman Catholic backgrounds. Some came against the wishes of their parents after being reached through revival campaigns and other evangelistic efforts. Pattee personally recruited students on his frequent evangelistic campaigns to the lowlands. On the other hand, in a few cases, parents sent seemingly incorrigible sons and daughters to the Bible college in hopes that it might reform them. Often it did.

In 1953 a young man in the Baguio church befriended Antonio Lumiqued, then a student at La Trinidad High School and a native of remote Lo-o Valley in northern Benguet Province. Pattee persuaded Lumiqued to attend the Bible College, and he was converted in 1954. He became a student pastor in Lo-o Valley and persuaded his friend Paul Bay-an also to attend Bible College. Soon missionaries were traveling across the mountains with these two Kankanaey students. A congregation was organized there in November 1959.[20]

Pastor Miguel Zambrano, who had been a member of Church of the Nazarene in California and then had started the Pilgrim Holiness Church in the Philippines, rejoined the Church of the Nazarene in the Philippines in 1950. While in the States he had evangelized widely among Filipinos and had attended the Pacific Bible College, which was affiliated with the Pilgrim Holiness Church. He left the Nazarene church at Pasadena and joined the Pilgrim Holiness church in Alta Loma, where other Filipinos also attended. Zambrano returned to the Philippines in 1932 with the encouragement of the Pilgrim Holiness Church, but was also supported in part by local Nazarene missionary societies in California. He organized the first Pilgrim Holiness church in the Philippines in June 1932 in San Francisco, La Union, his hometown. He vowed to the members to erect a large church building with funds from America, but he was unable to fulfill his promises. The support he thought he would be able to get for the project did not come. Within two years several other Filipino Pilgrims, also converted in California and members of the Alta Loma church, started returning to the Philippines. They began planting other churches. One of them, C. T. Bolayog, a Visayan, was appointed to lead the church in the Philippines. Zambrano served the Pilgrim Holiness church as a pastor and evangelist and eventually was ordained, but he felt that church leaders prevented his rise otherwise into leadership positions. Pilgrim leaders believed that he had "lost out completely," and by the late 1940s Zambrano was inactive. Then, with the encouragement of Encarnacion, Jamandre and other former Pilgrim Holiness leaders he knew, he rejoined the Church of the Nazarene in 1950. Zambrano went on to pastor the churches in Balacag, La Trinidad and San Francisco, and opened the work in Bangar.[21]

The fact that Encarnacion, Zambrano and Jamandre each had been active in the Pilgrim Holiness Church prior to the Church of the Nazarene's entry into the Philippines strained early relations between the two holiness denominations. Both Encarnacion and Zambrano had been Nazarenes in the States before becoming Pilgrims, and Jamandre had exited the Methodist Church before becoming a Pilgrim, but Nazarene work in Cabanatuan and in both La Union and Pangasinan provinces overlapped the Pilgrims' work. The Pilgrim Holiness Church tended to be even stricter than Nazarenes on matters of dress and (as seen in the case of Seth Rees and his follower Minnie Staples in Japan) wary of ecclesiastical control and desirous of the freedom of the Spirit.

Another leader for a time was a former Roman Catholic priest, Jose F. Lallana. He had been a former secretary to a bishop and was living in Bangar when Pattee held a revival there. After several personal conversations with Pattee, Lallana accepted Protestantism. In 1956 the Nazarenes employed him at the Bible College to teach Greek and English, and the church granted him a district minister's license in 1957.[22]

The church expanded through various means of evangelism in the early years. Pattee's method was the same as he had found successful in China: open-air preaching. Commonly he brought pastors or students with him to either play an accordion or translate his messages, though he attempted to speak Ilocano. He secured permission in various localities to set up a loudspeaker system, preach and show slides on the plaza during these evangelistic campaigns—in many places right across from the Roman Catholic church! One time the Catholic priest tried to drown out Pattee's loudspeakers with ones of his own. However, Pattee was careful not to directly criticize Catholicism. The message he preached was positive, centering on the necessity of exercising faith for salvation and right moral living.

In Binalonan, Pangasinan, for instance, four to five hundred heard Pattee preach over several nights, and he soon organized a congregation made up of new converts. In one year Pattee might typically preach over three hundred evangelistic messages and see two thousand persons "seek the Lord."

The church also grew through lay members contacting relatives who lived in other towns or through members themselves moving from one place to another, but in many cases new members came from older denominations. In Carusocan, Asingan, Pangasinan, many in the congregation that emerged had formerly been in another Protestant denomination (probably Methodist), but had been without a pastor for some time and drifted back to Roman Catholicism before the Nazarenes came.

The church in Baguio was composed of former members of various denominations. At San Francisco, the members were largely taken from the Pilgrim Holiness Church, which, years before, had taken members from the Evangelical United Brethren Church. The Cabanatuan Church contained former Methodists and the Balacag church former Independent Methodist Church members. But in other localities by far the majority of lay Nazarenes were "converted" from Roman Catholicism.[23]

The work in Manila itself commenced only in 1952, in Malate. In 1954 Gil Sevidal transferred there from Cabanatuan. Wilfredo and Rosita Suyat, former Nazarene Bible College students, remained active lay members across the years, but not until 1968 did a second church begin in Manila.[24]

New missionaries arrived in the 1950s. Among them were Frances Vine and Roy Copelin, both seminary graduates with masters-level degrees who strengthened the Bible College staff, and Erna Copelin, who served as treasurer of the mission for several years. Roy Copelin assumed leadership of the school in 1955 after being stationed for a year in Manila. Vine taught Christian education and began an extensive daily Vacation Bible School program for the denomination. Meanwhile Lillian Pattee opened a medical clinic at the Bible College.[25]

In 1955 the mission held the first District Assembly with Remiss Rehfeldt, foreign missions secretary, in attendance and presiding. Pitts reported, as district superintendent, that seven churches were fully organized: Baguio, Balacag, Binalonan, Cabanatuan, Iloilo, Loac and San Fernando. A Filipina, Rachel Carentes, served as district treasurer. Seven Filipinos held district ministerial licenses at this time but none were ready yet for ordination. (That required both completion of the course of study and two years of full-time pastoral service. It also required that a general superintendent do the ordaining.) Most of the licensed ministers were pastoring local churches. Zambrano pastored the largest of these, Balacag, which had 125 members. However, the pastors received almost all of their financial support from the mission. The Baguio church paid Encarnacion 30 pesos per month as their pastor, and rural churches provided rice and vegetables to their pastors, but that was about all.[26]

Lay members were expected to live by strict moral codes upon joining the Church of the Nazarene. The prohibitions of the *Manual* disallowed attending the movies, dancing, smoking cigarettes and drinking alcohol. The Philippine District Assembly added prohibitions on planting tobacco, cockfighting, and chewing betel nuts. Though prohibiting these aspects of Filipino communal life might have seemed countercultural, they were in keeping with the strict puritanism of Nazarene rules. In addition, Pitts had his own rules.[27]

## The Pitts Schism

It was over some unwritten taboos that serious controversy developed within the church. Pitts was among the most conservative Nazarenes to represent the church abroad. Like conservatives in the Church of the Nazarene in the United States, Pitts was worried about trends in the church that signified to him accommodation to culture or what might be called the "embourgeoisement" of the holiness lifestyle. Pitts agreed with common sentiment that "holiness people should neither look like, nor act like the world."[28] He was afraid that holiness people were losing their distinctiveness and was determined that whatever the American church might do or become he would see that the Church of the Nazarene in the Philippines remained pure. There were several issues that to him were crucial indicators of purity. He told the Filipinos from the beginning that consistent holy living demanded that women not cut their hair, wear make-up, or adorn themselves with any sort of jewelry (not even wedding rings). The basis of this teaching rested upon a literal reading of I Timothy 2:9 and I Peter 3:3-5. One by one as Nazarenes missionaries such as the Pattees, the Copelins and Frances Vine entered the country, Pitts and his wife persuaded each to toe this line; women missionaries allowed their hair to grow long and married women took off their wedding rings. The Church of the Nazarene in America still had some who were as conservative as Pitts, who worried about modern trends. But the church as a whole was not so strict on these issues. Sunday School and other periodical literature from the Nazarene Publishing House clearly depicted women with short, "bobbed" hair. Pitts persuaded the Filipino workers that these trends were contrary to biblical holiness, and to the true Church of the Nazarene. But how long could Pitts run counter to the real movement of the Church of the Nazarene away from such narrow legalism?[29]

By 1956 the general superintendents had decided that either Pitts must loosen his strictness or be replaced. The Pattees furloughed that year and reported legalistic extremes to these leaders (though the Pattees themselves had gone along with Pitts on these matters while on the field). Though Remiss Rehfelt was sympathetic to Pitts's extreme conservatism, the general superintendents pushed through the appointment of Robert and Mathilda McCroskey as missionaries, knowing that "Tilly" McCroskey had short hair and that neither she nor her husband were disposed to her removing her wedding band.

When Pitts heard through sources in Kansas City of the McCroskeys' appointment to the Philippines, he protested to the general superintendents. One of the crucial tests for new missionaries was their willingness to adjust to situations on the field. That was in the missionary contract, Pitts reminded them, and Kansas City knew full well the standards of the Philippines field. In a letter to Pitts, the General Board stated that the McCroskeys were sent to the field with the "full backing" of the church—a clear signal that the church's leaders were ready to confront the issue.

The McCroskeys arrived in 1956 and, unlike the previous missionaries, refused to obey Pitts's dictates on these matters. Tilly McCroskey would cut her hair and wear her wedding ring. Pitts assigned them to Manila, where, he believed, they would have the least influence upon the Filipino Nazarenes. At the 1957 District Assembly, with the McCroskeys sitting right there, and in front of all the delegates who knew full well to whom he was referring, Pitts declared: "We regret to speak about worldliness coming into our mission work. When the late General Superintendent Dr. James B. Chapman was editor of the *Herald of Holiness*, we went on record in his editorials against the bobbing of hair and the wearing of rings as well as other forms of worldliness, and we want to go on record against these things also. We regret that a double standard now exists in our mission work: one for the nationals in our Bible School and churches and another among the missionaries."[30]

He went on to declare that the Filipino pastors would stand by him 100 percent. He sent a letter to the general superintendents stating: "If my stand upholding the standards set on this field is not upheld by the Board of General Superintendents, I will consider it as sufficient grounds to resign and request to be brought back to the States."[31] He advised that one of the general superintendents visit the field to investigate. Clearly he was laying down a challenge, and he convinced Encarnacion, Lallana, Jamandre, and other licensed ministers to stand with him.[32]

The general superintendents directed Pitts to return to the United States in order to report to them personally. Before departing, however, and anticipating the probable outcome, he organized a "Filipino Nazarene Ministers Association," made up of most of the pastors, which could stand with him against the mission, if it came to that. After arriving in Kansas City, Pitts met behind closed doors with the general superintendents and long and heated discussions ensued. The issue of greatest matter to him was "bobbed" women's hair. It was a symbol of their submission both to God and to their husbands. The general superintendents knew that few of the church's members in the United States were concerned about women's hair. At least one-half of the Nazarene women in the United States were cutting their hair, one general superintendent estimated. The general superintendents believed that the Nazarene church in the Philippines must, like the rest of the denomination, resist legalistic tendencies. In 1956 at the quadrennial General Assembly, the church had turned back a movement led by reactionaries to ban television from Nazarene homes, and the generals were bolder, sensing a mandate of the delegates not to be ruled by the consciences of a few. After the Assembly some on the extreme right wing of the church bolted and formed the Bible Missionary Church.[33]

The generals decided not to reappoint Pitts to the Philippines. They were willing to appoint him to Barbados, however, so as not to make a martyr of him with radicals in the denomination. Pitts countered that the Lord himself had called him to the Philippines. He was willing, he told them, to work in Lo-o Valley, in the mountains, and resign leadership to other missionaries, but to the Philippines he would go. The generals did not trust him to take such a reticent role. Pitts rallied his lay supporters, particularly around Lake Charles, Louisiana, where his brother Paul Pitts pastored, and in Wilmore, Kentucky, who were as disconcerted as he that the Church of the Nazarene was becoming too modern. He secured regular financial support and began sending money directly to several of the Filipino pastors who sided with him—more money, in fact, than what the Nazarene mission had been paying them.[34]

The Filipino pastors were caught in a dilemma. There was loyalty to Pitts, who had brought several of them into the church, and there was a debt of gratitude to him for supplying their needs. Pastors who came out of the Pilgrim Holiness Church had, like Pitts, associated holiness with strict standards on dress and hair. Furthermore, there may have been cultural affinities between what he stood for and what they naturally believed about women's attire. Most Filipino women in the rural areas where the Church of the Nazarene was strongest did not cut their hair. It was not a moral issue, just a social custom not to cut their hair. A wedding ring was not so much a part of their customs either—women might wear many rings, but none with special significance. Pitts's standards on make-up made little difference on rural farms. And, after all, how could it be morally wrong one Sunday for women to cut their hair, and permissible the next? How could pastors who had preached strongly on these issues from Bible texts face their congregations without shame and tell them they had been wrong? Was the Bible changeable? The Church of the Nazarene was distinctly known for these standards. At Pitts's prompting several pastors wrote along these lines to the leaders in Kansas City. Epifania Encarnacion stated for them: "We only want worldliness banned and a little voice in the running of the mission field, because we feel we know our people and our country."[35] Marciano Encarnacion knew well that the extreme legalism that Pitts preached was not truly representative of the American Church of the Nazarene. Yet, after working with him for ten years, Encarnacion felt indebted to Pitts. The older pastors already had changed denominations more than once, so they sensed no particular loyalty to the general superintendents. The pastors sympathized with Pitts because it seemed as though he was standing with them as Filipinos against impersonal forces in faraway Kansas City.[36]

That perception became even clearer to some when General Superintendent Hugh C. Benner presided over the 1958 District Assembly. Some pastors were still wavering between the general church and Pitts. Encarnacion himself hoped that Benner would listen to the Filipino side. He thought that the denomination had been too hasty in making decisions that affected the Filipino church without conferring with its own leaders. Kansas City administrators could not possibly understand Filipino customs, Encarnacion believed. But Benner's method of handling the difficulty seemed brusque. He refused even to meet with Filipino leaders to discuss the situation or the issues. This wounded Encarnacion all the more. Benner had no sympathy for legalists like Pitts and felt that it was better for the mission to make a decisive break with him. His actions caused Encarnacion and several others to walk out of the Assembly and out of the Church of the Nazarene.[37]

Pitts returned to the Philippines the same year, supported independently by sympathetic Nazarenes and other holiness people throughout the States. He published a newsletter, *Echoes from the Philippines*, to raise money and keep his supporters abreast of the work he was establishing. He received financial help through an organization called the "Holiness Evangelical Covenanters," which was composed of holiness people from several denominations who were convinced that their denominations were becoming too worldly.[38]

He gathered Encarnacion, Lallana (whom the other missionaries had prevented from teaching at the Bible College because he had sided with Pitts), Ciriaco Jamandre, Victoriano Luzong, who was then pastoring the Manila church, and some other licensed ministers and formed the "Holiness Church of the Nazarene." Pitts served as "chairman," with Encarnacion as vice chairman, Luzong as district secretary and Rachel Carentes as district treasurer. Within months of the 1958 Assembly the mission dropped those who left from local church membership rolls. In some places Pitts began local congregations very close to the Nazarene churches and attempted to lure members away. The split most affected seven locations: Baguio, Cabanatuan, Balacag and Laoac among organized churches, and Binalonan, Paniqui and Manila among unorganized groups. (Jamandre, for instance, pastored the Holiness Church of the Nazarene in Binalonan.) However, as late as 1960 general church leaders held hope that the schismatic group would return. In late 1961 a conservative Nazarene evangelist, Helen Mooshian, toured the Philippines (without the endorsement of the general church), and preached to both groups. Although other missionaries were afraid she would cause problems, she tried to build bridges between the two groups but became critical of Pitts's work.[39]

Pitts raised legal problems for the Church of the Nazarene. There were two deeds to the Bible College property, one in Pitts's name, and he claimed ownership. He also claimed ownership of furniture, chapel benches, chairs, lumber, a piano, and a host of other items. Pitts incorporated the Holiness Church of the Nazarene in December 1961, but somehow remained a minister in good standing on his home district in the States until 1962. (Then, like R. R. Miller, later, in regards to his work in Taiwan, Pitts was expelled for initiating an independent church.) In 1968 Pitts announced his retirement from the Philippines and turned over the Holiness Church of the Nazarene to the Church of the Bible Covenant. The Church of the Bible Covenant had been founded the previous year by former foreign missions secretary Remiss Rehfeldt and some other breakaway Nazarenes who protested the perceived breakdown of standards on such matters as hair, dress, and the allowance of television. Not until 1969 did the Philippine courts resolve the case involving the Bible College property and award full ownership to the Church of the Nazarene.[40]

In 1961 Encarnacion wrote a remorseful letter to Harry Wiese, by then mission director, regarding his wrong attitudes. "I want to have peace with God and I owe you an apology," Encarnacion said. Though he stayed with Pitts as long as Pitts remained in the Philippines, Encarnacion and his family did not join the Church of the Bible Covenant. Some others of those who split did likewise.[41]

In 1968 the Church of the Bible Covenant sent Charles and Lottie Tryon to the Philippines. They had served as Nazarene missionaries in the Philippines from 1961 to 1967 and had been active in evangelism. During a furlough in 1967 World Missions decided not to reappoint them to the Philippines. They had been involved in some conflicts with other missionaries and had sided with the McCroskeys on a number of issues. The church would have sent them to Taiwan if the Tryons had been willing. But just as Pitts, they believed that their calling was to the Philippines.[42]

## Church Building

Meanwhile, the Philippine Church of the Nazarene regained its balance. Benner ordained seven in 1958: Prisco Contado, Gil Sevidal, Carlino Fontanilla, Geronimo Galindez, Jaime Galvez, Castillo Ongogan and Andres Valenzuela. Each became a leader in succeeding years. All except Contado were quite young, and each had ties to the newer missionaries.

Contado, the only Visayan among the group of ordinands, was from a long-time Protestant family in Samar, where Presbyterians had held comity. Before the Second World War he studied at Silliman University (sponsored by the Presbyterian and Congregationalist denominations) in Dumaguete and accepted a pastorate in the United Evangelical Church on the eastern coast of Samar. However, the growing "liberalism" within the denomination disturbed him. When American forces returned to the Philippines toward the close of the war Contado became acquainted with Nazarene serviceman Adrian Rosa, who, with other Americans, held evangelistic services alongside Contado in Samar. Rosa secured a promise from Contado that should he return to the Philippines as a missionary, Contado would join him. Rosa stayed in touch with Contado and notified him when he arrived as a newly appointed Nazarene missionary in 1952. Contado journeyed to Baguio to greet him. Rosa held him to his earlier promise and immediately appointed him to help open the work in Bacolod City. Contado took an indefinite leave of absence at the next United Church of Christ Assembly, of which he was a prominent member, and worked with Rosa in both Bacolod City (though the church there was not organized until several years later) and Iloilo. He became pastor of the Iloilo church in late 1954 and remained there nine years. When Pitts stationed the Pattees in Iloilo in 1956, Contado and Pattee began services in Samar. Contado eventually moved there, to pioneer a church in Balagiga, in 1963. He also had contacts in Mindanao, where some of his relatives lived, and helped to begin Nazarene work on the island at Mahayag,

Zamboanga del Sur. In 1967 he began the church on Leyte, at Tacloban City, then after two years he returned to Samar, where he pastored at San Antonio until his retirement in 1977.[43]

The others ordained in 1958 were all from Luzon, but came from various religious backgrounds and possessed different skills. Not all stayed with the Church of the Nazarene.

Sevidal had been previously affiliated with an independent Protestant group in Cabanatuan called the Christian Mission. He became acquainted with Encarnacion and through him joined the Pilgrim Holiness Church, and, later, the Church of the Nazarene. Like Encarnacion, he was Tagalog. He was slightly older as well as among the better educated of the first ordinands, a strong leader in potential. He pastored in Manila; La Trinidad; Binday, San Fabian, Pangasinan; and Baguio City; and he served as the district evangelist several years in the early 1960s. During his pastorate in Manila he pursued education at Far East University, where, eventually, he received a master's degree. Disagreements with missionaries over his desire for higher education along with some other personal conflicts led him to leave the church in 1969. By this time Sevidal had begun teaching at the Lyceum University in Baguio. Briefly he affiliated with Charles Tryon in the Bible Covenant Church, but Sevidal soon left him also.

Fontanilla served as the district secretary, 1955–1957, and pastored churches in Agbannawag, Rizal, Nueva Ecija; San Fernando, La Union; Baguio; Carosucan, Asingan, Pangasinan; and La Trinidad. While pastoring in Baguio and La Trinidad he attended secular colleges, despite missionaries' opposition to this.[44] As pastor, Fontanilla encouraged his local congregations to be self-supporting. While he was pastoring the La Trinidad church, because of his education and success as a pastor, missionaries asked him to teach at the Bible College. In 1972, he became a full-time faculty member and in 1974 the first Filipino president of the Nazarene Bible College (serving 1974–1976 and 1980–1983).

Galindez to many was a rising star. Like Fontanilla, Galindez was Ilocano. He had been raised in the Philippine Independent Church, a national denomination that had broken with Roman Catholicism in 1902 but which had retained many of its forms. Galindez pastored Nazarene congregations in Aringay and Bangar, La Union; and for ten years, 1958–1968, in Cabanatuan. He was the first Filipino to hold a major district-wide office as president of the Nazarene Young People's Society, 1962–1965, and Filipino pastors sensed that the missionaries were grooming him for the district superintendency. He pastored the college church for a year, 1968–1969. The missionaries recommended and received approval from World Missions for him to study at Nazarene Theological Seminary in Kansas City. While in the States he raised some of his support speaking in local churches.[45] He received the master of religious education degree from NTS in 1973. He returned to teach at the Bible College, but personal conflicts arose. He left the Church of the Nazarene in 1977 and joined the Social Brethren Church. He became that denomination's first "missionary" to the Philippines, but used Nazarene literature.

Galvez had been converted from Roman Catholicism in the Pilgrim Holiness Church before joining the Church of the Nazarene. He pastored in La Trinidad and Agbannawag, and then in Binalonan, Pangasinan, where he stayed for about ten years. In 1967 he moved to Hawaii, and for more than thirty years pastored a Nazarene Filipino congregation there.

Ongogan also was raised in the Philippine Independent Church, but frequently attended both the Evangelical United Brethren and Pilgrim Holiness churches in his hometown, San Francisco. He joined the Roman Catholic Church while attending a Catholic high school, and aimed for the priesthood. He was brought into the Nazarene Church through his uncle, Miguel Zambrano, and John Pattee, who encouraged him to attend the Nazarene Bible College. Ongogan pastored several places, including a year in Manila, but for more than twenty years he remained pastor of the Bangar church. He also served frequently as an evangelist for other congregations.

Valenzuela, the youngest of the 1958 ordinands, was from a Roman Catholic family. He pastored in San Fernando and Baguio, and from 1961 to 1967 in Agbannawag. In 1967 the District Assembly elected him assistant national district superintendent on the third ballot (the runner-up was Galindez); during the following year he traveled extensively with McCroskey, then mission director, throughout the field. The 1968 District Assembly elected Valenzuela as district superintendent through a "yes or no" ballot. He received 62 "yes" votes out of 65 ballots cast. At that time the district, which still included the entire Philippines, had 21 organized and 18 unorganized churches with 677 full and probationary members. He became superintendent of the Metro Manila District when it divided from the Luzon District in 1980, and remained as such until he accepted a position that involved ministry to Filipinos with the Nazarene district in northern California in 1987.

Each of the first ordinands except for Contado and Sevidal were among the first two classes of graduates of the Bible College. In a country dominated by Roman Catholicism, they represented a variety of religious backgrounds. Three had attended Pilgrim Holiness churches. However, in ethnicity, they were more alike. Only one was from outside Luzon, and all but two were Ilocano.[46]

There was no more mention of wedding rings and bobbed hair among either the missionary or national leaders, but the other standards of the church remained intact. Leaders zealously proved through both revivals and preaching that theirs was still a holiness church and vitally alive.

Even before Pitts had left the mission, church leaders already planned to send Harry Wiese, then working among Chinese in California, to the Philippines as mission director. Upon arriving, as he was later to do in Taiwan in relation to the problems with Miller, Wiese helped to put the church, suffering from the Pitts split, back together. Wiese complained that his five years in the Philippines (1957–1962) were frustrating. He had to close his ears, as he once said, to taunts that the Nazarene church had "gone modern." He spent much of his time clearing the titles to property. As much as Pitts, he also wanted to maintain a pure church. He wanted a "glorious church, without spot or wrinkle," he said.[47]

To do so, as he had in China, he imposed high standards for church membership. Prospective members spent at least one year on "probation" before the church granted full membership. They had to prove during this year or more that they were over their vices—that they were not smoking or drinking, or attending cockfights, or playing mahjong or gambling. For a time Wiese personally interviewed every person who wished to unite with the church. He also either implied or stated that before joining the church each person should first be in the experience of entire sanctification, the "second blessing" (even though the church's *Manual* required simply that members be in the experience of salvation and be seeking "earnestly to perfect holiness of heart and life").[48] Wiese wanted to emphasize a positive Christian message—that Christians were marked by what they did rather than what they avoided—but perhaps it remained easier to preach against various personal sins than about spiritual life and growth.

Under him the mission provided money for church properties, but Wiese purposely kept pastors' salaries low so that local congregations would be compelled to pay them more. That was the only way, he felt, toward self-support. He prevented pastors from taking part-time work so that they would depend only upon the Lord and would devote themselves fully to the ministry.[49]

Though national leaders took increasingly important roles in the 1960s, the administration of the church remained largely in the hands of missionaries. The missionaries began to weary of Wiese's leadership as district superintendent. Until the district was more fully organized under a Filipino, the election of the district superintendent rested with the missionary council. At the 1961 council meeting Wiese failed to garner the necessary two-thirds. But neither could any of the other missionaries, so the general superintendents reappointed Wiese to the position. When General Superintendent V. H. Lewis visited in March 1962, the missionaries agreed that they were willing for Wiese to remain as district superintendent until his furlough in early 1963, and elected Copelin to take his place at that time. However, at their October 1963 meeting the missionaries changed their minds and elected McCroskey over Copelin as district superintendent. The McCroskeys and the Tryons created an alliance. They were opposed to Copelin's handling of some of the legal matters with Pitts and felt that he had been too willing to compromise. They pushed for an emphasis upon evangelism. To Ronald Beech, a new missionary on the field who was not yet able to vote in council decisions, this "division of God's people" was a "deep surprise and shock." He wondered what the Filipinos' perception would be of this.[50] Even the Pattees, who had seen divisions before in their long missionary careers, worried that the tensions between the missionaries would afflict the Filipino church and bring "shame to the cause of holiness."[51] But Kansas City reversed the decision of the council and appointed Copelin as district superintendent until his furlough in September 1964. Then McCroskey took over.

Copelin and McCroskey see-sawed between the top leadership assignment for most of the next decade. They symbolized the interplay between focuses upon ministerial education and evangelism in the Philippine mission. Copelin represented the importance of the Bible College and McCroskey that of evangelism. McCroskey held revivals and established churches, while Tilly McCroskey evangelized children. Both Copelin and McCroskey also alternated, in their long missionary careers, between stations in Luzon and the Visayas. Usually Copelin remained close to the Bible College in Baguio, and, later, in the Visayas.

Meanwhile, John Pattee stayed as much as he could away from administration. He was content for Lillian Pattee to lead the Bible College while he taught subjects such as New Testament Greek at the Bible College on weekdays. On the weekends he either preached at the College Church or held meetings in the lowlands that resulted in the planting of a number of churches.[52]

He and several of the other missionaries found mission council meetings tedious and boring. The missionaries met together twice a year for long sessions that went on for days. The newer missionaries endured these sessions even though (as it was a general church policy) they were not allowed to vote during their first term of service. Each council meeting produced twenty to thirty pages of single-spaced, typed minutes. The meetings covered every conceivable aspect of the mission and its property (including kitchen appliances), as well as local church arrangements and pastoral assignments. It was a case of micromanagement. One disgruntled missionary complained to E. S. Phillips that he could endure any hardship in the Philippines except council meetings and characterized the meetings as "meaningless, fruitless pettiness."[53] Yet the missionaries also addressed larger issues such as how to raise up an indigenous church.[54]

District organization progressed. At the 1964 District Assembly Lewis ordained seven (the first ordination ceremony since 1958) and recognized the ordination papers of Zambrano. (He retired in 1970.) The 1965 District Assembly elected one of the new ordinands, Meliton Bernabe, district treasurer, and for the first time, a Filipina to head the Missionary Society, Rebecca Fontanilla. During the next year the society collected money among Filipinos for the Nazarene hospital in Papua New Guinea.[55]

As the church matured organizationally, it spread to various parts of the country. While the Pattees were stationed in Iloilo from 1956 to 1959 they began contacts in Negros Occidental that led to a church in Binalbagan. As mentioned above, Pattee and Contado began holding revivals in Samar in 1958, although a church was not firmly planted there until 1963.

By 1958 there already was talk of beginning a second Bible college, this one in the Visayas. Baguio was a distance in both kilometers and culture, and misunderstanding frequently arose between students from distinct language groups. The church purchased property for a missionary residence across from the church in Iloilo, on Zamora Street. Under the leadership of missionaries Stanley and Flora Wilson, both with masters' degrees in education, a two-year program began there with twelve students in 1964. The idea was for graduates to complete their college training in Baguio. In 1973 the school, Visayan Nazarene Bible College, initiated its own baccalaureate program.

Iloilo and the island of Panay was the center of Nazarene work in the Visayan islands. Unlike Cabanatuan, where Methodists had held comity, the Eastern Visayas, where Iloilo was located, had been evangelized by American Baptists (known as Convention Baptists in the Philippines). The Baptists maintained Central Philippine University in Iloilo and, with the cooperation of the Presbyterians, a hospital. Like

Methodists earlier in the century, Baptists in the Visayas originally emphasized to converts the necessity of giving up vices such as gambling and cockfighting. But some Baptist missionaries disagreed with the emphases the mission placed on education and medicine. A fundamentalist Baptist faction separated from the Convention Baptists over these issues as well as Baptist participation in comity arrangements and interdenominational projects. Raphael Thomas, a medical doctor, established the Association of Baptists for World Evangelism (ABWE) in 1927 and Doane Evangelistic Institute in Iloilo in 1928.[56]

The Nazarene Bible College transferred to Cebu City, the largest city in the Visayan islands and more centrally located, in 1986.[57]

The school in Baguio, Luzon Nazarene Bible College, remained strong. When Filipino teachers in the Bible colleges emerged in the mid-1960s (Carlino Fontanilla and Wilfredo Manaois in particular) they were paid low salaries. Their reward, said Copelin, was in "working with the best church [they] could find."[58] Graduation with the bachelor of theology degree required a rigorous five years and 145 credits. A similarly rigorous bachelor of religious education program began in 1966.[59]

In 1965 Ronald and Neva Beech, who had arrived in January 1963, started a soon-thriving church in Angeles City, Pampanga, with the help of Nazarene servicemen stationed at nearby Clark Air Force base. Though servicemen helped substantially to pay for the property where the church was located, it was not an American church. In both membership and giving, under Angelito Agbuya, it became one of the strongest congregations in the country.[60]

The congregation in Manila, however, faced difficulties. The church building had been erected on property for which the church had only a 10-year lease. Pitts had met a Filipino woman in the United States who allowed the Church of the Nazarene to lease and build on property her mother owned on Singalong Street in Malate, an old section of Manila. She assured him that she would inherit the property and donate it to the Church of the Nazarene. The mother lived adjacent to the property. By 1965 the lease was over and the situation had changed. The daughter in the United States had become a Pilgrim Holiness pastor and the family refused to renew the lease. The Nazarenes had to secure a restraining order to keep the family from demolishing the building, but, finally, decided to give up the property and look for another location. The missionaries decided on Parkway Village in Quezon City and the general church committed about $60,000 to this project. The Suyats, but few others of the original members, transferred to the new location.[61]

The role of Filipino women as leaders emerged naturally, since the Church of the Nazarene had always ordained women as elders and women missionaries preached and took other active roles in the mission. Both Katherine Wiese and Lillian Pattee were ordained ministers. Lillian Pattee served as president of the Bible College for several years in the 1960s. Norma Armstrong served as a district evangelist in the 1960s and 1970s, complementing Frances Vine's work in education. The Philippines, unlike other Asian countries, allowed women prominent leadership roles in society. So the Church of the Nazarene had little hesitancy encouraging women to attend Bible college (where they often met their future husbands) and using them as pastors of local churches. In 1961 the Filipino church licensed its first female minister, Ricareda Valenzuela, and she was ordained in 1971. In fact, the strength of her character and influence was one factor leading Filipinos to elect her husband as assistant superintendent in 1967.[62]

The ethical positions of the church led it to focus more on personal than social morality. The list of prohibited behavior grew by 1964 to include attendance at dancing halls, cockpits, theaters; canyaos (feasts to honor dead ancestors); gambling and participation in any games of chance, including lotteries, sweepstakes, jueting, mahjong, bingo and the "daily double"; the planting, wrapping or any other labor involved in raising tobacco, or chewing betel nut or tobacco, or smoking tobacco; and the use of alcoholic or intoxicating liquor, including fermented tuba, or using benubodan (fermented rice) as a beverage. Most of these items were introduced by the Filipino pastors themselves as amplifications and adaptations that applied *Manual* strictures to the Filipino context. It showed that members of the Church of the Nazarene would be known primarily among their neighbors by the limitations the church placed on their behavior, and that obedience to these morals would be the sign of holiness. The Church of the Nazarene was even stricter than other evangelical groups in the Philippines. Behavior clearly separated them from the rest of society.[63]

Only a few other social issues in the 1960s drew Nazarenes' interest. Filipino Nazarenes viewed a proposal to allow religious instruction in public schools by teachers on a voluntary basis as an attempt of the Roman Catholic hierarchy to control education in the Philippines, and opposed it.[64]

In the 1960s, World Missions Secretary E. S. Phillips encouraged greater indigenization. The missionaries' decision in November 1965 to secure permission for the election of a national district superintendent seemed to him overdue. The missionaries themselves were increasingly aware of the necessity of reducing dependency on the mission, and of creating a greater sense of responsibility among the local churches for both their pastors' salaries and their church buildings. The missionaries hoped that each existing church would be able to fully support its pastor within six years. In 1966 the missionaries proposed a 10 percent per year phase-out of support for any new work. But Phillips thought that this was too slow and cabled them to reduce the time period to only three years.[65]

Missions Secretary Jerald Johnson was critical of what he found in the Philippines on a trip to the country in 1974. He believed that the missionaries were too paternalistic. Even at that late date, only the missionary council chairman could approve who would be baptized or received into membership. Valenzuela enjoyed few of the provisions of his office, as nearly all aspects of the work, it seemed to Johnson, were firmly under missionary control. Johnson also found divisions and poor relationships among the missionaries themselves. He wished that the church would do more with literature in the dialects and concentrate more on Manila.[66]

The missionaries decided to divide the Philippine district in 1977. They had talked about this since the mid-1960s, and it made sense from geographic, cultural and church growth standpoints. Valenzuela remained as district superintendent of the Luzon District. The missionaries appointed Wilfredo Manaois to lead the Visayan–Mindanao District. After the division of the district, the Church of the Nazarene experienced comparatively rapid growth in numbers, with most of it occurring in the South. Manaois was an Ilongo from Negros Occidental who had been a public school teacher and principal before being recruited by John Pattee for the ministry. Manaois had been both a student and teacher at the Bible college in Baguio and went on to earn several advanced degrees. Manaois attended extensions of Fuller Theological Seminary and attempted to apply the church growth principles of Donald McGavran. For the first few years after the division, the growth in the Visayas and Mindanao was among the fastest in the country among evangelical groups and in the Nazarene denomination as a whole. Most of the growth was in Panay and the Western Visayas, where many of the new members formerly had been Convention Baptists. As a result of this growth, Manaois came to the attention of Jerald Johnson, then mission secretary, and tapped to serve on a team of persons who went into countries where permanent missionaries were not allowed in order to introduce local leaders to the Church of the Nazarene. Manaois served briefly as a missionary to Nigeria in the mid-1980s, then as a professor at Asia Pacific Nazarene Theological Seminary.[67]

The Luzon District matured. A survey in 1979 found that 94 percent of the district's full-time workers were Bible college graduates, and that 41 percent had earned secular college degrees, even though missionaries had discouraged this. The pastors made very little income, and the mission prevented them from pursuing outside work. Nine of the 28 organized churches were still receiving subsidies from the mission. There were 1,442 full and probationary members on the district. This number reflected only about one-half of the average weekly attendance on the district. The Church of the Nazarene's Filipino leaders retained the reluctance of early missionaries to quickly accept church members. Each member had to give up vices and testify to the experience of entire sanctification. Of the 36 full-time workers, 16 were ordained. Nearly all were affiliated with other groups before becoming Nazarene. Fourteen of the 36 were Roman Catholic in background; seven were Philippine Independent Church; four Methodist; four Pilgrim Holiness; and the rest from a variety of other groups. The Church of the Nazarene used women as pastors and ordained them. Of the 29 pastors on the district in 1979, seven were women.[68]

The Luzon District reached self-support and "regular" district status under the leadership of Meliton Bernabe in 1985. Following the policy of growth by division, the mission continued to divide the districts. The Metro Manila District was carved out of the Luzon District in 1980.

The Church of the Nazarene was slow in building up emphasis in Metro Manila. It may have been due to the rural backgrounds of both the missionaries and the Filipino leaders. The church decided to enter the city in earnest in the mid-1970s under the leadership of David Browning, Peter Burkhart and Andres Valenzuela. They brought in key pastors from the Luzon District, almost all of whom were Ilocano. These pastors ministered mostly to fellow Ilocanos who had migrated to Metro Manila from the provinces rather than to the dominant Tagalog population or Visayan subgroups. This meant that outside of the older Manila First Church the church members also were Ilocano. However, the church found its greatest source of growth in the Tagalog area east of Taytay, Rizal, and gradually the balance of members and leaders shifted.[69]

The history of the Church of the Nazarene in the Philippines indicates that most converts were formerly Roman Catholics, but the leaders by and large had Protestant backgrounds. Two had had contacts with the Nazarene church in America, several others came out of the Pilgrim Holiness church, a very similar denomination, and one from the United Church of Christ. Others as young men had belonged to the

Philippine Independent Church. This shows the indebtedness of the denomination to earlier Protestant work in the country. It also may have been one factor that led some of the older ones to leave the Church of the Nazarene with Joseph Pitts.

Like other evangelical groups, if not more so, the Church of the Nazarene was countercultural in its expectations for Christian life among both pastors and laity. While that may have limited early growth, it was both consistent with the doctrinal distinctives of the church and compensated for by the boldness and zeal of American missionaries' pursuit of converts and Bible college students. In typical evangelical fashion the organization conserved converts through local congregations and trained pastors in denominational Bible colleges.

The educational program of the church from the early years was strong, including a full collegiate program with competent, well-educated teachers. By the 1960s the Bible colleges were producing Nazarene pastors and the earlier dependency upon leaders who had transferred from other denominations waned. Of course it also meant that, unlike the older leaders, many of whom left with Pitts, there was a paternalistic relation between the Filipino leaders and the somewhat older missionaries. The missionaries expected all of the pastors to have graduated from either one of the Bible colleges. Almost exclusively, missionaries had been their teachers. They were guarded about the possible influences of secular education and employment. They expected that pastors would devote themselves full-time to the ministry yet realized that the pastors would be underpaid.

The exit of strong leaders with Pitts and the paternalist relationship among those who remained may have delayed greater measures of autonomy. But there were other factors as well. The church mostly worked in the provinces among lower-class people with Roman Catholic backgrounds who had little familiarity with or capability for tithing, the principal means by which Nazarene congregations are financed. With subsidies from America going for both property and pastors' salaries, there seemed to be little need for tithing anyway. So the relationship of dependency persisted for many years.

Although other groups grew faster, in the context of the Philippines, Protestantism in general failed to advance much against Roman Catholicism. Considering the ethnic, linguistic and social diversity of the people, Roman Catholicism was one of the few commonalities holding the people together as a culture. Since Protestantism was associated with American colonialism, nationalist impulses in the Philippines associated Roman Catholicism, in spite of its Spanish orientation, with what it meant to be a Filipino. In that sense Roman Catholicism in the Philippines functioned in fact, if not in law, as a state religion—something like Shintoism in Japan.

A historian is not allowed to ask "what if," but perhaps the readers can imagine what might have happened if the early, older leaders had stayed; or if the church had concentrated early on building strong urban congregations in Manila and elsewhere. Nevertheless, as it was the Church of the Nazarene in the Philippines in the early decades maintained the mission and character of the worldwide church as a conservative evangelical denomination known for its theological fidelity to Wesley's doctrine of entire sanctification, and its strict moral prohibitions.

# Notes

1. Steve Brouwer, Paul Gifford, and Usan D. Rose, *Exporting the American Gospel: Global Christian Fundamentalism* (New York: Routledge, 1996), chapter five. On the economic and cultural ties between the Philippines and the United States see Stephen R. Shalom, *The United States and the Philippines: A Study of Neocolonialism* (Reprint, Quezon City: New Day, 1986), especially chapter two. On the question of the relation of Protestantism to colonialism in the early part of the century see Kenton J. Clymer, *Protestant Missionaries in the Philippines, 1898–1916: An Inquiry into the American Colonial Mentality* (Urbana: University of Illinois Press, 1986), and Mariano Apilado, *Revolutionary Spirituality: A Study of the Protestant Role in the American Colonial Rule of the Philippines, 1898–1928* (Quezon City: New Day, 1999).

2. Benjamin I. Guansing, "Developments in the Philippines," *The Philippine Faith and Life* (1950), 25–26; Enrique Sobrepena, "The State of the Church," *Philippine Christian Advocate* (June 1953), 5–6; Richard Bush, "The Sectarian Challenge," *Philippine Christian Advocate* (January 1954), 4–5; "Mindanao in the Making," Richard L. Deats, *The Story of Methodism in the Philippines* (Manila: Union Theological Seminary, 1964), 111–112; Peter G. Gowing, *Islands Under the Cross: The Story of the Church of the Philippines* (Manila: National Council of Churches in the Philippines, 1967), chs. 7–8; Douglas Elwood, *Churches and Sects in the Philippines: A Descriptive Study of Contemporary Religious Group Movements* (Dumaguete City: Silliman University, 1968); Dionisio D. Alejandro, *From Darkness to Light: A Brief Chronicle of the Beginnings and Spread of Methodism in the Philippines* (N.p.: Philippines Central Conference, United Methodist Church, 1974), 254–256; Jose L. Valencia, *Under God's Umbrella: An Autobiography* (Quezon City: New Day, 1978), 97–107; Clymer, *Protestant Missionaries in the Philippines*, 32–61; T. Valentino Sitoy, *Several Springs, One Stream: The United Church of Christ in the Philippines*, vol. 1: *Heritage and Origins (1898–1946)* (Quezon City: United Church of Christ in the Philippines, 1992), 10–12, 321–328, 498.

See also Arthur Tuggy, *The Philippine Church: Growth in a Changing Society* (Grand Rapids, Mich.: Eerdmans, 1971), 150–156.

3. H. Orton Wiley, editorial, *Other Sheep* (November 1928), 2. See also [J. G. Morrison], "Wants to Open a Mission in the Philippines," *Other Sheep* (May 1935), 4.

4. *The Oasis* (Nampa, Idaho: Northwest Nazarene College, 1922), 40, 81; *The Oasis* (1923), 44; *The Oasis* (1926), 34. On Methodist organization in Cabanatuan see Alejandro, *From Darkness to Light*, 66.

5. Interview with Castillo Ongogan, December 2, 1991. On the Pilgrim Holiness group, which merged with the Wesleyan Methodists in the Philippines in 1970 (two years after the merger in the United States), see Paul Westphal Thomas and Paul William Thomas, "The Philippine Islands," in *The Days of Our Pilgrimage: The History of the Pilgrim Holiness Church*, ed. Melvin Dieter and Lee Haines (Marion, Ind.: Wesley Press, 1976), 194–201; *Wesleyan World* (July/August 1987); and Paul W. Thomas, "The Philippines," 526–555. The Free Methodist Church, another group much like the Church of the Nazarene, entered in 1949. The Free Methodists were about the only group among those entering after the war to secure approval from the Protestants' Philippine Federation of Christian Churches before arriving. The Federation assigned them to a remote area on the Surigao coast of Mindanao at Lianga and in Agusan Valley. The Free Methodists later established their headquarters at Butuan City. See Ruby Schlosser and Gertrude Groesbeck, eds., *Lighting the Philippine Frontier* (Winona Lake, Ind.: Woman's Missionary Society, Free Methodist Church, 1956), 24–25.

6. Joseph Pitts, *Mission to the Philippines* (Kansas City, Mo.: Beacon Hill, 1955), 7–8; Ely S. Encarnacion, "Bible School Student's Testimony," *Other Sheep* (February 1953), 7; *The Church Abroad: A Quadrennial Review of Missions, 1948-52* (Kansas City, Mo.: Nazarene Publishing House, 1952), 86–87; [Epifania] Encarnacion to Carol Bestre, March 11, 1989; interview with Castillo Ongogan, December 2, 1991; Paul W. Thomas, "The Philippines," in *Reformers and Revivalists: The History of The Wesleyan Church*, ed. Wayne E. Caldwell (Indianapolis: Wesley Press, 1992), 528; Robert A. Bickert, "Perception and Response to Receptivity: The History and Growth of the Wesleyan Church in the Philippines, 1932–1994," D.Miss. dissertation, Asbury Theological Seminary, 1996, 195–196.

7. For holiness emphases in Philippine Methodism see D. D. Alejandro, "Evangelism for the Philippines," *The Philippine Faith and Life* (1950), 15–18; Alejandro, "Evangelism: Its Methods," *The Philippine Faith and Life* (1951), 11–14; and Alejandro, "The Holy Spirit in Christian Experience," in Estanislao Abainza, et al., *Selected Philippine Sermons* (Manila: National Council of Churches in the Philippines, 1967), 68–82; Alejandro, *From Darkness to Light*, 104–107, 133, 243. See David Y. Santiago, "Keeping Our Body Holy," *Philippine Christian Advocate* (February 1959), 9–10, on the Methodists' prohibition of smoking, dancing and drinking.

8. Pitts, *Mission*, 7; John W. Pattee, "Tenth Anniversary of Nazarene Work in the Philippines," 1958 *District Assembly Journal*, 29.

9. Eckel, "Our Trip to Manila," *Other Sheep* (September 1939), 12–15.

10. J. E. Moore, Jr. "The Philippines and the Islands," in *The Chaplains See World Missions*, ed. Lauriston J. DuBois (Kansas City, Mo.: Nazarene Publishing House, 1946), 53–54; H. C. Powers to H. V. Miller, June 10, 1946 (file 920-62); Pattee, "Tenth," 30; Purkiser, *Called*, 185–186; Carol Bestre, "Baguio First Church of the Nazarene: A Historical Sketch," term paper for the History of Nazarene Missions class, APNTS, March 14, 1989. See also the study of Ernesto N. Rulloda, "The Church of the Nazarene in the Philippines: Her Role in Nation Building" (Ed.D. dissertation, Baguio Central University, 1990).

11. Pitts, *Mission*, 18–23.

12. "Philippine Islands Scrap Book" (two volumes in the Asia Pacific Nazarene Theological Seminary Library, Taytay, Rizal, Philippines), contains undated clippings. For the context see Purkiser, *Called*, ch. 8.

13. Pitts, "A New Church in Iloilo City," *Other Sheep* (December 1948), 6–7; Pitts, "Pioneering in the Philippines," *Other Sheep* (July 1949), 7.

14. Powers to Remiss Rehfeldt, July 27, 1951, and August 20, 1951; Rehfeldt to Powers, September 26, 1951, World Mission Division Office.

15. Pitts, *Mission*, 51.

16. See Elwood, *Churches and Sects*, 67–73. See also Raul Pertierra, *Religion, Politics and Rationality in a Philippine Community* (Quezon City: Ateneo De Manila University Press, 1988), 153–181.

17. C. C. Jamandre, "How God Saved and Sanctified Me," *Other Sheep* (1951); *The Church Abroad*, 86–87; Pitts, *Mission*, 30–40, 74–78; Jose F. Lallana, "Report," 1957 *Journal*, 45; Copelin, "Report," 1957 *Journal*, 51; Billy Verceles, "The Life and Ministry of Rev. Carlino Fontanilla," term paper for the History of Nazarene Missions class, APNTS, March 15, 1989; interview with Carlino Fontanilla, November 3, 1991; interview with Castillo Ongogan, December 2, 1991.

18. Pattee, *Hazardous Days in China* (Pasadena, Calif.: the author, n.d.), 39–43; C. Ellen Watts, *John Pattee of China and the Philippines* (Kansas City, Mo.: Beacon Hill, 1984), 51–56, 77–78, 92–93.

19. Joseph Pitts, *Voices from the Philippines* (N.p., 1958), 4; Pattee, "Preachers' Institute," *Other Sheep* (1951); Copelin, *Life in a Nazarene Bible College: The Story of Missionary Education in the Philippines* (Kansas City, Mo.: Nazarene Publishing House, 1962), 18–22; Donald Owens, *Sing Ye Islands: Nazarene Missions in the Pacific Islands* (Kansas City, Mo.: Nazarene Publishing House, 1979), 57–61. For the context see Benedict J. Kerkvliet, *The Huk Rebellion: A Study of Peasant Revolt in the Philippines* (Berkeley, Calif.: University of California Press, 1977), esp. ch. 6.

20. Eleuterio Pitong, "From Communism to Christ," *Other Sheep* (July 1952), 11; Pitts, "Lo-o Valley," *Other Sheep* (August 1955), 2; Wiese, "Superintendent's Report," September 1960; Copelin, *Life*, throughout; Abdon Butag,

"History of the Church of the Nazarene in Zone Eight, North-Central Luzon District," term paper for the History of the Nazarene Missions class, APNTS, October 1989, based on interviews with key leaders. The Missouri Synod Lutherans had begun work in Abatan and Lo-o in 1951 and established a hospital in Abatan. See Herbert Kretzmann, "Lutheranism in the Philippines, 1952–1966," S.T.M. thesis, Concordia Seminary, 1966, 214–215, 268, 279, 284–287, 301.

21. Pitts, *Mission*, 8–9; Thomas and Thomas, "The Philippine Islands," 195–196; interview with Castillo Ongogan, December 2, 1991; Thomas, "The Philippines," 526–527.

22. Lillian Pattee to Mary Scott, May 20, 1955; 1957 *Journal*, 1, 44, 46; Watts, *Pattee*, 108–109.

23. Interviews with Carlino Fontanilla, Nov. 3, 1991, and Castillo Ongogan, December 2, 1991.

24. Nease to Rehfeldt, July 1, 1949, and Rehfeldt to Nease, July 22, 1949, General Board of Foreign Missions; 1955 *Journal*, 26–28; 1958 *Journal*, 32; Pattee, "A New Chapel at Aringay," *Other Sheep* (June 1956), 4; Wilfredo Manaois, "What Revival Means to Me," *Other Sheep* (January 1959), 3; John and Lillian Pattee to Friends, September 17, 1957, and June 9, 1958; Lillian Pattee, "Revival in Binalonan," *Other Sheep*, clipping; interview with Carlino Fontanilla, Nov. 3, 1991; interview with Castillo Ongogan, December 2, 1991; Watts, *Pattee*, 95–97.

25. "Meet Your Missionaries," *Other Sheep* (September 1955), 11; "Frances Vine," *Other Sheep* (February 1953), 15.

26. "Licensed Ministers," 1955 *Journal*, 5; Pitts, "Report," 1955 *Journal*, 21; statistics, 1957 *Journal*, 38f; Rehfeldt, "Our Philippine Work," *Other Sheep* (September 1955), 1.

27. Encarnacion, "Report," 1955 *Journal*, 35. Compare Purkiser, *Called*, 256–286.

28. *Echoes from the Philippines* (May 1961).

29. Pitts, *Voices* (1958), 6–7, 17–18. See Wallace Thornton, *Radical Righteousness: Personal Ethics and the Development of the Holiness Movement* (Salem, Ohio: Schmul, 1998), 122–131.

30. Pitts, "Report," 1957 *Journal*, 35–36. See Copelin's "Report," p. 49.

31. Pitts, *Voices* (1958), 12.

32. Pitts to Rehfeldt, November 2, 1957, World Mission Office; Lillian Pattee to Mary Scott, January 9, 1958; Pitts, *Voices* (1958), 4–5, 8–9, 11–12.

33. Thornton, *Radical Righteousness*, 140–142.

34. Rehfeldt to Pitts, January 15, 1958, World Mission office; Pitts, *Voices* (1958), 12, 18; Wiese to Rehfeldt, March 7, 1958; Pitts to Rehfeldt, May 2, 1958; Pitts to Department of Foreign Missions, May 17, 1958; Wiese to Rehfeldt, December 16, 1958, World Mission Office; Vanderpool to Rehfeldt, June, 1958; Thornton, *Radical Righteousness*, 142.

35. Pitts, *Voices* (1958), 23–24.

36. Pitts, *Voices* (1958), 6, 9, 13–14; Paul Pitts, *Pentecost Rejected* (N.p., [1956]), mimeographed, 24; Pattee to Board of General Superintendents and Remiss Rehfeldt, October 9, 1957, World Mission Office; Epifania Encarnacion to Carol Bestre, March 11, 1989. Respected Filipino educator and jurist Jorge Bocobo thought "bobbed" hair a dangerous, imported American vice. See *Philippine Christian Advance* (November 1958), 7.

37. Yet the Pattees stated that Benner had acted wisely. John and Lillian Pattee to Friends, June 9, 1958. See Pitts, *Voices* (1958), 22–23 and Paul Pitts, *Pentecost*, for some of the other issues within the church as a whole.

38. *Echoes from the Philippines* (May 1961).

39. Wiese to Benner, August 23, 1961; *Echoes from the Philippines* (September 4, 1961).

40. Pitts, *Voices* (1958), 19, 25; Wiese to Rehfeldt, September 23, 1958, World Mission Office; Annual Council Meeting, Philippine Mission, October 13–18; Vanderpool to Pitts, April 15, 1960, and Vanderpool–Rehfeldt correspondence regarding the "Historic Enon Covenant" (file 906-9); 1958 Annual Council Meeting; *Echoes from the Philippines*, ed. J. S. Pitts, May 1961 and September 4, 1961 issues; Philippine Security and Exchange Commission (registration of Holiness Nazarene Mission), December 14, 1961 (file 1385-22); Pitts to Wiese, January 24, 1962; Wiese, "Pitts Sparks More Trouble," February 7, 1962 (file 1361-13); Lillian Pattee to Mary Scott, May 20, 1962; John and Lillian Pattee to Mary Scott, December 28, 1964; Council Meeting, March 1962; Copelin to Phillips, May 21, 1969. See Charles E. Jones, *A Guide to the Study of the Holiness Movement* (Metuchen, N.J.: Scarecrow, 1974), 474–475; Arthur C. Piepkorn, *Profiles in Belief: The Religious Bodies of the United States*, vol. 3: *Holiness and Pentecostal* (New York: Harper and Row, 1979), 60–61; Thornton, *Radical Righteousness*, 142.

41. Wiese to Benner, August 23, 1961, in which was attached the letter from Encarnacion and others.

42. John and Lillian Pattee to Coulter and Lewis, October 19, 1963; Tryon to Phillips, September 29, 1967; McCroskey to Coulter [1968] (file 1357-23); Pattee to Coulter, June 8, 1968.

43. Various issues of the District Assembly *Journal*; Ciriaco Ganchoree, "Iloilo City Ministers for Evangelical Fellowship," *Philippine Christian Advocate* (October 1959), 29–31; Gilbert Montecastro, "A Brief History of the Western Visayas District," term paper for the History of Nazarene Missions class, APNTS, October 1989; Prisco G. Contado to Cunningham, October 28, 1991. For a negative assessment of the UCCP during this time see Donald McGavran, *Church Growth in the United Church of Christ in the Philippines*, vol. 1: *Multiplying Churches in the Philippines* (N.p., n.d.), 66–77.

44. Mission Council Meeting, November 1965.

45. Coulter to McCroskey, January 26, 1967.

46. Wiese to Benner, November 15, 1958, World Mission office; Benner, "Revival in the Philippines," *Herald of Holiness* (September 17, 1958), 10–11; Frances Vine, "Bible School Revival in the Philippines," *Herald of Holiness*

(September 17, 1958); Wiese, "Revival Spirit Continues," *Herald of Holiness* (July 1959). For details on the lives of these seven ordinands see various issues of the *District Assembly Journal*. The preceding paragraphs are also based on interviews with Carlino Fontanilla, November 3, 1991; and Castillo Ongogan, December 2, 1991.

47. Wiese, District Superintendent's Report, 1958 *Journal*, 23; 1962 *Journal*, 32.

48. *Manual of the Church of the Nazarene 1960*, 51, 250–252.

49. Pitts to Rehfeldt, March 4, 1957, World Mission office; Philippine Council Minutes, September, 1959; Wiese, "Report to the Council Meeting," October 12, 1959; "The Wieses," *Other Sheep* clipping (1958), 12; Wiese, "Report," 1958 *Journal*, 25; Wiese, "Report," 1961 *Journal*, 31; Honorio Mateo, "Report," 1961 *Journal*, 47; "Minutes," 1962 *Journal*, 26–27; Mateo, in *Journal* (1962), 38.

50. McCroskey to Lewis, October 28, 1963, enclosing Beech to McCroskey, October 24, 1963.

51. John and Lillian Pattee to Coulter and Lewis, October 29, 1963.

52. 1963 Mission Council Meeting; Pattee to Lewis, January 1, 1965; McCroskey to Coulter, September 26, 1966, and October 17, 1966; Coulter to McCroskey, November 7, 1966; Watts, *Pattee*, 122–127.

53. Bob Lathram to Phillips, May 10, 1969.

54. For examples, see "Minutes of March 1962 Council Meeting"; "Mission Council Meeting—1963"; "Council Meeting—1964"; "Mission Council Mid-Year Meeting," April 1966.

55. 1959 Council Minutes; 1960 Mission Council Minutes; 1962 Council Meeting; October 1963 Council Meeting; Copelin to Lewis, November 5, 1963; September 1964 Council Meeting.

56. Enrique C. Sobrepena, *That They May Be One* (Manila: UCCP, [1955]), 32–33, 74; Jesse E. Posey, "A Historical Study of Baptist Missions in the Philippines, 1900–1967," Th.D. dissertation, New Orleans Baptist Theological Seminary, 1968, 63–66, 69; Raymond W. Beaver, *Partners in Mission: American Baptists and Philippine Baptists in Mission Together, 1900–1988* (Iloilo: ABC Printing, 1988), 77–92, 356–359; Nestor D. Bunda, *A Mission History of the Philippine Baptist Churches 1898–1998 from a Philippine Perspective* (Aachen: Verlag an der Lottbek, 1999), 101–103.

57. Copelin to Lewis, October 7, 1964; Copelin to Phillips, October 7, 1964; Parker, *Mission*, 338, 340.

58. Copelin to Lewis, October 20, 1964. See also "Philippine Islands Budget Breakdown 1961–62."

59. "Philippine Mission Council Mid-Year Meeting," April 1966; meeting of the missionaries, February 25, 1967 (file 1361-14).

60. Annual Council Meeting (1958); John and Lillian Pattee to friends, December 1958; Minutes of the 1962 Council Meeting; 1964 *Journal*, 1; McCroskey, "More than 7,000 Islands," *Other Sheep* (October 1965), 4–5; McCroskey to Coulter, May 3, 1966; Neva Beech, "The Answer to Angeles,"

*Other Sheep* (October 1967), 4–6; Ana Maria Gabrido, "History of the Binalbagan Church of the Nazarene Negros Occidental," term paper for the History of Nazarene Missions class, APNTS, 1991.

61. McCroskey to Phillips, April 17, 1965; Coulter, "The Philippines" [n.d.] (file 1361-14); Council Minutes, October 9–11, 1967.

62. Wiese, "Report," 1961 *Journal*, 45; Virginia Fontanilla, "Report," 1962 *Journal*, 53; Wiese, "Report," 1962 *Journal*; "Ordained Elders," 1971 *Journal*, 11; interview with Castillo Ongogan, December 2, 1991.

63. Mateo, "Report," 1964 *Journal*, 42. See F. Landa Jocano, *Folk Christianity: A Preliminary Study of Conversion and Patterning of Christian Experience in the Philippines* (Quezon City: Trinity Research Institute, 1981), 52–70; and Raul Pertierra, *Religion, Politics, and Rationality in a Philippine Community* (Quezon City: Ateneo de Manila University Press, 1988), 138–139, 153–169. See also Thornton, *Radical Righteousness*, 208.

64. "Minutes," 1965 *Journal*, 27. See also Camilo Osias, *Separation of Church and State* (Manila: N.p., 1965), 117–130.

65. Mission Council Meeting, November 1965; Mission Council Mid-Year, April 1966; McCroskey to Coulter, April 14, 1966; Annual Council Meeting, October 1966.

66. Jerald Johnson, "Tentative Observations: Philippine Islands, Hong Kong, Taiwan, and Korea—1974" (file 568-4).

67. McCroskey to Coulter, November 8, 1966; James Montgomery and Donald McGavran, *The Discipling of a Nation* (Santa Clara, Calif.: Global Church Growth Bulletin, 1980), 121–123; Manaois, "Church Growth in the Philippines: The Visayan District," ms.; Manaois, "The Next Ten Years: A Strategy for Church Growth in the Visayas and Mindanao," ms.

68. Beech, "Luzon District Survey," ms. (March 1979).

69. Browning to Edward Lawlor, March 20, 1972; various issues of the Metro Manila District Assembly *Journal*.

# Conclusion

In China one missionary responsible for touring a number of villages was passing from town to town in his "Model T" Ford. At one village stop a mother brought to the missionary a child whose head was covered with sores. The missionary was not a doctor, but the people still expected him to know what to do. Indeed, almost every missionary was called upon to treat diseases. They passed out soda mints, dressed sores, opened abscesses with jackknives, and pulled teeth—all to relieve some of the intense misery of the people. On this occasion the missionary had no medical supplies at all. But the growing crowd of people watched him and expected him to do something for the child. The only thing he had was motor oil. So he requested the mother to bring the child to him and the missionary doused the child's head with the motor oil. He gave the mother the can and told the mother to rub some on the child's head every day. Then the missionary went on his way. A few weeks later, when the missionary next returned to the village, he was greatly surprised. As he pulled up people from everywhere came bringing bowls. The child had gotten well and they too wanted some of that amazing miracle-working elixir.[1]

Perhaps that was something of a parable of Nazarene missions. Missionaries came in vehicles foreign to the places where they served. They seemed *deus ex machina*. The people had little understanding of motivations. But they found that the missionaries did have something to offer, which they took. It helped them in some way, even if it was not particularly in the way that the missionaries intended. But, however misunderstood the giving and the receiving, there was an impact whether brief or lasting of missionaries upon the lives they touched. Nazarenes drew small groups of people together in congregations, divided them from others in their own cultures, and united them organizationally with men and women around the world with similar beliefs.

Missions maintained the support of Nazarene laypersons. By the end of the century, the Church of the Nazarene was the fifth largest United States-based denomination in its giving for overseas ministries (about $40 million). It was among the ten or twelve largest denominations in number of missionaries who had served overseas more than four years. In both giving and missionaries it had surpassed the United Methodists. The Church of the Nazarene was second only to the Southern Baptists in the number of short-term and volunteer workers.[2]

There were 1.4 million members in the Church of the Nazarene around the world by the end of the century. More than 740,000 Nazarenes—53 percent—lived outside the United States and Canada. In numbers, if not yet in other ways, the church had become international. Among the first Asian countries that the church entered, in 2000 there were 53,000 Nazarenes in India and Bangladesh, 5,600 in Japan, 32,500 in Korea, and 15,000 in the Philippines. In China, there were 2,000 members in Taiwan, and 150,000 believers attending registered churches in the Hebei Province side of the area over which the Church of the Nazarene had responsibility.[3]

These believers in China as well as members in other countries knew that their religious roots were in the Church of the Nazarene and its holiness movement background. Missionaries and early local leaders implanted among these believers, to greater or lesser extents, a specific heritage of theology, polity, behavior and ethos. Members had seen the importance the church placed on a reasonably educated clergy, and compassionate ministries as well as evangelism. They had seen methods of leadership and decision-making. Yet, missionaries and the general church could not determine the inner workings of mature, self-supporting local bodies, and cultural patterns ultimately prevailed.

Nazarene mission leaders, like their counterparts in other denominations, expected converts to know what made their church distinct, what it stood for theologically and ethically, and, in general, what it meant to be a member of it. As Nazarenes, members identified themselves distinctively within the larger fabric of Protestantism in their own countries. The church provided a subcultural and sometimes countercultural worldview. Missionaries wanted converts to define themselves primarily within the church, and only secondarily within the converts' own nation. To be a Nazarene, leaders hoped, would be a category of self-identity transcending national ties.[4]

Judging from records, it would appear that the Church of the Nazarene existed in its own peculiar enclave, nearly oblivious to the outside world. Nazarene leaders rarely wrote to administrators about political and social issues. This reflected the call to separate from the "world," and at the same time to build a community that would transcend national barriers. The Nazarene ethos was so attached to separateness that the church's missionaries, unlike representatives of larger denominations, did not see themselves as part of broader world events. Nazarenes accommodated themselves to political realities.

In India, Nazarenes worked under a British colonial system that gave way to nationalism. Missionaries there did not look upon themselves as Indians did, as members of the colonial establishment. The Indian government, for geopolitical reasons, restricted the number and activities of American missionaries by the 1970s. In China they worked under unsettled political situations. Most Chinese members carried on under communism and joined the Three Selfs Patriotic Movement. In Japan, the church before the war accepted the idea of bowing to the Emperor. After the war, the church remained nationalistic. The strength of Japanese leaders, the comparative economic wealth of the country, and nationalism meant less control than leaders in Kansas City would have liked. In Korea, proud and tested local pastors who came into the Church of the Nazarene with their own ways curtailed the role of missionaries from the start. In the Philippines missionaries remained longer in control. The church lost an older generation of Filipinos with the Pitts split, and those who stayed did not articulate nationalist aims. The neocolonial relation between the Philippines and the United States abetted paternalism, even if there was little public reflection upon this.

In each of these situations, more than they realized, in spite of their separateness, the church's ministry was shaped by social and political factors.[5]

The missionaries were products of a Western culture that they considered superior, it is true, but this bore little on their minds. Their greater sense of superiority and self-esteem came religiously, in the message of holiness. As outsiders in their own culture, and even, they sensed, in Christianity as a whole, they thought themselves superior on moral grounds to the shallowness and sinking depravity of their own country and its nominal Christianity.

Indeed, more than social and political factors, the personal characteristics and backgrounds of missionaries determined much about the development of the local churches. Even those from meager homes found themselves not only well off financially relative to the people they went to serve, but in positions of control and authority that were easy to grow accustomed to and difficult to relinquish.

One senses this in the lives of missionaries as dissimilar as A. D. Fritzlan, William Eckel and R. R. Miller. But the backgrounds of missionaries such as Minnie Staples and Ida Vieg led as often to a ready identification with the people. Whether it was out of duty or compassion, missionaries engaged in deeds aimed to uplift the people not only spiritually but in every way they could. The mission situation forced them into certain social roles and functions, such as dam and road building and relief efforts, that they would not have been called upon to do if they were ministers in their own country. They started schools, hospitals, clinics, and literacy programs, and distributed clothing.[6]

Nazarene missionaries did not carry grand notions of social reform, but were controlling over their own small fields.[7] They concentrated on religiously and morally transforming converts. Their world was the church they made. They built churches abroad that conformed to American holiness churches. Whether it was in China, the Philippines or Taiwan, Harry Wiese was more concerned about creating pure Nazarene churches—ones, indeed, more pure in standards than churches in North America—than in numbering hundreds of converts.

The personalities of missionaries affected the shape of the churches they planted. Though there was a diverse character to missionaries, the pioneer days of mission fields tended either to employ or to produce men and women of a very independent temperament. The church's leaders expected them to be not only church planters and administrators, but also preachers, pastors and teachers, building contractors and masons, and even dispensers of medicine. This also was the image in the minds of the lay members of churches who sent money to support the work abroad. M. D. Wood, Peter Kiehn, A. J. Smith, Minnie Staples, R. R. Miller and Joseph Pitts exhibited the "rugged individualism" and "self-reliance" of American cultural values. Often, when most isolated from other missionaries, the pioneers identified with the people, learned from them, and, in some ways, came to be like them. Probably more than they realized, the culture and, particularly, the respect of the converts and local leaders among whom they lived and worked affected them daily. They were the first converts' spiritual mothers and fathers. That parental role carried both affection and domination. Asian leaders supported missionaries such as Peter Kiehn, Minnie Staples and Joseph Pitts long after other missionaries and church leaders had turned against them. Early local leaders followed them, not remote leaders and an abstract denomination. The test of missionaries' patience came not in dealing with the subjects of their ministry, but in dealing with other missionaries. Interrelationships with other missionaries, more than cultural adjustments, sorely tested holiness and perfect love.[8]

Strong independency as a personality characteristic did not long suit the bureaucratic structure of the Church of the Nazarene. The very qualities that made men and women sturdy pioneers led them into conflicts with higher authorities. Reynolds and his successors preferred missionaries such as Leighton Tracy, Harry Wiese and William Eckel, who were willing to cooperate with church leaders, to the rugged individualists. In the process, structure triumphed over spirit.

Conflicts involved national leaders' protests against missionaries who seemed to them autocratic. It resulted from the political changes of the early and mid-twentieth century, the rising sense of nationalism that affected nearly all non-Western societies, and the normal processes of church development and growth. Partly, tension between national church leaders and missionaries was a sign of maturity, as when Indians questioned the practices of Fritzlan in the 1920s, or when Japanese leaders during the 1930s and again in the 1960s wondered why they needed to retain ties to the denomination, or when Chinese clamored for some sort of self-governance in 1940. When tensions between missionaries and Asian leaders arose, Asian leaders thought of the conflict situation in the terms of colonialism, but the missionaries in terms of spiritual shortcomings on the part of the Asians who challenged them.

The irony is that while attempting to preach holiness abroad, the missionaries themselves fell far short of the ideal. Sometimes they fell short by blatant immorality, but usually it was in more subtle ways—in struggles for domination and control and in the breakdown of civil interpersonal relations among themselves. There was an obvious credibility gap if one could profess holiness and live in daily conflict with fellow Christians. The failure of Eckel and Staples to work together in Japan split the church for decades, long after both of these leaders retired.

Sometimes the rancor among missionaries was not merely personal, as was mostly the case in the conflict between Reynolds and Wood. Their struggle clarified the structure of the church's government and control of missions and churches abroad. As structure dominated over spirit, the church lost the freedom to make the message of holiness culturally meaningful.[9]

Missionaries practiced both the "Bresee" and "Reynolds" paradigms throughout the church's history. At times it seemed just a matter of emphasis. Both Bresee and Reynolds were committed to evangelism, and both saw the necessity of schools and hospitals on mission fields—although from different perspectives. Bresee and Reynolds represented the tensions within the holiness movement between churchly and sectarian tendencies. Reynolds represented structure and power, Bresee, Spirit and purity.

When the church emphasized empowerment with the Holy Spirit, the passion to win souls by whatever means possible was intense. Means of advancing the gospel were not only revivals, but compassionate deeds as well. It was the same gospel story as presented by other evangelicals. Nazarenes simply added entire sanctification to the order of salvation. There was room for cooperation with other denominations.

When the church emphasized purity, the mission focused on establishing places where perfect love was manifest among the marginalized. The Spirit welcomed spontaneity and compassionate works. Other churches needed this purity, leaders such as Bresee felt, and the Church of the Nazarene was raised up in some way to motivate other Christians to pursue holiness.

Since it was Reynolds rather than Bresee who oversaw missions, Reynolds's personality and ideas shaped the larger church. Reynolds expected respect for the authority of the church and its leaders. He fretted whenever missionaries became too independent. Even reported revivals in India and China worried Reynolds. He wanted guarantees that the movement of the Spirit fit Nazarene patterns. The emphasis upon conformity to structure was passed on to local church bodies.

At the same time, through the struggle in Japan between Lulu Williams and the other missionaries over the presence of Kitagawa and Nagamatsu on the mission council, Reynolds established another principle: the church would incorporate local workers into positions of leadership. The principle prevailed decades later when Rehfeldt championed Chung rather than Owens for the top position in Korea.

Through conflict on policy issues, consensus and compromise often emerged. Conflict, when it was focused on the church's mission and direction, propelled the church forward. Missionaries' struggles with Pitts in the Philippines clarified the relationship of holiness to certain rules. On another front, some missionaries in the Philippines believed too much emphasis was being placed on the Bible college and not enough on evangelism. Similarly, in India, by the 1960s Bronnell Greer faced what he thought was a great imbalance in the mission away from direct evangelism and contact between missionaries and Indian people, toward institutionalism.

The balance between education and evangelism was integral to the identity of the Church of the Nazarene. In Japan there was a balance between evangelism and education because Staples was most responsible for evangelism in the church and her co-worker, Kitagawa, was in charge of the school. In China, too, there was balance. Though the church built a hospital and established village schools, a number of missionaries were involved in evangelism. Then, in the late 1930s, all saw the immediate necessity for a well-prepared core of Chinese ministers and placed emphasis on theological education. The importance of education in Taiwan, Korea and the Philippines was unquestioned. In these "second-generation" mission fields, Bible colleges were established as soon as possible. In both Korea and Taiwan the Presbyterian model of a well-educated ministry prevailed in all Protestant churches. Chung saw it as so necessary to the work in Korea that he called for a missionary to initiate and lead it. John and Lillian Pattee had seen the benefit of ministerial education in China, and feared Communist insurgency in the Philippines, so rapidly set up a strong school near Baguio. By their ministries and involvements, both Lillian and John Pattee contributed directly to the synthesis of education and evangelism.

The importance of having trained and loyal local leaders was obvious to administrators and missionaries alike. In some countries such as Japan and Korea there were strong local leaders from the beginning. In India, they developed over time. It took four decades to raise up Bhujbal and his generation of leaders. In any case, these leaders strengthened the sense that missionaries were dispensable and that the Asian churches could effectively carry on without them—as the situation in China effectively proved. Hsu and Wiese cooperated harmoniously in China, yet missionaries had not yet seen young leaders emerge when they were forced out. Kitagawa and Chung stood shoulder to shoulder with American missionaries in Japan and Korea. Pitts relied upon and built upon Encarnacion's contacts—but when Encarnacion sided with Pitts it proved his disloyalty and the church, though it took time, found other Filipino leaders. Indeed, leaders sought denominational loyalty among all its workers and local bodies.

In theory, Nazarene missionaries imbibed the "three-selfs" missions mantra of self-propagation, self-support and self-government. When mission fields reached the three-selfs goals, at least in principle, the mission would desist and the local districts would stand on their own. Not only were these established missiological principles, and ones evident in early as well as late Nazarene missions policies, but they were ones in accord with Anglo-American virtues of independency, hard work and self-determination. They fitted Ralph Waldo Emerson's philosophy of self-reliance and Woodrow Wilson's ideas of national self-determination as well as the missions theories of Rufus Anderson and J. Hudson Taylor. Nazarenes accepted them, but putting them into practice was difficult. Asking when these goals had been reached, the answer seemed always to be "not yet." Missions-established churches needed to wait for spiritual purity and doctrinal maturity, however the missionaries gauged these, as well as self-support.

Self-support at least was measurable, but with expanding districts, schools, literature development, and other concerns, elusive. The longer a mission remained in a country the more institutionalized it became, and the less likely that local leaders could take over its enterprises in the same way. The missionaries' goals were not self-perpetuation, either by policy or by conscious inclination.

Beneath the surface of the "not yet" answer were missionaries who had stayed in India, Japan or China for decades. They considered themselves at home in those cultures and strangers in their own lands. Missionaries demanded in some cases a spiritual and emotional maturity among the people in excess, many times, of what they themselves exhibited to each other, or what was true in their own countries, before they would leave them on their own. As long as missionaries remained they were perceived to be in positions of authority.

In regard to self-government, due to the centralized nature of Nazarene polity, the commitment of the church toward developing fully self-governing bodies, in the sense that Henry Venn, Rufus Anderson and John Nevius meant it, was partial. Unlike Baptists and other congregationally oriented denominations and faith missions, the church retained a structure that kept churches around the world tied together. Nazarene polity kept the quadrennial General Assembly at the pinnacle of its democratic processes. Assembly delegates, elected by districts, in principle represented all of the geographic areas of the church. Local groups of believers either at home or abroad were not fully independent, but, rather, bound to the General Assembly, the districts, the general superintendents, and the *Manual*. Although Methodists and Anglicans were similarly governed, unlike them Nazarene missionaries did *not* go with the goal of establishing national and autonomous bodies. More like the Roman Catholics, Nazarenes aimed to remain one organic whole, governed from a central headquarters. The Nazarene church composed itself of districts spread around the world, rather than national churches. The Japanese Nazarenes, among others, chafed under this, because it seemed only to perpetuate North American domination.[10]

To make a comparison, Nazarene polity more closely resembled French than British imperial philosophies. The French went into their colonies with a governmental code or constitution that would be universally applicable. They glorified French language and culture, art and architecture. They taught the French language to Africans and Asians. They saw their colonial holdings as overseas departments or extensions of France itself. The culmination of assimilation was representation from the colonies in the National Assembly. The British system, by contrast, was more flexible, allowing adaptations of its codes and precedents based on local situations. The British groomed national leaders, administrators and high-level bureaucrats in British law in British schools, but the goal was home rule. Their colonies could become autonomous members of the Commonwealth.

Like the French, Nazarenes were "assimilationists" rather than contextualists about the extension of their holiness language and code of behavior. Like them, Nazarenes envisioned a centralized, representative world government. The Church of the Nazarene maintained one constitution and set of rules for all. They were not aiming for "home rule" for any segment of the church. Theoretically, all Nazarenes were equal. They were equally capable of the same spiritual and moral attainments. But, as it was for the French, for Nazarenes, the localization of leadership was slow to actually take place.[11]

Edward Said defined colonialism as "the expansive force of a people; it is its power of reproduction; it is its enlargement and its multiplication through space; it is the subjection of the universe or a vast part of it to that people's language, customs, ideas and laws."[12]

In a sense, this also describes Nazarene missions, which represented the church's "expansive force," in contrast to its reflective and intellectual side. The church pushed outward, and attempted to "replicate" itself among peoples far from and unlike those in the center. The mission became the "multiplication" of the church. In the case of the church the stated reasons for the expansiveness and reproductiveness were spiritual. "We" was expanded. Something deep was confirmed in the movement itself about its transcendent and spaceless message.[13]

Both French and Nazarene colonialism replaced indigenous customs with ones thought to be nobler. The customs of Nazarenes were incorporated in the holiness code contained in its *Manual*, and passed on through missionaries, leaders and pastors to local members. If colonialism introduced people to a new language, for the Church of the Nazarene it was the peculiar language of second blessing holiness. Its terms, phrases, and ways of interpreting the Bible are transmitted in other tongues, but the theology or worldview of the church was supposed to be the same everywhere. Along with church structure and behavioral boundaries, missionaries taught the people holiness theology. They translated the church's teachings into local languages. How these teachings were received was less obvious, since there was little direct attempt to contextualize holiness theology. There was no doubt among Nazarenes at home and abroad that "we," defined by a common theology as well as experience and morality, could be universalized. Leaders from Hiram Reynolds to Remiss Rehfeldt assumed this to be self-evident. Nazarenes were a people of one code that leaders believed was suitable for all cultures. The Nazarene theory of "internationalization," therefore, remained "colonial," albeit assimilationist.

Nazarene missionaries were not British or French in their imperialism but American. In a typically American way they were guided by their sentiments, by their hearts. They thought of assimilation as William McKinley had in regards to taking the Philippines, in terms of benevolence. They faced, in their own terms, a lost and dying world. They took various evangelistic means toward others not out of a desire to dominate or control, but in order to save the world for Christ.[14]

# Notes

1. Henry C. Wesche, *Medical Missions: What? Why? How?* (Kansas City, Mo.: General Board, Church of the Nazarene, n.d.), 8–9.

2. John Siewart and Edna Valdez, eds., *Mission Handbook: U.S. and Canadian Christian Ministries Overseas*, 1998–2000 ed. (Monrovia, Calif.: MARC, 1997), 76–79.

3. General Secretary, "Annual Church Statistical Reports," December 4, 2000; conversations with Handan North Church Pastor Lee Ling En and others in China, March 13, 1999.

4. William R. Hutchison, *Errand to the World: American Protestant Thought and Foreign Missions* (Chicago: University of Chicago Press, 1987), 1–14; Patricia Hill, "The Missionary Enterprise," in *Encyclopedia of the American Religious Experience: Studies of Traditions and Movements*, ed. Charles H. Lippy and Peter W. Williams (New York: Charles Scribners Sons, 1988), 3: 1683–1696; Joel A. Carpenter and Wilbert R. Shenk, eds., *Earthen Vessels: American Evangelicals and Foreign Missions, 1880–1980* (Grand Rapids, Mich.: Eerdmans, 1990).

5. For the context of missionaries amid American expansionism see Emily S. Rosenberg, *Spreading the American Eagle: American Economic and Cultural Expansion, 1890–1945* (New York: Hill and Wang, 1982), 8, 28–33, 41, 100, 108, 119–120.

6. Timothy L. Smith, *Called Unto Holiness; The Story of the Nazarenes: The Formative Years* (Kansas City, Mo.: Nazarene Publishing House, 1962), 87–88, 113–114, 140, 149–150; early missionary application forms in the Nazarene Archives, Kansas City, Mo. See also Amy N. Hinshaw, *Messengers of the Cross in China* (Kansas City, Mo.: Woman's Foreign Missionary Society, Church of the Nazarene, n.d.) and *Messengers of the Cross in India* (Kansas City, Mo.: Woman's Foreign Missionary Society, Church of the Nazarene, n.d.), for biographical profiles.

7. Compare Lois W. Banner, "Religious Benevolence as Social Control: A Critique of an Interpretation," *Journal of American History* 60 (June 1973), 23–41.

8. Compare Kenelm Burridge, *In the Way: A Study of Christian Missionary Endeavors* (Vancouver: University of British Columbia Press, 1991), xiii-xiv, 3–11, 31–34.

9. The American Board faced similar issues in its early years and found solutions fitting to Congregationalist polity. See *To Advance the Gospel: Se-*

*lections from the Writings of Rufus Anderson*, ed. R. Pierce Beaver (Grand Rapids, Mich.: Eerdmans, 1967), 122–138.

10. See Jerald Johnson, *The International Experience* (Kansas City, Mo.: Nazarene Publishing House, 1982); Paul Orjala, "Communicating to Ourselves as Nazarenes about the Nature, Need and Future of Internationalization," (outline) presented to Internationalization Commission, February 13–14, 1987. The Nazarene structure is noted by Ralph D. Winter, "Protestant Mission Societies and the 'Other Protestant Schism'," in *American Denominational Organization: A Sociological View*, ed. Ross P. Scherer (Pasadena, Calif.: William Carey, 1980), 211. For the context of this issue in missions theory see Charles Forman, "A History of Foreign Mission Theory in America," in *American Missions in Bicentennial Perspective*, ed. R. Pierce Beaver (Pasadena, Calif.: William Carey, 1977), 69–140; Hutchison, *Errand to the World*, 77–90, 112–118; and Charles E. Van Engen, "A Broadening Vision: Forty Years of Evangelical Theology of Mission, 1946–1986," in *Earthen Vessels*, ed. Carpenter and Shenk, 203–232.

11. See Winfried Baumgart, *Imperialism: The Idea and Reality of British and French Colonial Expansion, 1880–1914*, revised ed. (Oxford: Oxford University Press, 1982), 1–3, 14–17, 51–57, 180–181; Raymond F. Betts, *Assimilation and Association in French Colonial Theory, 1890–1914* (New York: Columbia University Press, 1961), 8–9, chs. 2, 6 and 9; Jo W. Saxe, "Dilemmas of Empire: The British and French Experience," in *The Idea of Colonialism*, eds. Robert Strausz-Hupe and Harry W. Hazard (New York: Frederick A. Praeger, 1958), 50–57, 65–67.

12. Edward W. Said, *Orientalism* (New York: Vintage, 1978), 219; see 211–216.

13. For similar ideas see Lamin Sanneh, *Translating the Message: The Missionary Impact on Culture* (Maryknoll, N.Y.: Orbis, 1989), 4–8, and *Encountering the West; Christianity and the Global Cultural Process: The African Dimension* (Maryknoll, N.Y.: Orbis, 1993), 15–28; Jonathan Bonk, *The Theory and Practice of Missionary Identification, 1860–1920* (Lewiston, N.Y.: Edwin Mellen, 1989), vi, 237–265; Charles R. Taber, *The World Is Too Much with Us: "Culture" in Modern Protestant Missions* (Macon, Ga.: Mercer University Press, 1991), 71–86, 166–169.

14. See James Thomson, Peter Stanley and John Perry, *Sentimental Imperialists: The American Experience in East Asia* (New York: Harper, 1981).

# Bibliography

The following list of books, theses and articles does not include reports, correspondence, District Assembly and mission council journals, and other records held at Nazarene Archives, Kansas City, Missouri. File numbers of significant documents are indicated in the endnotes. Among the papers of the general superintendents, the papers of Hiram F. Reynolds were the most helpful. Also useful were those of Phineas F. Bresee, James B. Chapman, Samuel Young and George Coulter. The General Church Officers collection included the papers of E. G. Anderson. The General Board Foreign Missions section includes reports from the fields, publications and pamphlets, policies, reports of the general superintendents, correspondence with the mission fields (categorized by missionary), and general correspondence (categorized by foreign missions secretary). The correspondence and papers of such missionaries as Leighton Tracy are included here. Also under the General Board Foreign Missions material are District Assembly journals of non-North American areas, and mission council journals.

On microfiche held in the Church of the Nazarene's Division of World Mission offices in Kansas City are records of Korea and Taiwan not held elsewhere. Materials related to the constituent bodies that went into the formation of the Church of the Nazarene are on microfilm, and are more accessible to the public.

The following list does not include numerous articles taken from *The Other Sheep* and its successor, the *World Mission* magazine (the official organ of the Church of the Nazarene's Missionary Society and World Mission Division). Likewise it does not include articles from the *Herald of Holiness*, the earlier *Nazarene Messenger*, or from *Zion's Outlook*. It does not include later issues of the Nazarene *Manual*. Likewise, it does not include the student term papers that are mentioned in the endnotes.

In addition to the Nazarene Archives, I consulted certain records at the United Methodist Archives in Madison, New Jersey, and also used the Drew University Library. These materials were especially helpful for the India chapter.

## General

Allen, Roland. *Missionary Methods: St. Paul's or Ours?* Reprint, Grand Rapids, Mich.: Eerdmans, 1962.

Anderson, E. G. *Annual Report and Survey of the Fields Occupied by Missionaries of the Pentecostal Church of the Nazarene, 1917–1918.* Kansas City, Mo.: General Foreign Missionary Board, [1918].

Armstrong, Ken. *Face to Face with the Church of the Nazarene.* Boulder, Colo.: Johnson, 1958.

Association of Pentecostal Churches of America. *Minutes of the Eleventh Annual Meeting.* Providence, R.I.: Pentecostal Printing, 1906.

———. *Minutes of the Tenth Annual Meeting.* Providence, R.I.: Pentecostal Printing, 1907.

Baldwin, Deborah J. *Protestants and the Mexican Revolution: Missionaries, Ministries, and Social Change.* Urbana: University of Illinois Press, 1990.

Bangs, Carl. *The Communist Encounter.* Kansas City, Mo.: Beacon Hill, 1963.

———. *Our Roots of Belief: A Biblical and Faithful Theology.* Kansas City, Mo.: Nazarene Publishing House, 1981.

———. *Phineas F. Bresee: His Life in Methodism, the Holiness Movement, and the Church of the Nazarene.* Kansas City, Mo.: Beacon Hill, 1995.

Banner, Lois. "Religious Benevolence as Social Control: A Critique of an Interpretation." *Journal of American History* 60 (June 1973): 23–41.

Barclay, Wade C. *History of Methodist Missions.* Part II. *The Methodist Episcopal Church, 1845–1939.* Vol. 3: *Widening Horizons, 1845–1895.* New York: Board of Missions of the Methodist Church, 1957.

Bassett, Paul. "Culture and Concupiscence: The Changing Definition of Sanctity in the Wesleyan/Holiness Movement, 1867–1920." *Wesleyan Theological Journal* 28 (Spring/Fall 1993): 59–127.

———. "The Fundamentalist Leavening of the Holiness Movement, 1914–1940." *Wesleyan Theological Journal* 13 (Spring 1978): 65–91.

———. "The Theological Identity of the North American Holiness Movement." In *The Variety of Evangelicalism*, ed. Donald Dayton and Robert K. Johnston. Knoxville: University of Tennessee Press, 1991.

Baumgart, Winfried. *Imperialism: The Idea and Reality of British and French Colonial Expansion, 1880–1914.* Rev. ed. Oxford: Oxford University Press, 1982.

Beaver, R. Pierce. *All Loves Excelling: American Protestant Women in World Mission.* Grand Rapids, Mich.: Eerdmans, 1968.

———. *Ecumenical Beginnings in Protestant World Mission: A History of Comity.* New York: Thomas Nelson, 1962.

———, ed. *American Missions in Bicentennial Perspectives.* Pasadena, Calif.: William Carey, 1977.

———, ed. *To Advance the Gospel: Selections from the Writings of Rufus Anderson.* Grand Rapids, Mich.: Eerdmans, 1967.

Bendroth, Margaret L. *Fundamentalism and Gender: 1875 to the Present*. New Haven, Conn.: Yale University Press, 1993.

Benner, Hugh C. *Rendezvous with Abundance*. Kansas City, Mo.: Beacon Hill, 1958.

Benson, John T., Jr. *Holiness Organized or Unorganized? A History 1898–1915 of the Pentecostal Mission*. Nashville, Tenn.: Trevecca, 1977.

Betts, Raymond F. *Assimilation and Association in French Colonial Theory: 1890–1914*. New York: Columbia University Press, 1982.

Bonk, Jonathan. *The Theory and Practice of Missionary Identification, 1860–1920*. Lewiston, N.Y.: Edwin Mellen, 1989.

Bosch, David. *Transforming Mission: Paradigm Shifts in Theology of Mission*. Maryknoll, N.Y.: Orbis, 1991.

Boyer, Paul. *Urban Masses and Moral Order in America, 1820–1920*. Cambridge, Mass.: Harvard University Press, 1978.

Bresee, Phineas. *Sermons from Matthew's Gospel*. Kansas City, Mo.: Nazarene Publishing House, n.d.

———. *Sermons on Isaiah*. Kansas City, Mo.: Nazarene Publishing House, 1926.

———. *Soul Food for Today*. Comp. C. J. Kinne. Kansas City, Mo.: Nazarene Publishing House, 1929.

Brouwer, Steve, Paul Gifford, and Susan D. Rose. *Exporting the American Gospel: Global Christian Fundamentalism*. New York: Routledge, 1996.

Burridge, Kenelm. *In the Way: A Study of Christian Missionary Endeavors*. Vancouver: University of British Columbia Press, 1991.

Cameron, James R. *Eastern Nazarene College: The First Fifty Years, 1900–1950*. Kansas City, Mo.: Nazarene Publishing House, 1968.

Campbell, Joseph E. *The Pentecostal Holiness Church, 1898–1948*. Franklin Springs, Ga.: Pentecostal Holiness Publishing, 1951.

Carpenter, Joel A., and William R. Shenk, eds. *Earthen Vessels: American Evangelicals and Foreign Missions, 1880–1980*. Grand Rapids, Mich.: Eerdmans, 1990.

Chandler, Ward B., comp. *Sayings of Our Founder*. Houston: Chandler and Roach, 1948.

Chapman, J. B. *Ask Doctor Chapman*. Kansas City, Mo.: Nazarene Publishing House, 1943.

———. *A History of the Church of the Nazarene*. Kansas City, Mo.: Nazarene Publishing House, 1926.

———. *Thirty Thousand Miles of Missionary Travel*. Kansas City, Mo.: Nazarene Publishing House, [1931].

Chiles, Robert E. *Theological Transition in American Methodism, 1790–1935*. Reprint. Lanham, Md.: University Press of America, 1983.

*Constitution of the Association of Pentecostal Churches of America*. Providence, R.I.: Beulah Christian, 1897.

Cook, R. Franklin. *The International Dimension: Six Expressions of the Great Commission*. Kansas City, Mo.: Nazarene Publishing House, 1988.

———. *Water from Deep Wells: A Survey to the Church of the Nazarene in India, Korea, Taiwan, Hong Kong, Australia, New Zealand.* Kansas City, Mo.: Nazarene Publishing House, 1977.

Cook, R. Franklin, and Steve Weber. *The Greening: The Story of Nazarene Compassionate Ministries.* Kansas City, Mo.: Nazarene Publishing House, 1986.

Corbett, C. T. *Pioneer Builders: Men Who Helped Shape the Church of the Nazarene in Its Formative Years.* Kansas City, Mo.: Beacon Hill, 1979.

Corlett, D. Shelby. *Spirit-Filled: The Life of the Rev. James Blaine Chapman, D.D.* Kansas City, Mo.: Beacon Hill, n.d.

Curtis, Olin A. *The Christian Faith Personally Given in a System of Doctrine.* New York: Eaton and Mains, 1905.

Damsteegt, Gerard. *Foundations of the Seventh-day Adventist Message and Mission.* Grand Rapids, Mich.: Eerdmans, 1977.

Dayton, Donald W. *Theological Roots of Pentecostalism.* Grand Rapids, Mich.: Zondervan, 1987.

DeLong, Russell V. *We Can If We Will: The Challenge of World Evangelism.* Kansas City, Mo.: Nazarene Publishing House, 1947.

DeLong, Russell V., and Mendell Taylor. *Fifty Years of Nazarene Missions.* Vol. 2: *History of the Fields.* Kansas City, Mo.: Beacon Hill, 1955.

Department of Foreign Missions. *Missionary Policy.* Kansas City, Mo.: Nazarene Publishing House, 1951.

Department of World Missions, comp. *Ministering to the Millions.* Kansas City, Mo.: Nazarene Publishing House, 1971.

Dieter, Melvin. *The Holiness Revival of the Nineteenth Century.* Second ed. Lanham, Md.: Scarecrow, 1996.

———. "Primitivism in the American Holiness Tradition." *Wesleyan Theological Journal* 30 (Spring 1995): 88–91.

DuBois, Lauriston, ed. *The Chaplains See World Missions.* Kansas City, Mo.: Nazarene Publishing House, 1946.

Dunning, H. Ray. "Nazarene Ethics as Seen in a Theological and Sociological Context." Ph.D. dissertation, Vanderbilt University, 1969.

Eighmy, John L. *Churches in Cultural Captivity: A History of the Social Attitudes of Southern Baptists.* Knoxville: University of Tennessee Press, 1972.

Escobar, Samuel, and John Driver. *Christian Mission and Social Justice.* Scottsdale, Pa.: Herald, 1978.

Fiedler, Klaus. *The Story of Faith Missions.* Oxford: Regnum, 1994.

Fitkin, Susan N. *Grace Much More Abounding: A Story of the Triumphs of Redeeming Grace Through Two Score Years in the Master's Service.* Kansas City, Mo.: Nazarene Publishing House, n.d.

———. *Holiness and Mission.* Second ed. Kansas City, Mo.: Nazarene Publishing House, 1940.

Fitkin, Susan N., and Emma B. Word. *Nazarene Missions in the Orient.* Kansas City, Mo.: Nazarene Publishing House, n.d.

Fleming, E. J., and M. A. Wilson, eds. *Journal of the Seventh General Assembly of the Church of the Nazarene*. Kansas City, Mo.: Nazarene Publishing House, 1928.

Flemming, Leslie A., ed. *Women's Work for Women: Missionaries and Social Change in Asia*. Boulder, Colo.: Westview, 1989.

Frankiel, Sandra Sizer. *California's Spiritual Frontiers: Religious Alternatives in Anglo-Protestantism, 1850–1910*. Berkeley: University of California Press, 1988.

Girvin, E.A. *Phineas F. Bresee: A Prince in Israel; A Biography*. Kansas City, Mo.: Nazarene Publishing House, 1916.

Godbey, W. B. *Around the World: Garden of Eden, Latter Day Prophecies and Missions*. Cincinnati, Ohio: God's Revivalist, 1907.

Goodnow, Edith P. *Hazarded Lives*. Kansas City, Mo.: Nazarene Publishing House, 1942.

Gould, Joseph Glenn. *Missionary Pioneers and Our Debt to Them*. Kansas City, Mo.: Nazarene Publishing House, [1935].

Gould, J. Glenn, Basil Miller, and Amy Hinshaw. *The Dynamic of Missions*. Kansas City, Mo.: Nazarene Publishing House, [1932].

*Government and Doctrines of New Testament Churches*. Milan, Tenn.: Exchange Office, 1903.

Greathouse, William. "The Church of the Nazarene." *The Ecumenical Review* (July 1971): 303–316.

———. "Nazarene Theology in Perspective." Inaugural Address, Nazarene Theological Seminary, January 6, 1969.

Gresham, L. Paul. *Waves Against Gibraltar: A Memoir of Dr. A. M. Hills, 1848–1935*. Bethany, Okla.: Southern Nazarene University Press, 1992.

Grider, J. Kenneth. *Entire Sanctification: The Distinctive Doctrine of Wesleyanism*. Kansas City, Mo.: Beacon Hill, 1980.

Griffith, Glenn. *A Voice in the Midnight Hour*. Comp. Donald Hughes. Denver: N.p., n.d.

Gusfield, Joseph R. *Symbolic Crusade: Status Politics and the American Temperance Movement*. Urbana: University of Illinois Press, 1966.

Gutman, Herbert. *Work, Culture and Society in Industrializing America: Essays in American Working-Class and Social History*. New York: Vintage, 1977.

Hauerwas, Stanley, and William H. Willimon. *Resident Aliens: Life in the Christian Colony*. Nashville, Tenn.: Abingdon, 1989.

Higham, John. "Hanging Together: Divergent Unities in American History." *Journal of American History* 61 (June 1974): 5–28.

Hill, Patricia. "The Missionary Enterprise." In *Encyclopedia of the American Religious Experience: Studies of Traditions and Movements*, vol. 3, ed. Charles H. Lippy and Peter W. Williams. New York: Charles Scribner's Sons, 1988.

———. *The World Their Household: The American Woman's Foreign Mission Movement and Cultural Transformation, 1870–1920*. Ann Arbor: University of Michigan Press, 1985.

Hills, A. M. *Fundamental Christian Theology: A Systematic Theology.* 2 vols. Reprint. Salem, Ohio: Schmul, 1980.

———. *Pentecostal Light.* Reprint. Salem, Ohio: Schmul Publishers, n.d.

———. *The Secret of Spiritual Power.* Nashville, Tenn.: Pentecostal Mission, n.d.

Hinshaw, Amy N. *In Labors Abundant: A Bibliography of H. F. Reynolds.* Kansas City, Mo.: Nazarene Publishing House, n.d.

———. *Messengers of the Cross in Africa.* Kansas City, Mo.: Woman's Foreign Missionary Society, [1928].

———. *Messengers of the Cross in Latin America.* Kansas City, Mo.: Woman's Foreign Missionary Society, 1927.

———. *Native Torch Bearers.* Kansas City, Mo.: Nazarene Publishing House, 1934.

*History of the Foreign Missionary Work of the Church of the Nazarene.* Kansas City, Mo.: General Board of Foreign Missions, Church of the Nazarene, 1921.

Hofstadter, Richard. *The Age of Reform: From Bryan to F.D.R.* New York: Knopf, 1955.

———. *The Paranoid Style in American Politics and Other Essays.* Chicago: University of Chicago Press, 1965.

*Holiness Association of Texas Yearbook 1904–1905.* Greenville, Tex.: Texas Holiness Advocate Print, [1905].

*Holiness Association of Texas Yearbook, 1906–1907.* N.p., [1907].

Hopkins, C. Howard. *John R. Mott, 1865–1955: A Biography.* Grand Rapids, Mich.: Eerdmans, 1979.

Houseal, Richard. "Women Clergy in the Church of the Nazarene: An Analysis of Change from 1908 to 1995." M.A. thesis, University of Missouri–Kansas City, Mo., 1996.

Hurn, Raymond W. *Mission Possible: A Study of the Mission of the Church of the Nazarene.* Kansas City, Mo.: Nazarene Publishing House, 1973.

Hutchison, William R. "Americans in World Mission: Revision and Realignment." In *Altered Landscapes: Christianity in America, 1935–1985*, ed. David W. Lotz. Grand Rapids, Mich.: Eerdmans, 1989.

———. *Errand to the World: American Protestant Thought and Foreign Missions.* Chicago: University of Chicago Press, 1987.

———. *The Modernist Impulse in American Protestantism.* Oxford: Oxford University Press, 1976.

Hynd, David. *Africa Emerging.* Kansas City, Mo.: Nazarene Publishing House, 1959.

———. "The Healing of the Church." In *For the Healing of the Nations: Ten Missionary Sermons*, ed. C. Warren Jones. Kansas City, Mo.: Nazarene Publishing House, 1954.

*Important Information Concerning Mission Work and Missionaries of the Pentecostal Church of the Nazarene, October 1, 1910 to September 30, 1911.* Chicago: General Missionary Board, [1911].

Ingersoll, Stan. "Christian Baptism and the Early Nazarenes: The Sources That Shaped a Pluralistic Baptismal Tradition." *Wesleyan Theological Journal* 25 (Fall 1990): 24–38.

———, ed. *Rescue the Perishing, Care for the Dying: Sources and Documents on Compassionate Ministry in the Nazarene Archives.* Second ed. Kansas City, Mo.: Nazarene Archives, n.d.

Ingle, Robert L. "The Changing Spatial Distribution of the Church of the Nazarene." M.S. thesis, Oklahoma State University, 1973.

Jared, Robert. "The Formation of a Sunday School Philosophy for the Church of the Nazarene, 1907–1932." Ed.D. dissertation, Southern Baptist Theological Seminary, 1989.

Jernigan, C. B. *Pioneer Days of the Holiness Movement in the Southwest.* Kansas City, Mo.: Nazarene Publishing House, 1919.

Johnson, B. Edgar, et al., editing committee. *Manual/1985 Church of the Nazarene: History, Constitution, Government, Ritual.* Kansas City, Mo.: Nazarene Publishing House, 1985.

Johnson, Jerald. *The International Experience.* Kansas City, Mo.: Nazarene Publishing House, 1982.

———. *Hardy C. Powers: Bridge Builder.* Kansas City, Mo.: Nazarene Publishing House, 1985.

Jones, Charles E. *A Guide to the Study of the Holiness Movement.* Metuchen, N.J.: Scarecrow, 1974.

———. *Perfectionist Persuasion: The Holiness Movement and American Methodism, 1867–1936.* Metuchen, N.J.: Scarecrow, 1974.

Jones, C. Warren, comp. *For the Healing of the Nations: Ten Missionary Sermons.* Kansas City, Mo.: Beacon Hill, 1954.

———, ed. *Missions for Millions.* Kansas City, Mo.: Nazarene Publishing House, 1948.

Jones, C. Warren, and Mendell Taylor, ed. *Journal of the Tenth General Assembly of the Church of the Nazarene.* N.p., [1940].

Kinne, C. J. *The Modern Samaritan: A Presentation of the Claims of Medical Missions.* Kansas City, Mo.: Nazarene Publishing House, n.d.

Kirby, J. E. "Matthew Simpson and the Mission of America." *Church History* 36 (1967): 299–307.

Kirkemo, Ronald. *For Zion's Sake: A History of Pasadena/Point Loma College.* San Diego: Point Loma, 1992.

Knott, James P. *History of Pasadena College.* Pasadena, Calif.: Pasadena College, 1960.

Lamson, Byron S. *Venture! The Frontiers of Free Methodism.* Winona Lake, Ind.: Light and Life, 1960.

Latourette, Kenneth S. *Christianity in a Revolutionary Age.* Vol. 5: *The Twentieth Century Outside Europe.* New York: Harper and Row, 1962.

Lavely, John L. "Personalism's Debt to Kant." In *The Boston Personalist Tradition in Philosophy, Social Ethics, and Theology*, ed. Paul Deats and Carol Robb. Macon, Ga.: Mercer University Press, 1986.

Levine, Lawrence. *Defender of the Faith: William Jennings Bryan: The Last Decade, 1915–1925*. New York: Oxford University Press, 1965.

Lindsell, Harold. *Missionary Principles and Practice*. Westwood, N.J.: Fleming H. Revell, 1955.

Littel, Franklin. "The Anabaptist Theology of Mission." In *Anabaptists and Mission*, ed. Wilbert R. Shenk. Scottsdale, Pa.: Herald, 1984.

Ludwig, S. T., and Greta Hamsher, ed. *Journal of the Twelfth General Assembly of the Church of the Nazarene*. N.p., 1948.

Magnuson, Norris. *Salvation in the Slums: Evangelical Social Work, 1865–1920*. Metuchen, N.J.: Scarecrow, 1977.

Manikam, Rajah B., ed. *Christianity and the Asian Revolution*. New York: Friendship, 1954.

*Manual of the Church of Christ*. Greenville, Tex.: Holiness Associates, 1905.

*The Manual of the Church of the Nazarene, Promulgated by the Assembly of 1898*. N.p., [1898].

*Manual of the Church of the Nazarene, 1903*. Los Angeles: Nazarene Publishing House, 1903.

*Manual of the First Pentecostal Church of Lynn, Massachusetts*. Providence, R.I.: Pentecostal Printing, 1898.

Marsden, George M. *Fundamentalism and American Culture: The Shaping of Twentieth-Century Evangelicalism, 1870–1925*. New York: Oxford University Press, 1980.

Messenger, F. M. *The Coming Superman*. Kansas City, Mo.: Nazarene Publishing House, 1928.

Metz, Donald S. *Some Crucial Issues in the Church of the Nazarene*. Olathe, Kans.: Wesleyan Heritage, 1994.

Miller, Basil. *Dreams Fulfilled: My Mission Career*. Pasadena, Calif.: World-Wide Missions, 1971.

———. *Susan N. Fitkin: For God and Missions*. Kansas City, Mo.: Nazarene Publishing House, n.d.

———. *Those Were the Days: Remembering My Youth*. Pasadena, Calif.: World-Wide Missions, 1971.

Miller, B[asil], and G. F. Owens. *Behold He Cometh: Inspirational Messages on the Second Coming*. Kansas City, Mo.: Nazarene Publishing House, 1924.

Miller, Basil, and U. E. Harding. *"Cunningly Devised Fables": Modernism Exposed and Refuted*. N.p., n.d.

*Minutes and Yearbook of the Eastern Council Holiness Church of Christ*. Pilot Point, Tex.: Evangel Publishing, [1907].

*Minutes of the Annual Conferences of the Methodist Episcopal Church: Spring Conferences 1935*. New York: Methodist Book Concern, [1935].

Moore, Paul, and Joe Musser. *Shepherd of Times Square*. Nashville, Tenn.: Thomas Nelson, 1979.

Moorhead, James. "The Erosion of Postmillennialism in American Religious Thought, 1865–1925." *Church History* 53 (March 1984): 61–77.

Morgan, Edmund S. *The Puritan Family: Religion and Domestic Relations in Seventeenth-Century New England*. Revised ed. New York: Harper and Row, 1966.

Mowry, George E. *The California Progressives*. Berkeley, Calif.: University of California Press, 1951.

Murch, James DeF. *Cooperation Without Compromise: A History of the National Association of Evangelicals*. Grand Rapids, Mich.: Eerdmans, 1956.

*Nazarene Biography Index*. Nampa, Idaho: Northwest Nazarene College, 1984.

Neill, Stephen. *A History of Christian Missions*. Second ed. New York: Penguin, 1986.

Niklaus, Robert L., John S. Sawin, and Samuel J. Stoesz. *All for Jesus: God at Work in the Christian and Missionary Alliance over One Hundred Years*. Camp Hill, Pa.: Christian Publications, 1986.

*The Oasis*. Nampa, Idaho: Northwest Nazarene College, 1922, 1926.

Olsen, M. Ellsworth. *A History of the Origin and Progress of Seventh-day Adventists*. Washington, D.C.: Review and Herald, 1925.

Orr, J. Edwin. *The Flaming Tongue: Evangelical Awakenings, 1900–*. Chicago: Moody, 1975.

Owens, Donald. *Sing Ye Islands: Nazarene Missions in the Pacific Islands*. Kansas City, Mo.: Nazarene Publishing House, 1979.

Park, Ruth Miriam, comp. *The Church Abroad: A Quadrennial Review of Missions, 1948–52*. Kansas City, Mo.: Nazarene Publishing House, 1952.

Parker, J. Fred. *Mission to the World: A History of Missions in the Church of the Nazarene through 1985*. Kansas City, Mo.: Nazarene Publishing House, 1988.

———. "Those Nazarenes Cared: Compassionate Ministries of the Nazarenes." *The Preachers Magazine* 59 (September/October/November 1983).

Parker, Michael. *The Kingdom of Character: The Student Volunteer Movement for Foreign Missions (1886–1926)*. Lanham, Md.: University Press of America, 1998.

Parr, F. O. *Perfect Love and Race Hatred*. N.p., [1964].

Patterson, James. "The Kingdom of the Great Commission: Social Gospel Impulses and American Protestant Missionary Leaders, 1890–1920." *Fides et Historia* 25 (Winter/Spring 1993): 48–61.

*Pentecostal Mission and Missionaries*. Providence, R.I.: Pentecostal Printing, 1905.

Perkins, Phyllis H. *Women in Nazarene Missions: Embracing the Legacy*. Kansas City, Mo.: Nazarene Publishing House, 1994.

Peters, John L. *Christian Perfection and American Methodism*. New York: Abingdon, 1956.

Philips, Clifton J. *Protestant America and the Pagan World: The First Half-Century of the American Board of Commissioners of Foreign Missions, 1810–1860*. Cambridge, Mass.: Harvard University Press, 1969.

Phillips, E. S. *Man of Missions: Messages from the Pulpit of E. S. Phillips*. Kansas City, Mo.: Nazarene Publishing House, 1974.

Piepkorn, Arthur C. *Profiles in Belief: The Religious Bodies of the United States*. Vol. 3: *Holiness and Pentecostal*. New York: Harper and Row, 1979.

Pierce, Robert, ed. *Proceedings of the Tenth Annual Assembly of the Church of the Nazarene*. Los Angeles: Nazarene Publishing House, 1907.

Price, Ross. *H. Orton Wiley: Servant and Servant of the Sagebrush*. Kansas City, Mo.: Nazarene Publishing House, 1968.

Primer, Ben. *Protestants and American Business Methods*. Ann Arbor, Mich.: UMI Research Press, 1979.

*Proceedings of the First General Assembly of the Pentecostal Church of the Nazarene*. Los Angeles: Nazarene Publishing House, 1907.

*Proceedings of the General Board of the Church of the Nazarene*. Special Sessions. Kansas City, Mo.: General Board of the Church of the Nazarene, [1929].

*Proceedings of the Ninth Annual Assembly of the Church of the Nazarene*. Los Angeles: Nazarene Publishing House, 1904.

*Proceedings of the Second General Assembly of the Pentecostal Church of the Nazarene*. Los Angeles: Nazarene Publishing House, 1908.

Purkiser, W. T. *Called Unto Holiness*. Vol. 2: *The Second Twenty-Five Years, 1933–1958*. Kansas City, Mo.: Nazarene Publishing House, 1983.

*Quadrennial Reports to the Eleventh General Assembly of the Church of the Nazarene*. N.p., [1944].

Reasoner, Victor. "The American Holiness Movement's Paradigm Shift Concerning Holiness." *Wesleyan Theological Journal* 31 (Fall 1996): 132–146.

*Records of the Annual Meetings of the Central Evangelical Holiness Association*. Providence, R.I.: George A. Wilson, 1896.

Reed, James. *The Missionary Mind and American East Asia Policy 1911–1915*. Cambridge, Mass.: Harvard University Press, 1983.

Rees, Paul S. *Seth Cook Rees: The Warrior Saint*. Indianapolis, Ind.: Pilgrim, 1934.

Rees, Seth Cook. *The Holy War*. Cincinnati, Ohio: God's Bible School and Revivalist, 1904.

Reynolds, Hiram F. *World-Wide Missions*. Kansas City, Mo.: Nazarene Publishing House, [1915].

Reynolds, Hiram F., comp. *History of the Foreign Work of the Church of the Nazarene*. Kansas City, Mo.: General Board of Foreign Missions, 1921.

Reza, H. T. *Our Task for Today*. Kansas City, Mo.: Nazarene Publishing House, 1963.

———. *Prescription for Permanence: The Story of Our Schools for Training Ministers in Latin America*. Kansas City, Mo.: Nazarene Publishing House, 1968.

Riley, John, et al., editing committee. *Manual of the Church of the Nazarene: History, Constitution, Government, Ritual: 1960*. Kansas City, Mo.: Nazarene Publishing House, 1960.

Robert, Dana L. *American Women in Mission: A Social History of Their Thought and Practice*. Macon, Ga.: Mercer University Press, 1996.

Rosenberg, Emily S. *Spreading the American Eagle: American Economic and Cultural Expansion, 1890–1945*. New York: Hill and Wang, 1982.

Said, Edward W. *Orientalism*. New York: Vintage, 1978.

Sanneh, Lamin. *Encountering the West; Christianity and the Global Cultural Process: The African Dimension*. Maryknoll, N.Y.: Orbis, 1993.

———. *Translating the Message: The Missionary Impact on Culture*. Maryknoll, N.Y.: Orbis, 1989.

Saxe, Jo W. "Dilemmas of Empire: The British and French Experience." In *The Idea of Colonialism*, ed. Robert Strausz-Hupe and Harry W. Hazard. New York: Frederick A. Praeger, 1958.

Seamands, John T. *Tell It Well: Communicating the Gospel Across Cultures*. Kansas City, Mo.: Beacon Hill, 1981.

Shenk, Wilbert R. *Henry Venn: Missionary Statesman*. Maryknoll, N.Y.: Orbis, 1983.

Smee, Roy F., S. T. Ludwig, and Alpin P. Bowes. *Enlarge Thy Borders: The Story of Home Missions in the Church of the Nazarene*. Kansas City, Mo.: Nazarene Publishing House, 1952.

Smith, A[aron] J. *Bible Holiness and the Modern, Popular, Spurious*. N.p., 1953.

Smith, Harold Ivan, comp. *The Quotable Bresee*. Kansas City, Mo.: Beacon Hill, 1983.

Smith, Timothy L. *Called Unto Holiness; The Story of the Nazarenes: The Formative Years*. Kansas City, Mo.: Nazarene Publishing House, 1962.

Smith, Tony. *America's Mission: The United States and the Worldwide Struggle for Democracy in the Twentieth Century*. Princeton, N.J.: Princeton University Press, 1994.

Stanley, Susie C. "Wesleyan/Holiness Churches: Innocent Bystanders in the Fundamentalist/Modernist Controversy." In *Re-Forming the Center: American Protestantism, 1900 to the Present*, ed. Douglas Jacobsen and William V. Trollinger, Jr. Grand Rapids, Mich.: Eerdmans, 1998.

Strickland, William J., with H. Ray Dunning. *J. O. McClurkan: His Life, His Theology, and Selections from His Writings*. Nashville, Tenn.: Trevecca Nazarene University, 1998.

Sweet, Leonard. "A Nation Born Again: The Union Prayer Meeting Revival and Cultural Relativism." In *In the Great Tradition: Essays on Pluralism, Voluntarism and Revivalism*, ed. Joseph D. Bon and Paul R. Deckar. Valley Forge, Pa.: Judson, 1982.

Swim, Roy. *A History of Missions of the Church of the Nazarene*. Second ed. Kansas City, Mo.: Nazarene Publishing House, 1936.

Taber, Charles R. *The World Is Too Much with Us: "Culture" in Modern Protestant Missions*. Macon, Ga.: Mercer University Press, 1991.

Taylor, Clyde W. *A Glimpse of World Missions: An Evangelical View*. Chicago: Moody, 1960.

Taylor, Mendell. *Fifty Years of Nazarene Missions*. Vol. 1: *Administration and Promotion*. Kansas City, Mo.: Beacon Hill, 1952.

———. *Fifty Years of Nazarene Missions.* Vol. 3: *World Outreach through Home Missions.* Kansas City, Mo.: Beacon Hill, 1958.

Taylor, Richard S. "A Theology of Missions." In *Ministering to the Millions,* comp. Department of World Missions. Kansas City, Mo.: Nazarene Publishing House, 1971.

Thomson, James C., Jr., Peter W. Stanley, and John C. Perry. *Sentimental Imperialists: The American Experience in East Asia.* New York: Harper and Row, 1981.

Thornton, Wallace. *Radical Righteousness: Personal Ethics and the Development of the Holiness Movement.* Salem, Ohio: Schmul, 1998.

Timberlake, James H. *Prohibition in the Progressive Movement, 1900–1920.* Reprint, New York: Athenaeum, 1970.

Tucker, Ruth A. *From Jerusalem to Irian Jaya: A Biographical History of Christian Missions.* Grand Rapids, Mich.: Zondervan, 1983.

Verkuyl, J. *Contemporary Missiology: An Introduction.* Trans. and ed. Dale Cooper. Grand Rapids, Mich.: Eerdmans, 1978.

Wainwright, Geoffrey. "Ecclesial Location and Ecumenical Vocation." In *The Future of Methodist Theological Traditions,* ed. M. Douglas Meeks. Nashville, Tenn.: Abingdon, 1985.

Walls, Andrew. *The Missionary Movement in Christian History: Studies in the Transmission of Faith.* Maryknoll, N.Y.: Orbis, 1996.

Warren, Max, ed. *To Apply the Gospel: Selections from the Writings of Henry Venn.* Grand Rapids, Mich.: Eerdmans, 1971.

Weber, Steve, and R. Franklin Cook. *The Greening: The Story of Nazarene Compassionate Ministries.* Kansas City, Mo.: Nazarene Publishing House, 1986.

Weber, Timothy P. *Living in the Shadow of the Second Coming: American Premillennialism, 1875–1982.* Rev. ed. Grand Rapids, Mich.: Zondervan, 1983.

Weisman, Neil B., ed. *To the City with Love: A Source Book of Nazarene Urban Ministries.* Kansas City, Mo.: Beacon Hill, 1976.

Wesche, Henry C. *Medical Missions: What? Why? How?* Kansas City, Mo.: General Board, Church of the Nazarene, n.d.

White, J. Timothy. "Hiram F. Reynolds: Prime Mover of the Nazarene Mission Education System." Ph.D. dissertation, University of Kansas, 1996.

Wiebe, Robert M. *The Search for Order, 1877–1920.* New York: Hill and Wang, 1967.

Wiley, H. Orton. *Christian Theology.* Vol. 3. Kansas City, Mo.: Beacon Hill, 1943.

Williamson, G. B. "The Mission of the Church." *Preachers Magazine* (January 1954).

Wilson, Mallalieu. *William C. Wilson: The Fifth General Superintendent.* Kansas City, Mo.: Nazarene Publishing House, 1995.

Winston, Diane. *Red-Hot and Righteous: The Urban Religion of the Salvation Army.* Cambridge, Mass.: Harvard University Press, 1999.

Winter, Ralph D. *The Twenty-Five Unbelievable Years, 1945–1969*. South Pasadena, Calif.: William Carey, 1970.

———. "Protestant Mission Societies and the 'Other Protestant Schism.'" In *American Denominational Organization: A Sociological View*, ed. Ross P. Scherer. Pasadena, Calif.: William Carey, 1980.

Worcester, Paul W. *The Master Key: The Story of the Hephzibah Faith Missionary Association*. Kansas City, Mo.: Nazarene Publishing House, 1966.

Wynkoop, Mildred Bangs. *A Theology of Love: The Dynamic of Wesleyanism*. Kansas City, Mo.: Beacon Hill, 1972.

———. *The Trevecca Story: 75 Years of Christian Service*. Nashville, Tenn.: Trevecca Nazarene College, 1976.

# India

Beals, Prescott. *India's Open Door*. Kansas City, Mo.: Nazarene Publishing House, 1940.

———. *India Reborn: The Story of Evangelism in India*. Kansas City, Mo.: Beacon Hill, 1954.

Bishop, Steve. "Protestant Missionary Education in British India." *Evangelical Quarterly* 69 (July 1997): 245–266.

Bugge, Henriette. *Mission and Tamil Society: Social and Religious Change in South India (1840–1900)*. Richmond, Surrey, England: Curzon, 1994.

Bundy, David. "Bishop William Taylor and Methodist Mission: A Study in Nineteenth Century Social History, Part I: From Campmeeting to International Evangelist." *Methodist History* 27 (July 1989): 198–212.

———. "Bishop William Taylor and Methodist Mission: A Study in Nineteenth Century Social History, Part II: Social Structures in Collision." *Methodist History* 28 (October 1989): 3–21.

Burgess, Stanley. "Pentecostalism in India: An Overview." *Asian Journal of Pentecostal Studies* 4 (January 2001): 88–89.

Copley, Antony. *Religions in Conflict: Ideology, Cultural Contact and Conversion in Late-Colonial India*. New Delhi: Oxford University Press, 1997.

Cunningham, Floyd T. "Mission Policy and National Leadership in the Church of the Nazarene in India, 1898–1960." *Indian Church History Review* 25 (June 1991): 17–48.

Daniels, A. G. "The Bombay Mission." *The Adventist Review and Sabbath Herald* 92 (April 29, 1915).

Daniels, W. H., ed. *Dr. Cullis and His Work: Twenty Years of Blessing in Answer to Prayer*. Boston: Willard Tract Repository, 1885.

David, M. D. "American Missionaries in India: A Difference." *Indian Church History Review* 30 (December 1996): 115–116.

———. "Indian Attitude Towards Missionaries and Their Work with Special Reference to Maharashtra." *Indian Church History Review* 29 (December 1995): 93–105.

Dyer, Helen S. *Pandita Ramabai: The Story of Her Life*. New ed. London: Morgan and Scott, 1907.

Eaton, Emma, comp. *Our Work in India: Hallelujah Village, Hope School Calcutta*. Portland, Ore.: Boyer Printing, 1913.

Ekvall, Robert B., et al.. *After Fifty Years: A Record of God's Working Through the Christian and Missionary Alliance*. Harrisburg, Pa.: Christian Publications, 1939.

Gibson, Julia. *A Cry from India's Night*. Kansas City, Mo.: Nazarene Publishing House, 1914.

Greer, Bronnel. "Nazarene Troika." Mimeographed, [1969].

Harper, Susan B. *In the Shadow of the Mahatma: Bishop V. S. Azariah and the Travails of Christianity in British India*. Grand Rapids, Mich.: Eerdmans, 2000.

Heideman, Eugene P. *From Mission to Church: The Reformed Church in America Mission to India*. Grand Rapids, Mich.: Eerdmans, 2001.

Hinshaw, Amy N. *The Messengers of the Cross in India*. Kansas City, Mo.: Woman's Foreign Missionary Society, Church of the Nazarene, n.d.

Holmes, Brian. "British Imperial Policy and the Mission Schools." In *Educational Policy and the Mission Schools: Case Studies from the British Empire*, ed. Brian Holmes. London: Routledge and Kegan Paul, 1967.

Hudson, D. Dennis. *Protestant Origins in India: Tamil Evangelical Christians, 1706–1835*. Grand Rapids, Mich.: Eerdmans, 2000.

India Nazarene Mission Council. *New India and the Gospel*. Kansas City, Mo.: Nazarene Publishing House, 1954.

Kawashima, Koji. *Missionaries and a Hindu State: Travancore 1858–1936*. Delhi: Oxford University Press, 1998.

Lee, Hazel C. *Treasures of Darkness*. Kansas City, Mo.: Beacon Hill, 1954.

Manickam, Sundararaj. *The Social Setting of Christian Conversion in South India: The Impact of the Wesleyan Methodist Missionaries on the Trichy-Tanjore Diocese with Special Reference to the Harijan Communities of the Mass Movement Area, 1820–1947*. Wiesbaden, Germany: Franz Steiner Verlag, 1977.

Marak, Krickwin. "Christianity Among the Garos: An Attempt to Re-read Peoples' Movement from a Missiological Perspective." In *Christianity in India: Search for Liberation and Identity*, ed. F. Hrangkhuma, 155–186. Delhi: ISPCK, 1998.

Martin, Paul A. J. *The Missionary of the Indian Road: A Theology of Stanley Jones*. Bangalore: Theological Book Trust, 1996.

McGee, Gary B. "'Latter Rain' Falling in the East: Early-Twentieth-Century Pentecostalism in India and the Debate over Speaking in Tongues." *Church History* 68 (September 1999): 648–665.

Miller, Basil. *Mother Eaton of India*. Los Angeles: Bedrock, 1951.

*The Missionary Policy in India of the Methodist Episcopal Church: Recommendations of the Asonol Conference*. N.p., [1927].

Myatt, Carolyn. *A Tapestry Called Orpha*. Kansas City, Mo.: Nazarene Publishing House, 1991.

Oddie, Geoffrey A., ed. *Religious Conversion Movements in South Asia: Continuities and Change, 1800–1900.* Richmond, Surrey, England: Curzon, 1997.

*Official Minutes of the Fourth Session of the Bombay Annual Conference of the Methodist Episcopal Church.* Madras, India: Methodist Episcopal Publishing, 1896.

Orr, J. Edwin. *Evangelical Awakenings in Southern Asia.* Minneapolis, Minn.: Bethany, 1975.

Osborn, Lucy Drake. *Heavenly Pearls Set in a Life: A Record of Experiences and Labors in America, India, and Australia.* New York: Fleming H. Revell, 1893.

*Our Missionaries to India: The Christian Experiences of the Four Persons Recently Approved by the Association of Pentecostal Churches of America for Missionary Work in India.* Providence, R.I.: Beulah Christian, 1899.

Pardington, G. P. *Twenty-Five Wonderful Years, 1889–1914: A Popular Sketch of the Christian and Missionary Alliance.* New York: Christian Alliance, 1914.

*Report of the Third Decennial Missionary Conference.* Vol. 2. Bombay: Education Society's Steam Press, 1893.

Scott, J. E. *History of Fifty Years: Comprising the Origin, Establishment, Progress and Expansion of the Methodist Episcopal Church in Southern Asia.* Madras, India: Methodist Episcopal Press, 1906.

Sherring, M. A. *The History of Missions in India: From their Commencement in 1706 to 1881.* New edition. Ed. Edward Storrow. London: Religious Tract Society, 1884.

Singh, Maina Chawla. *Gender, Religion and "Heathen Lands": American Missionary Women in South Asia (1860s-1940s).* New York: Garland, 2000.

Tracy, Olive G. *Tracy Sahib of India.* Kansas City, Mo.: Beacon Hill, 1954.

Williams, Christine. "Nazarene Missions in India." M.A. thesis, George Washington University, Washington, D.C., 1930.

Williamson, G. B., and Audrey Williamson. *Yesu Masiki Jay: A First-Hand Survey of Nazarene Missionary Progress in India.* Kansas City, Mo.: Beacon Hill, 1952.

Witthoff, Evelyn, and Geraldine Chappell. *Three Year's Internment in Santo Tomas.* Kansas City, Mo.: Beacon Hill, n.d.

Witthoff, Evelyn M. *Oh Doctor! The Story of Nazarene Missions in India.* Kansas City, Mo.: Nazarene Publishing House, 1962.

Wood, M. D. *Fruit from the Jungle.* Mountain View, Calif.: Pacific, 1919.

———. "India Famine Conditions: How Charlie Found the Third Angel's Message." *The Adventist Review and Sabbath Herald* 94 (May 10, 1917): 14–15.

———. *A Life Saving Station.* Igatpuri, India: Watchman Press, n.d.

———. "Two Testimonies." *The Adventist Review and Sabbath Herald* 92 (April 29, 1915): 11.

# Japan

Aoki, Yoshiaki, et al., ed. [*The Ninety Year History of the Japan Church of the Nazarene*]. Tokyo: Japan Nazarene District, 1999.

Baker, Richard T. *Darkness of the Sun: The Story of Christianity in the Japanese Empire*. New York: Abingdon-Cokesbury, 1947.

Cary, Otis. *A History of Christianity in Japan: Roman Catholic, Greek Orthodox, and Protestant Missions*. Reprint. Rutland, Vt.: Charles E. Tuttle, 1976.

Cary, W. W. *The Story of the National Holiness Missionary Society*. Chicago: National Holiness Missionary Society, 1940.

*The Christian Movement in Its Relation to New Life in Japan*. Third issue. Tokyo: Methodist Publishing, 1905.

Clement, Ernest W., and Glaen M. Fisher, ed. *The Christian Movement in Japan*. Sixth ed. Tokyo: Methodist Publishing, 1908.

Cove, Mary E. *Friends on the Islands*. Kansas City, Mo.: Nazarene Publishing House, n.d.

Cowman, Lettie. *Charles E. Cowman: Missionary-Warrior*. Los Angeles: Oriental Missionary Society, [1928].

Cunningham, Floyd T. "Mission Policy and National Leadership in the Church of the Nazarene in Japan, 1905–1965." *Wesleyan Theological Journal* 28 (Spring/Fall 1993): 128–164.

Davidann, Jon T. "The American YMCA in Meiji Japan: God's Work Gone Awry." *Journal of World History* 6 (Spring 1995): 107–125.

Drummond, Richard H. *A History of Christianity in Japan*. Grand Rapids, Mich.: Eerdmans, 1971.

Eckel, Catherine P. *Kitagawa of Japan*. Kansas City, Mo.: Nazarene Publishing House, 1966.

Eckel, William A. *When the Pendulum Swings*. Kansas City, Mo.: Beacon Hill, 1957.

Eckel, William D. *Japan Now*. Kansas City, Mo.: Nazarene Publishing House, 1949.

Furuya, Yasuo, ed. *A History of Japanese Theology*. Grand Rapids, Mich.: Eerdmans, 1997.

Hirai, Kiyoshi, ed. *Japan Christian Yearbook 1957*. Tokyo: Christian Literature Society, [1957].

Howes, John P. "The Marunouchi Lectures of Uchimura Kanzo (1861–1930)." *Fides et Historia* 24 (Winter/Spring 1992): 25–32.

Iglehart, Charles W. *A Century of Protestant Christianity in Japan*. Rutland, Vt.: Charles E. Tuttle, 1959.

Isayama, Nobumi. *Consider Nippon: Incidents from My Life*. Kansas City, Mo.: Beacon Hill, 1957.

Kida, Ross. *The Many Faces of Japan*. Kansas City, Mo.: Nazarene Publishing House, 1964.

Kitagawa, Hiroshi. *The Guiding Hand*. Trans. Jun Ooka. Unpublished manuscript, 1987.

Manabu, Ishida. "Doing Theology in Japan: The Alternative Way of Reading the Scriptures as the Book of Sacred Drama in Dialogue with Minjung Theology." *Missiology* 22 (January 1994): 55–63.

———. "Live Peace! A Commentary on the Confession of Responsibility of the Church of the Nazarene in Japan During the Second World War." English ed. Oyma-shi: Department of Social Affairs of the Church of the Nazarene in Japan, July 1994.

Merwin, John J. "The Oriental Missionary Society Holiness Church in Japan." D.Miss. thesis, Fuller Theological Seminary, 1983.

Miller, Basil. *Standing on the Promises in Japan: The Story of Pearl Wiley Hanson*. Pasadena, Calif.: International Gospel League, n.d.

———. *Twenty-Two Missionary Stories from Japan*. Kansas City, Mo.: Beacon Hill, 1949.

Miura, Hiroshi. *The Life and Thought of Kanzo Uchimura, 1861–1930*. Grand Rapids, Mich.: Eerdmans, 1996.

Myers, Ramon H., and Mark R. Peattie, ed. *The Japanese Colonial Empire, 1895–1945*. Princeton, N.J.: Princeton University Press, 1984.

Parker, F. Calvin. *The Southern Baptist Mission in Japan, 1889–1989*. Lanham, Md.: University Press of America, 1991.

Phillips, James M. *From the Rising of the Sun: Christians and Society in Contemporary Japan*. Maryknoll, N.Y.: Orbis, 1981.

Rightmire, R. David. *Salvationist Samurai: Gunpei Yamamuro and the Rise of the Salvation Army in Japan*. Lanham, Md.: Scarecrow, 1997.

Sachs, William L. "Self-Support: The Episcopal Mission and Nationalism in Japan." *Church History* 58 (1989): 489–501.

Schildgen, Robert. *Toyohiko Kagawa: Apostle of Love and Social Justice*. Berkeley, Calif.: Centenary, 1988.

Smith, Frank B. *The Dual System in Nazarene Missionary Activity on Japan District: Unparalleled, Unbelievable, True*. N.p., n.d.

Spangenberg, Alice. *Oriental Pilgrim: Story of Shiro Kano*. Kansas City, Mo.: Beacon Hill, 1948.

Toland, John. *The Rising Sun: The Decline and Fall of the Japanese Empire*. New York: Bantam, 1971.

Trevor, Hugh. *Japan's Post-War Protestant Churches*. Monrovia, Calif.: MARC, 1995.

Tsuchiyama, Tetsuji. *From Darkness to Light (My Testimony)*. New York: N.p., 1917.

Tyner, Juliatte, and Catherine Eckel. *God's Samurai: The Life and Work of Dr. William A. Eckel*. Kansas City, Mo.: Nazarene Publishing House, 1979.

Widmeyer, Maud F., Everette D. Howard and Pearl Wiley. *Our Island Kingdoms*. Kansas City, Mo.: Nazarene Publishing House, 1939.

Wilkes, Paget. *Missionary Joys in Japan; or, Leaves from My Journal*. London: Morgan and Scott, 1913.

Wood, Robert D. *In These Mortal Hands: The Story of the Oriental Missionary Society; The First Fifty Years*. Greenwood, Ind.: OMS, 1983.

Yamamori, Tetsunao. *Church Growth in Japan: A Study of the Development of Eight Denominations, 1859–1939*. Pasadena, Calif.: William Carey, 1974.

Yoshinobu, Kumazawa, and David L. Swain, ed. *Christianity in Japan, 1971–1990*. Tokyo: Ko Bun Kwan, 1991.

# China

Bays, Daniel H., ed. *Christianity in China from the Eighteenth Century to the Present*. Stanford, Calif.: Stanford University Press, 1996.

———. "Christian Revival in China, 1900–1937." In *Modern Christian Revivals*, ed. Edith L. Blumhofer and Randall Balmer. Urbana: University of Illinois Press, 1993.

———. "Indigenous Protestant Churches in China, 1900–1937: A Pentecostal Case Study." In *Indigenous Responses to Western Christianity*, ed. Steven Kaplan. New York: New York University Press, 1995.

———. "The Modern Protestant Missionary Establishment and the Pentecostal Movement." In *Pentecostal Currents in American Protestantism*, ed. Edith L. Blumhofer, Russell P. Spittler, and Grant A. Wacker. Urbana: University of Illinois Press, 1999.

Borg, Dorothy. *American Policy and the Chinese Revolution, 1925–1928*. Reprint, New York: Octagon, 1968.

———. *The United States and the Far Eastern Crisis of 1933–1938: From the Manchurian Incident through the Initial Stage of the Undeclared Sino-Japanese War*. Cambridge, Mass.: Harvard University Press, 1964.

Broomhall, A. J. *Hudson Taylor and China's Open Century*. Book 3: *If I Had a Thousand Lives*. London: Hodder and Stoughton, 1982.

Brown, G. Thompson. *Earthen Vessels and Transcendent Power: American Presbyterian Missionaries in China, 1837–1952*. Maryknoll, N.Y.: Orbis, 1997.

Brown, William A. "The Protestant Rural Movement in China (1920–1937)." In *American Missionaries in China: Papers from Harvard Seminars*, ed. Kwang-Ching Liu. Cambridge, Mass.: Harvard University Press, 1966.

Carpenter, Joel, ed. *Modernism and Foreign Missions: Two Fundamentalist Protests*. New York: Garland, 1988.

Cochrane, Thomas. *Survey of the Missionary Occupation of China*. Shanghai: Christian Literature Society for China, 1913.

Cohen, Paul. A. *China and Christianity: The Missionary Movement and the Growth of Chinese Antiforeignism, 1860–1870*. Cambridge, Mass.: Harvard University Press, 1963.

———. *History in Three Keys: The Boxers as Event, Experience, and Myth*. New York: Columbia University Press, 1997.

Covell, Ralph. *Pentecost of the Hills in Taiwan: The Christian Faith Among the Original Inhabitants*. Pasadena, Calif.: Hope, 1998.

Esherick, Joseph E. *The Origin of the Boxer Uprising*. Berkeley: University of California Press, 1987.

Fairbank, John K., ed. *The Missionary Enterprise in China and America*. Cambridge, Mass.: Harvard University Press, 1974.

Flynt, Wayne, and Gerald W. Berkley. *Taking Christianity to China: Alabama Missionaries in the Middle Kingdom, 1850–1950*. Tuscaloosa: University of Alabama Press, 1997.

Forsythe, Sidney A. *An American Missionary Community in China, 1895–1905*. Cambridge, Mass.: Harvard University Press, 1971.

Friedman, Donald J. *The Road from Isolation: The Campaign of the American Committee for Non-Participation in Japanese Aggression, 1938–1941*. Cambridge, Mass.: Harvard University Press, 1968.

Fritz, Maxine F. *But God Gives a Song: The Story of Dr. and Mrs. R. G. Fitz, Pioneer Missionaries to China and Alaska*. Kansas City, Mo.: Nazarene Publishing House, 1973.

Hammond, Robert. *Bond Servants of the Japanese*. San Pedro, Calif.: Sheffield, 1943.

Hinshaw, Amy N. *The Messengers of the Cross in China*. Kansas City, Mo.: Woman's Foreign Missionary Society, Church of the Nazarene, n.d.

Hunter, Alan, and Kim-Kwong Chan. *Protestantism in Contemporary China*. Cambridge: Cambridge University Press, 1993.

Hunter, Jane. *The Gospel of Gentility: American Women Missionaries in Turn-of-the-Century China*. New Haven, Conn.: Yale University Press, 1984.

Kane, J. Herbert. "The Legacy of J. Hudson Taylor." *International Bulletin of Missionary Research* 8 (April 1984).

Ketler, Isaac. *The Tragedy of Paotingfu*. Second ed. New York: Fleming H. Revell, 1902.

Kiehn, Peter. "The Legacy of Peter and Anna Kiehn." N.p., 1970.

King, Marjorie. "Exporting Femininity, Not Feminism: Nineteenth-Century U.S. Missionary Women's Efforts to Emancipate Chinese Women." In *Women's Work for Women: Missionaries and Social Change in Asia*, ed. Leslie A. Flemming. Boulder, Colo.: Westview, 1989.

Kinne, C. J. *Our Field in China: The Field and the Mission of the Church of the Nazarene in China Briefly Described and Illustrated*. Kansas City, Mo.: Nazarene Publishing House, n.d.

Kwok, Pui-lan. *Chinese Women and Christianity, 1860–1927*. Atlanta: Scholars, 1991.

Lambert, Tony. *The Resurrection of the Chinese Church*. Wheaton, Ill.: OMF, 1994.

Latourette, Kenneth S. *A History of Christian Missions in China*. New York: Macmillan, 1929.

Leung, Beatrice, and John D. Young, ed. *Christianity in China: Foundations for Dialogue*. Hong Kong: University of Hong Kong Press, 1993.

Lian, Xi. *The Conversion of Missionaries: Liberalism in American Protestant Missions in China, 1907–1932*. University Park: Pennsylvania State University Press, 1997.

Liao, Kuang-sheng. *Anti-Foreignism and Modernization in China: 1860–1980*. Second ed. Hong Kong: Chinese University Press, 1986.

Lobenstine, E. C., and A. L. Warnshuis, eds. *China Mission Year Book*. Shanghai: Kwang Hsueh, 1920.

Lodwick, Kathleen L. *Crusaders Against Opium: Protestant Missionaries in China, 1874–1917*. Lexington: University Press of Kentucky, 1996.

Lutz, Jessie. *China and the Christian Colleges, 1850–1950*. Ithaca, N.Y.: Cornell University Press, 1971.

Lutz, Jessie, ed. *Christian Missions in China: Evangelists of What?* Boston: D. C. Heath, 1965.

Lyall, Leslie T. *John Sung*. London: China Inland Mission, 1954.

MacGillvry, D., ed. *China Mission Year Book*. Fourth ed. Shanghai: Christian Literature Society for China, 1913.

Malatesta, Edward J. "China and the Society of Jesus: An Historical–Theological Essay." Unpublished, 1996.

Miller, Basil. *Generalissimo and Madame Chiang Kai-Shek: Christian Liberators of China*. Second ed. Grand Rapids, Mich.: Zondervan, 1943.

Miller, Ruth A. *The Darkest Side of the Road*. Kansas City, Mo.: Nazarene Publishing House, 1962.

Miller, Stuart C. "Ends and Means: Missionary Justification for Force in Nineteenth Century China." In *The Missionary Enterprise in China and America*, ed. John K. Fairbank. Cambridge, Mass.: Harvard University Press, 1974.

[National Holiness Association]. *Holiness Unto the Lord*. N.p., 1913.

Neils, Patricia, ed. *United States Attitudes and Policies Toward China: The Impact of American Missionaries*. Armonk, N.Y.: M. E. Sharpe, 1990.

Nevius, John L. *Demon Possession and Allied Things*. Third ed. New York: Fleming H. Revell, n.d.

Osborn, L. C. *The China Story: The Church of the Nazarene in North China, South China, and Taiwan*. Kansas City, Mo.: Nazarene Publishing House, 1969.

———. *Christ at the Bamboo Curtain*. Kansas City, Mo.: Beacon Hill, 1956.

———. *Hitherto! 1914–1939: Silver Anniversary of the Church of the Nazarene in China*. Tientsin, China: Peiyang Press, 1939.

Pattee, John W. *Hazardous Days in China*. Pasadena, Calif.: Author, n.d.

Preston, Diana. *The Boxer Rebellion: The Dramatic Story of China's War on Foreigners that Shook the World in the Summer of 1900*. New York: Walker, 1999.

Price, Frank Wilson. *The Rural Church in China: A Survey*. New York: Agricultural Missions, 1948.

Rabe, Valentin H. *The Home Base of American China Missions, 1880–1920*. Cambridge, Mass.: Harvard University Press, 1978.

Raber, Dorothy A. *Protestantism in Changing Taiwan: A Call to Creative Response*. Pasadena, Calif.: William Carey, 1978.

Reed, L. A., and H. A. Wiese. *The Challenge of China*. Kansas City, Mo.: Nazarene Publishing House, 1937.

Rees, D. Vaughan. *The "Jesus Family" in Communist China*. Chicago: Moody, 1956.

Rubinstein, Murray A. *The Protestant Community on Modern Taiwan: Mission, Seminary and Church*. Armonk, N.Y.: M. E. Sharpe, 1991.

———. "Witness to the Chinese Millennium: Southern Baptist Perceptions of the Chinese Revolution, 1911–1921." In *United States Attitudes and Policies Toward China: The Impact of American Missionaries*, ed. Patricia Neils. Armonk, N.Y.: M. E. Sharpe, 1990.

Scott, Mary L. *Kept in Safeguard*. Kansas City, Mo.: Nazarene Publishing House, 1977.

Shaw, Yu-ming. *An American Missionary in China: John Leighton Stuart and Chinese-American Relations*. Cambridge, Mass.: Harvard University Press, 1992.

Smith, A[aron] J. *Jesus Lifting Chinese: Marvelous Spiritual Awakenings in China*. Cincinnati, Ohio: God's Bible School and Revivalist, n.d.

Spence, Jonathan. *The Gate of Heavenly Peace: The Chinese and Their Revolution, 1895–1980*. New York: Viking, 1981.

Sung, John. *My Testimony: The Autobiography of Dr. John Sung*. Reprint, Hong Kong: Living Books for All, 1977.

Sutherland, Francis C. *China Crisis*. Kansas City, Mo.: Nazarene Publishing House, 1948.

Sutherland, Robert, and John Sutherland. *Behind the Silence: The Story of Frank and Ann Sutherland*. Kansas City, Mo.: Nazarene Publishing House, 1999.

Swanson, Allen J. *The Church in Taiwan: Profile 1980: A Review of the Past, A Projection for the Future*. Pasadena, Calif.: William Carey, 1981.

———. *Mending the Nets: Taiwan Church Growth and Loss in the 1980's*. Pasadena, Calif.: William Carey, 1986.

———. *Taiwan: Mainline Versus Independent Church Growth: A Study in Contrasts*. Pasadena, Calif.: William Carey, [1970].

Sweeten, Alan R. *Christianity in Rural China: Conflict and Accommodation in Jiangxi Province, 1860–1900*. Ann Arbor: University of Michigan, 2001.

Tashjian, Jirair. *Taiwan in Transition*. Kansas City, Mo.: Nazarene Publishing House, 1977.

Taylor, Geraldine. *Pastor Hsi (of North China): One of China's Christians*. London: Morgan Scott, 1903.

———. *The Triumph of John and Betty Stam*. Philadelphia: China Inland Mission, 1935.

Thomson, James C. *While China Faced West: American Reformers in Nationalist China, 1928–1937*. Cambridge, Mass.: Harvard University Press, 1969.

T'ien, Ju-k'ang. *Peaks of Faith: Protestant Mission in Revolutionary China*. Leiden, Netherlands: E. J. Brill, 1993.

Tong, Hollington K. *Christianity in Taiwan: A History*. Taipei, Taiwan: China Post, 1961.

Troxel, Mrs. Cecil, and Mrs. John J. Trachsel. *Cecil Troxel: The Man and the Work*. Chicago: National Holiness Missionary Society, 1948.

Uhalley, Stephen, and Xiaoxin Wu, ed. *China and Christianity: Burdened Past, Hopeful Future*. Armonk, N.Y.: M. E. Sharpe, 2001.

Varg, Paul A. *Missionaries, Chinese, and Diplomats: The American Protestant Missionary Movement in China, 1890–1950*. Princeton, N.J.: Princeton University Press, 1958.

Wickeri, Philip L. *Seeking the Common Ground: Protestant Christianity, the Three-Self Movement, and China's United Front*. Maryknoll, N.Y.: Orbis, 1988.

Williams, Jim. "Accurate Contextualization: Prerequisite to Church Growth in Taiwan." M.A. thesis, Asia Pacific Nazarene Theological Seminary, 1987.

Yang, Martin C. *A Chinese Village: Taitou, Shantung Province*. New York: Columbia University Press, 1945.

# Korea

Baldwin, Frank. "Missionaries and the March First Movement: Can Moral Men be Neutral?" In *Korea Under Japanese Control: Studies of the Policy and Techniques of Japanese Colonialism*, ed. Andrew C. Nahm. Kalamazoo: Western Michigan University Press, 1973.

Bradley, Floyd N. *Red Terror; or Robert Chung's Escape*. Louisville, Ky.: Pentecostal Publishing House, 1951.

Brown, G. Thompson. "Why Has Christianity Grown Faster in Korea than in China?" *Missiology* 22 (January 1994): 77–88.

Cho, Eun Sik. "Korean Church Growth in 1970s: Its Factors and Problems." *Asia Journal of Theology* 10 (1996): 348–362.

Choi, Myung Keun. *Changes in Korean Society Between 1884–1910 as a Result of the Introduction of Christianity*. New York: Peter Lang, 1997.

Choy, Bong-youn. *Korea: A History*. Rutland, Vt.: Charles E. Tuttle, 1971.

Clark, Allen D. *History of the Korean Church*. Seoul: n.p., [1961].

Clark, Charles A. *The Nevius Plan for Mission Works: Illustrated in Korea*. Seoul: Christian Literature Society, [1937].

Cobb, A. Brent. *Tried and Triumphant: Testimonies of Twelve Korean Nazarenes*. Kansas City, Mo.: Beacon Hill, 1984.

Cox, Harvey. *Fire from Heaven: The Rise of Pentecostal Spirituality and the Reshaping of Religion in the Twenty-first Century*. Boston: Addison-Wesley, 1995.

Crose, Lester A. *Passport for a Reformation*. Anderson, Ind.: Warner Press, 1981.

Cummings, Bruce. *Korea's Place in the Sun: A Modern History*. New York: W. W. Norton, 1997.

Cunningham, Floyd T. "The Beginnings of the Church of the Nazarene in Korea (1932–1966)." *Bokyum Gwa Shinhak* [Gospel and Culture] 4 (1992): 145–170.

Hong, Harold S., Won Young Ji, and Chung Choon Kim. *Korea Struggles for Christ: Memorial Symposium for the Eightieth Anniversary of Protestantism in Korea.* Second ed. Seoul: Christian Literature Society of Korea, 1973.

Hong, Ki Young. "Planting an Indigenous Nazarene Church in Korea as a Basis for Church Growth." *The Mediator* (January 1996): 37–63.

Hong, Paul Yong Pyo. "Spreading the Holiness Fire: A History of the OMS Korean Holiness Church, 1904–1957." D.Miss. dissertation, Fuller Theological Seminary, 1996.

Hunt, Everett N., Jr. *Protestant Pioneers in Korea.* Maryknoll, N.Y.: Orbis, 1980.

Huntley, Martha. *Caring, Growing, Changing: A History of the Protestant Mission in Korea.* New York: Friendship, 1984.

Kang, Sam Young. [*A History of the Church of the Nazarene in Korea*]. N.p., n.d.

———. "[An Historical Study of the Denominational Event That Brought Crisis in the Korean Church of the Nazarene]." *Bokyum Gwa Shinhak* [Gospel and Culture] 4 (1992): 41–66.

Kang, Wi Jo. *Christ and Caesar in Modern Korea: A History of Christianity and Politics.* Albany: State University of New York Press, 1997.

Kim, Byong Suh. "The Explosive Growth of the Korean Church Today: A Sociological Analysis." *International Review of Mission* 74 (1985): 59–72.

Kim, John T. *Protestant Church Growth in Korea.* Belleville, Ontario: Essence, 1996.

Kim, Sung Won. "A Critical Reflection on the History of the Church of the Nazarene in Korea." Paper presented at the Global Theology Conference, Guatemala City, April 4–7, 2002.

Kong, Chang Sul. "[The Historical Research of the Church of the Nazarene in Korea]." M.A. thesis, United Graduate School of Theology, Yonsei University, 1970.

Ogle, George E. *Liberty to the Captives: The Struggle Against Oppression in South Korea.* Atlanta: John Knox, 1977.

Owens, Donald. *Challenge in Korea.* Kansas City, Mo.: Beacon Hill, 1957.

———. "Church Growth in Korea." In *Ministering to the Millions*, comp. Department of World Missions. Kansas City, Mo.: Nazarene Publishing House, 1971.

———. *Revival Fires in Korea.* Kansas City, Mo.: Nazarene Publishing House, 1977.

Paik, Lak-geoon George. *The History of Protestant Missions in Korea, 1832–1910.* Second ed. Seoul: Yonsei University Press, 1971.

Ro, Bong Rin, and Marlin L. Nelson. *Korean Church Growth Explosion.* Seoul: Word of Life Press, 1983.

Shin, Min-gyoo. "An Analysis of the Variable[s] that Affect the Financial Support of Korea Nazarene Theological College by the Korean Church." *Bokyum Gwa Shinhak* [Gospel and Culture] 1 (1989): 89–191.

Stults, Donald LeRoy. "A Plan for a Continuing Education Program of Pastors of the Church of the Nazarene in the Republic of Korea." D. Miss. thesis, Trinity Evangelical Divinity School, 1982.
Thomas, Emily. "What God Hath Wrought in Korea." *The Way of Holiness* (November 1915).
Underwood, Lillias H. *Underwood of Korea.* New York: Fleming H. Revell, 1918.
Wells, Kenneth M. *New God, New Nation: Protestants and Self-Reconstruction Nationalism in Korea, 1896–1937.* Honolulu: University of Hawaii Press, 1990.
Yoo, Boo-Woong. *Korean Pentecostalism: Its History and Theology.* Frankfurt am Main, Germany: Velag Peter Lang, 1987.

# Philippines

Abainza, Estanislao, et al. *Selected Philippine Sermons.* Manila: National Council of Churches in the Philippines, 1967.
Alejandro, D. D. *From Darkness to Light: A Brief Chronicle of the Beginnings and Spread of Methodism in the Philippines.* N.p.: Philippines Central Conference Board of Communications and Publications, United Methodist Church, 1974.
———. "Evangelism for the Philippines." *The Philippine Faith and Life* (1950).
Bickert, Robert A. "Perception and Response to Receptivity: The History and Growth of the Wesleyan Church in the Philippines 1932–1994." D. Miss. dissertation, Asbury Theological Seminary, 1996.
Bunda, Nestor D. *A Mission History of the Philippine Baptist Churches 1898–1998 from a Philippine Perspective.* Aachen, Germany: Verlag an der Lottbek, 1999.
Bush, Richard. "The Sectarian Challenge." *The Philippine Christian Advocate* 6 (January 1954).
Clymer, Kenton J. *Protestant Missionaries in the Philippines, 1898–1916: An Inquiry into the American Colonial Mentality.* Urbana: University of Illinois Press, 1986.
Copelin, Roy E. *Life in a Nazarene Bible College: The Story of Missionary Education in the Philippines.* Kansas City, Mo.: Nazarene Publishing House, 1962.
Cunningham, Floyd T. "The Early History of the Church of the Nazarene in the Philippines." *Philippine Studies* 41 (First Quarter 1993): 51–76.
Deats, Richard L. *The Story of the Methodism in the Philippines.* Manila: Union Theological Seminary, 1964.
Elwood, Douglas. *Churches and Sects in the Philippines: A Descriptive Study of Contemporary Religious Group Movements.* Dumaguete City, Philippines: Silliman University, 1968.

Galang, Fred. "Evangelism Program of the Methodist Church." *The Philippine Christian Advocate* 11 (February 1959).

Ganchoree, Ciriaco. "Iloilo City Ministers for Evangelical Fellowship." *The Philippine Christian Advocate* 11 (October 1959).

Gowing, Peter G. *Islands Under the Cross: The Story of the Church in the Philippines.* Manila: National Council of Churches in the Philippines, 1967.

Groesbeck, Gertrude, and Ruby Schlosser, eds. *Lighting the Philippine Frontier.* Winona Lake, Ind.: Woman's Missionary Society, Free Methodist Church, 1956.

Guansing, Benjamin I. "Developments in the Philippines." *Philippine Faith and Life* (1950).

Hayden, Joseph R. *The Philippines: A Study in National Development.* New York: Macmillan, 1947.

Jocano, F. Landa. *Folk Christianity: A Preliminary Study of Conversion and Patterning of Christian Experience in the Philippines.* Quezon City, Philippines: Trinity Research Institute, 1981.

Kerkvliet, Benedict J. *The Huk Rebellion: A Study of Peasant Revolt in the Philippines.* Berkeley: University of California Press, 1977.

Kretzmann, Herbert. "Lutheranism in the Philippines, 1952–1966." S.T.M. thesis, Concordia Seminary, 1966.

McGavran, Donald. *Church Growth in the United Church of Christ in the Philippines.* Vol. 1: *Multiplying Churches in the Philippines.* N.p., n.d.

Montgomery, James H., and Donald A. McGavran. *The Discipling of a Nation.* Santa Clara, Calif.: Global Church Growth Bulletin, 1980.

Moore, J. E., Jr. "The Philippines and the Islands." In *The Chaplains See World Missions*, ed. Lauriston J. DuBois. Kansas City, Mo.: Nazarene Publishing House, 1946.

Osias, Camilo. *Separation of Church and State.* Manila: n.p., 1965.

Pertierra, Raul. *Religion, Politics, and Rationality in a Philippine Community.* Quezon City, Philippines: Ateneo de Manila University Press, 1988.

Pitts, Joseph, ed. *Echoes from the Philippines.* [Various issues].

———. *Mission to the Philippines.* Kansas City, Mo.: Beacon Hill Press, 1955.

———. *Voices from the Philippines.* N.p., n.d.

Pitts, Paul. *Pentecost Rejected.* N.p., 1956.

Posey, Jesse E. "A Historical Study of Baptist Missions in the Philippines 1900–1967," Th.D. dissertation, New Orleans Baptist Theological Seminary, 1968.

Rulloda, Ernesto N. "The Church of the Nazarene in the Philippines: Her Role in Nation Building." Ed.D. dissertation, Baguio Central University, 1990.

Schlosser, Ruby, and Gertrude Groesbeck, ed. *Lighting the Philippine Frontier.* Winona Lake, Ind.: Woman's Missionary Society, Free Methodist Church, 1956.

Shalom, Stephen R. *The United States and the Philippines: A Study of Neocolonialism.* Reprint, Quezon City, Philippines: New Day, 1986.

Sitoy, T. Valentino, Jr. *Several Springs, One Stream: The United Church of Christ in the Philippines.* Vol. 1: *Heritage and Origins (1898–1948).* Quezon City, Philippines: United Church of Christ in the Philippines, 1992.

Sobrepena, Enrique. "The State of the Church." *The Philippine Christian Advocate* 5 (June 1953).

———. *That They May Be One.* Manila: United Church of Christ in the Philippines, [1955].

Thomas, Paul W. "The Philippines." In *Reformers and Revivalists: The History of the Wesleyan Church,* ed. Wayne E. Caldwell. Indianapolis, Ind.: Wesley Press, 1992.

Thomas, Paul Westphal, and Paul William Thomas. "The Philippine Islands." In *The Days of Our Pilgrimage: The History of the Pilgrim Holiness Church,* ed. Melvin Dieter and Lee Haines. Marion, Ind.: Wesley Press, 1976.

Tuggy, Arthur. *The Philippine Church: Growth in a Changing Society.* Grand Rapids, Mich.: Eerdmans, 1971.

Valencia, Jose L. *Under God's Umbrella: An Autobiography.* Quezon City, Philippines: New Day, 1978.

Watts, C. Ellen. *John Pattee of China and the Philippines.* Kansas City, Mo.: Beacon Hill, 1984.

# Index

Africa, 1, 17, 29–30, 80, 178, 223, 276
African Americans, 25, 27, 73
Agbuya, Angelito, 256
Ahn, Hyung Chu, 212, 215, 216
Allen, Roland, 8, 84
American Board of Commissioners for Foreign Missions, 146, 160
Amolik, B. D., 69, 70, 75, 76
An, Chang Ho, 209
Anderson, E. G., 60, 107, 110–111, 113, 127, 180, 281
Anderson, Mary, 80
Anderson, Rufus, 8, 21, 64, 75, 83, 217, 275, 276
Anglican (*see* Church of England)
Anti-American (*see* Nationalism)
Antiforeignism (*see* Nationalism)
Apostolic Holiness Union, 96
Armstrong, Norma, 257
Asbury College, 210, 238
Asia Pacific Nazarene Theological Seminary, 258
Assimilation, 277
Association of Pentecostal Churches of America (APCA), 4–14, 15, 17, 50, 51, 53–57, 63, 103, 111, 206
Australia, 28, 205
Avetoom, A. A., 58

Babu, Dwarka, 61
Babu, Samed, 61, 62
Baguio, 238, 239–240, 241, 242, 244, 249, 251, 252, 255–256, 258, 275
Ban, Takeshi, 114
Banarjee, Sukhoda, 13, 57–59, 64, 98, 109
Bangladesh, 60, 61, 62, 270
Bangs, Carl, 31
Baptists, 8, 55, 61, 63, 127, 156, 180, 255, 256, 276
Barnes, Nellie, 53, 55
Bartel, Henry, 147
Bates, J. E., 108–109, 110
Bay-an, Paul, 242
Beals, Prescott, 62, 71, 75–79, 84
Beech, Neva, 256
Beech, Ronald, 254, 256
Benner, Hugh C., 28, 31, 127, 129, 221, 248, 250
Benson, John T., 18
Bernabe, Meliton, 255, 259
Bethany Nazarene College, 147, 187, 213, 216, 217, 225–226
Bhujbal, David, 75, 76
Bhujbal, Samuel, 69–70, 75, 76, 79–82, 218–219, 275
Bible and theological schools and colleges, 22, 70–71, 82, 98, 102, 113, 114, 116–118, 127–129, 147, 155, 156, 159, 169, 174, 177, 178–180, 183–191, 193–196, 203, 205, 207, 210, 212, 213, 216, 218, 220, 224, 225, 238, 241–244, 249, 251, 254–260, 274

## Index

Bible women, 30–31, 73, 109, 147, 151, 155–156, 158, 172, 173, 207, 215
Biswas, P. B., 13, 57, 60, 98
Bolayog, C. T., 242
Booth, William, 96
Borde, G. S., 75, 76, 79, 81
Bowes, Alpin, 30
Boxer Rebellion, 144–145
Bresee, Phineas F., 11–14, 17, 19, 20, 26, 30, 34, 57–58, 97–98, 103, 108–109, 111, 145, 156, 273, 274, 281
Browning, David, 259
Buldana, 50, 52, 56, 69–70, 71, 75–76, 78, 83, 206
Bultmann, Rudolph, 128–129
Burgess, Pat, 187
Burkhart, Peter, 259
Buxton, Barclay, 96

Cabanatuan, 237, 238, 239, 240, 243, 249, 251, 255
Calcutta, 13, 58–63, 66, 99, 109
California, 4, 10, 11, 17, 19, 30, 56, 57, 60, 96–98, 101, 103–104, 108, 112, 114, 126, 128, 154, 156, 174, 180, 209–210, 238, 242, 252, 253
Campbell, L. A., 56
Cape Verde, 7, 17
Carentes, Rachel, 244, 249
Carpio, Ricardo, 241
Chang, Chien-hsun, 151
Chang, Chin, 165–166, 172
Chang, Hsi-tien, 151
Chang, Hua-hsin, 151
Chang, Hua-huw, 151
Chang, Hung-en, 146
Chang, Sung Oak, 207–209, 212–213
Chaocheng, 147–155, 161, 162, 164
Chapman, J. B., 5, 20, 21, 25, 26, 49, 75, 84, 115–116, 124, 162, 163, 164, 207, 246, 281

Chenault, J. A., and Minnie, 96–97
Chengan, 152, 165, 168, 170, 173
Chi, Yuew-han (John Chi), 166, 173, 180, 184
Chiang, Kai-shek, 25, 159, 160, 173, 189
China, 8, 10, 13, 17, 18, 19, 25, 28, 101, 118–120, 122, 143–203, 205, 206, 209, 214, 217, 241, 243, 253, 270–276
China Famine Relief, 153
*Chinese Characteristics*, 152
Cho, Jung Hwan, 207, 208
Cho, Moon Kyung, 218, 221, 222, 225
Cho, Seigyoku (*see* Chang, Sung Oak)
Chonan, 229
Choudhury, Samed, 62
Chow, Ko, 13
Christian and Missionary Alliance (CMA), 17, 50–52, 56, 66, 71
Christian Church of Japan, 122, 123
*Christian Theology*, 176
Chung, Lin-ching (Samuel Chung), 177, 179
Chung, Nam Soo, 205, 207, 209–216, 217, 219–221, 225, 227, 229
Church Missionary Society, 52, 96
Church of England (*see also* Episcopal Church), 14, 52, 96, 276
Church of God (Anderson, Indiana), 211, 212, 215, 216, 220
Church of South India, 78
Church of the Bible Covenant, 249–250
Church of the Nazarene (1895–1907), 11–14, 55, 56
Codding, Roy G., 66, 67
Colonialism, 11, 32, 70, 77, 78, 80, 118, 260, 271, 273, 277

Comity, 7–8, 26, 52, 56, 61, 63, 69, 72, 143, 146, 149, 150, 237, 250, 255
Committee of Twenty-Four, 167, 170
Communism, communists, 28, 81, 144, 165, 170–173, 177, 205, 211, 214, 241, 271, 275
Congregational church polity, 55, 215, 276
Congregationalism, Congregationalists, 4, 7, 25, 55, 146, 157, 250
Conrad, Howard, 188
Contado, Prisco, 250–251, 252, 255
Copelin, Erna, 244, 245
Copelin, Roy, 244, 245, 254, 256
Cornett, Eldon, 224, 226
Coulter, George, 31–32, 82, 181–185, 188, 281
Cowman, Charles and Lettie, 96–97, 98
Cox, Hilda, 83
Cox, Ira, 82
Cullis, Charles, 73, 74

Dai, Chun-de, 187
Daming, 119, 144, 145, 146, 151, 152–159, 161, 162, 163–167, 170, 172, 176, 180, 188
Davis, Harrison, 121
Deacons, 167, 177, 179, 226–227, 228, 229
Deale, Otis, 151, 153
Deale, Zella, 151
DeLong, Russell V., 29, 84
Dennis, James, 8, 25
Diaz, John J., 6–7
Ding, Hsin, 177, 179
Document 19, 172
Dongerdive, S. P., 83
Drake, Lucy (*see* Osborn)
Dzau, Phillip, 186
Dzau, Timothy, 186

East Asia Christian Mission, 120
Eastern Nazarene College, 123–124
Eaton, E. G., 57, 60
Eaton, Emma, 57–60, 109
Eckel, Florence, 101, 103, 107, 111, 122
Eckel, Howard, 103, 111
Eckel, William, 95, 101, 103–111, 113–114, 117–118, 120–122, 129–131, 185, 207–208, 209, 211, 223–224, 238, 271–273
Emerson, Ralph Waldo, 275
Encarnacion, Epifania, 240, 248
Encarnacion, Marciano, 237–240, 243, 246, 248–249, 251, 275
Episcopal Church, Episcopalians, 8, 73, 146, 173
Esselstyn, William, 29
Evangelical Fellowship of India, 84
Evangelical Fellowship of Japan, 130
Evangelical United Brethren, 244, 252
Evangelism, 1–2, 4, 6, 7, 13, 14, 15–16, 20, 23–32, 49, 50, 56, 63, 64, 70, 73, 75, 76, 77, 79, 81, 82–84, 96, 100, 101, 102, 106, 109, 110, 112, 113, 114, 117, 126, 129, 143, 144, 147, 149, 150–160, 161, 172, 175, 177, 179, 181, 184, 186, 210–211, 213, 215, 217, 222, 224, 243, 249–253, 254, 255, 270, 273, 274, 278
Existentialism, 128–129

Faith missions, 7, 10, 12, 50
Farmer, W. A., 17
Fellowship of Asian Evangelicals, 130
Feng, Lan-xin, 164
Feng, Yu-hsiang, 165
Ferries, Celia (*see* McMurry)

Fetters, Fred, 238
Fitkin, Susan, 6, 111, 127, 207, 241
Fitz, R. G., 156, 157, 164, 173
Fontanilla, Carlino, 250, 251, 256
Fontanilla, Rebecca, 255
Formosa (*see* Taiwan)
Formosa Gospel Mission (*see* Taiwan Gospel Mission)
Fowler, C. J., 146
Franklin, George, 61–63, 110
Franklin, Hulda, 59, 60, 61
Free Methodism, Free Methodists, 56, 73, 76, 78, 98, 106, 113, 114, 122, 123, 127, 129, 150, 184, 186–187, 210
Friends, Friends Church, 7, 101, 103, 110, 177, 186
Fritzlan, Andrew, 56, 67, 69–70, 77, 271, 273
Fritzlan, Daisy, 67, 74, 77
Fritzlan, Leslie, 77
Fukuchiyama, 98, 99, 102, 106, 107, 108, 112
Funagoshi, Takichi, 130
Fundamentalism, 27, 109, 267

Galindez, Geronimo, 250, 251–252
Galvez, Jaime, 250, 252
Gandhi, Mohatma, 77, 80
Gardner, Agnes, 77
Garos, 60–61
Gay, Leslie, 97–98, 101, 105, 109, 110
Ghordpade, S. D., 69
Ghose, Hermanto (*see* Banarjee)
Gibson, Julia, 53, 56
Goodwin, John W., 62, 71, 113, 116, 161
Gould, J. Glenn, 24, 26, 29, 84, 113
Graham, Billy, 223
Grebe, Hulda (*see* Franklin)
Grebe, Leoda, 59, 60
Greer, Bronnel, 83, 84, 274

Greer, Paula, 83, 84
Guatemala, 18, 32, 33, 67
Guillermo, Federico, 32, 33

Hallelujah Village, 58, 59, 60
Hammond, Robert, 177–179
Handan, 119, 153, 157, 168, 171, 172
Hang, Hung-yu, 146
Hanson, Pearl Wiley, 112, 121, 122, 126–127
Hardie, R. A., 206
Hawkes, E. L., 109
Haynes, B. F., 14
Healing, 14, 30, 73, 83, 114, 155
Heart of India Mission, 60
Hebei, 118, 143, 144, 145, 164, 172, 270
Hephzibah Faith Missionary Association, 96
Herrell, N. B., 20
Heslop, Norah and William, 206
Hill, J. I., 109
Hill, Mary, 13, 145–146
Hills, A. M., 4, 24, 96
Hinshaw, Amy, 152
Hitchens, Priscilla, 53, 56
Hofstadter, Richard, 28
Holiness (*see also* Perfect love), 1–4, 6–8, 9, 11, 12, 13–16, 17, 21, 26, 31, 34, 55, 56, 58, 67, 76, 79, 82, 96, 98, 99, 102, 113, 118, 146, 153, 158, 160, 172, 175, 184, 186, 205, 206, 209, 210, 211, 213, 219, 228, 238, 253, 254, 259, 261, 270, 272–275, 277
Holiness Association of Texas, 11
Holiness Church of Christ (HCC), 4, 9–11, 17, 21, 56, 64, 96, 125
Holiness Church of the Nazarene, 249
Holstead, John, 178–181, 185–186, 188

Holstead, Natalie, 178, 179, 181, 188
*Holy Fire*, 211
Holy Spirit, 4, 7, 9, 22, 24, 29, 34, 50, 54, 55, 72, 99, 157, 158, 206, 273, 274
Hong Kong, 120, 144, 171, 194, 209
Hoople, William H., 50
Hope School, 59
Hospitals, 16, 19, 24, 29, 30, 49, 74, 77, 78–80, 82, 83, 143, 154, 156–157, 164, 165, 168, 169, 172, 255, 272, 274
Houlding, Horace (*see also* South Chili Gospel Mission), 13, 145–146, 151, 153, 157
Hsu, Kwei-pin, 161, 165, 167, 168, 169, 170, 173–174, 275
Hull, Cordell, 166
Humphrey, L. H., 98, 99, 104, 105
Hwang, Paul, 187
Hynd, David, 30

Ichihara, E., 112
IEMELIF, 240
Igatpuri, 51, 52, 55, 56, 66
Ilocanos, 243, 251, 259
Immanuel Gospel Mission, 125, 129
India, 5, 8, 9, 13, 16–18, 28, 49–94, 95, 98, 99, 100, 106, 109–110, 111–114, 143, 145, 149, 153, 157, 206, 210, 218, 236, 270, 271, 274–276, 281
India Gospel League (*see* International Gospel League)
International Gospel League, 60, 127, 180
International Holiness Mission, 206
Inter-Varsity, 177
Isayama, Nobumi, 95, 102, 104, 105, 106, 107, 110, 112–113, 115–117, 120–126, 127, 144–146, 208

Jackson, K. Hawley, 67
Jacques, V. J., 57–59
Jamandre, Ciriaco, 240, 242, 243, 246, 248–249
Jamandre, Edison, 240
Japan, 9, 15–17, 28, 63, 95–142, 143, 148, 149, 157, 166, 169–170, 173, 187, 189, 206–209, 211–212, 215–216, 237, 239, 240, 270, 271, 273–275
Japan Evangelistic Band, 96
Japan Holiness Church, 96, 113, 129, 207
Japan Holiness Church of Christ, 123
Japan Nazarene Theological Seminary, 128
Jen, Chin-ya, 151
Jenkins, Orville, 225
Jesuits (*see* Society of Jesus)
*Jesus Lifting Chinese*, 158
Jiangxi, 144, 171, 173, 176–177, 188
Johnson, Jerald, 31, 174, 258
Jones, Charles Warren, 26, 27–28, 113, 120–122, 167, 168, 169, 209, 211
Jones, E. Stanley, 210

Kagawa, Toyohiko, 100
Kakihara, Paul, 98
Kaku, K., 112, 119
Kano, Shiro, 123–124
Kao, E-feng, 166, 170, 180
Karns, Bertie, 117, 122
Kawabe, T., 98
Kellerman, Darlene and Phillip, 186–187
Kennedy School of Missions (Hartford Seminary), 71
Kharat, D. M., 83
Kharat, W., 52, 57, 75–76

Kida, Aishin, 130
Kiehn, Anna, 147–149, 151, 153, 162–164, 168–169, 171, 174, 177–179, 182
Kiehn, Peter, 147–151, 153, 157, 160–164, 167, 168–169, 171, 173, 174, 176–180, 182, 185, 187, 223, 272
Kierkegaard, Soren, 128–129
Kilbourne, E. A., 98
Kim, Chong Soo, 222–223, 225, 226
Kim, Hwan Sun, 218
Kim, Young Baek, 221
Kim, Yung Chin, 215, 216
Kinne, C. J., 19–20, 26, 30, 156
Kishorganj, 61–63, 72
Kitagawa, Hiroshi, 95, 97, 101–106, 115, 116, 118–132, 162, 275
Kitagawa, Shin, 132
Kitagawa, Shiro, 102, 117, 119, 120, 121, 134
Knapp, Martin, 96
Korea, 28, 82, 96, 97, 118, 119, 123, 205–235, 270, 271, 274–275, 281
Korea Holiness Church, 209, 211
Korean War, 212
Kumamoto, 97, 101, 102, 105, 108, 112, 127
Kuo, Min-hua, 188
Kyoto, 96–99, 104–106, 108, 110–113, 115, 116, 118, 119–121, 124–126, 207

Lallana, Jose, 243, 246, 248
Lasam, Elijah, 239
Laubach, Frank, 25
Leadership, 4, 9, 20, 23, 32–34, 49–50, 54, 55, 63–78, 79, 83, 95, 99, 101–118, 122, 129, 131, 166, 167–168, 173–175, 180, 182, 188–189, 190, 207, 215–217, 222, 241, 260, 265, 270, 274, 277

Lee, Bong Hwan, 218
Lee, Byung He, 215
Lee, Young Jun, 218
Legalism, 20, 27, 28–29, 30, 182, 245–249
Lewis, V. H., 181–183, 254, 255
Li, Ching-ho, 149, 150
Li, Ching-i, 151
Li, Mary, 174
Li, Sui-chung, 166
Lin, Adam, 181
Lin, Betty, 187
Little, J. T., 109
Little Flock, 187
Liu, S. E., 168
London Missionary Society, 146
Lo-o Valley, 242, 247
Ludwig, S. T., 30
Lumiqued, Antonio, 242
Lutherans, 154
Luzong, Victoriano, 248–249

Ma, Hsueh-wen, 170, 173
Magar, John, 71
Manaois, Wilfredo, 256, 258
Manila, 238, 239, 240, 244, 249, 251, 252, 256, 259
Manmothe, Luther, 74, 76, 80, 81
Mao, Ze-dong, 144, 170
Mass Education Movement, 152
Mayhew, Clinton, 125
McClurkan, J. O., 11, 17, 18
McCroskey, Mathilda, 246, 250, 254
McCroskey, Robert, 246, 250, 252, 254
McDonald, D. J., 5
McKay, Bartlett, 131
McKinley, William, 6, 278
McMurry, Celia, and V. G., 73
McPhearson, Ethel, 106
McReynolds, Mae, 13, 109
Mennonites, 147, 151, 153, 157, 159, 171
Meshramkar, Kamalakar, 83
Meshramkar, Padu, 83

Methodism, Methodists, 1, 5, 6, 9, 11–12, 13, 14, 20–21, 31, 50, 51, 55, 72–74, 75, 76, 96, 103, 104, 126, 146, 151, 154, 160, 173, 206, 207, 210, 212, 215, 217, 237, 238, 239, 240, 255, 259, 276
Mexico, 9, 10–11, 16, 17, 107
Millennialism
  (see Second Coming)
Miller, Basil, 25, 26, 127, 180
Miller, Howard V., 79, 80
Miller, Ray, 178–183, 187, 188, 249, 253, 271, 272
Miller, Ruth, 178–183
Miss Choe Orphanage, 215
Missionary Society (Nazarene), 3, 6, 81, 154, 156, 174, 207, 208, 223, 255, 281
Missions Board (Nazarene), 5, 6, 10, 13, 15, 17, 50–57, 65, 68–69, 101, 111, 112, 125, 148, 281
Missions Committee
  (see Missions Board)
Missions Department (Nazarene), 22, 33, 34, 109–113, 130, 162, 174, 177, 181, 182, 188, 215, 218, 219
Modernism, 20, 25, 153
Moody Bible Institute, 96
Moody, Dwight L., 50
Moore, J. E., Jr., 239
Moore, Laura and William, 73
Mooshian, Helen, 249
Morning Light School, 153
Morrison, Henry C., 9, 11, 210
Morrison, J. G., 21, 113, 114–115, 117, 160–161, 162, 207
Moses, Arthur, 169
Muslems, 61–63, 145, 149

Nagamatsu, J. I., 95, 97–100, 102, 104–108, 274
Nagase, Kikuo, 125

Nagase, Rika, 129
Nakada, Juji, 96, 98, 114, 118
Nakada, Ugo, 126
National Campmeeting Association for the Promotion of Holiness (see National Holiness Association)
National Christian Council: China, 172–173; Japan, 129, 130
National Holiness Association (NHA), 5, 13, 146, 147, 150, 151, 154, 169
Nationalism, 34, 69–70, 76, 79, 81, 83, 145, 156–157, 160, 162, 273
Nazarene Theological Seminary, 29, 83, 186, 187, 252
Nease, Orval, 125, 126, 171, 173, 180, 190, 209, 212–214, 215, 217, 240
Nease, Orval, Jr., 125
Nee, "Watchman," 187
Neesima, Joseph H., 98
Neo-Orthodoxy, 27, 128–129
Nevius, John, 217–218, 276
New Century Crusade, 130
New Zealand, 28, 205
Noah's Ark, 158
Northwest Nazarene College, 24, 70, 191, 238
Oh, Jung Hwan, 218, 221
Olivet Nazarene College, 31, 103
Ongogan, Castillo, 250, 252
Ordination, 10, 74, 76, 81, 152, 173, 176, 180, 207, 221, 228, 255, 259
Oriental Missionary Society (OMS), 96, 98, 113–114, 186, 206–208, 210–211
Orphanages, orphans, 4, 10, 13, 16, 21, 24, 50–55, 57, 61, 63, 69, 70, 73, 78, 83, 147, 214
Osborn, Emma, 146, 151, 164, 165, 169, 174, 180, 182

# Index

Osborn, Leon C., 119, 146, 151, 153, 158, 165, 168, 169, 174, 177–178, 180, 181, 182, 187
Osborn, Lucy (Drake), 73
Oura, S., 112
Owens, Adeline, 205, 216, 218, 224
Owens, Donald, 205, 213, 218–224, 222–224, 225–226, 274

Pakistan, 92
Pan, Ming-ding, 177, 179, 187–188
Papua New Guinea, 28, 29, 205, 255
Park, Chung Hee, 226
Park, Ki Suh, 212, 217, 218–219, 222–223
Park, Nah Won, 218
Pasadena College, 13, 58, 95, 97, 98, 103, 117, 119, 127, 128, 170, 174, 241
Pattee, John, 166, 169, 170–171, 172, 173, 241, 242, 243, 245, 250, 252, 254, 255, 258, 275
Pattee, Lillian, 173, 241, 244, 245, 250, 254, 255, 257, 275
Peking Union Medical College, 165, 168
Pentecost, 4, 24, 158
Pentecostal Church of Scotland, 19, 69
Pentecostal Collegiate Institute, 9, 54, 55
Pentecostal Mission, 4, 11, 16, 17–18, 55, 65, 66, 71, 157
Pentecostalism, 9, 24, 54, 103, 109, 117, 157, 227–228
Perfect love, 12, 14, 20, 31, 34, 53, 58, 82, 153, 272, 274
Perry, Ella, 53, 56
Pettit, Lyman, 9, 55
Philippine Independent Church, 242, 251, 252, 260
Philippines, 6, 25, 28, 120, 161, 182, 205, 237, 237–267, 271, 272, 281, 271, 278
Phillips, E. S., 31–32, 225, 253, 257
Pilgrim Holiness Church, 103, 178, 238, 239, 240, 242, 238, 247, 251–253, 256
Pitts, Joseph, 125, 182, 239–241, 245–250, 253, 254, 256, 260, 272–275
Pitts, Paul, 247
*A Plain Account of Christian Perfection*, 157
Point Loma Nazarene University (*see* Pasadena College)
Poole, Lillian, 96, 98
Powers, Hardy C., 81, 214, 239, 241
Presbyterian Church, Presbyterians, 8, 17, 55, 146, 159, 161, 166, 174, 184, 209, 210, 218, 227, 250, 255, 275
Pyongyang, 123, 205, 207–208, 209
Pyun, Nam Sung, 211

Quak, Chae Kun, 212, 215, 216
Quakers (*see* Friends Church)

Ramabai, Pandita, 54, 55
Red Cross, 153
Rees, Seth, 96, 101, 103, 243
Rehfeldt, Remiss, 28, 30–31, 214–216, 215–220, 239, 244, 246, 249, 274, 277
Rench, Donna, 181
Rench, George, 181, 186, 188
*Re-Thinking Missions*, 24
Reynolds, Hiram F., 3, 5, 7–9, 11, 12, 15–17, 18, 21–26, 29, 34, 50–57, 62, 66, 68–69, 59, 60, 61, 63, 74, 75, 84, 97, 98–100, 102, 103, 105–112, 113, 115, 147–148, 149, 150, 157, 272–274, 277, 281
Reza, H. T., 32

# Index

Rhee, Syngman, 211–212
Roberts, Evan, 206
Roman Catholicism, Roman Catholics, 144, 145, 173, 223, 242, 243, 244, 251–253, 259, 260, 276
Rosa, Adrian, 250
Rural, 3, 5, 10, 19, 20, 26, 141, 143, 152, 153, 155, 209, 218, 223, 241, 242, 244, 247, 259
Russian Orthodox Church, 97, 101
Ruth, C. W., 147, 148, 169

Sachs, William, 132
Said, Edward, 277
Salvation Army, 50, 96, 119, 126, 171
Salve, S. Y., 70, 71–72, 74, 75–76
Samoa, 28, 211
Sanctification (*see* Holiness)
Santee, Helen, 106
Santin, V. G., 107
Schmidt, Anna (*see* Kiehn)
Schools (*see also* Bible and theological schools and colleges), 8, 10, 16, 21, 24, 31, 81, 82, 95, 101, 103, 127, 145, 147, 149, 150, 153, 155, 156, 161, 170, 172, 173, 180, 186, 213, 214, 228, 238, 278
Scott, Mary, 169, 173, 174
Second Coming, 18, 21, 25, 114, 124
Sect, sectarianism, 4, 9, 12, 14, 20, 26, 27, 30
Self-government, 3, 16, 32, 71, 95, 99, 131, 143, 170, 218
Self-propagation (*see also* evangelism), 71, 162, 170, 175, 180
Self-support, 10, 16, 23, 26, 32, 33, 53, 64, 65, 71, 81–83, 99, 116, 129, 132, 143, 149, 153, 162, 163, 166–167, 182, 170, 171, 173, 175, 180, 183, 187– 188, 251, 253, 258, 259, 275– 276
Seoul, 123, 205, 208, 211, 212– 213, 214, 218, 219, 228–229
Seung, Hak Su, 212–214
Seventh-day Adventists, 8, 55, 173
Sevidal, Gil, 240, 244, 250, 251, 252,
Shandong, 143–145, 147, 149, 156, 157, 164, 173, 175
Shang, Chih-rung, 166, 170
Sharpe, George, 69
Shintoism, 101, 102, 121, 128, 261
Simpson, A. B., 114
Simpson, Matthew, 13
Sims, Glennie, 147, 148, 150, 153
Smee, Roy, 30
Smelser, F. L., 96
Smith, Aaron J., 157–159, 272
Smith, Amanda, 73
Smith, Arthur, 152
Smith, Frank, 114–116, 117
Snider, Cora, 97–99, 109
Social Brethren Church, 252
Social concern (*see also* hospitals, orphanages), 14, 16, 21, 100, 152–153, 272
Social Gospel, 20, 24, 153
Society of Jesus, 144, 145, 151, 153
Society of the Divine Word, 144
Son, Shin Gu, 208
Song, Jung Mahn, 228
Song, Shang-jie (John Sung), 165– 166
South Chili Gospel Mission, 13, 145, 146, 147, 155, 161, 166
South China Peniel Holiness Mission, 177
Southern Nazarene University (*see* Bethany)
Speicher, Orpha, 74, 82, 83
Sprague, Lillian, 51, 53–55, 106

# Index

Stafford, S. M., 10
Stalker, Charles, 96
Stam, John and Mary, 170
Staples, Isaac, 101, 102, 106, 107–109, 117
Staples, Minnie, 95, 97–98, 101–118, 121, 122, 126, 129, 131, 162, 223, 243, 271–274
Star Hall, 206
Stockton, John, 239
Storey, R. K., 238
Student Volunteer Movement, 7, 159
Suh, Jae Chul, 212
Sun, Yat-sen, 145, 159
Sung, John (*see* Song, Shang-jie)
Sutherland, Francis, 152, 159, 165, 174
Suyat, Rose and Wilfredo, 244, 256
Swaziland (*see* Africa)
Swim, Roy, 24–25

Tagalogs, 251, 259
Taiwan, 28, 119, 144, 191, 176–189, 191, 205, 216, 223, 249, 253, 270, 272, 274, 275
Taiwan Gospel Mission, 176–180
Taiwan Holiness Church, 186
Taiwan Leprosy Relief Association, 177, 182, 186
Taiwan Missionary Fellowship, 186
Taylor, Carrie, 51
Taylor, James, 184
Taylor, James Hudson, 10, 50, 275
Taylor, William, 7, 52, 56
Taylor, Woodford, 146, 148–149
Tei, Ki-sho, 123, 208
Thana, 65, 70–72, 75, 76
Thatcher, Gertrude and Paul, 105–106
Theological colleges (*see* Bible and theological schools and colleges)
Theology, 1, 4, 7, 19, 27, 114, 128, 127, 172, 218, 229, 270, 277
Thomas, David, 206
Thomas, Emily and John, 206
Thomas, Raphael, 256
Three Selfs Patriotic Movement, 172, 271
Tode, Runza, 71
Tokyo, 96, 113, 117–118, 121, 123–126, 130
Tongues (*see* Pentecostalism)
Trachsel, John, 184
Tracy, Gertrude, 53, 56, 67, 70–71
Tracy, Leighton, 53–63, 66–69, 70–72, 74, 76, 78, 81, 84, 105, 110, 223, 226, 272, 281
Trevecca Nazarene College, 129
Troxel, Cecil, 146
Tryon, Charles and Lottie, 249–250, 251, 254
Tsuchiyama, Tetsuji, 114, 122, 123
Tsutada, David, 125

United Church of Christ in the Philippines, 237, 250, 259
United Nations, 171, 214
Upperman, Minnie (*see* Chenault)
Urban, 1, 3, 5, 11, 13–14, 16, 17, 20, 26, 61, 105

Valenzuela, Andres, 250, 252, 257–259
Valenzuela, Ricareda, 257
Varnedoe, Maude, 62
Varro, Michael and Elizabeth, 173, 178–179
Venn, Henry, 8, 21, 64, 75, 83, 217, 276
Vieg, Ida, 151, 154, 156, 271
Vine, Frances, 244, 245, 257
Visayans, 255–256, 258, 259
Voice of China, 177, 178

# Index

Waghamari, Lucas, 57
Wagner, H. H., 106
Walker, E. F., 103
Washim, 55, 72–74, 75, 78, 79
Welsh Revival, 206
Wesche, Henry, 164–165
Wesley, John, 1, 14, 51, 157
Wesleyan Church (*see* Pilgrim Holiness Church)
West, C. E., 157
Wheeler, Laura (*see* Moore)
Widmeyer, C. B., 177
Wiese, Harry, 153, 155, 162, 163, 164, 166–168, 170, 171–173, 181–185, 188, 249, 253, 254, 272, 275
Wiese, Katherine, 155, 173, 168, 257
Wiley, Fred, 51
Wiley, H. Orton, 24, 27, 31, 112, 174, 177
Wiley, Pearl (*see* Hanson)
Williams, L. Milton, 108
Williams, Lulu, 96, 98, 105, 281
Williams, Roy T., 20, 21, 62, 71, 113, 116, 127, 161
Williamson, G. B., 30, 80
Wilson, Flora and Stanley, 255
Wilson, W. C., 101
Wilson, Woodrow, 148, 275
Winans, Roger, 25
Women (*see also* Bible women), 6, 13, 14, 18, 20, 28, 31, 55, 56, 57, 61, 63, 73, 74, 109, 110, 129, 151, 152, 154–156, 174, 245–247, 259
Wong, Pao-hsi, 168
Wood, Anna, 53–55, 106
Wood, M. D., 9, 50–56, 106, 157, 223, 272, 273
Woodruff, A. Bond, 239, 247
Word, Emma, 207
World Evangelical Fellowship Conference, 130
World Gospel Mission (*see* National Holiness Association)
World War I, 2, 4, 19, 21
World War II, 27, 28, 29, 49, 74, 77, 84, 80, 95, 108, 189, 205, 237, 241, 250
Worldwide Evangelization Crusade, 177
Wu, Tung-tai, 161
Wynkoop, Mildred Bangs, 127–128, 130

Yamamuro, Gunpei, 96
Yoda, Terry, 121
Young Men's Christian Association (YMCA), 66, 127
Yu, Wan-ch'ien, 167, 169, 170, 173
Yuan, Hsuan-ch'un (Allen Yuan), 166, 170
Yuan, Shi-kai, 148
Yunnan, 184

Zambrano, Miguel, 238, 242, 243, 244, 252, 255

# About the Author

**Floyd T. Cunningham** is academic dean and professor of the history of Christianity at Asia Pacific Nazarene Theological Seminary, Taytay, Rizal, Philippines, where he has served since 1983.

In 1984 he earned a Ph.D. in American religious history at the Johns Hopkins University. He also is a graduate of Eastern Nazarene College and Nazarene Theological Seminary. He is an ordained minister in the Church of the Nazarene.

Dr. Cunningham has published articles in *The Drew Gateway, Asbury Theological Journal, Asia Journal of Theology, Indian Church History Review, Methodist History, Philippine Studies, Wesleyan Theological Journal*, and other journals and magazines. He has contributed chapters to *Church and Community Among Black Southerners, 1865–1900*, edited by Donald G. Nieman, and *Grounds for Understanding: Ecumenical Resources for Responses to Religious Pluralism*, edited by S. Mark Heim.